THE WORLD OF
PERSIAN
LITERARY HUMANISM

———◆◆◆———

HAMID DABASHI

HARVARD UNIVERSITY PRESS
Cambridge, Massachusetts
London, England
2012

For the memories of my mother's lullabies,
and the whispers of the woman I love:

For Golbarg. For Good.

Library of Congress Cataloging-in-Publication Data

Dabashi, Hamid, 1951–
The world of Persian literary humanism / Hamid Dabashi.
  p. cm.
Includes bibliographical references and index.
ISBN 978-0-674-06671-7
1. Persian literature—History and criticism.
2. Humanism in literature.   I. Title.
  PK6412.H86D33 2012
  891'.5509—dc23   2012022225

Contents

Preface

The Karun River runs through the Khuzestan province in southern Iran, where I was born and raised, like an immortal serpent whose head and tail are lost in the subterranean sinews of the earth or else deleted from the terrain of history. All that has remained and flowing is the body—bold, braving the elements, corporeal, canonic, mythic—as if it began in the infinity of a nowhere and is headed toward the immortality of somewhere else. Karun is some 450 miles long on the map and the only navigable river in my homeland. It originates in the Zard Kuh mountain range of the Bakhtiari region in the Zagros Mountains, and after receiving many tributaries it flows through my hometown of Ahvaz on its way to the Persian Gulf. The blood of our homeland in southern Iran is brown, you might say, by the commanding color that Karun so convincingly projects in and of itself. Karun is the color and conviction of faraway mountains—invisible, imagined, dormant in the twists and turns of the silent river. It is ponderous, meditative, and confident, knows where it is going, minds its own business—all the while generously nourishing us as if entirely unbeknownst to itself.

Is it because of the enduring memories of Karun, the invisible matrix of its time and space mapped repeatedly on the dawning of its visible aspects, now all carved with confidence and assurance into the rhythm and flow of my being, that I also have an atemporal and yet tactile sense of my mother tongue, and the literature, prose, and poetry that goes with it, at once flowing and stationary, timeless and timely, evident and effusive—the enduring music of a language and literature that I began sensing and then learning from my mother's lullabies, continued learning until the day I decided what quatrain from Omar Khayyam should be carved on her gravestone, and then learned again in the nights I sang the same lullabies to my own children in New York or taught Persian literary masterpieces to my students at Columbia University, and will continue to learn until the day that they will be lost but still palpable to me in the invisibility of my own death and dying, and from there to the memories that my children will carry from me?

> But helpless pieces in the game He plays
> Upon this chequer-board of Nights and Days
> He hither and thither moves, and checks . . . and slays
> Then one by one, back in the Closet lays.

I write this book on Persian literary humanism *(Adab)* as it has emerged and spread over the last 1,400 years, like a mighty and magnificent river, from Bengal to Istanbul and from central Asia to the eastern coasts of Africa, and with the contemporary map of Iran as its epicenter, by way of a historical retrieval of an otherwise ahistorical phenomenon code-named "literature." What you will see and sense is a river running under your feet, like Karun under mine, while what you will feel and form in your mind is the abiding presence of where it has been and where it is headed: that is the paramount image in my mind as I begin to tell my story of Persian literature, a river whose mighty and majestic aspect will soon dawn on you and you will have an abiding sense of where it has been and where it is headed. I will have you sail on that river— claiming, naming, feeling, sensing it. Persian literature is a living organism, just like a river, and telling its story requires a fluidity of narrative that comes to terms with its existential immediacy, as if it had no history, and yet is fully aware of the expansive history that it tacitly flaunts. Like the Karun River, Persian literature is flowing from an infinity of historical sources, comes to you with the massive volume of its abiding presence, and leads to the immortality of a yet-to-be-named sea.

Adab is one of the richest and aesthetically most provocative words in Arabic, Persian, Urdu, and Turkish. In all of these languages, with slight variations in both pronunciation and connotations, it suggests a commanding allusion to proper etiquette, finesse, flair, grace, or the art of living gracefully—a grace that extends from the way you speak and think, to the manner in which you clothe and carry yourself, to the disposition of your character and culture. The German *Bildung* is probably the closest word in any European language to what *Adab* means in Persian and its adjacent languages. But *Adab*, at the same time, categorically relates to literature as *belles-lettres*, literature as the summation of all linguistic arts that are beautiful and make for equally beautiful living, an art that informs a literature that becomes a testimony of your having achieved (not inherited) a living grace. It is this rich range of the connotations of *Adab*, which I translate as "literary humanism," that I wish to convey in this book as the running leitmotif of Persian literary imagination, and thereby the Iranian cultural heritage. *Adab* is apt for the literary disposition of the writing we call "literature," because it embraces life and letters, body and book, manners and matters, society and solitude, wish and will, code and character.

What I ultimately plan to demonstrate in this book is that the literary subconscious of a civilization is its paradoxical undoing, which may in fact account in part for the active hostility of the masculinist aspect of the dominant Arabic culture early in Islamic history against the consistently feminized Persian language and literature, character and culture, "accusing" Persians not only of effeminate delicacy and sexual misconduct (as now aptly demonstrated by Joseph Massad in his *Desiring Arabs*) but also of scientific and philosophical inaccuracy—a charge that may in part at least account for such leading Iranian scholars and scientists as al-Biruni, Ibn Sina, and al-Ghazali opting to write most of their important and canonized work in Arabic. This theological, philosophical, and scientific shunning of the Persian language (to which, of course, there are a number of exceptions), ipso facto posited Persian literary humanism as the modus operandi of a mode of being, writing, and reading safely distanced from the sanctified language of the Qur'an and the masculinist rectitude of Islamic scholasticism that it had historically occasioned. This historic condition thus ascribes to Persian literary humanism an effectively feminine disposition, even as it remained in a by-and-large male-dominated domain. That effectively feminine subconscious of a decidedly masculinist civilization has given Persian literary humanism a subversive disposition by being ipso facto narrated from a hidden and denied, repressed, and thus paradoxically flamboyant and defiant vantage point. The proposition of *Adab* as the literary subconscious of a masculinist civilization posits the subject that it invokes as creatively unstable and always already somewhere else, beyond the command and control of any sacred certitude.

The name *Karun* is probably a modern corruption of *Kuhrang*, which means "the color of mountain." A river that looks like a mountain in motion and carries the memories of its mountainous origins in the running fluency of its color is the image that Persian literature has projected of itself throughout its long and generous history. Karun is also identified with the Biblical river of Pishon, which along with the Tigris, Euphrates, and Karkheh ("Gihon") constitutes the four rivers of Eden. To think that the river that runs quietly through my hometown and over which I traveled all my childhood and adolescent years was also one of the four rivers that ran through Eden! The idea radically compromises one's sense of time and space, rhythm and harmony, and sense and sensibility, and teaches you, above all, humility, as you pick up your proverbial pen, dip it into Karun, and write the *aleph* that anticipates the *beh*, dreaming of the sea with no name.

. . . and thus I put one brick upon another
In the house of the blind
So when the sun rises tomorrow
I can sit them down under a canopy . . .

Nima Yushij (1896–1960)

Introduction

The Making of a Literary Humanism

ONCE UPON A TIME, so says the sagacious and always jovial poet Sheykh Mosleh al-Din Sa'di (ca. 1209–1291) in his *Golestan* (composed in 1258), there was a king who one day in a rage ordered the execution of a foreign slave in his custody. The condemned man began cursing the king in his native tongue, for he was now convinced he would be killed, and so he let go his fears and told the monarch what he thought of him. The king did not understand the language in which the condemned man spoke, so he turned to his courtiers and asked for a proper translation. There was a good-hearted vizier in attendance who said, quoting a passage from the Qur'an (3:134), "Your Majesty, he says: 'Those who spend in prosperity and in adversity, who repress anger, and who pardon men; verily, Allah loves the good-doers.'" The King was pleased with this translation and, properly admonished by its wisdom, summoned his magnanimity and forgave the condemned man. There was another vizier in attendance who was an adversary of the good-hearted vizier. He instantly turned to the king and said, "People of our rank and position should never lie to His Majesty. This man was not praising you or asking for forgiveness; he was cursing His Majesty and abused His Most Royal name." The king was saddened by this remark and said, "That lie was far more appeasing to me than this truth, for that lie was meant to solicit a good deed, while the source of your truth was to do evil, and wise men have said, 'a judicious lie is better than a seditious truth.'"[1]

Sa'di: The Mind of the Moralist

They say if something catastrophic were to happen, and the entire Persian literary culture were to disappear from the face of the earth, and all that remained was the text of Sa'di's *Golestan*, that lost civility could be constructed anew.[2] There are those who even believe that claim need not be limited to Iranian civilization—that civility as such, justice, grace, tolerance, and a harmonious and happy humanity at large are all embedded in Sa'di's poetry and prose, in the *Adab* that he personified and helped make into a literary-humanist institution in Iranian (and by extension Islamic) culture. Medieval Persian literature, as best represented by and in Sa'di, is replete with gems of worldly wisdom, at the heart of which always dwells the twist of a verbal pun informing a moral paradox, where harmful truth-telling, for example, must yield to the wisdom of a white lie. Only in the literary space—with poetic license—thus crafted and made viable can a lie be celebrated and privileged over truth, by way of a mere parabolic coil whipping at the adjectival spin of a morally superior lie to an ethically compromised truth.

But how is that possible, and what would such a paradox do to the commanding mandates of a religion like Islam, a holy text like the Qur'an, or a divine emissary like Prophet Muhammad? How do we, or can we, account for a sustained legacy of literary humanism in the bosom or context or even the neighborhood of commanding doctrinal beliefs, strict juridical injunctions, expansive metaphysical mandates—all summoned under the word "Islam"? Were Iranians—or even more widely those who composed, spread, read, and celebrated Persian literature, Sa'di chief among other poets and prose stylists—not Muslims? Of course they were—not all of them, but most of them. Persian literary humanism, I propose, was neither despite nor because of Islam. It was, as it remains, the literary manifestation of a cosmopolitan urbanism, rooted in successive empires, that emerged in the aftermath of the Muslim conquest of the mid-seventh century. Persian literary humanism—where those who produced and received it have come into being—spells out an entirely different universe of moral and ethical obligations, where, if you can poetically stage it, "a judicious lie," as Sa'di says, "is better than a seditious truth." To dwell in that universe, to come to terms with the possibilities of such noble lies, we need to know who and what and where and under what circumstances was conceived and crafted this wise and perspicacious poet and prose stylist: Sheykh Mosleh al-Din Sa'di Shirazi.

The Master, the Perfect Model, the Truthful, the Prince of Speech, the Most Eloquent Speaker: medieval and modern biographers cannot praise Sa'di enough when naming or citing him. Abu Muhammad Moshref al-Din Mosleh ibn Abdullah ibn Musharraf al-Sa'di al-Shirazi was his full honorific name.[3] He is the singularly celebrated poet and master prose stylist of the thirteenth century—the very model of eloquence that defined the beauty and grace of the language that to this day carries his seal and signature. As one literary historian put it, it is not very strange that the Persian-speaking world today speaks the same language that Sa'di wrote some 750 years ago, for we simply mimic his Persian.[4] Sa'di was widely known and deeply loved and admired by his contemporaries. Royal courts sought his company, and poets from around the Muslim world paid him homage and imitated his poetry or else admonished themselves for daring to put pen to paper while he was still living. His two most famous books, *Bustan* (1257) in poetry and *Golestan* (1258) in highly stylized prose and poetry, universalized his fame, while his Persian lyrics and Arabic panegyrics made him a household name among the literati from one end of the Islamic world to the other.

Now: Who exactly was this Sa'di—and what do we know about his life? Not much—and what is known is not entirely reliable. He was born and raised in Shiraz, went to Baghdad to study at the famous Nizamiyyah university, traveled widely in the region, and eventually returned to Shiraz, where he was very popular at the royal courts in the Fars region. Consulting all the extant biographical and hagiographical dictionaries about Sa'di, two factors are paramount in any reading of his life: first, that throughout his writings he keeps placing himself in his stories with such an easy matter-of-factness that you think he was indeed there and was a participant observer in what he is describing—he is in the Grand Mosque of Damascus in one story, arrested by the Crusaders in another, and wandering in India or central Asia in yet another story. But generations of scholars have long since determined that these are in fact narrative tropes for dramatic purposes and should not be taken at face value.[5] The second factor is that Sa'di's admirers and successive generations of biographers have kept adding items to his biography out of love and admiration for him. If we were to take all these anecdotes at face value, we would believe he traveled widely from India to Syria and from central Asia to Yemen and North Africa—and once he was even arrested by the Franks in Syria during the Crusades, whereupon a friend rescued him from bondage and gave his daughter to him in marriage. When we say "Sa'di," we refer to a narrative trope made up of all these citations and posited as the master poet of a vast literary tradition that has consistently canonized and celebrated him.

These two conflating factors need to be summoned and added to the historical circumstances of Sa'di's time and place. The almost century-long life of Sa'di was spent during the tumultuous epoch of the Mongol invasion, when the Islamic (Iranian) world saw the deeply traumatic collapse of the Seljuqid dynasty, which ruled over much of the Muslim world from the early eleventh to the late twelfth century, and with it the final demise of the Abbasid caliphate (750–1258). Consider the major landmarks of the Mongol conquest to recognize a new meaning for the term fin de siècle: the fall of Bokhara (1219) in the northeasternmost part of the Seljuqid empire, followed by the fall of Samarqand (1220), Neishabur (1221), and Isfahan (1227), the destruction of the Isma'ili strongholds (1256), and ultimately the sack of Baghdad and the fall of the Abbasids (1258)[6]—and you can imagine the range and depth of the seismic changes that effectively ended the classic age of Islam. Sa'di was a product of this time—with the urgency of the time written into the fabric of his prose and poetry.

What has remained for posterity about Sa'di as a person is a strange but joyous mélange of biography, hagiography, and mythology through which a people's favorite poet was assimilated and absorbed into his texts, whereby he was transformed from a person and a name into a phenomenon and a citation. On this collectively creative site, *history* is made effective and meaningful only to the degree that it is at the service of the *literary* event, which has enabled that history by way of implicating it into a *story* that makes more sense for a poet who is then collectively canonized. On the site of that canonization, Sa'di as a poet and prose stylist is transformed into the mind of a moralist who in turn posits a vast topography of sentiments and ideals for a people to behold and uphold. As Philip Rieff demonstrated in his *Freud: The Mind of the Moralist* (1959), Freud had turned the classical take on body/mind and individual/society upside down in his psychoanalytic theories and thus crafted a constellation of the psychic drama driven by instinct that drove the world in one direction or another. Similarly, Sa'di as a moralist became a mirror of an entire people in which they saw and upon which they projected what they were and what they wanted to see at one and the same time. This primacy of the literary act over the historical narrative, the sovereignty of the poetic over the political, is what I believe to be the guiding principle of coming to any historical terms with a literary imagination a people continue to believe to represent what is best in them. Sa'di was willed—in person, persona, poetry, and prose—by the collective subtext of Persian literary humanism.

The assimilation of Sa'di's biography into the mind of the moralist that he was and the prose and poetry that he left behind produced a literary *heteroglossia* through what Bakhtin would call "the dialogical imagination," which was subsequently embedded in the hybrid nature of the language (*polyglossia*) with which he is remembered.[7] On the surface of that literary act, the mind of the moralist becomes the *nexus classicus* of a people's moral imagination (their Durkheimian collective consciousness incarnate) in which a noble lie will be understood as better than a troubling truth without any moral qualms—and on the basis of which an entire literary humanism is made possible and sui generis. The heteroglossia that results from the historical dialectic between the context and the text translates into the hybridity (polyglossia) of literary utterances that makes up a literary tradition. In such utterances, Sa'di's words are always already animated by the emerging intentions of their readers. This is how, in Sa'di's case, the mind of the moralist was at once literary in its disposition and moralizing in the collective consciousness of the people, who in loving and quoting and procreating him in effect celebrated their own repressed aspirations and thus collectively enacted a nonprophetic, self-revelatory act of prophecy, which in turn ipso facto detranscendentalized the sense of the sacred.

Literary History sans Historicism

Perhaps the most famous poem of Sa'di known globally is one from his *Golestan*, in which he speaks of the brotherhood/sisterhood of humankind:

> The children of Adam are limbs of but one body,
> Having been created of but one essence.

> When the calamity of time afflicts one limb,
> The other limbs will not remain at ease.
> If thou hast no sympathy for the troubles of others,
> Thou art unworthy to be named human.[8]

In the Persian original, that very last word, which is usually translated as "human" (the same word at the root of "humanism"), is *Adami.* The last two lines of the poem in the original are:

> To kaz mehnat-e digaran bi-ghami,
> Nashayad keh namat nahand Adami.[9]

Literally:

> Thou who art indifferent to others' misfortune,
> You are unworthy to be named human.

The very last word of the last hemistich, "human being," marks a peculiar construction in Persian. The word *Adami*, which is usually translated as "humanity" or "being named human," escapes immediate attention but (perhaps precisely for that reason) demands a closer scrutiny. I say the construction is "peculiar," because that last "i" after Adam posits a very strange intonation in the Persian original. "Adam" quite obviously means Adam, the first human being in the Bible and in the Qur'an, the man God created from naught and in his own image, and into whom he breathed from his own breath. From the word *Adam* we have the abstract noun of *Adamiyat*, which means—now degendered beyond the "Adam-Eve" divide—humanity or humanism or the condition and quality of being a human being. But instead of the usual *Adamiyat*, the simpler and more poetic (though less philosophical) construction of *Adami* cast onto that little "i" at the end of the word the daunting task of creating an attribute out of Adam—for *Adami* means both a human being and the state of being a human being, or just "humanity" or even "humanism," if we were to allow ourselves a bit of leeway. Paramount in the word *Adami*, however, is Adam—biblical and Qur'anic, prehistoric and atemporal, and yet precisely in that designation the atemporal origin of temporality, of time, of history. Time begins with Adam and so does history. So in the word *Adami* we have embedded Adam, the first human being, from time immemorial, that makes the memorial time possible, history afoot. Humanity, as evident and present in the word *Adami*, is thus made historical by its ahistoricality, a literary act, in other words, exuding with temporality made temporal. In being so fragile, *Adami* fragments its own history into indeterminate pieces.

Adami is a literary act, a poetic implosion, that makes the evidence of historicality embedded in the verbal utterance without yielding to historicism. That literary fact implicates any attempt at literary historiography. If the literary history of a people ought to be told more like an open-ended epic than a closed-circuit panegyric, then that epic is habitually punctuated with lyricism. This is not to suggest that lyricism, in and of itself, has no narrative place in literary history. Quite to the contrary: almost everything about Persian literature—modern and medieval—carries an indelible mark of lyricism on it. It has emerged as something of a second nature to the subtext of the language and its self-perception of itself. Be that as it may, the drama of a national, regional, and above all imperial literature, long in the making, demands a certain global awareness of its epic proportions. But does the epic disposition of a people's literature amount to a "literary history"? That little "i" that gives a literary disposition to the biblical and Qur'anic ahistoricality of Adam/human is the answer—and so is the hidden miracle of any language and literature that gives birth and breeding to that very little sound that makes the apparition of an immortal humanity suddenly emerge out of the mortal human.

Evident in that one word—*Adami*, humanity and humanism—and mapped out on a global scene, as the vast and mighty Abbasid and Seljuqid empires were crumbling and the Mongol empire was flexing its overextended muscles, Sa'di performs the Persian language and stages the literary prowess of his mother tongue with equal might and commanding manner. In doing so, and for ages to come, Sa'di becomes Persian literary humanism incarnate: precise, graceful, expansive, delicate, balanced, and judicious, exhibiting the brevity that is the soul of his wit, and above all wise and worldly. He performs Persian prose and poetry like two melodious instruments, harmoniously staging that performance, and thriving at showing off his command of the language, which becomes performative in his capable hands and serves, at face value, no other purpose than that very performance, the audible delight of the reader/performer of Sa'di. Sa'di becomes exemplary for generations of poets and prose stylists to come; he cast his shadow upon the literary masters who preceded and followed him—bringing them all under the wide and spacious canopy of one single literary event: *Adab-e*

Farsi (Persian literary humanism). "Sa'di is the absolute ruler of the realm of speech," in the judicious and rare words of Mohammad Ali Foroughi, "and no one else can compare with his command of elocution. Speech is like wax in his hands, expressing every meaning with phrases that are impossible to surpass in beauty and brevity. . . . His prose tastes like poetry, his poetry is as fluent as prose. . . . In other words, because of Sa'di, Persian poetic and prose diction were rescued from a false binary and became one."[10] To emphasize Sa'di's penchant for the surface beauty of the language, and his happiness in dwelling there, is not to ignore his uplifting ideas and graceful thoughts, for he is full of morals and manners, but they are entirely tangential to that paramount performativity of the language itself—and all else becomes poignant and powerful by virtue of Sa'di's performance. That performance is literary, ahistorical, a temporal pause running through its atemporality.

Embedded in that literary performativity of Sa'di, and the literary humanism that he best represents, is an always already hidden core of evident historicality that need not be exhausted, exposed, or overextended by or in any historical narrative. Humanism as the prose and poetry of historicality is something that becomes evident in and through the course of Persian literary humanism.[11] That thrust of historicality on the act of the literary amounts to a literary history without historicism—lyricism keeping historicism at bay, thus recognizing the decentered subject at the heart of the literary act. Here the literary act has no history, and subjecting it to history (as practically all "histories of Persian literature" do) inadvertently assigns a false totalizing subject to its amorphous narrative, whereby the historical narrator becomes the historical narrative of the literary. The literary act would command and claim that effective (and affective) history, as it must, if by *history* we were to mean more *a genealogy of here and now* rather than an *archeology of there and then*—and it does not, if we were to dwell on the moment of its creative spontaneity (which is here now and gone the next moment)—however framed within the institutions of power and formality that craft and canonize it. Can the twain meet—the historicity of the craft and the spontaneity of its creative moment? Much of Persian literary historiography, as we have received it and keep producing it today, is precisely one of an archeology of *what was* rather than a genealogy of *what is*. By keeping historicism at bay, seeing through the historicality of the literary act, we will not only retrieve the literary act as and for what it is, but also refrain from inadvertently ascribing to it a false organizing subject.

Literary humanism as the modus operandi of a dialogical imagination that thrived on its polyglossia to become a self-revelatory reality, and thus flaunting a self-evident historicality minus historicism, is what will drive this sustained reflection on one of the most magnificent manifestations of an aesthetic subtext trying to make sense of a senseless universe. Keeping historicism at bay while retrieving the historicality of this literary imagination will also prevent attributing to it a false organizing subject.

Humanism sans Scholasticism

One of the most memorable and oft-quoted passages in *Golestan* is the story of a quarrel between Sa'di and a belligerent Interlocutor who was denouncing the rich and the powerful for being selfish and obnoxious, against Sa'di's insistence that they were in fact generous, kind, and worthy of the gratitude of the poor and the weak. In *Jedal-e Sa'di ba Modda'i* (*The Quarrel of Sa'di with the Interlocutor*), we witness Sa'di at his absolute storytelling best—in effect telling a whole drama in a few short strokes with wit, precision of dialogue, and full dramatic diction, using an almost uncanny cinematic technique to tell an entire episode in a few judicious cuts. Sa'di, as the narrator, chances upon a Dervish who had launched a fierce denunciation of rich and powerful people in a gathering. Sa'di intervenes and mildly admonishes him, testifying that rich people are in fact kind, generous, and attentive to their duties to the needy and the weak. Sa'di the narrator then proceeds to give an account of the crescendo of their heated debate that soon becomes a fierce quarrel and eventually degenerates into physical assault. The two are then taken to a judge, who upon hearing the story admonishes them both by telling Sa'di that there are indeed selfish among the rich and not all are generous, and then turning to his Interlocutor and telling him that yes there are such selfishly rich and powerful people, and yet there are exceptions among them.[12]

Who is the narrator and who are the actors in this short drama? There is one narrator (Sa'di) and three actors (Sa'di, his Interlocutor, and the Judge), and they are all the creatures of Sa'di's storytelling mind, and yet they are all there as the dramatis personae of a literary realism unsurpassed in brevity and power of persuasion. At the hidden heart of the drama—all three protagonists of which are represented with almost identical conviction—is the creative effervescence of that very fragile *Adami* who sits at the center of Sa'di's moral imagination. Even Sa'di himself is implicated in the act of narration—when he says "I," that "I" is already implicated inside the narrator's story and compromised by it, its subjection metamorphic. The autonomous fragility of that *Adami*, entirely independent of the God/man binary and their respective reflections upon each other, which sustains the course of Islamic metaphysics, is what makes Sa'di's literary humanism plausible. Done in a swift and solid *parabolic* language, and above all through the indeterminacy of a knowing subject who is telling all these stories with equal conviction (and thus with no conviction at all), the teller of these tales becomes a self-effacing narrator dissolved into naught precisely at the moment when he is telling his tale. The frivolity of the teller of tales—that he too becomes a persona in the dramatis personae—translates into the indeterminacy of the knowing subject, exposing the fragility of *Adami* at the heart of its humanism.

Persian literary humanism (*Adab*) is a narrative institution unto itself, irreducible to any metaphysical certainty that is Zoroastrian, Manichean, Jewish, Christian, Hindu, Buddhist, Gnostic, agnostic, or above all Islamic in origin and destination—though all these religious traditions, in one way or another, lend their mores and metaphors to its creative and effervescent making. That this literary humanism developed almost simultaneously with Islamic scholasticism (from jurisprudence and theology to philosophy and mysticism) was the result of a social and intellectual history that afforded one otherworldly and the other worldly audacity. What also makes literary humanism historically anchored and yet immune to reductionist historicism is its classical juxtaposition against Islamic scholasticism. Literary humanism and Islamic scholasticism have been posited as the two legs, the yin-yang, of medieval intellectual history—well beyond the boundaries of the Muslim world and into Christendom.[13] In my reading of Persian literary humanism, I will mark it as being distinctly at the opposite end of Islamic scholasticism, informed by but categorically irreducible to it, if by no other force than by virtue of the critical factor of the primacy of language and the fragility of the subjects (in plural) that have occasioned it. The principal language of Islamic scholasticism was Arabic; Persian literature was in Persian—a constitutionally noncanonical language when placed next to the canonized Arabic. The systematization of religious learning into Islamic scholasticism, which extended from theology to jurisprudence and from there to philosophy and mysticism, had an entirely different vision of the world than that of literary humanism. Their location adjacent to each other marked their differences even more clearly.

A principal inspiration behind the writing of this book on Persian literary humanism is the magisterial work of my late teacher George Makdisi (1920–2002) and his two seminal volumes *The Rise of Colleges* (1981) and *The Rise of Humanism* (1990), the former about Islamic scholasticism and the latter about literary humanism (both with references to the Latin West)—the two institutions that he saw as a twin project.[14] Makdisi considered "humanism and scholasticism . . . [as] two movements that dominate the intellectual history of classical Islam." Whereas scholasticism required "a study of the scholastic movement, with its representatives, its institutions, its 'license to teach,' the doctorate, and the scholastic method leading to it," the study of humanism dealt "with its representatives, its institutions, its 'art of dictation,' and its emphasis on books for autodidacts."[15] In Makdisi's correct estimate, scholasticism was geared toward a "license to teach," while humanism was for "the autodidacts," meaning the institution of the former was formal and legislative, while the practice of the latter was informal and out of joint. In relation to power, one might suggest scholasticism was definitive and stabilizing, while humanism was definitely indeterminate and paradoxically destabilizing—serving and subverting power at one and the same time.

George Makdisi believed that "in classical Islam, each of the two movements has its *raison d'être*, distinct from the other; yet both sprang from concern for a common source: the Sacred Scripture."[16] I disagree with this presupposition—and during the time I was George Makdisi's student and for years later, we had many lively discussions over this crucial matter. While the Sacred Scripture did indeed provide the raison d'être of scholasticism, I believe this was not the case with humanism. Though perfectly respectful of the Muslim Sacred Scripture, as of that of others, the humanists did not take it as their raison d'être. I believe that not the Sacred Scripture but the social conditioning of the vast and diversified Abbasid empire (750–1258) was the raison d'être of the rise of humanism. George Makdisi did make his case in the case of

Arabic humanism, and very eloquently so, and now I would like to make mine with Persian, though with a perspective rooted in and yet divergent from his. Without his exquisite scholarship, I must acknowledge at the very outset, none of these discussions about Persian or any other literary humanism would have been possible.

Makdisi believed that "the history of their [scholasticism and humanism] developments is one of interaction in which there was conflict, but never a clean break." The notion of a "break" (let alone a "clean break") between scholasticism and humanism implies an effective epistemic codependency, with which assumption I disagree, for I see the rise of these two institutions from two different provenances. Islamic scholasticism emerged from the formal and organic need for the foundation of Islamic doctrines at the heart of the successive Islamic juridical regimes laying claims on successive empires; humanism was the result of the societal formation of a multicultural and polyvocal urbanism entirely independent of the political needs of those empires and deeply rooted in their cosmopolitan characters. Scholasticism was the active formation of an "ideological" disposition to sustain multiple Islamic empires; humanism was the organic growth of a cosmopolitan societal formation that gave expression to its extra- and nondenominational intellectual urbanism. Every time empires reached for scholasticism, they received something in return (legitimacy); every time empires sought to appropriate humanism, they did so at the risk of losing something (legitimacy). In *Golestan* Sa'di says, "One cannot trust either the friendship of monarchs or the good humor of infants, for one is changed with a mere suspicion and the other after a short nap."[17] He was of course right—but he was also projecting, for the same is true about the friendship and humor of poets: they would praise a monarch to high heaven one day and cast him to the lowest depth of hell the next. In no uncertain terms, Sa'di knew that "kings are much more in need of the good advice of the wise than the wise in need of proximity to kings."[18]

Makdisi believed that humanism "arose because of deep concern for the purity of the classical Arabic of the Koran as the living language, as well as the liturgical language, of Islam." I concur with the concern for classical Arabic that literary humanism in its Arabic vintage harbored, but not necessarily, or exclusively, as a medium of the Qur'an, but in and of itself, language qua language, language as the modus operandi of eloquence, of art, as the material of a literary project. Makdisi held, and rightly so, that "scholasticism owed its rise to a struggle between opposing religious forces, the conflict coming to a head in the third-/ ninth-century inquisition (*mihna*), over a century after the dawn of humanism." In other words, Makdisi dates the formation of humanism (as a project and a mode of thinking and being) over a century before the rise of scholasticism. This point I in fact use as proof of my position, that the rise of humanism was entirely independent of those religious concerns and arose long before them. Makdisi put the argument succinctly and beautifully with the centrality of the Holy Scripture but disregarded that the Qur'an was a "sacred" text for scholasticism, while it was the mere model of linguistic and literary eloquence for humanism. Makdisi held that "both movements aimed for orthodoxy: humanism, for 'orthodoxy' in language; scholasticism, for orthodoxy in religion."[19] Precisely. Humanism had no concern for or against religious orthodoxy.

Makdisi was wrong when he said, "The two movements had their roots in religion" but partially right when he said these movements "owed their impetus to external forces. For humanism the external force was the influence of foreign tongues on that of the Arabians. For scholasticism it was the influence of Greek philosophy on the development of the Prophet's religion."[20] For humanism, I believe, the influence of foreign tongues was of course crucial, but those foreign tongues—from Syriac and Greek to Pahlavi and Sanskrit—were themselves the result (as much as the consequence) of a massive imperial cosmopolitanism that was conditioned by successive Islamic empires, that of the Abbasids (750–1258) in particular. For the formation of Islamic scholasticism the influence of Greek philosophy was of course equally crucial, but so was the influence of Jewish theology, Buddhist monasticism, or Persian Zoroastrianism. All these external factors were calibrated by the internal dynamics of an "Islamic" empire that had to connect its emperor/caliph to some sort of ideological explanation for which the scholasticism that he chiefly sponsored became a crucial conduit. But he also, through the intermediary office of his (mostly Persian) vizierate, promoted humanism as the more immediate modus operandi of his might and majesty.[21] The Persian vizierate became the conduit of transformation of tribally based Islamic conquests—from the Arab Abbasids to the Turkish Seljuqids—on the Sassanid model of cosmopolitan world empires.

George Makdisi was partially correct that "humanism began as a scholarly philological movement back to the purity of the Arabian language, at its source in the Arabian Peninsula, untouched by foreign matter"—but the implication that "foreign matter" may indicate a certain sense of xenophobia or anxiety of untouchability on the part of the humanists is categorically wrong, for humanism in fact began as a revolt against patently racialized tribalism of the Umayyad period (661–750), paving the way for the literary cosmopolitanism of the Abbasids. Humanism—in both its Arabic and Persian vintages—remained true to the centrality of language and eloquence only so far as it served its raison d'être within a vast multicultural and cosmopolitan empire, for which Arabic had become a lingua franca, in the making of which expansion of tribal Arabic Persian-speaking Arabist humanists were key elements. The transformation of tribal Arabic into the lingua franca of a vast empire had its own power and purpose, in which "the purity of the Arabian language" had certain worldly limitations—not just in Arabic humanism but in fact in the Arabic used by scholasticism as well.

Makdisi was also partially right that "scholasticism was a scholarly religious movement, away from the excesses of a philosophical theology inspired by Greek thought, towards a juridical theology more in conformity with the nomocracy of Islam." Partially, I say, because that nomocracy (primacy of law) was only one of the authorizing discourses of Islam, which Makdisi privileged (for reasons peculiar to his intellectual predisposition and not definitive to the vast panorama of Islamic intellectual history) over the logocentrism of Islamic philosophy and the homocentrism of Islamic mysticism. Makdisi looked at Greek philosophy only as an impetus for the reactive formation of Islamic scholasticism, and that only so far as Islamic nomocentrism (Fiqh, Shari'ah, and Ash'ari Kalam in particular) sought to overcome it, and never took Islamic philosophy (logocentrism) or mysticism (homocentrism) seriously into his full vision of Islam. Even more flawed was Makdisi's attempt to assimilate even humanism into the bosom of Islamic scholasticism. Makdisi was entirely correct that "the Sacred Scripture supplied the substance of Scholasticism" but partially wrong that it also "served as a model for humanistic eloquence."[22] For that model was always already stripped of its divine disposition and brought into the mundane human domain of humanism. For scholasticism the Sacred Scripture was divine revelation; for humanism it was a superior model of linguistic eloquence. These speak of two vastly different normative dispositions—

one posits an absolute alterity as the absolutist subject of being; the other dismantles any authorial subjection that comes its way.

Makdisi confused the raison d'être of humanism and scholasticism because of their common source in Arabic language. He made that mistake because he never seriously considered the equally important domain of Persian (or Turkish or Urdu) literary humanism. The Arabic language of Arabic literary humanism and the Arabic language of the Qur'an and of the scholasticism it caused and occasioned confused Makdisi to the point that he did not see the categorical difference of language in one vis-à-vis the other. Makdisi by intellectual disposition and linguistic competence had an Arabic-centered and westward view of Islamic civilization, which was both the source of his exquisite scholarship and the blind spot in his insights. He believed that "the combined periods of rise and development of both movements [humanism and scholasticism] stretch roughly from the first/seventh century to about the eighth/fourteenth. Both movements begin in eastern Islam, and move westward from Iraq, to Syria, Egypt and the rest of North Africa, Spain and Sicily, and from there to other parts of the Christian West."[23] This was his crucial mistake, that he looked westward and that as a Christian he was preoccupied with the movement of humanism westward and toward Christianity and the Latin West. In doing this, he categorically missed the Persian domain of literary humanism, eastward from Baghdad, to Shiraz and Isfahan, Hamdan and Khurasan, Herat, Tashkent, and Samarqand, and all the way to Bengal and back eastward to the Ottoman domains. This eastward movement of literary humanism on its Persian wings had nothing to do with the Latin West. It had everything to do with the multifaceted domains of Islamic civilization itself. The undue anxiety of influence, that "Islam" had influenced "the West," and the flawed Arab-centric reading of the spectrum of Islamic civilization combined to send the great Makdisi off on the wrong track.

Makdisi's preoccupation with proving the influence of Islamic humanism on the Latin West was a major animus of his scholarship. "The arrival of the two movements in the Christian West was at about the same time, in the second half of the eleventh century; but the sequence of their full development was the reverse of that of Islam." His attention to the Latin West inevitably forced the direction of his reading of both humanism and scholasticism westward, where he was adamant to prove Islamic influence. "The evidence is overwhelmingly," he believed, "in

favor of the reception of both movements, scholasticism and humanism, from classical Islam by the Christian Latin West. It is generally
known that this influence existed in such fields as philosophy and
medicine, mainly because of the translation of books in those and other
fields of the sciences, from Arabic to Latin, as well as the adoption of
Arabic terms. It is however not generally known that books in the field
of humanistic studies have also been translated from Arabic to Latin
and other European languages, and that terms of humanism in the
West are terms of classical Arabic humanism."[24]

Makdisi's preoccupation with the direction of that influence in
humanism and scholasticism was of course a reaction to the presumed
centrality of "the West" in the Mediterranean cultural universe and
would make sense by way of offering a different take on the genesis
and disposition of that universe. But it becomes positively distracting
and distorting when the focus is shifted to the character and disposition of both scholasticism and humanism in the Muslim world itself.
Here Makdisi made the crucial mistake of not seeing humanism as an
institution sui generis, because he never considered Arabic humanism
in its immediate neighborhood of Persian (or Turkish or Urdu) literary
humanism, and the Arabic language of Arabic literary humanism and
the Arabic language of the Qur'an and the scholasticism it had occasioned misdirected him toward a common course of causality for both.

Persian literary humanism—as indeed Arabic, Turkish, or Urdu—
emerged as the self-revelatory aesthetic subtext of an entire civilization
with an assured historicality that was embedded in its parabolic language. The overriding indeterminacy of the knowing subject at the
heart of this literary humanism—an always self-effacing narrator (an
Adami) that becomes the alter ego of his audience—made of this literary humanism an institution that was the binary opposition of nothing,
for it was rooted in the cosmopolitan character of successive empires
with a worldly disposition to their will to power. If Islamic scholasticism was in the business of sustaining and regulating those empires,
multiple literary humanisms (in the plurality of languages and cultures
that peopled those empires), the Persian included, were in the habit of
disturbing their dreams, while entertaining their courts. Persian literary humanism was a Trojan horse—world conquerors invited Persian
poets and literati to their courts as their victory trophies at their own
risk, for they never knew—no one ever knows—when the courtiers

were fast asleep what swordsmen existed in the belly of those handsomely crafted panegyrics to wreak havoc on what delusions of power.

Literary Humanism in the Face of Philosophical Antihumanism

It is impossible to exaggerate the beauty, elegance, and Dionysian ecstasy running through Sa'di's lyrical poetry. There are three undisputed masters of Persian *ghazal*: Sa'di, Rumi, and Hafez. But while Hafez's *ghazals* exude a powerful philosophical resonance, and Rumi's a mystical, Sa'di's flaunt a robust and physical worldliness. Physical love and expansive eroticism—an eroticism that is unabashedly and freely bisexual and homoerotic at one and the same time (for in Persian there is no gender-specific pronoun)—are the defining tropes of Sa'di's lyrical poetry. Not a knowing but a lyrical subject remains evasively at the center of Sa'di's *ghazals*. The notion of a unitary—autonomous and purposefully conscious—subject entirely disappears at the instant of reading a *ghazal* by Sa'di. As the author of all metaphysical certainties, the knowing subject will get lost in the labyrinth of Sa'di's lyricism, where he chases after a butterfly that makes him dance to its colorful rhythm entirely unbeknownst to himself. The lyrical undoing of the unitary subject (as the core concept of all metaphysics) is definitive in Sa'di's poetry. The inebriated consciousness and the worldly unreliability of that lyrical subject displace the all-knowing subject at the center of all scholasticism—Islamic or otherwise. The multiply split lyrical subject is constituted by not just a double, but a manifold, bind—at once alienated from itself (for it is always somewhere else) and yet paradoxically self-discovering (for there it discovers its alterity). As it leaves the realm of the real and enters into the imaginary, the lyrical subject becomes self-metaphorizing, allegorical to itself. Here the subject is a lyrical construct, interpolated by the effects of a soft power it imagines and dismantles at one and the same time. Notice the poetic dissolution of the lyrical "I" as I do an almost verbatim translation of one of Sa'di's most famous *ghazals*:

> I will never rise from this drunkard ecstasy for as long as I live
> For I did not even exist when you sat so sovereign upon my heart.
> You are not like the sun, now visible now not,
> Others come and go, you just stay the same.
> So many sad stories I had to tell when I am away from you,
> But once you showed up you close all doors to complaint.

Come and visit your friends for seeing you once
Is a thousand times better than writing a greeting or sending a gift.
Come and see me now that you have broken my heart
    from separation,
And be a cure to my ailing heart, caught in your snare.
No wonder you will strike at the heart of your enemies
    on the day of battle,
When you break the heart of your friends when away from them.
As for you the learned man of law—leave us to God!
You have your abstinence and piety, and leave me to my
    love and ecstasy.
You should abandon your knowing heart to a person you love,
For once you have a direction to pray to, you will never take yourself
    so seriously.
When fortune and success are not gained by striving too hard,
What are we to do except to serve and be obedient.
Complaining from separation from those you love and the hardship of
    the world
Is unbecoming of you, Sa'di, cut yourself short and be free.[25]

Sa'di's lyrical subject is epiphenomenal. That lyrical subjective is definitive to the makeup of Persian literary humanism. But how would that
lyrical subject posit the literary humanism that it sustains vis-à-vis a
historical antihumanism that today dismantles any solid supposition of
a knowing subject—the writer or the reader—who will encounter and
counter that literary humanism? There is no writing (about) any literary humanism today without facing that philosophical conundrum.
The active retrieval of Persian literary humanism for a contemporary
audience living consciously in the present age faces the fact of a philosophical antihumanism that would make it look, ipso facto, archaic,
exotic, or at best a casual walk down the halls of a museum. It is not. It
should not be. That philosophical antihumanism, deeply rooted in contemporary self-awareness of the globe, must be faced directly before
that literary humanism is allowed to present and posit itself.

The death of the Christian God (Nietzsche) as an omniscient subject
of the European history in the nineteenth century and the subsequent
death of the European man (Foucault) as an autonomous subject in the
twentieth on the same continent and upon the same moral clime are
matters of domestic European provenance and scarce have had reason to
reach the metaphysical underpinning of worlds stretched to the colonial

edges of that self-centered metropolitan imagination. When the Christian God and his counterpart the European man were declared dead, the news barely reached or when it did even less did it matter at the colonial edges of European postmodernity. Though the philosophical propensity toward antihumanism took a particular poignancy in the post-Holocaust anxiety of Europe, and rightly so, the challenge that the centrality of an all-knowing subject at the heart of Enlightenment humanism of Jean-Jacques Rousseau (1712–1778) and Immanuel Kant (1724–1804) faced goes back to the middle of the nineteenth century. As early as 1843, Karl Marx had criticized the notion of an abstract "human" in "On the Jewish Question," in which he had questioned the entire notion of "rights" as an expression of the capitalist mode of production, a proposition that had reduced humans to mere abstraction. By 1887, in his *Genealogy of Morals*, Nietzsche too had equated "humanism" with the theology of the weak. Later in the nineteenth century, in his psychoanalytic theories, Sigmund Freud (1856–1939) had excavated deep into the unconscious of the knowing subject and demonstrated its nonrational disposition. If the European Enlightenment invented the "human" in particularly poignant and powerful and all-knowing terms, almost coterminous with that momentous event were the critics of that assumption, from Marx and Nietzsche to Freud and Dostoyevsky, who exposed the fault lines of the "human" that had made that very narrative possible.

Midway through the twentieth century, philosophical antihumanism was to find even deeper grounds. In his philosophical project, Martin Heidegger rejected the notion of humans as autonomous agents and criticized the grounding of philosophy in abstract consciousness, most ostensibly in fact in his "Letter on Humanism" (1946). Addressing the question Jean Beaufret had addressed to him, "Can we restore meaning to the word 'humanism,'" Heidegger responded, "I wonder whether that is necessary. Or is the damage caused by all such terms still not sufficiently obvious?"[26] For Heidegger the assumption of "I think" as the condition of human liberty and autonomy is fundamentally flawed, given his philosophical rejection of the Cartesian *cogito*. After Heidegger, Louis Althusser (1918–1990) revived the Marxist rejection of individual consciousness and retrieved its reliance on social relations and collective behavior in the manufacturing of the dialectical making of the knowing subject. After Althusser, Jacques Derrida outlined, beginning in 1967 with his *De la grammatologie* (*Of Grammatology*), the philosophical contours of the decentered subject due to the uncertain disposition of language that enables the very possibility of speech. Almost simultaneous with Derrida, Foucault underlined in his *Les Mots et les choses* (*Order of Things*) (1966), as had in fact Thomas Kuhn in his *Structure of Scientific Revolution* (1962) before him, the epistemic/paradigmatic nature of knowledge production that has accidentally centered "man" as its knowing subject and that it was about to overcome it. By declaring "The Death of the Author" (1967), Roland Barthes pronounced the death of the selfsame man.

In telling the story of Persian literary humanism one cannot pretend that this long and powerful philosophical antihumanism did not exist, for that pretension will ipso facto render any such history as an exercise in either Orientalist fantasy or else nationalist historiography of an entirely outdated provenance. Positing Iran or Islam in its current postcolonial condition does not entirely resolve the issue either, for the larger philosophical problem of antihumanism is not the only obstacle that the writing of a Persian literary humanism faces. There is another, even more urgent, issue that is more immediate in its own vicinity. It is impossible to imagine the making of Persian literary humanism in the context of successive imperial iterations without coming to terms with the fact that "Persian" literary humanism has been achieved at the heavy cost of repressing, denying, dismissing, belittling, and denigrating the non-Persian elements within the Iranian cultural universe. The eloquence of Persian literary humanism, precisely by virtue of its successive imperial iterations, is predicated on the silencing of non-Persian languages and dialects under the reign of the same dynasties that enabled and privileged Persians as the ornament of their courts. Based on Middle (Pahlavi) and Ancient (Avestan) Persian, the Modern Persian (the Islamic period) was intensely aware of its imperial pedigree and thus fed itself into successive dynasties in its Islamic history. As an ancient imperial language, Persian posited itself against the emerging dominance of Arabic, which soon became the lingua franca of successive Muslim empires. Next to Arabic (which in both scholasticism and humanism emerged as the imperial language of successive Islamic empires), Persian was soon to be rivaled by Turkish—after Persian served generations of Turkic dynasties such as the Ghaznavids and the Seljuqids as their courtly language of administration—as the imperial language and literature of three almost simultaneous empires: the Ottomans, the Safavids, and the Mughals. Persian was thus no mere "vernacular cosmopolitanism" settled to and satisfied with that dubious designation. It always carried its cosmopolitan imperialism up its sleeve, as it were. Equally important is the emplotment of the rise of Persian literary humanism next to the politically dominant Arabic cosmopolitan imperialism—in administrative, scientific, scholastic, and humanist traditions. It is only next to that Arabic cosmopolitan imperialism that Persian would look like a "vernacular cosmopolitanism" by virtue of its decidedly peripheralized neighborhood with respect to Arabic. Retrieving Persian literary humanism during an antihumanist philosophical age thus posits a double bind: marking its modern anticolonial humanism as a bona fide project by way of recognizing its ancient and medieval imperial pedigree.

As Persian became peripherally vernacular and the language of cultural resistance to Arabic imperialism next to an imperial Arabic in the western Islamic world, so non-Persian languages and dialects became equally (if not more) peripheralized and silenced next to the imperial Persian in the eastern Islamic world. That historical fact gave Persian language and literature their innately paradoxical and split subject positions, which in addition to the centrality of the lyrical subject in its narrative makeup have posited Persian literary humanism as a mimetically transient act predicated on both politically unstable and aesthetically contingent modes of subjection. These historical particularities of Persian literary humanism give it a uniquely poignant position when it comes to facing the philosophical antihumanism of our own time, for the rise of antihumanism in its European context was predicated on the constitution of the sovereign subject—from Aristotle to Kant—as the prima facie evidence of the all-knowing *cogito* facing an all-knowable world. The multiply split subject—from its lyrical to its conflicted dispositions—at the heart of Persian literary humanism was never predicated on an all-knowing, self-appointed agency, nor did that absolutist assumption of agency ever cause any havoc around the globe (from colonialism to the Holocaust), for it to be now reprimanded and robbed of its troublesome sovereignty. The lyrical subject is constitutionally amorphous, and the paradoxical subject position—weak and vernacular next to imperial Arabic, imperial and cosmopolitan next to all other subimperial languages to the east of the Islamic world—disallows any assumption of absolutist sovereignty. The result is the centrality of a fragile *Adami* who was never imagined to have the illusion of sovereignty to begin with for a philosophical rise of antihumanism—from Nietzsche and Heidegger to Derrida and Foucault—to come and put it in its right place. In its self-rupturing fragility, *Adami* is the epitome of what the contemporary Italian philosopher Gianni Vattimo calls "il pensiero debole" (weak thought). It thinks, but softly.[27]

To see more clearly through these particularities of Persian literary humanism, we will greatly benefit from a closer look at one of the most astute theorists and staunchest defenders of (literary) humanism of our own time. In the age of philosophical antihumanism of varied origins and as a leading literary critic of his generation, Edward Said remained a politically steadfast and theoretically beleaguered humanist. In this theoretical belligerence he was of course up against some mighty philosophical forces—from Husserl and Heidegger to Derrida and Foucault, from poststructuralism to postmodernism. On many occasions, Edward Said responded extensively to charges of "residual humanism" in his work, in his groundbreaking *Orientalism* in particular. In his 1995 afterword to *Orientalism*, he wrote, "among American and British academics of a decidedly rigorous and unyielding stripe, *Orientalism*, and indeed all of my other work, has come in for disapproving attacks because of its 'residual' humanism, its theoretical inconsistencies, its insufficient, perhaps even sentimental, treatment of agency. I am glad that it has! *Orientalism* is a partisan book, not a theoretical machine."[28] This was of course a decidedly political response and not a theoretical argument—a reaction that nevertheless remains a testimony to the centrality of the issue in Edward Said's work. In his 2003 preface to *Orientalism*, Said continued to insist on this humanistic predilection: "My idea in *Orientalism* is to use humanistic critique to open up the fields of struggle. . . . I have called what I try to do "humanism," a word I continue to use stubbornly despite the scornful dismissal of the term by sophisticated post-modern critics."[29] Said's "stubborn humanism," as he put it, came to a final theoretical articulation in his first posthumous book, *Humanism and Democratic Criticism* (2004), in which he resumes a dialogue with James Clifford's detection of the central paradox of the sovereign subject and essentialism in *Orientalism*. Early in *Humanism and Democratic Criticism*, Said admits:

> In many ways Clifford was right, since during the 1960's and 1970's the advent of the French theory in the humanistic departments of Ameri-

can and English universities had brought about a severe if not crippling defeat of what was considered traditional humanism by the forces of structuralism and post-structuralism, both of which professed the death of man-the-author and asserted the preeminence of antihumanist systems such as those found in the work of Lévi-Strauss, Foucault himself, and Roland Barthes. The sovereignty of the subject—to use the technical phrase for what Enlightenment thought did with Descartes' notion of the cogito, which was to make it the center of all human knowledge and hence capable of essentializing thought in itself—was challenged by what Foucault and Lévi-Strauss carried forward from the work of thinkers such as Marx, Freud, Nietzsche, and the linguist Ferdinand de Saussure. This group of pioneers showed, in effect, that the existence of systems of thinking and perceiving transcended the power of individual subjects, individual humans who were inside those systems (systems such as Freud's "unconscious" or Marx's "capital") and therefore had no power over them, only the choice either to use or be used by them. This of course flatly contradicts the core of humanistic thought, and hence the individual cogito was displaced, or demoted, to the status of illusory autonomy or fiction.[30]

Having made this admission, Edward Said then proceeds to articulate his vision of humanism, pointing out that he did not agree with "the argument put forward in the wake of structuralist antihumanism by postmodernism or by its dismissive attitudes to what Jean-Francois Lyotard famously called the grand narratives of enlightenment and emancipation."[31] Instead, he insists that there is a kind of nontotalizing, nonessentializing humanism that he advocates and describes as being critical of humanism in the name of humanism, and that schooled in its "abuses by the experiences of Eurocentrism and empire, one could fashion a different kind of humanism that was cosmopolitan and text and language-bound in ways that absorbed the great lessons of the past from, say, Erich Auerbach and Leo Spitzer and more recently from Richard Poirier."[32] Said then spends the rest of his book articulating the particular terms of his democratic criticism, "text and language-bound" (literary) as it is, paving the way toward a more inclusive humanism by opening it up to other, repressed, forms of humanism.

This defense of humanism by Edward Said, in effect trying to separate humanism as such from European and Eurocentric humanists, did not sit well even with his closest followers. "So, who is responsible for the divorce of the cultural realm from questions of power," asks Rajagopalan

Radhakrishnan in a poignant criticism of Edward Said's persistent defense of humanism, in which he points "the finger quite steadily at humanists and intellectuals. These are the folks who have set up a kind of 'camouflage' whereby literature is always already exonerated from its real, and often brutal, implications in the real world of power, empire, dominance, exploitation, suffering, and subjugation."[33] Radhakrishnan rightly identifies the root cause: "If humanists and intellectuals . . . are to blame, what then of 'humanism' as a historic-political, cultural-ideological, and epistemic domain that generates these humanists?"[34] While Michel Foucault had systematically targeted humanism as the modus operandi of a beleaguered modernity that ipso facto also entailed ethnocentrism, Eurocentrism, and colonialism, Edward Said took pains to make a distinction between humanism and humanists. But Radhakrishnan insists that "the abuses that were committed in the name of humanism, contrary to Said, I would argue were very much in the spirit of humanism: the abuses are a form of compliance in the 'essentialism of humanism,' its anchorage in the a priori of the dominant discourse of the West."[35]

As Radhakrishnan rightly recognizes, Said's answer to this dilemma was never even to his own full theoretical satisfaction. But at the end, "Said does give us an answer," Radhakrishnan admits, "and that answer is profoundly literary. The cosmopolitan reality is text and language bound. It is in the domain of literature and aesthetics that the cosmopolitan worldview is realized as an ideal order. . . . Cosmopolitanism is aesthetic/literary humanism at its subtle best."[36] This direction of humanism toward literary humanism opens a liberating venue, for in it both Said and Radhakrishnan are paving the ground for a much wider and potentially more globally democratic domain of dealing with philosophical antihumanism and the epistemic crisis that the assumption of a sovereign subject has faced.

To face that challenge, Said, to be sure, did more than just posit the literary as the domain in which humanism can be salvaged. To see the significance and the direction of Said's solution, however, we first need to remember Fanon's. "Leave this Europe," Fanon demanded, "where they are never done talking of Man, yet murder men everywhere they find them, at the corner of every one of their own streets, in all the corners of the globe. For centuries they have stifled almost the whole of humanity in the name of a so-called spiritual experience. Look at them today swaying between atomic and spiritual disintegration. . . . When I search for Man in the technique and the style of Europe, I see only a succession of negations of man, and an avalanche of murders." Predicated on this bitter and battle-fatigued recognition, Fanon's solution was inaugural: "Let us waste no time in sterile litanies and nauseating mimicry. . . . Let us decide not to imitate Europe; let us combine our muscles and our brains in a new direction. Let us try to create the whole man, whom Europe has been incapable of bringing to triumphant birth."[37]

One might argue that Edward Said spent a lifetime trying to answer Fanon's last call in the making of his own literary humanism, the democratic supplementarity of European humanism, and not a radical reversal or abandonment or dismantling of it altogether. The supplementarity that Said contemplated might be considered a potential summation between the empirical of Eurocentrism and the transcendental of an open-ended literary humanism that sublated Europe to the world. His project in the end was to help transform humanism into multiple sites of varied humanisms (in plural) and thus turn the project into an open-ended organicity that consistently corrected its own blind spots. Said's criticism of the limited imagination of Eurocentric humanism pushed forward by calling for the organic growth of the project by multiplying it into other non-European humanities. Referring specifically to the two works of George Makdisi on the rise of humanism in Islam, Said joins him in criticizing Eurocentric scholars like Jakob Burckhardt and Paul Oskar Kristeller for having located the rise of humanism exclusively in Europe, disregarding at least 200 years of history of humanism in Muslim contexts.[38] Literary humanism for Said thus emerged as the modus operandi of overcoming the conundrum of antihumanism— a form of literary humanism, of course, that itself did not fall into the trap of nationalist identitarianism of one kind or another.

> It therefore seems to me that we must begin to rid ourselves, consciously and resolutely, of the whole complex of attitudes associated not just with Eurocentrism but with identity itself, which can no longer be tolerated in humanism as easily as it was before and during the Cold War. Taking their cue from the literature, thought, and art of our time, humanists must recognize with some alarm that the politics of identity and the

nationalistically grounded system of education remains at the core of what most of us actually do, despite charged boundaries and objects of research.[39]

That warning is particularly noteworthy in the case of Persian literary historiography, which has been invariably tied to Iranian nation-building projects and national identity politics, whether sponsored by the Pahlavi monarchy (1926–1979), the Islamic Republic, or even anticolonial and anti-totalitarian literary narratives. Contrary to these projects, the historical fact of Persian literary humanism is that its worldly domain has always been cross-national and transnational, and in fact, it has been the poetic subtext of successive imperial mappings of the region and attained at the heavy cost of silencing subnational languages and literatures.[40] So as the literary canons and varied iterations of humanism are multiplied and expanded, so Edward Said thought, so must the emancipatory politics of literary humanism be wedded to larger domains beyond national boundaries.

In the course of this book I will demonstrate that Edward Said's project for expanding and multiplying humanism in varied, "non-Western," directions, and thus saving it, ultimately fails and does not resolve the far more serious theoretical problem that humanism as such faces today. At the heart of contemporary philosophical antihumanism remains the enduring crisis of the all-knowing subject, a crisis that by simply driving the site of humanism in multiple directions we are not resolving, but are in fact exacerbating. The literary answer to that philosophical crisis must be sought elsewhere. It is the nature of the literary act and the precarious disposition of its varied and multiple subject positions that are the defining modes of literary humanism, and it is in those terms that literature qua literature does not face the cul de sac of philosophical antihumanism. What will sustain my course of argument throughout this book is the proposition that Persian literary humanism was an epiphenomenon, for no false authorizing subject, partaking in the absolute alterity of any viable God-term as its absolutist transcendence, had authorized either its *nomos/law* or its *logos/reason* (not to be confused with logos/sokhan of Persian literary humanism)— for it had claim to none.

All of these varied strategies can be, by way of a poetic metaphor, seen as predicated on the moment when Sa'di admonishes his readers:

"You should abandon your knowing heart to a person you love / For once you have a direction to pray to, you will never take yourself so seriously." Redirecting the presumption of the knowing self to the certainty of an unknown alterity: precisely there, upon that lyrical turn is the subject forever decentered.

The Decentered Subject of Persian Literary Humanism

Sa'di's *Golestan* is divided into eight chapters. That division is not by later editors and is integral to the text. Sa'di in his introduction, and in his own narrative voice, says that he has divided his book into the following eight chapters: "On the Manners of Kings," "On the Ethics of Ascetics," "On the Virtues of Abstinence," "On the Benefits of Silence," "On Love and Youth," "On Weakness and Aging," "On the Influence of Education," and "On the Proper Etiquette of Companionship." He has divided his *Golestan* into eight chapters, he says, just like Paradise, which has eight gates.[41] Eight gates into Paradise—and eight entries into *Golestan*.

It is easy to see a number of formal binaries in operation in these titles and divisions—kings and beggars, youth and aging, eloquence and silence, companionship and solitude, and so on. In each set of binaries, and indeed throughout the text, Sa'di seeks to strike a balance, a golden mean, that comes together from avoiding the extremities of two goods that become evil when carried too much to their own ends—such as in his famous dictum that "two things are the signs of a dull wit: speaking when you ought to be silent, and silence when you ought to speak!" The lyrically and loquaciously fragile subject, narratively held together for the fleeting moment at the heart of Sa'di's moral imagination to suggest a dictum, is thus posited not by an avoidance of two evils in the vacated space of their absence, but in fact by the ability to hold two divergent and opposing goods (silence in its time and eloquence in its time) from running to their evil consequences. The judicious choice, as a result, requires a constant vigilance that enables a versatile agency, a supple subject.

What is evident but dispersed in the logic and rhetoric of the organization of the *Golestan* chapters is also a narratively hidden balance that holds the whole text, and with it the moral of all its stories, together. There is also a more immediate (again hidden) metaphor that anticipates all these narrative mis-en-scènes in *Golestan*. The whole structural architecture of the text, as it is, is contingent on the preparatory staging of it in a famous prolegomena in which Sa'di informs his readers how it happened that he decided to write this book. After an elaborate, exceedingly verbose, and patently eloquent introductory showcasing and flaunting of his exquisite command of Persian and Arabic prose and poetry, Qur'anic allusions, and ancient wisdom, Sa'di informs his readers that at the age of fifty, when his reputation as a great poet and prose stylist was in fact at its height, he decided to become a recluse and to live the rest of his life in solitude and silence. One of his friends (here partaking in a very common narrative trope) comes to pay Sa'di a visit precisely at the moment when he had sworn to solitude and silence. Initially Sa'di refuses to talk to this friend. But after a while he yields to his friend's request and speaks and tells him of his decision. The friend is of course astounded and saddened to hear this decision and insists that Sa'di should do no such thing and must resume being the model of eloquence that he is, for "a tongue hidden in a mouth is like a key to the treasure trove of an eloquent person."[42]

While they are engaged in this conversation, the two friends leave Sa'di's house for a walk. This incident is happening during the season of spring in Shiraz and the two friends go for a casual stroll around the city and end up spending the night in a beautiful garden of a mutual friend, where they have a memorable banquet. In the morning, when they are about to leave, Sa'di notices that his friend has put together a bouquet of freshly cut flowers to take home. At this point Sa'di turns to his friend and tells him not to bother with these fresh flowers for in a few days they will perish. "What am I to do," the friend asks, to which Sa'di says, "for the delight of those who will observe and to teach eloquence to those who will read it I will write my *Golestan*, upon whose flowers the wind of autumn will have no affect, and the passage of time will never turn the feast of its spring to the frigidity of the winter." *Golestan*, literally "flower garden" (or "rose garden"), is thus composed of flowers that will never perish. Sa'di finishes his introduction by telling his readers that the spring season in Shiraz was still around and fresh flowers abounding when he had finished his *Golestan*.

There is something metaphorically urgent, fragile, and ephemeral at the heart of Sa'di's *Golestan* and the narrative cause of its composition—so that one reads every line, every poem, every story with that lingering sense of urgency (of a flower now beautiful and aromatic and gone the next moment) on one's mind. The entire opening gambit of *Golestan* begins by offering eight chapters of the book as if offering eight gates to Paradise, sustains the agential autonomy of the moralist entirely contingent on the delicate balance of not allowing two contrary goods (silence and eloquence) to result in evil consequences, continues with a paradoxical citation of eloquence describing a poet's decision to be silent, and concludes with leaving the enduring memory of fragile and perishable flowers lingering on every word and phrase that is gathered in *Golestan*. What remains throughout the text is the idea of eloquence emerging from silence and creating metaphoric flowers (in prose and poetry) that will never die, and yet precisely by virtue of the aroma of that metaphor the allegory of the freshly cut flowers remains hanging from the diction of the prose and poetry that is *Golestan*—celebrating endurance in impermanence, beauty in fragility, immortality in mortality. The fractured subject that permeates this narrative is definitive to the fictive transparency of Persian literary humanism.

When we look at Persian literature in general, a number of key factors define its particular idiomaticity—all of them coming together to constitute an entirely uncertain and wavering subject defining the horizons of its open-ended manners and modes of significations, intelligibilities, and symbiosis of signs and meanings. If *lyricism* were to be considered the defining moment of this literature (Sa'di, Rumi, and Hafez), the uncertain gender of the beloved emerges as the destabilizing force that ascertains its poetic disposition, in which masculinity and femininity are decidedly undecided. The lyrical subject—thus made metaphorically fragile—at the heart of Persian lyricism is ipso facto decentered, unreliable, evasive. That already decentered subject is further fragmented and made uncertain by the gender-neutral Persian pronoun, which becomes frivolously interpolated with the bisexuality and homoeroticism vastly evident in Persian lyrical poetry. This homoeroticism becomes particularly poignant in the *ghazals* of Rumi, whose poetry further exacerbates, obfuscates, and camouflages this decentered subject.

If, alternatively, we were to consider the *epic* proportions of Persian literature (Ferdowsi in particular), it will emerge as the literary heritage of an imperial confidence now cast in the form of figuratively dominated subjects when placed next to the triumphant (colonizing) Arabic language and literature—a fact that paradoxically casts Ferdowsi's *Shahnameh* as the triumphant memory of a rebellious people remembering themselves at the time of their political defeat. This exposes yet another layer of a split subject writing Persian literary humanism—at once politically defeated and poetically triumphant. The entire spectrum of Persian literature thus appears as an expansive event spreading eastward into successive empires from Iran to central to south Asia, and yet localized by virtue of its neighborhood to the political triumphalism of Arabic literary, scientific, and scholastic traditions moving westward into the Mediterranean domain. In the very same vein, Persian literary imagination appears as an imperial cosmopolitanism made to look vernacular by virtue of being adjacent to the mighty Arabic cosmopolitanism that had already laid a solid claim on the Mediterranean. Meanwhile, in the body politic of three globalized empires of the Ghaznavids (tenth to twelfth century), the Seljuqids (early eleventh to late twelfth century), and the Mongols (thirteenth to fourteenth century) Persian literature flourished into a manifest imperial imagination staging its otherwise latent defeats—a paradox that made Persian poets and literati creatively passive-aggressive in overcoming and outstaging their Arab counterparts.

The fragmentation of the authorial subject moves from lyrical and epic into *panegyric* (chief among its medieval master practitioners Manouchehri, Onsori, and Asjadi) *romance* (Nezami Ganjavi in particular), and finally comes to a crescendo, in terms of its varied narrative dispositions, in the abundance of the *karamat* literature dealing with saintly miracles (with Sana'i, Attar, Rumi, and Jami as the main beacons). The magic/realism that informs the creative imagination of the *karamat* (miracle literature) dances around any possibility of a centered subject that might come its way. What in fact we are witnessing in the *karamat* literature, with Farid al-Din Attar's (1145–1221) *Tadhkirat al-Awlia* (*Biographies of Saint*) and Muhammad ibn Munawwar's *Asrar al-Tawhid fi Maqamat al-Sheikh Abu Sa'id* (*Secrets of Unification: On the Spiritual Attainments of al-Sheykh Abu Sa'id*), composed in 1178, is the complete breakdown of any presumed logical connection between the signifier and the signified—in which the act of signification can mean very little outside the sacred narrative. As is evident in these seminal texts, which are among the absolute masterpieces of Persian prose, the *karamat* literature basically attributes the knowledge of the unseen and of the unheard to Sufi saints and also attributes to them solid command over the animal kingdom and other strange and extraordinary abilities that simply break down any and all assumptions of reason. Whether these attributions are read literally or figuratively, their allegorical disposition gives them the character of a magic/realism that suspends any assumption of a centered reason or a knowing subject.[43]

There are many other aspects of Persian literary humanism—when considered as a miasmatic movement across genres, generations, and historic spans—that speak to the amorphous disposition of their multiple narrating subjects, such as the fact that in the case of the *karamat* literature many miraculous attributions have been added to the text by subsequent generations, which fact makes the question of single and identifiable authorship entirely untenable. The result of all these varied factors in the making of Persian literary humanism is that the narrating subjects are not just always figuratively decentered—they are in fact positively miasmatic, narratively performative, dialogically imperceptive, and above all hermeneutically contingent on shifting audiences that receive or canonize them in one way or another. Compared to the vast whirlwind of decentered subjectivity thus narratively and poetically performed in Persian literary humanism, what today passes as a radical critique of the subject is in fact exceedingly limited and even arrested. The combined effect of multiple and metamorphic modes of decentered subjection feeds on itself to make the emotive center of Persian literary humanism always amorphous, invariably somewhere else, with never a single all-knowing subject in sight to question and/or dismantle. In contemporary deconstructive works of theorists like the distinguished feminist philosopher Judith Butler, in which the site of the body is examined as the stage of gendered performances, this playful mode of decentered subjection in literary arts placed outside the horizons of "English and Comparative Literature" (by way of what Gayatri Spivak has aptly called "sanctioned ignorance") results in a critique of the subject that has been entirely fixated into just one form or another (race, gender, or class) and not the combined effect of all and more. Judith Butler's move to emphasize the role of *acting* in performing gender appears as critical only when compared to the foundational metaphysical thinking that Derrida (the principle philosophical inspiration for Butler) has sought to dismantle. But compared with the playful frivolity of incessant and open-ended desubjections definitive to a literary imagination that like many others has been made alien, inaccessible, exotic, and peripheral—or else turned into an object of curiosity for "world literature"—such moves in fact remain limited within a very narrow European philosophical provincialism.

Take the homoerotic and cross-sexual ambiguity of the object of desire in Persian lyricism alone (one among a multitude of other literary idiomaticities) and see how it preempts any notion of a fixed, gendered, and autochthonic subject position, the way that, for example, Judith Butler proposes gender, sex, and sexuality are socially performed and ritually fixated. The proposition that "the materiality of sex is constructed through a ritualized repetition of norms"[44] leaves much more than "sex" outside of similarly ritualized repetitions, to which the subject, dodging here, might retreat. The principal target of Butler's critique, and quite rightly so, is of course the formation of a mode of "humanism" that is predicated on that repressively solidified, identified, undifferentiated, and consolidated subject:

> The ideal of transforming all excluded identifications into exclusive features—of appropriating all difference into unity—would mark the return to a Hegelian synthesis which has no exterior and that, in appropriating all difference as exemplary features of itself, becomes a figure for imperialism, a figure that installs itself by way of a romantic, insidious, and all-consuming humanism.[45]

That identification of humanism with imperialism, through the intermediary functioning of an undifferentiated subject, is the central and poignant issue here, an obstacle that Edward Said dies not being able to resolve, except through stubborn persistence on trying "to correct" humanism. But the presumption of that undifferentiated subject is also where Persian literary humanism radically—far more radically than anything imagined here in Butler's critique—parts ways with her (and others') critique of humanism. The lyrically depunctuated subject of a literary act that is always already decentered is not autochthonic, because it never originated where it is found, whereas in the ritualized subject position of gender and sexuality, the way Judith Butler understands it, it is. Borrowing from Foucault's notion of "regulative discourse," Judith Butler in her widely celebrated *Gender Trouble* (1990), and later in her *Bodies That Matter: On the Discursive Limits of "Sex"* (1993), has argued that through the repetitively stylized social acts, performances of gender, sex, and sexuality are ritually produced, regulated, and made to look natural, and thus manage to masquerade themselves as ontologically solid. In the received and reconstituted "frameworks of intelligibility" socially sanctioned behaviors thus become innately "natural." Performing regular and regulated stylized actions stages the gender for political foregrounding in relations of power. The performative disposition of the act makes it at once natural and even ontically self-evident. The iterability (Derrida's term) of the act, meanwhile, systematically ritualizes the social production of gender and sexuality under the constant threat of ostracism. By being effectively heterochthonic (as opposed to auto- and not homo-), the lyrically emancipated subject at the heart of Persian literary humanism mimetically camouflages its evasive positions. It is nowhere to be found.

The idea of subject formation as *performance* was of course not entirely new or original, and some three to four decades before Judith Butler, the Canadian sociologist Erving Goffman had already done extensive work in the field of symbolic interactionism in such groundbreaking works as *Interaction Ritual: Essays on Face-to-Face Behavior* (1967), *The Presentation of Self in Everyday Life* (1959), and ultimately in his *Behavior in Public Places: Notes on the Social Organization of Gatherings* (1963), he sought to decode the "body idiom" in various daily interactions. The advantage of Goffman's much more socially (rather than discursively) based arguments, which even he in 1959 thought "hardly novel,"[46] are that he had theorized the theatricality and the performative disposition of selves in varied public domains, emphasizing the dramaturgical analysis in social interactions. Goffman considered these public performances as integral to the socialization process, performances that are "idealized" in multiple ways. That these performances are codified and hegemonic (and thus gender and sexuality forming, among other things) is perfectly evident in Goffman's assertion that "when the individual presents himself before others, his performance will tend to incorporate and exemplify the officially accredited values of the society, more so, in fact, than does his behavior as a whole." That very fact is equally evident in an earlier American sociologist Charles Cooley's assertion, made back in 1922 and upon which Goffman relies, that "if we ever tried to seem a little better than we are, how could we improve or 'train ourselves from outside inward?'"[47] That training "from outside inward" is precisely where performativity of the public act becomes integral to the formation of the subject and her/his socially constituted corporeality. That corporeality is always contingent on public performances. Goffman had in fact likened social interaction to theatrical performances in which we even have a front stage, where the social actors perform what they gather to be positive and acceptable roles, in front of an audience, while in the backstage they kept what they thought was a more hidden or private repertoire of who and what they were—a place where the persons of the public personae, as it were, can be themselves and discard their public personae.

In both Butler and Goffman, and before them in Charles Cooley, we are of course entirely in bourgeois (or what Goffman rightly called "Anglo-American")[48] social domains, and the crucial factors of literary traditions in imperial formations do not enter their reading of subject formation. In specifically European philosophical terms, the critique of humanism in contemporary European philosophy is ultimately predicated on a radical questioning of the unitary, autonomous, and undifferentiated subject that was at the center of the Cartesian (and later Kantian) *cogito* as a core concept of metaphysics. Following the Freudian explorations of the unconscious and Heidegger's positing of *Dasein*, any notion of the autonomous (all-knowing) subject was altogether suspect. Jacques Lacan, building on Freud's psychoanalytics, posited a "split subject" that is always limited by a double bind when leaving the real and entering the imaginary. Meanwhile, in the political and social realm, the combined effect of Althusser, Foucault, and Bourdieu was to posit the subject as an ideological construction and as the "effect" of power and "disciplines."[49] But beyond the limits of these legitimate critiques of the subject and the humanism that it posits, retrieving a literary humanism that at once informed and subverted vast cosmopolitan empires—by always remaining their alter ego, so that the very empires they helped legitimize carried within them the seeds of their own undoing—points to an entirely different mode of subject de/formation.

When we open the domain of subject formation to Persian literary humanism, we find that the decentered subject has a much wider spectrum of operation and never presumed to be unitary, autonomous, or undifferentiated. Quite to the contrary, the decentered subject was expressed in multiple terms, not the least of which was the miasmatic cross-gendering of Persian language and literature. What I ultimately plan to demonstrate in this book is that the literary subconscious of a civilization is its paradoxical undoing, which may in fact in part account for the active hostility of the Arabic masculinist culture against the consistently feminized Persian language and literature and character and culture, "accusing" Persians not only of effeminate delicacy and sexual misconduct[50] but also of scientific and philosophical inaccuracy—a charge that may in part at least account for such leading Iranian scholars and scientist as al-Biruni, Ibn Sina, and al-Ghazali opting to write most of their important and canonized work in Arabic.

The Case for Literary Worldliness

Early in his *Bustan*, Sa'di describes the reasons behind the composition of one of his two most famous texts—this entirely in poetry. "I have traveled all around the world," he says, "Have been in the company of many people."

> I have much learned from every corner of this world,
> From every crop I have gathered a share.
> I know of no people more noble
> Than the people of Shiraz—may their land be blessed!
> To anoint the noble people of this land,
> I have recollected what I have learned from Syria to Anatolia!
> For I thought it unfair from all those orchards
> To go empty-handed to my friends.[51]

Sa'di is the worldliest of Persian poets and literati—so much so that traveling and getting to see the world, crossing boundaries, dwelling in alien or familiar, inhospitable or even hostile territories became metaphoric to his name, literary reputation, and work. Not only in his *Bustan* and *Golestan*, but throughout all his prose and poetry, a worldly disposition, a global vision, animates his vast cosmopolitan wisdom. Shiraz remains his hometown, which he deeply loves, and to which he always returns, both physically and metaphorically. But he always returns to Shiraz only to leave it. Not just the specific places that he visited, or imagined himself to have visited, but the world, *the idea of the world*, found a happy and wise habitat in his work and through it in the literary humanism that he best represented.

In his cosmopolitan worldliness, Sa'di is definitive to Persian literary humanism—a multifaceted, cross-historical, and self-transformative phenomenon that was produced by generations of poets and prose stylists in dialectical negation of their location at successive imperial and dynastic courts, from the Samanids (819–1005) to the Qajars (1794–1925)—in effect a Trojan horse too precious for monarchs and emperors to ignore, and yet too unruly to rein in with any courtly culture. The decentered and polysemous subjects that animated Persian literary humanism ultimately resolve themselves via an aesthetic cosmopolitanism, an expansive worldliness, that becomes the poetic subtext of a universalizing history. The language and diction of Persian literary humanism were and remained courtly, formal, and imperial, serving the cause of political imperialism, claiming a pre-Islamic pedigree, and yet at the same time positing a moral imaginary that ipso facto discredited any political power that laid a claim to them. While the mosque/madrasah (colleges) became the site of Islamic scholasticism, the court emerged as the domain of literary humanism, which served and subverted it at one and the same time.

The making of Persian literary humanism over the last 1,400 years was the product of a creative imagination institutionally embedded in an imperial worldview that politically facilitated and normatively engendered its worldly character. The most immediate memory of Iran after the Arab conquest of the mid-seventh century was that of the Sassanid empire (224–651), which assumed wider and more fantastic proportions the more Iran as a self-conscious world plunged deeper into its Islamic universe. The initial conquests of the Umayyad dynasty (661–750) soon dissolved into the making of the Abbasid empire (750–1258), in which the Iranian vizierate and Persian literati played an ever larger and seminal role. Retrieving its cosmopolitan disposition—it was formed in conversation with Arabic before it went global into both the Ottoman and the Mughal empires—exposes the worldly character of Persian literary humanism as it was narrated over a millennium and a half of its sustained history.

Imperial cosmopolitanism is what informs and sustains Persian literatures and gives it at one and the same time both its decorous formalism and its hidden subversive disposition. At the expansive heart of Persian literature is a lyrical subject that oscillates between miasmatic creativity and a defiant critical judgment. The literary humanism that is thus projected is not predicated on an all-knowing subject that can be either immediately identified or else held responsible for one thing or another, for the multiple subjects that write through that humanism are always already conflicted, heterogeneous, and subversive precisely at the moment of precarious services to courtly powers, a Trojan horse even despite the poets themselves. The paradoxical disposition of the subject is definitive to the worldliness of Persian literary humanism, as it is occasioned by the imperial imagination that it served and yet achieved a mode of desacralized transcendence beyond the political limits of any empire, for it reminds the ruling elite of their mortality precisely as it celebrates its own immortal ideals. At the courtly center of these empires always dwelled the decentered subject of a literary humanism that served and subverted that court at one and the same time—and thus mapped its own fragile worldliness.

In the context of these imperial cosmopolitanisms, Persian literary humanism was formally courtly and politically accommodating, and yet the seeds of dissent, predicated on a tropically decentered, amorphous, and miasmatic subject was always evident in it—narratively in Ferdowsi's *Shahnameh*; romantically in Nezami's *Khamseh*; formally in Omar Khayyam's subversive quatrains; thematically in Naser Khosrow's politically defiant poetry; metaphysically in Sana'i, Attar, and Rumi's mystical poetry; and indeed lyrically in Rumi, Sa'di, and Hafez's *ghazals*. These varied and variegated seeds of embedded discontent finally became paramount in the making of the nineteenth- and twentieth-century transmutation of Persian literary humanism into a robust, transgressive, and revolutionary version of itself. Thus, even before the advent of colonial encounter with European modernity, Persian literary worldliness had a long history of navigating through multiple narrative tropes that at one and the same time gave the humanism that it conditioned its historic poignancy and its imperial dis/services.

The Poet and the World Conqueror

In one of the apocryphal stories told about Sa'di, we read how once, returning from a Hajj pilgrimage, he stopped in Tabriz to visit some of his old friends who were now high-ranking dignitaries at the court of Abaqa Khan (1234–1282), the mighty Mongol warlord of the Ilkhanid dynasty. One day he sees them in attendance on the sultan and tries to evade them, so as not to put them on the spot while they are in royal company. But the two old friends notice Sa'di and descend from their horses, rush toward him, and embrace and honor him in an exceedingly reverential manner. The sultan is surprised by this and turns to

the two revered courtiers and tells them that for so many years they
have been at his court, but they have never treated *him* with the same
reverence they had shown Sa'di. "Who is he?" the sultan wonders. "He
is our father, your majesty!" "Father?" the sultan asks in amazement.
"Yes, sire, our father and master Sa'di, whose reputation has certainly
reached Your Majesty!" The sultan summons Sa'di to his court. Sa'di
initially declines, but finally accepts and pays the monarch a visit. As
Sa'di is leaving the court, the Sultan asks him to grace him with an
advice. Sa'di tells him just to remember one thing: "You cannot take
anything from this world to the next except the consequences of good
and bad deeds. Now you do as you wish." The Sultan asks him to compose a poem to that effect. Sa'di accepts and extemporaneously says:

> A king who attends to the well-being of his subjects
> Deserves the taxes he collects, for they are like the wages
>   that a shepherd receives.
> And if he were not to attend to the needs of his subjects,
> May that wealth be like poison to him for he is abusing Muslims.

Upon hearing these two lines, the Sultan bursts into tears from fear and
pleads with Sa'di to tell him if he is like that shepherd or not, to which
Sa'di repeatedly responds that if he is like that shepherd in the first line
of the poem, then he is, or else he befits the second line. The moral of
the story is even more poignant when we notice that the author of this
apocryphal story is unknown (though the story does appear in many
manuscripts and critical editions) and that in effect Persian literary
humanism has willed and authored it in absentia of any particular or
known poet. To top it all, the anonymous author adds at the end of the
story that in his own time no poet could have advised any reigning monarch like that, for at that time "greengrocers and butchers" had ascended
the throne![52]

    This apocryphal story about Sa'di and Abaqa Khan, recorded and
repeated in the oldest extant manuscripts, reveals the sovereignty of the
literary humanism he best represents over the moral imagination of
the empires that sought its endorsements. The point of the story is not
just the fear and trembling of a world conqueror of what Sa'di thought
of him, but the fear and trembling of all other warlords of what any other
poet (recollecting Sa'di) thought of them. In the shadow of world conquerors and vast empires was created a worldly literature, a cosmo-

politan literary humanism, that consisted of multiple universes coming together to form a moral constellation of its own making. In Ferdowsi's *Shahnameh* a universal epic became the defining moment of this literary humanism; that same defining moment is found in Nezami's *Khamseh* and Jami's *Haft Awrang* cosmogonies of love and adventure; in Sana'i, Attar, and Rumi's mystical universes that point humanity to an intuition of transcendence beyond the domain of all doctors of law; in Rumi, Sa'di, and Hafez's lyrical poesies that hanged the world on a conception of love that made life meaningful and trustworthy; and in Omar Khayyam and Baba Taher Oryan's quatrains and their whisperish doubts of the very assumption of any metaphysics beyond the reach of the here and even the now.

Adab, as literary humanism, thus functions as the successive traces of empires that have mislaid a claim on it and given it their dynastic designation—the Taherids, the Saffarids, the Samanids, the Ghaznavids, the Seljuqids, the Mongols, and so on. Upon these traces, the presence of *Adab* is always epiphenomenal, the similitude of what it says it is, and as such it remains in a perfect position to dislocate that which lays any claim to it—from a sovereign monarch to a sovereign subject. *Adab* effaces itself as it announces itself and demands and exacts readership, attention, and a political pause that punctuates its literary character. *Adab* jeopardizes the other than itself, the court that seeks to claim it, as it recites its disclaimers. *Adab* is the undecidability of the literary manners momentarily legislated. On that plane of traces, the literary act is self-revelatory: its signs mean nothing beyond themselves and thus embrace everything, and its hermeneutic circles are expansive and open-ended. The practitioners of *Adab* achieve this literary feat by speaking from the depth of a knowing subject that does not know itself, and in that unknowingly enabling proposition it denies itself agency, and as such it is read by an unknowing audience that always delays and defers its own agency.

As the collective subtext of successive empires, Persian literary humanism served and subverted, at one and the same time, any imperial claim on it: it served them by praising the reigning monarch at the court beyond any human limit or possibility, and it subverted that court precisely by positing a hyperbolic ideal that no mortal monarch could ever match or rival. When these poets went mystical in their poetry, in the manner and memory of the eleventh-century poet Baba Taher

Oryan, then mighty warlords like the Seljuqid Sultan Tugrul (990–1063) would plead with them for their blessings. "What can I give you in return for your blessing," Tugrul is believed to have asked Baba Taher, while mounted on his horse. "Just get out of the way of the sunshine!" The more mortal the political might of empires appeared, the more immortal looked the worldly disposition of *Adab* (particularly when it flaunted otherworldly rhetoric in it mystical guise) as an institution running its own independent, autonomous, and even sovereign course, for the Persian literati posited themselves and what they did as "the judgment of history" on the passing realm, and thereby crafted a literary continuity that became a reality sui generis, an arbiter of truth and beauty that royal courts courted at their own peril or else shunned at heavy cost. The whole world may have been at the mercy of Abaqa Khan or Tugrul Khan, but Abaqa Khan and Tugrul Khan were at the mercy and grace of one poetic allusion that Sa'di or Baba Taher planted in one hemistich as opposed to another.

The story of Persian literary humanism and the cosmopolitan worldliness that it embraced ought to be told in a manner that neither yields the spontaneity of its creative effervescence to historicism nor makes it falsely contingent on the presumed primacy of a scholasticism that was altogether tangential to its nature and disposition. Working toward a literary history without falling into historicism and retrieving a literary humanism without reducing it to a binary of Islamic scholasticism are both to be posited by way of thinking through a defiant humanism against the legitimate objections of a robust philosophical antihumanism. The theoretical foregrounding of that project would then prepare the way toward the recognition of the literary subtext of a civilization—though this time not in Arabic but in Persian, where the subtext is doubly repressed, for it was doubly removed from any sacred certitude and as such made ipso facto transgressive—a transgressive disposition that then moves from Persian to Turkish and Urdu. Working toward a reading of Persian literature as a mode of literary humanism thus puts it beyond the distorting reaches of both Orientalism and nativism at one and the same time by wedding it to a cosmopolitan worldliness that has always been its natural habitat.

The story of Persian literary humanism begins violently with the Muslim conquest of Iran but ends happily with the open-ended sovereignty of the literary act, and in between that violent beginning and that triumphant ending it gives birth to one of the greatest stories ever told. Iranians are born to their mothers' lullabies, live by the lyrics of their poets from one end of eternity to another, and die to the lamentations of yet another lullaby that gently soothes and assures them back to mother earth, just before they rise again in the ethereal songs of their mystics. In their poetry they seem, always seem, to have found eternity. Upon the full spectrum of that open-ended eternity, I sometimes think there are as many stories of Persian literature as there are Persian-speaking people around the globe. This is mine.

1

The Dawn of an Iranian World in an Islamic Universe

The Rise of Persian Language and Literature (632–750)

THE TRAUMATIC BIRTH of Persian language and literature in the violent aftermath of the Muslim conquest of Iran was predicated on the aggressive transmutation of the more sedentary social and economic conditions of the Sassanid empire into the far more aggressive supremacy of the nascent Islamic triumphalism that was soon consolidated in the Umayyad caliphate (661–750) and then the Abbasid empire (750–1258). The Sassanid empire (224–651), extending from central Asia to the Mediterranean, was vastly urbanized and sedentary; the Islamic triumphalism that invaded and conquered it was lightweight, agile, and initially divided along patrimonial communalism. The Sassanid imperial haughtiness lost; the nascent Muslim agility won. The conquering Muslims had Islam as their deriving moral momentum (God had promised them victory), and before long the emerging Islamic scholasticism in general, and Sunni jurisprudence (*fiqh*) in particular began to consolidate, justify, codify, and systematize the ideological foregrounding of their conquest—almost at the same time that Persian language and literary humanism emerged as the site and citation of moral and imaginative resistance to that total and absolute domination. As Islamic scholasticism consolidated the Arab conquest, and Arabic literary humanism beautified and smoothed its rough edges, Persian literary humanism emerged as a site of cultural resistance and literary opposition to the Arab conquest—if by nothing else then at least by being in the language of the vanquished against the will of the victorious. As Islamic scholasticism helped the conquering Arabs rule "in the Name of Allah, the Merciful, the Compassionate," and Arabic literary humanism, to which

Iranians contributed immensely, globalized that domination, Persian literary humanism allowed Iranians as a people to resist that rule in the humble name of humanity, the fragile, the forgetful. This is not to suggest that Iranians had ceased to be Muslims at the gate of their literary creativity—on the contrary, Persian language and literature became the vessel of the selfsame faith to navigate uncharted territories. But nevertheless, even as Muslims, Iranians were now the liberated architects of a whole new vantage point on the worldly fragility of being merely human.

Before long, and against all odds, as successive dynasties and empires in eastern Muslim lands began adopting Persian as their courtly language, Persian literary humanism emerged as the vanguard and the vista of a rising cosmopolitan worldliness in the farthest reaches of Islamic civilization as the creative imagining of a new world, crafted by poetry and politics alike, to make life habitable for a whole new familiarity with it. This was the prose of a renewed historicality, the poetry of defiance, and thus the traumatic birth of a literary humanism in which was embedded (always already) a *deferred and differed defiance.* As both Islamic scholasticism and Arabic literary humanism sustained the course of Arab imperial conquest of both the Umayyad and the Abbasid dynasties, Persian literary humanism emerged as the lingua franca of either Iranian or Persianized Turkic dynasties—at once serving and promoting a different brand of imperialism, and yet subverting it via this deferred and differed defiance. This paradoxical disposition of Persian literary humanism, rooted in its traumatic birth as the defiant language of a defeated people that in turn becomes triumphant in rival courts, stayed the course with it until the advent of European colonial modernity, when it finally exited the royal court and faced a vastly different horizon of cosmopolitan worldliness.

The Trauma of an Imperial Defeat

The Sassanid empire came crumbling down like a house of cards—as if all that it needed was a snap. All that remained was dust—as if it never were.[1]

The vast Sassanid empire, which lasted for over 400 years and stretched from the Mediterranean to the Himalayas, was already deeply weakened by a quarter-century-long war with the eastern Roman

Empire. Their days of might and glory far behind them, between 603 and 628 the Sassanids were barely holding their own against the advancing Byzantines.[2] The two aging empires were at it, weakening each other, entirely oblivious to a gathering storm to their south. The deeply corrosive wars on both sides ended with the victory of the emperor of the eastern Roman Empire Heraclius (r. 610–641) and the defeat and subsequent murder of Khusraw II, the twenty-second Sassanid king (r. 590–628). After this fateful defeat, for some 4 years (628–632) the Sassanid court collapsed into absolute chaos and anarchy until it fell into the equally incompetent hands of Yazdegerd III (r. 632–651), the twenty-ninth and last king of the dynasty, the emperor during whose reign the Sassanid empire finally buckled under the advancing Arab armies—a bizarre and undignified end to an imperial adventure that to this day traumatizes Iranian nationalists and baffles historians.[3]

The successive battles that ultimately ended the Sassanid empire in defeat and disgrace came in relentless waves and with whipping force. The Prophet of Islam, Muhammad ibn Abdullah (570–632), had just died, having barely unified Arabia. Invading vast and prosperous northern territories was the principal way out of internal strife in the aftermath of the Prophet's death and the problem of succession that the nascent Muslim community faced. The Sassanid empire, whatever was left of it in will and wherewithal, was caught by surprise. Battles followed, one ignominy after another: the Battle of al-Qadisiyyah (636), the Battle of Jalula (637), the Battle of Nahavand, also known to Muslims as *Fath al-Futuh*, or Victory of Victories (642), are all indelibly marked on the historical memory of Iranians as the undecipherable signs of a seismic change in world history and in their grasp of their place in the world.[4] The prolonged wars between the Sassanids and the Byzantines, the deeply fractious Sassanid dynasty, divided along class conflicts and aristocratic privileges, religious conflicts between Zoroastrianism and its contenders, facing the ferocity of a zealous army winning small but effective battles that gnawed at a great empire until it brought it down—these are some of the enduring explanations that historians provide as to how and why was it that the mighty Sassanids collapsed and the Arabs succeeded in bringing their new faith into a vast empire. There remained some pockets of aristocratic resistances here and there to save the empire, but the last princes of the Sassanids escaped to China and for years lived as refugees in the Chinese royal courts of Emperor Gaozong of Tang (r. 649–683). The Sassanid empire was no more.[5]

What about the people who were at the mercy of one defeated empire and now the subjects of a new and triumphant one? Subjected to a colonial conquest and imperial occupation by a military might that was aided by a solid religious triumphalism, a period of massive and forced acculturation commenced in the former Sassanid realm—a period that later historians would dub "two centuries of silence."[6] The trauma of defeat was to remain with the land for generations to come—a trauma underlined by excessive brutality and widespread violence. The name and reputation of al-Hajjaj ibn Yusuf al-Thaqafi (661–714), an Arab warlord, is synonymous for historians of early Islamic Iran with brutish treatment of Iranians by the reigning Umayyad caliphate. Al-Hajjaj's reputation as a murderous conqueror is accentuated by the report that he evidently detested Persian language. Not just al-Hajjaj ibn Yusuf, but all conquering Arab generals treated Iranians (as indeed all non-Arabs) "with undisguised contempt."[7] Iranian historians still remember and record with horror[8] the manner in which Arab conquerors (bringing along the message of Islamic brotherhood of mankind) would put a heavy metal yoke around the neck of an Iranian peasant, recording on it the amount of tax he had paid, what village he was from, and how much he still owed the Arab warlords in charge of those villages.

To be sure, it was also at the very same time that the conversion of conquered people to Islam began gradually to forge a transregional Muslim identity that glossed over these racialized hostilities between the Arab conquerors and their non-Arab subjects. But what also remains paramount is the defeat of one massive empire (the Sassanids), the rise of successive Arab empires (the Umayyads and the Abbasids), and the gradual rise of Persian as the lingua franca of eastern provinces and later dynasties against the imperial imposition of Arabic as both a sacred language and the language of a conquering culture. As Muslims, Iranians were now among the most active participants in the making of the triumphalist Islamic culture—in both scholastic and literary terms. But at the very same time, Persian language, and eventually literary humanism, were carving an emotive and soon imperial space for themselves—a force and phenomenon that would mark their own history.

With the surviving Sassanid princes running away to China, the new generation of Iranian elite soon joined their conquerors and found a defining (and even lucrative) presence in the emerging Islamic empire in both political and intellectual domains. Politically they were instrumental in transforming the tribal leadership of the Umayyad dynasty into the cosmopolitan imperialism of the Abbasids.[9] Intellectually, the Iranian elite soon mastered the Arabic language and began contributing voluminously to the ideological foregrounding of the Islamic empire in both Islamic scholasticism and Arabic literary humanism.[10] The emerging Islamic civilization was in a considerable part their handiwork. "The most eminent of the early grammarians," observed the great historian Ibn Khaldun (1332–1406) generations later, "traditionalists, and scholastic theologians as well as those learned in the principles of Law and in the interpretation of the Koran, were Persian by race or education and the saying of the Prophet was verified—'If Knowledge were attached to the end of the sky, some amongst the Persians would have reached it.'"[11] In both scholastic and humanist terms, the recently converted Iranian scholars and literati were instrumental in consolidating the ideological foregrounding of their Arab/Muslim conquerors. These achievements notwithstanding, they still faced unabated racialization, because of which many of them "provided themselves with fictitious pedigree, on the strength of which they passed for Arabs."[12] These luminary Iranians, having in effect given birth and momentum to not just Islamic scholasticism but also Arabic literary humanism, became the signposts of a cosmopolitan worldliness beyond any racialized distinction. For such towering figures as Bashar ibn Burd, Abu Nuwas, Ibn Qutaybah, al-Tabari, al-Ghazali, "and hundreds of others"[13] were in fact Iranian by birth and upbringing.

Such racialized binaries, however, ultimately dissolved themselves in the material and moral expansion of successive Islamic empires, for the intellectual feat was accompanied by emerging political power to produce a transnational cosmopolitanism. The rise of the Barmecide family of viziers to power and prominence during the early Abbasid period is the political hallmark of this renewed prominence for the Iranian elite. The Barmecide were a noble Persian family that became exceedingly powerful during the reign of the Abbasids. Yahya the Barmecide was the vizier to the legendary Harun al-Rashid (r. 786–809) and a key force in transforming the administrative apparatus of the Abbasids from tribal patrimonialism to a cosmopolitan empire. While the Iranian intellectual elite and Persian vizierate were instrumental in transforming the Umayyad tribalism into the Abbasid cosmopolitan imperialism and in contributing massively to both Islamic scholasticism and Arabic literary humanism, the weight of the imperial acculturation was so massive that there was still plenty of defiant energy left in both political and intellectual terms.

Resisting the New Empire

Not all leading Iranian intellectuals joined forces with their conquerors, or even converted to Islam, or if they did abandoned their autonomous moral and intellectual aspirations, or faked Arab credentials for themselves. There were crucial and consequential exceptions to those who did. One of the most significant cultural aspects of the emergent intellectual elite was their resistance to both Umayyad tribalism and even Abbasid patrimonialism, perhaps best expressed in the rise of the Shu'ubiyyah movement—a cultural, literary, and poetic uprising principally initiated by Iranians late in the Umayyad period and well into the Abbasid period, which subsequently extended as far east as Andalusia in later centuries.[14] In direct response to the racialized Arab domination, the Shu'ubiyyah movement received its name from its proponents' favorite Qur'anic passage (49:13) about equality of nations and peoples. They even went so far as fabricating prophetic traditions to buttress their call for equality among Arabs and non-Arabs. "He that speaks Arabic," they believed the Prophet had said, "is thereby an Arab." "Whoever of the people of Persia accepts Islam," they believed another Prophetic tradition had said, "is [as much an Arab as] one of Quraysh."[15] Because of their insistence on the equality of all Muslims regardless of being Arabs or non-Arabs, the Shu'ubiyyah were also known as the Levelers (*Ahl al-Taswiyah*).[16] In response to the racialized discriminations they faced, such early representatives of the Shu'ubiyyah sentiments as Bashar ibn Burd (714–784) and Ibn al-Muqaffa' (d. 756) openly flaunted their Persian heritage and boasted of their noble origins. The unabashed racialized prejudices of the prominent Arab literary figure al-Jahiz (781–869) resulted in reverse racism among some of the Shu'ubiyyah poets too. The Shu'ubiyyah movement was the most significant early sign that within Islamic empires were voices of cultural and revolutionary dissent—that all was not well with the states of Islam and that the Prophet's message of equality and brotherhood of all Muslims had failed to register with the overriding imperial racism of the conquerors. The presence of Iranian cultural elite in the Shu'ubiyyah movement was perhaps the most significant sign of a rising and resounding site of resistance against the new imperialism that had supplanted the Sassanids.

The Iranian reaction to the Arab conquest was not limited to cultural terms in one way or another. The heavy-handed tribalism of the Umayyads generated widespread popular revolts by the urban poor and the abused peasantry of the conquered territories. These popular dissents were initially expressed in sectarian uprisings under the banner of such Islamic movements as those of the Kharijites and the Shi'is. The generic class of the Mawali (the Clients) became a derogatory designation for non-Arab Muslims who were treated like second-rate subjects of the Umayyad dynasty, assigning primacy of status to their own tribal lineage. The Mawali class, emerging as subjects of a new empire but disenfranchised from its privileges, soon became the recruiting crowd for various forms of uprising against the Umayyads. All these sectarian social uprisings were ultimately channeled to a massive revolt against the Umayyads led by their tribal rivals the Banu Hashim, which was politically manifested in the Abbasid revolution, led by their Iranian general from Khurasan, Abu Muslim. Abu Muslim led the Abbasid Revolution in 747 and came to power in 750, but he was subsequently murdered by the second Abbasid caliph, al-Mansur, in 754. The murder of Abu Muslim by the Abbasid caliph was the cause of even more widespread revolt against their dynasty throughout their Iranian territories.

Not all political uprisings against the Umayyad and Abbasid dynasties were in sectarian Islamic terms. Syncretic, proto-Zoroastrian, religious ideas and sentiments soon began to give ideological momentum to these movements. Most of these uprisings, waged by the urban poor and the abused peasantry against their Arab conquerors, were variations on the theme of Abu Muslim's revolt—though this time around not in support of the Abbasid cause but in fact against their empire and in revenge for their cold-blooded murder of Abu Muslim. In the aftermath of his death, Abu Muslim became a prototype for a succession of chiliastic uprisings in northern Iran, from Khurasan and Sistan to Gilan and Azerbaijan. The former Sassanid territories were not easily ruled by the new Arab warlords.[17]

One of the earliest such uprisings was led by Sundbath (d. 755), a man from Neishabur who led a major revolt against the Abbasids. Sundbath was a friend and comrade of Abu Muslim and led his revolt by way of avenging Abu Muslim's death, in fact claiming that Abu Muslim had not died and was in hiding. Proto-Zoroastrian and Mazdakite colors were widely evident in these so-called Bu-Muslimiyyah uprisings— ostensibly to avenge Abu Muslim's murder but mostly the indices of a widespread urban and rural dissatisfaction with the Abbasid rule. In Sundbath's preaching, Islam and Zoroastrianism were fused to meet the revolutionary demands of his movement. The revolt of Sundbath, crushed by the Abbasids, was followed by those of Ustadhsis (d. 768) and then al-Muqanna' (d. 779)—both of which manifested themselves again in markedly proto-Zoroastrian terms, for they too claimed prophethood, as the reincarnations of Abu Muslim and epiphanies of God. Al-Muqanna', the more esoteric leader, wore a mask by way of hiding his own identity and adding to the mysterious disposition of his uprising. These movements formed what would later be known as the Khorramiyah millenarianism, even going so far as claiming divinity for Abu Muslim. The same was with the revolt led by Babak Khorram-Din (795–838), who led yet another uprising against the Abbasids, which lasted for almost two decades, again fueled by a proto-Zoroastrian syncretic ideology—ideologies of revolt that were clearly stated against the Islamic disposition of the Arab empire that sought to subdue and silence the lands it had scarcely conquered.

These scattered but persistent uprisings in eastern Muslim lands eventually led to the formation of the first Persian dynasties. With the establishment of the Tahirid dynasty (821–873), the Persian-speaking world began to have its first autonomous royal court. Despite their nominal homage to the Abbasids, the Tahirids were effectively in charge of their own territories. Established by Taher ibn Husain, a general in the Abbasid caliph al-Ma'mun's army, the Tahirids ruled over a vast territory in eastern Iran that extended all the way to India and at some time even had the capital, Baghdad, under their military might. The Tahirid dynasty was followed by the Saffarids (867–1495), whose reign in southeastern Iran extended into modern Afghanistan and Pakistan and gave further political momentum to the cause of Iranian cultural autonomy and sovereignty.[18] Ya'qub bin Laith as-Saffar, the founder of the dynasty, is famed to have responded to a poet who praised him in Arabic, "Why do you praise me in a language I do not understand?"[19] Among these early dynasties the Samanids (819–1005) were the most avidly active in promoting Persian language and culture—but so were the Ziarids (931–1090) and the Buyids (934–1055).[20] The fate of Persian literature was now squarely interwoven with the emerging dynastic politics that sought to secure an autonomous niche for local and regional powers at the outer peripheries of a central Arab caliphate now increasingly drawn from and anchored in the western Islamic world.

As first the Umayyad and then the Abbasid dynasty sought to consolidate the Arab conquest of Iran, and a platoon of Muslim scholastics (leading among them the newly converted Iranian scholars) helped them do so in legal, juridical, and theological terms. But soon after, in the course of the Shu'ubiyyah movement, the Iranian cultural renaissance began to reassert itself in multiple terms—political and intellectual—the most important and enduring of which was the rise of Persian language and letters. From peasant uprisings with sectarian or syncretic ideologies to the Shu'ubiyyah-inspired prose and poetry, from Persian noble families infiltrating the Abbasid empire to the Iranian intellectual elite giving vast momentum to theological and philosophical rationalism—the resistance to Arab domination and dynastic feudalism was relentless, uncompromising, multifaceted. The crowning achievement of this moral uprising against political defeat was the Persian language and Persian literary humanism—at once deeply influenced and enabled by the thriving Arabic literary humanism, while cultivating and expanding its own literary and political domains.

The Rising Sovereignty of the Literary

The Persian court of these dynasties soon emerged as the principal site of literary production for primarily political reasons—for first and foremost Persian was and remained the language of the people, from the landed gentry to the peasantry, from the urban elite to the impoverished artisans, and to rule them their conquerors had to speak their language. The formation of Persian as a literary language, which began with the retrieval of its pre-Islamic heritage, occurred almost simultaneously with Persian literary humanism's emergence as part of resistance to Arab imperial domination and Arabic humanism. Although

Persian literature itself soon became imperial, this was always offset by its rebellious disposition, which was rooted in its response to the victorious Arab culture. So as mundane as the language of tax collectors, and yet as lofty as a poetry befitting kings and queens, as rebellious as the tongue of a defeated people reclaiming their collective dignity, and yet as accommodating as serving the political interests of successive empires, as distinct and self-referential as the idiomaticity of any literary tradition would demand, and yet as syncretic in its syntax and morphology as any language in the vicinity of the rich and triumphant Arabic would be: that is the definitive and paradoxical hybridity from which Persian literary humanism initially emerged and subsequently developed in multiple and varied terms.

What we of today call "Persian literature" is a variegated body of prose and poetry that was created over vast imperial territories from the Indian subcontinent through Iran to central Asia and Asian Minor. The epicenter of this literary production was what are now the boundaries of Iran and Afghanistan, pushing north into central Asian territories— and the birth pangs of its worldly formation were evident in the immediate aftermath of the Arab imperial conquest of Iran.[21]

In the context of varied Persianate imperial domains and their full and multifaceted participation in and contributions to Islamic civilization, Persian literature constitutes a rich, diversified, syncretic, and yet autonomous aesthetic event to which Persian-speaking literati and their historical audiences have actively contributed. In its language and rhetoric, aesthetic ideals and emotive dispositions, poetic sensibilities and creative imagination, this literature is not reducible to fundamental tenets and doctrines of Islam, or any other religion for that matter. Although the majority of Persian poets and literati were nominally or even believing Muslims of one sort or another, their universe of imagination and literary production constitutes a reality sui generis, a space of aesthetic experience irreducible to any particular religious worldview. Christianity has in some significant degree influenced anyone from Shakespeare to James Joyce. But we ordinarily do not remember them as Christian poets, dramatists, or novelists. Zoroastrianism, Judaism, Buddhism, Hinduism, Manichaeanism, Mazdakism, and all the major and minor sectarian divisions within Islam have also invariably contributed to the Persian literary imagination. But the totality and integrity of that imagination is principally an aesthetic phenomenon irreducible to any one of its religious or nonreligious informants. Persian literary humanism is a reality sui generis. It has historically fed on itself. It is markedly different from Islamic scholasticism, the major aspects of which were doctrinally mandated to be performed, and were performed, in Arabic.

Perhaps the single most significant aspect of the Persian literary imagination, as it was delivered in a colorful panorama of formal styles and aesthetic sensibilities, is the noncanonical nature of its language, which creatively posited itself next to the sacerdotal Arabic of the dominant Umayyad and Abbasid empires. As it gradually developed after the Arab invasion of the early seventh century, modern Persian (as distinct from Pahlavi, or Middle Persian, and Avestan, or Old Persian) was a language in which no sacred text was believed to have been revealed. As opposed to Hebrew and Arabic, in which the Bible and the Qur'an were believed to have been delivered, Persian remained a constitutionally vernacular language when placed next to Arabic, though entirely cosmopolitan when placed in its own subsequently imperial context in the eastern domains of the Islamic civilization. The successive transmutations of Persian from an imperial (Sassanid) to a vernacular (next to Arabic) back to imperial (in Iranian or Persianate dynasties) remained definitive to its paradoxical disposition. The memories of the sacred language of the Avesta and the exegetical language of Pahlavi having been surpassed and superseded by the absolutist hegemony of the Qur'anic Arabic, Persian language occupied a noncanonical space in which worldly and historical events could assume a poetic and literary character beyond the doctrinal inhibitions of the sacred certitude of the Muslim canonical text. In this historical context, Islamic scholasticism was *nomocentric*; Persian literary humanism was *homocentric*.

There were of course any number of syncretic religious movements launched immediately after the Arab invasion of the seventh century, such as the Khorramiyah and Beh-Afridiyah, that had occasional rhetorical claims to the revelation of a "Persian Qur'an." But with the political demise of such movements, the idea of a "Persian Qur'an" never materialized. The Arabic Qur'an remained the canonical text of all sacred imagination for Muslim Iranians who fully and productively participated in the narrative, historical, canonical, and scholastic unfolding of that imagination. The phrase "Persian Qur'an" was also later used by Abd al-Rahman Jami (1414–1492), who called Jalal al-Din

Rumi's *Mathnavi Ma'navi* "the Qur'an in Persian," meaning that Rumi's text had the sacred sanctity of the Qur'an expressed in Persian. Such hyperbolic expressions notwithstanding, the historical fact has always been that Persian remained a noncanonical language in which the literary imagination was paramount, autonomous, and even sovereign. This does not mean that Qur'anic allusions do not abound in Persian literature. But it means that those allusions are assimilated into the literary act and the poetic event, and not vice versa.

The Persian literary imagination has been acted out in the vicinity of multiple sacred imaginings. Zoroastrian, Manichaean, Mithraic, Mazdakian, Hindu, Buddhist, Judaic, Christian, Islamic, and a host of other less politically successful religions have emerged or arrived in historical succession and left their marks on Persian literary culture. But the very fact of their multiplicity, that they have come in succession and, in doctrinal hostility or mutual tolerance, have coexisted or tolerated one another, has also prevented any one of them from exercising absolutist or hegemonic power over the Persian literary imagination. Zoroastrian, Manichaean, and Buddhist imageries entered the aesthetic parlance of the Persian literary imagination and endured, even flourished, well into the Islamic period.[22] Even within the Islamic context, sectarian doctrinal differences continued to divide the active and passive loyalties of Persian literati throughout the ages. Whereas up until the fifteenth century the majority of Persian poets and literati could be identified as Sunnis, after the establishment of the Safavids (1501–1732), Shi'ism became at least the nominal faith of many poets and writers. But against all these religious, sectarian, and doctrinal divides, Persian literary humanism had its own sovereign presence as the literary subtext of successive empires and dynasties—all the way from the Tahirids in the ninth century to the advent of colonial modernity in the nineteenth century and then down to the Pahlavis in the twentieth century.

The active loyalties of Muslims (Iranian Muslims included) were divided also along variedly dominant scholastic grounds. Having theological/antitheological, philosophical/antiphilosophical, or mystical/antimystical predilections further added to the divisive orientations that loosened the active absolutism of any one particular ideological force over the Persian literary imagination. As for the oral and literary sources of this imagination, Iranian, Indian, Chinese, Arabic, and Turkish material converged to create a uniquely worldly and multicultural literary universe that went beyond the confines of any particular politics. The world was home to the Persian poet as he (mostly) or she (quite a good number of cases) sat to wonder on the nature and purpose of being-poetically-in-the-world.

There was a marked geographical demarcation in the formation of Persian literary humanism. As Iraq (Baghdad in particular) emerged as the cultural capital of the Arabic west, Khurasan (Neishabur in particular) became the cultural capital of the Persian east. From the central heartland of Khurasan, Persian literature eventually spread as far east as the Indian subcontinent, as far west as the Balkans, as far north as China, and as far south as the eastern coasts of Africa. Contemporary Iranians, Afghans, Tajiks, Indians, Pakistanis, Turks, and Arabs have almost as equal a claim on Persian literary history as they have on Arabic and Turkish. Today Iranians, Afghans, Tajiks, and Persian-speaking people anywhere around the globe have an identical claim on the heritage of Persian literature. Nationalization of Persian literature is a fairly recent and fundamentally flawed project. This literature is the heritage of a transnational imperial age, and as such has categorical difficulties being cut down and pasted onto nationalistic projects. Its formative forces—relations of power, changing features of royal patronage, revolutions, wars, invasions, and conquests—have had much more to do with literary productions than anything ethnic, racial, or linguistic. For the Turkish warlords of central Asia, in particular, Persian literature became the chief ideological legitimizer of their rule, without them necessarily having a taste for it.

As an apparatus of political legitimation, production of Persian literature functioned as one of the principal ideological forces at the disposal of any dynasty that patronized it, including the Turkish dynasties of the Ghaznavids (977–1186), the Seljuqids (1038–1194), and even the Ottomans (1281–1924). As a courtly artifact, Persian poetry was equally present and instrumental in India, particularly during the reign of the Mughals (1526–1858). Persian literary humanism was not wedded to any place or power and departed for greener pastures when patrons did not cater to it. Exacerbated by the coming to power of the Shi'i Safavids (1501–1732), who, having substituted Shi'ism as the state ideology, had no particular need, penchant, time, or taste for Persian poetry, Persian and Indian poets found India a far more congenial, hospitable, and rewarding place than Iran. The result of these varied historical replacements is that any history of Persian literature in the sixteenth and seventeenth centuries ought to be traced to India rather than Iran. Whether self-consciously or not, dynasties that considered themselves Turkish, Persian, or Indian throughout the medieval period adopted the political apparatus of Persian literary humanism to fulfill the major ideological task of state legitimation in a space adjacent to other, principally Islamic, modes and modalities of legitimacy. Whichever way these dynasties turned in their fame and fortune, Persian literary humanism was the beneficiary—the autonomous, even sovereign, apparatus of granting or withdrawing legitimacy to them.

Retrieving an Ancient Heritage

When the Arabs conquered the Sassanid empire, Iran was already a very ancient land. That ancient history was a matter of sacred recollection for Zoroastrian priesthood and a source of popular myth-making for people at large when the Arab conquest happened, and much later it became the subject of European Orientalist scholarship and Iranian nationalist pride and prejudice in the nineteenth and twentieth centuries. But beyond these uses and abuses of history, what remains most significant in the midst of all crosscurrents of historical memory is the fact that the gradual retrieval of ancient, pre-Islamic history was a matter of constructing a unified and pre-existing world against the emerging Islamic world of the Arab conquerors. While pre-Islamic Iranian history was a matter of Zoroastrian *doctrinal narratives* and later Persian *epic myths* at the time of the Arab conquest of the seventh and eighth centuries, in the aftermath of European Orientalist scholarship extensive archeological excavations gradually led to more detailed *historical* accounts that fed into the two complementary narratives of colonial Orientalism and ethnic nationalism, which effectively fed on each other. But if we look at the selfsame evidence from the vantage point of Persian literary humanism, we discover the preparatory stages of a cosmopolitan worldliness that was eventually brought home in the making of Persian language and literature.[23]

In that context, the first textual evidence of a literary tradition in Iran goes back to the royal inscriptions of the Achaemenid kings, Darius I (522–486 B.C.E.) and his son Xerxes, in particular.[24] Inscribed in old Persian, these royal texts indicate a proud, self-confident, assertive, and theocentric imagination: "A Great God is Ahura Mazda," reads one, "who created the earth, who created the sky, who created man, who created happiness for man, who made Darius the King."[25] Although theocentric, this royal self-conception remained consistently conscious of mortal beings: "Says Darius the King, by the favor of Ahura Mazda I am such a man who is friend to right. I am not a friend to wrong. It is not my wish that the weak man should have wrong done to him by the mighty; nor is it my wish that the mighty man should have wrong done to him by the weak."[26] In these inscriptions, the king as narrator extends his authority from the supreme deity, Ahura Mazda, and then acts as a moral agent full of ethical convictions. With an authority extended from God, Darius the king is the man, the lawgiver, the monarch, the chronicler, and the historian of the Achaemenids' glorious deeds. In an inscription, Darius gives a rather full, boastful account of how he overthrew Gaumata, a Magian who had pretended to be the slain brother of Cambyses, Smardis. Darius's account is swift, concise, and not entirely devoid of narrative elegance. The self-assured sovereignty of the king as the narrator would eventually become the suspenseful sovereignty of the subject in Persian literary humanism.

From the royal inscriptions of the Achaemenids to Zoroaster's own hymns, the *Gathas*, there lies a vast arena of imaginative oral traditions that are distilled and barely visible through the Avestan prism. This oral tradition was perpetuated by Iranian minstrels, who carried forward a fantastic tradition of narrative songs. As storyteller/magicians, these minstrels had a central social function in ancient, particularly Parthian and Arsacid, communities.[27] They sang songs, told stories, recited poems, delivered satires, mourned and celebrated on occasions, and carried forward a rich and rewarding tradition of songs and tales, legends and myths, stories and anecdotes. The traditions that these minstrels carried were obviously not suddenly disrupted in the aftermath of Arab conquest and must have still been alive, certainly in the northeastern part of the Iranian world in Khurasan.[28]

In the Avesta, the Gathas, and the pre-Zoroastrian hymns Zoroaster remembered later, the Yashts are the first, most comprehensive poetic narrative we have that remains principally at the service of the Zoroastrian sacred imagination. Gods, deities, and heroes, as well as their metahistorical relations to worldly being, are the subjects of these sacred narratives in which the poetic proclivity plays a vital role. But

the same poetic urge that partially served the sacred imagination of the
Avesta was equally at work in the epic narrative of ancient Iranians. As
evident through the prism of the Avestan Yashts, a flourishing oral tradition had given epic proportions to legendary rivalries between the
Iranian house of Kianian and its perpetual enemies, the Turanians.
Not until the time of Ferdowsi (d. ca. 1025) do we have textual evidence of this effervescent oral tradition, which must have been active
and widespread during the composition of the Yashts.[29] Iranian minstrels must have transmitted various versions of these epics from generation to generation. Under the patronage of the Parthians and the
Arsacids (247 B.C.E.–226 C.E.), this minstrel tradition was given enough
political momentum to permit the extension of a folkloric narrative
into a royal lexicon of cultural legitimacy. It has been suggested[30] that
the overwhelming, and politically successful, Eastern (Zoroastrian) tradition overshadowed the receding memory of the legends and histories
of the Achaemanids and the Medes, and that by the time of the Sassanids only the Kianian legends had been constituted as the legitimizing
force at the disposal of courtly scribes.

The Sassanid emperors were the direct beneficiaries of both the
sacred and the worldly imagination that had informed much of the sentiments of the earlier Iranian communities. Certainly by the time of
the composition of *Khwaday-namag* (*The Book of Lords*) during the reign of
Khusraw II, the renarration of already ancient legends and stories had
assumed legitimizing status. *Khwaday-namag* represents the earliest fictive renarration of a legendary history that puts the poetic occasion at the
service of ideological legitimation of the state apparatus and the Persian
court. As the first man/king, Gayomarth, in this narrative, presides over
the creation and succession of the rendition of much older stories. As
"the most important literary heritage of ancient Iran,"[31] *Khwaday-namag*
is a compendium of moral and philosophical injunctions as delivered
through the Persian poetic imagination. As such, however, it is as much
a distant memory of pre-Sassanid legends and stories as it is an immediate mirror of the moral and political imperatives of the Sassanid empire.
As a supreme example of storytelling, *Khwaday-namag* represents some
of the rhetorical features that have endured through subsequent variations in the epic genre.

The absence of textual evidence has permitted suggestions that pre-
Islamic Persian literature lacked any significant nonreligious literature.

"This judgment," Ehsan Yarshater has suggested, "ignores two basic facts: that the secular literature of Iran prior to Islam was essentially oral, and that much of the early New Persian literature was in fact only a new rendition or direct rendering of Middle Persian and Parthian creations."[32] As an example, Fakhr al-Din As'ad Gorgani's (d. ca. 1063) eleventh-century modern Persian renditions of the love story *Vis and Ramin* is our textual link to the Parthian version of the story available to the poet in Middle Persian and Georgian.[33] As an adventurous love story, *Vis and Ramin* reads in marked contrast to *Derakht-e Asurig*, which, extant in Middle Persian, provides one of the earliest examples of didactic dialogics in Persian poetry, in this case between a tree and a goat. Among an overwhelming body of religious verses that Manichaean and Zoroastrian priests produced in Parthian and Pahlavi, *Ayadgar-e Zariran* and *Derakht-e Asurig* are the textual examples of an autonomous literary imagination. Indirectly, however, we know of an even more elaborate literature. What in later sources is identified as *Fahlawiyat* refers to an extensive body of poetic traditions—*Surud*, *Chakamah*, and *Taraneh* among them—with which even the later Persian poets, whose prosody was considerably Arabized, were also familiar.[34]

The Persian literature produced after the Arab invasion of the seventh century was thus both textually and orally heir to a substantial body of literature that, whether in direct (written or oral) transmission or in continuation of literary imagination, persisted well into the later periods. As it gradually emerged as a noncanonical language, Persian evolved into a literary language of varied and fertile imagination. Always under the shadow of Arabic, modern Persian carried within its slanted relation of power to Arabic the traumatizing memory of a decisive defeat. As Arabic became the paternal language of the hegemonic theology, jurisprudence, philosophy, and science, the maternal Persian, the language of mothers' lullabies and wandering singers, songwriters, storytellers, and poets, constituted the subversive literary imagination of a poetic conception of being. The significance of the pre-Islamic literary heritage was the gradual but concerted retrieval of a *world* that was defeated and lost and yet gave historical legitimacy and momentum to the one that generations of Persian literati were constructing for themselves and for the future. In this heritage, Persian literary humanism in effect glossed over its dividing barrier along Islamic scholasticism and the Arab conquest. It now had a worldly lineage.

Permission to Narrate in Persian

The parameters of cultural resistance and enabling political prowess were both palpably present at the nascent moment of Persian literary humanism. Predicated on putting up stiff revolutionary resistances to the rising Arab empires, and determined to retrieve its linguistic, literary, and cultural heritage as part and parcel of that resistance to militant acculturation, Persian literary humanism soon began to sprout in divergent and multifaceted directions—in both prose and poetry. The evidence surviving the ravages of time with respect to the earliest texts produced in modern Persian prose is exceedingly scant.[35] Literary historians, however, are particular about the three earliest, almost simultaneous, prose narratives that have reached us from the tenth century. The first text is the Persian translation of the great Abu Ja'far Muhammad ibn Jarir al-Tabari's (838–923) *Tarikh al-Rusul wa al-Muluk* (*The History of the Prophets and Kings*) by Mohammad ibn Mohammad ibn Abdollah al-Bal'ami (d. 996). Bal'ami prepared this translation at the court and following the command of the Samanid monarch Mansur ibn Nuh ibn Ahmad ibn Isma'il (r. 961–976).[36] This Persian translation was done only a few decades after the original Arabic was written and is a solid evidence of both an advanced and precise Persian prose and a narrative interest in al-Tabari's *History.* The monarch who commissioned it, Mansur ibn Nuh the Samanid, thus sought to legitimize his court, designate its Iranian character, inevitably craft a space for Persian prose, and implicate Persian, and with it those who speak it, in a universal history that begins with the biblical/Qur'anic creation of the world and concludes with his own time. The crafting of this prose displays all the enduring notes of what will happen in Persian literature for the next millennium, just like the notes of a prelude in a musical composition.

The second extant text from this early period is the Persian translation of the monumental Qur'anic commentary by the same al-Tabari, *Jami' al-Bayan fi Tafsir al-Qur'an* (*Compendium of Commentary on the Qur'an*), again commissioned by the same Samanid monarch Mansur ibn Nuh. As the translator of this text testifies at the beginning, Mansur ibn Nuh had received a copy of the original Arabic *Commentary* but could not read or understand it properly. So he solicited the permission of religious authorities to have it translated into Persian. These authorities provided written permission to that effect, and he proceeded to command the

Persian translation to be prepared for him.[37] This translation also reads today as historic testimony that by this time Persian prose was very advanced and exquisitely capable of the most sophisticated Qur'anic commentary. The choice also indicates that while the translation of al-Tabari's *History* was a sign of interest in historical narratives, there was an equally compelling interest in scholastic discourses of Qur'anic hermeneutics. But evident and paramount in both translations is an attempt to secure pride of place for Persian as the courtly language of a major dynasty with sovereignty over a vast territory in the east.[38] That sovereignty was now made ideologically contingent on this freshly minted Persian prose.

The third earliest text of Persian prose that has reached us is an introductory treatise on medicine and pharmacy called *Al-Abniah 'an Hagha'iq al-Adwiah* (*Principles of the Attributes of Plants*) by Abu Mansur Movafaq ibn Ali al-Heravi, again commissioned by the very same Persian patron Mansur ibn Nuh, the Samanid monarch. This particular text is solid evidence of the earliest application of Persian prose to scientific writing. Again the prose is polished, effective, purposeful, and obviously drawn from a vast and varied scientific vocabulary that came naturally and melodiously to Abu Mansur al-Heravi. What the composition of this particular text at the Samanid court indicates is that on a small scale the nascent Iranian dynasty in the east was effectively positing itself as a counterpoint to the Abbasids in the west as a patron of arts and sciences—though this time entirely in Persian. This modality of the Persian or Persianate court as the haven of Persian literary humanism continues apace for the rest of Islamic history, extending from Iranian (Tahirids, Saffarids, and Samanids) to Turkish but Persianate (Ghaznavids and Seljuqids) courts and beyond.

There are a number of other texts from this nascent period, but perhaps the most important, written even earlier than these three books, is the text of a *Muqaddimah (Introduction)* to a prose *Shahnameh (Book of Kings)* that was composed in 957 by (or under the general editorship of) a certain Abu Mansur al-Mu'ammari, who was a learned scribe in the service of Abu Mansur Mohammad ibn Abd al-Razzaq al-Tusi (d. 962), who had specifically ordered the composition of this Shahnameh. This Abu Mansur Mohammad ibn Abd al-Razzaq al-Tusi was a prominent dignitary in the Samanid court, and the man he had commissioned to compose this prose Shahnameh, Abu Mansur al-Mu'ammari, had brought together an "editorial board" from all over Khurasan and Sistan with an astonishing command over both Persian prose and ancient histories and legends.[39] Except for this *Introduction*, the complete text of that prose *Shahnameh* has disappeared. But we know that the great Ferdowsi had direct access to it, and in fact based his poetic rendition of the *Shahnameh* precisely on that prose *Shahnameh*, so closely, in fact, that he even repeats some of its historical (anachronistic) mistakes.[40]

The story of this *Introduction* to *Shahnameh* as one of the earliest extant texts of modern Persian prose, which is later rendered in the Iranian national epic as composed by Ferdowsi, is coterminous with the rise of Persian literary humanism. In this *Introduction* we read that Abu Mohammad Abdollah Ruzbeh ibn Daduyah, known as Ibn al-Muqaffa' (d. 757), one of the greatest literary humanists of his time, who was murdered by the Abbasid Caliph al-Mansur (r. 754–775) because of his Zoroastrian inclinations, translated the text of *Khwaday-namag* (*The Book of Lords*), originally composed during the reign of Khusraw II (590–628), from Pahlavi into Arabic. *Khwada* here means "Lord" or "Shah," so this text is in fact the earliest indication of the genre of *Shahnameh* that was translated from a pre-Islamic source in the aftermath of the Arab invasion by leading Iranian literati.[41] Neither the original Pahlavi nor Ibn Muqaffa''s Arabic translation has reached us, except by various references from other corroborative sources. In fact none of these *Shahnameh* texts prior to Ferdowsi's masterpiece has survived. But the fact they existed is corroborated by many other sources. Even after Ferdowsi, historical references exist referring both to his poetic rendition and other extant prose versions of *Shahnameh*. So it is not unusual that just before the time of Ferdowsi we have yet another of these prose *Shahnamehs* ordered by Abu Mansur Mohammad ibn Abd al-Razzaq al-Tusi. The presence of these *Shahnamehs* so early in the Islamic history of Iran is a clear indication of a prose (and soon poetic) interest in both preserving the national mythology of a defeated people and using it as the modus operandi of successive dynasties to carve out a niche of legitimacy against foreign (Arab and Islamic) domination.

Reading this *Introduction* to that prose *Shahnameh* today gives a key contemporary context in which we can retrieve the spirit of Persian literary humanism and see how and in what particular terms it took shape and formed a formidable space. After praising God and the Prophet, Abu Mansur Abd al-Razzaq turns to praising two interrelated ideas,

danesh (knowledge) and *sokhan* (speech). "As long as the world has existed," he proposes, "people have been inclined towards knowledge and
have honored speech, considering it the most enduring legacy."[42] The
first example of such eloquent speech that Abu Mansur provides is—
and here is the very first indication of the cosmopolitan worldliness of
Persian literary humanism—the text of *Panchatantra*, as ordered by an
Indian monarch, which was subsequently brought to the Abbasid Caliph
al-Ma'mun's (813–833) attention by Ibn Muqaffa',[43] who interested the
caliph in this text by reporting to him that it was brought to Persia and
ordered translated into Pahlavi by Khusraw I Anushirvan (r. 531–579),
the Sassanid emperor. From this point forward, Anushirvan becomes
the prototype of just and magnificent kings to whose majesty and might
and proverbial justice all Abbasid and even other Muslim kings and sultans aspire. This Arabic text of *Panchatantra* is then brought to Nasr ibn
Ahmad Samani's attention, who in turn orders his vizier, the same al-
Bal'ami who had translated al-Tabari's *History*, to translate it into Persian, and also orders his court poet Rudaki Samarqandi (858–941), to
render it into Persian poetry. Upon hearing this story, Abu Mansur Abd
al-Razzaq wishes to do the same and commissions al-Mu'ammari with
the task of compiling a Shahnameh from various sources that existed in
Khurasan and Sistan so that kings and courtiers will learn the proper
decorum of imperial gathering of power and prestige.

Al-Mu'ammari, the author of the *Introduction*, then says that reading this book will teach other poets and scribes the techniques of writing books and its elements of composition and that it is also beneficial
to the kings as to how to rule properly. So the first beneficiaries of the
text are in fact the literati, and the kings are second. This intercon-
nected nexus of the literati and the monarchy becomes definitive to
Persian literary humanism—it gives it its cosmopolitan worldliness and
imperial reach, its tropes of just authority, and its penchant to lend or
withdraw its legitimizing power to that effect, making monarchy as a
result contingent on its narrative sovereignty, and its own institutional
legitimacy subject to the fate of empires. The net result: the formative
trauma of its birth and breeding transfuse its paradoxical relations to
political power.

The imaginative geography evident at the birth of Persian prose posits "Iran" as the center of universe. In the geography that al-Mu'ammari

presents in his *Introduction*, the world is divided into seven climes, and Iran is the seventh and central clime, and as such is the best and most habitable, and ancient kings have named it "Iranshahr/Persepolis."[44] Iranshahr, Abd al-Razzaq reports, extends all the way from Amu Darya (in central Asia) to the Nile River (in Africa)—and all other climes, from India to Europe, from Russia to Yemen, are all located around Iranshahr. Iranshahr is also "the most noble in every art," and all other climes have only certain aspects of its excellence. Though undoubtedly rooted in earlier and more ancient geography, this renewed centralization of Iran (Persepolis) in the universe has a newly found significance in the east in response to the rise of Baghdad in the west as the epicenter of Islamic universalism and Arab imperialism. There is a pride of place evident in al-Mu'ammari's imaginative geography that narratively pulls the center of the universe into Persian and the Iranian east and away from the imperially Arabized west, which extended into North Africa and Asia Minor.

The sources of al-Mu'ammari's information about ancient Iranian history and legends are from extant written sources such as the *Khwadaynamag*, as well as the old landed gentry (*Dehqan*) and other learned members of the literati from Khurasan and Sistan, some of whom he identifies by name.[45] The history that he relates begins with mythical king Gayomarth and then comes down to Houshang, which period is called the Pishdadian, followed by Kian, and then the Arsacids, and finally the Sassanids.[46] He then adds: "The prose is by Abu Mansur al-Mu'ammari, humble servant of Abd al-Razzaq who ordered the composition of this Shahnameh." This prose and pattern of historiography from this point on becomes definitive and even conventional to narratives of Persian literary humanism—a mode of historiography (or even one might call "historiosophy") that begins in time immemorial and comes down to the time of the reigning monarchy and the literary humanist at the court commissioned this particular narrative. What we have here is the first extant textual evidence of how it was that Persian literary humanism emerged as a bona fide project of dynastic and empire building in deliberate parallel construction with Arab tribal dynasties and the vast Islamic empire led by the Abbasids. The Persian prose of this nascent period is purposeful, confident, and self-assuring. It exudes a narrative competence that reveals generations of systematic development soon after the Arab invasion and long before these first extant texts were produced. But above all, their almost exclusive production in the Samanid court is a solid indication of a determined dynastic design to facilitate and cultivate a solid and enduring institutional base for Persian literary humanism as the modus operandi of Persian and Persianate dynasties.[47] The Samanid court at this time was functioning as the dynastic prototype and the microcosm of an empire, modeled on the Sassanids, facing up to the Abbasids, and providing a template for future empires—empires within which Persian literary humanism was to play a defining, albeit paradoxical, role.

Birthing Poetry

Would it not be strange, and paradoxically befitting, if the first Persian poetic composition turned out to actually be by an Arab poet who was in fact at the service of the Umayyads, before he turned against his patrons and started satirizing and scandalizing them?[48]

Modern (as opposed to Middle/Pahlavi or Ancient/Avestan) Persian poetry began by adopting Arabic prosody and modifying it. The chief theorist and systematizer of Arabic prosody was the great al-Khalil ibn Ahmad al-Farahidi (ca. 718–791), a prominent philologist best known as the person who invented the science of *al-ʿArud* (Arabic prosody). Among the earliest surviving pieces in Persian poetry is Abu al-Abbas al-Marvazi's panegyric for Caliph al-Maʾmun, composed in Marv in 808. Mohammad Qazvini (1877–1949), the leading literary historian of his time, dismisses the veracity of this claim, because he believes this poem to be too perfect and mature in its prosody to have been composed so early and so soon after al-Farahidi's systematization of Arabic prosody.[49]

What Qazvini offers as the very first poetic composition in Persian has a bizarre history that contains much about the early Islamic conquest of Iran. The earliest Persian poems, Qazvini proposes, are in fact much earlier than 808, and what the few lines that have survived reveal is that the origin of Persian poetry is not in any royal court but in fact (and quite naturally so) in common and folkloric songs sung in the streets and alleys of the newly conquered lands.

The story that Qazvini reconstructs is based on a variety of Persian and Arabic primary sources, which he summarizes solely for the purpose of giving the circumstances when these few lines were uttered. During the reign of Yazid ibn Muʾawiyah (r. 645–683), a certain Ubayd Allah ibn Ziyad had become the governor of Kufa and Basra, and later Khurasan in 673. By 674 he had crossed the Amu Darya. In 680, Yazid I ordered Ubayd Allah to keep order in Kufa as a reaction to increasing popularity there of the grandson of the Prophet, Hossein ibn Ali. Muslim historians (the Shiʾis in particular) remember this Ubayd Allah ibn Ziyad for executing Hossein ibn Ali's cousin Muslim ibn Aqil and persecuting his other supporters. He was also one of the leaders of the army of Yazid I during the famous Battle of Karbala (680) in which the grandson of the Prophet, Hossein ibn Ali, and his small band of followers were murdered. This very Ubayd Allah ibn Ziyad had a brother named Ibad ibn Ziyad, who was appointed as the governor of Sistan by Yazid I. A poet named Yazid ibn Mifraq wanted to accompany Ibad to Sistan. Ubayd is reported to have called the poet to a private meeting and told him that he was not happy with the idea of Ibad going with his brother to Sistan, because his brother was going to war and would not have time to attend to Yazid and as a result the poet would turn against his patron and satirize and ridicule him and give his family a bad name. The poet, however, assured Ubayd that would not be the case. Ubayd asked him to promise that he would write to Ubayd if his brother ignored him and before he started satirizing him. Yazid the poet agreed. What is already remarkable here is the fear of a ruthless warlord for a poet and the power that these poets had over their patrons.

So Yazid the poet goes with Ibad to Sistan. In Sistan, what Ubayd had feared happens. Ibad becomes preoccupied with his conquest. Yazid the poet is offended by the warlord's lack of favor to him and, precisely as Ubayd Allah ibn Ziyad had predicted, he becomes angry and starts composing satires about Ibad and his evidently very long beard. Ibad initially ignores Yazid but ultimately arrests and imprisons him on some trumped-up charges. Yazid the poet finally runs away from Sistan and goes to Syria, where he continues to scandalize both Ibad and Ubayd and their father and mother. Ubayd finally arrests him and wants to kill him, but Caliph Yazid intervenes on his behalf. So Ubayd arranges for a nasty torture and force-feeds the defiant poet sweet wine mixed with a diarrheic herb. Yazid the poet is thus afflicted with severe diarrhea—at which point Ubayd sends him into the streets tied to a cat and a pig to humiliate him. Persian-speaking kids gather around him

and ask him in jest and ridicule what was this coming out of him—to
which he responds in a Persian poem:

> Ab ast-o nabiz ast / It's Water and it's Wine;
> O osarat-e zabib ast / It's the juice of grape;
> O donbeh farbeh-o pi ast / [My] tail is greasy and fat;
> O Sumayyah rusebi ast / And Sumayyah is a whore.[50]

Sumayyah being Ubayd and Ibad's mother, who was putatively a famous whore. Yazid the poet endures much hardship from these two
powerful brothers, but ultimately Yazid the Umayyad caliph intervenes
on his behalf (for the poet's relatives served in his army and he does not
wish to alienate them), and Yazid the poet spends his last years in a safe
haven in Musil.

This incident was during the reign of Yazid ibn Mu'awiyah and thus
certainly before 683. The second case dates back to about a quarter of a
century later, in the year 726, when a Muslim general attacked a Turkish
territory in central Asia and was squarely defeated, and upon his return
from the battlefield children in the streets of Khurasan were greeting
him with satirical songs that began with the refrain:

> Az Khatalan amadhi / You have come back from Khatalan,
> Beh-ru tabah amadhi / You have come back shamed.[51]

Both these cases show the popular and even the folkloric dimensions of Persian poetic disposition before it became highly formalized
and stylized at various royal courts. Both these instances also reveal
the satirical, palpably political, and defiant poetic voices that were
heard in the streets and alleys, chanted by children and charged against
the powers that be. Both cases also report the carnivalesque occasions
under which the first recorded sounds of Persian poetry were audible to
early Muslim historians. As is evident in these two disparate cases, the
power of the poets against their princely patrons was publicly staged,
and the princes obviously feared it. If the origin of Persian prose has
been detected in the Samanid court and at the service of dynastic and
empire building, the first evidence of Persian poetry is in fact found
in the streets and alleys and in satirical defiance of power, uttered by
Persian-speaking and non-Persian-speaking children and poets poking
fun at the power of those ruling over them. The combination of these
two geneses of prose and poetry in fact points at the paradoxical disposi-

tion of Persian literary humanism that at one and the same time legiti-mized and delegitimized the power that it both served and subverted.

Logos *for* Ethnos

The case of an Arab poet having perhaps accidentally (and under dire circumstances) "composed" the first Persian poem points to the evolving societal formation of Persian language and literary humanism as a nar-rative site committed to the principal primacy of *language* rather than *race, ethnicity,* or *nationhood.* Persian belonged to those who spoke it, and Persian literary humanism to those who produced and celebrated it— Arab, Iranian, Turk, or Indian, if we were to use contemporary designa-tions. Good speech, *logos/sokhan,* rather than *ethnos/nezhad,* soon emerged as the key operating factor and the defining moment of Persian literary humanism. Persian literary humanism was thus a normative and moral *space* consistently cultivated within an imperial imaginary rather than a mere ethnic uprising replicating Arab tribalism. The more the early Islamic empires become tribal in their caliphal leadership, the more Persian literary humanism went precisely in the opposite direction, to-ward a vast literary cosmopolitanism in direct contradistinction with the politically privileged Islamic scholasticism. Persian literary human-ism was far more an expression of an emerging cosmopolitan civiliza-tion within which Persian-speaking people and literati wanted to as-sure themselves a pride of place, rather than a blind racialized response to the violent tribalism that was ushered in by the Umayyad (or later Abbasid) patrimonialism. To be sure, initially it was the formation of dynasties such as the Saffarids, the Samanids, or the Tahirids, which had distinct claim to Iranian heritage, that gave dynastic momentum to the formation of Persian literary humanism. But soon it was the Ghaznavids, and later the Seljuqids, namely Turkic dynasties, that became the prin-cipal patrons of Persian language and literature, and after them the Mongols, their descendents the Il-Khanids, and the Timurids, who had a Turko-Mongol lineage. For all of these dynasties, Persian literary hu-manism was the lingua franca of power and wisdom, grace and humility, admonition to justice and claim to legitimacy. Persian literary human-ism was a universe of imagination in which partook different imperial projects, with a vastly cosmopolitan, patently transnational, claim on earth and its inhabitants. Though a claim to a separate *ethnos/nezhad* was what triggered the Shu'ubiyyah movement, within which Persian literary humanism initially emerged, it was *logos/sokhan* that soon became the defining trope of *Adab*. The very raison d'être of this cosmopolitan humanism was transcending tribalism and dynastic hubris and reaching for an imperial globalism that reflected the worldly conquests of warlords who, at their own risk, sought to patronize it.

This vision of Persian literary humanism at its nascent moments posits an entirely different take on the mode of historicism that habitually accompanies Persian literary historiography—in alternatively Orientalist or nationalist parlance. As we try to keep historicism at bay to reach for the *literary* disposition of Persian literary humanism, it is important to keep in mind that "history" itself (any mode of historiography) has been exposed for its own literary predicates. In his *Allegories of History: Literary Historiography after Hegel* (1992), Timothy Bahti has extensively and persuasively argued the allegorical (literary) character of historiography, an argument that radically qualifies the truth-claims of all acts of writing history. Even before Timothy Bahti, Hayden White in his *Metahistory: The Historical Imagination in Nineteenth-Century Europe* (1973) had already sought to excavate the nature of historical imagination in the production of historical knowledge. White considered the writing of history as the plotting of any other story that is predicated on the formative force of an ideology. Based on the works of other theorists of ideology, such as Karl Mannheim, White narrowed in on the four archetypical genres of romance, comedy, tragedy, and satire to show the formist, organist, mechanicist, and contextualist modes of historiography. A historian may have an anarchist, conservative, radical, or liberal narrative bent that may opt for representation, reduction, integration, or negation of the plotted history, assimilated to one of four dominant tropes: metaphor, metonymy, synecdoche, and irony.

Similar narrative predilections are evident in both the Orientalist and nationalist historiography of Persian (as indeed any other Orientalized) literature. As the two dominant modes of Persian literary historiography, European Orientalism and nativist nationalism reflect and complement each other, one assimilated into a narrative Eurocentricity as one of its multiple civilizational others, while the other responded in kind by making it integral to an exclusionary literary nationalism. Lost to both was the paradoxical disposition of Persian literature that was rooted in its traumatic birth of a defeated minority (Persian) within a triumphant majority complex (Islam). That trauma has remained with Persian literary humanism and been the defining moment of its specific worldliness—so that the specific allegorical trope of Persian literary humanism is neither irony nor synecdoche, neither as a metaphor nor as metonymy, but in fact as a traumatic paradox. Neither as the civilizational other of the myth of "the West" nor as the literary allegory of the nation, but predicated on that traumatic birth, Persian literary humanism has posited its unique cosmopolitan worldliness, hitherto concealed to both Orientalist and nationalist narratives.

The self-realization of Persian literary humanism is ipso facto a syncretic act. The history of Persian *Adab* throughout the centuries has by its nature and disposition accommodated reciprocity with political and literary forces that have come its way. As a hybrid product of a cosmopolitan context, Persian *Adab* is rooted within changing imperial contexts, and not until the nineteenth and twentieth centuries would it be claimed by any nationalist sovereignty or imaginary—and as a result the medieval history of *Adab* in both Persian and Arabic is immune to later nativist nationalism and historiography, which lay a claim on that history. The fact that both Arab- and Persian-speaking worlds (plus many other worlds) were united in making their Muslim subjectivity possible paved the way for future fusions of the two. What separated Arabic and Persian literary humanism so early in their history would later come back to unite them when both the Arab- and the Persian-speaking worlds faced European colonialism, in the crucible of which both the Arab- and Persian-speaking literati ultimately left their habitual courtly and racialized locations and entered the *public space* of their common and renewed pact with history.

2

The Persian Presence in
the Early Islamic Empires

Resisting Arabic Literary Imperialism (750–1258)

IN THE FAMOUS Shah Tahmasp, or Houghton, illustrated *Shahnameh* (ca. 1522), there is a scene in which we see a young lad encountering three court poets of Ghazna. Here we see the three prominent court poets—Onsori (d. 1040), Farrokhi (d. 1037), and Asjadi (d. 1040)—sitting and having a picnic. Upon their august and dignified gathering stumbles a not-so-refined-looking fellow who asks politely to be allowed to sit down and join their gathering. These are world-renowned and exceedingly refined court poets and they obviously do not wish to sit in the same gathering with the young intruder. But being poets they decide to turn their refusal to allow the young man to sit with them into a poetic play, a challenge, a wager. You can join us, the three tell the young man, if, and only if, you can come up with the fourth hemistich of a quatrain for which we will provide the first three hemistichs. The young man readily agrees. Reluctant to accept him into their midst, the three mighty court poets deliberately choose a rhyming pattern they are sure, absolutely sure, that there are only three words in the Persian language that would fit the pattern—namely words that end in "-shan"—and they each offer a line:

Chon arez-e to mah nabashad roshan / Even moon is not as bright as your face;
Manand-e rokhat gol nabovad dar golshan / No flower in any garden is as beautiful as your face;
Mozhgant hami gozar konad az joshan / Your eyelashes pierce through any armor . . . ;

To which the young man instantly adds:

> Manand-e senan Give dar Jang-e Pashan / Just like the lance of
> Give in the Battle of Pashan!

The court poets have no idea who "Give" was and what and where was the "Battle of Pashan." They ask the mysterious intruder to explain who these people are, and how he comes to know about them when they did not. The young poet smiles and asks if he can now be permitted to sit down and explain.[1]

The history of Persian classical poetry of course remembers those three court poets with much reverence and admiration. But the name and dignity of that young man—one Hakim Abu al-Qasim Ferdowsi Tusi (940–1020)—today shines in the firmament of Persian literary humanism like no other. The figure of the anonymous poet—competent, caring, soon to outshine others—standing at a distance from the court poets and the court they serve will remain the defining moment of Persian literary humanism for centuries to come. That invisible line separating the solitary poet from the ceremonious co-opting of the court and the poets it employs is the demarcation of the tension that at once enables, compromises, and yet paradoxically liberates the emancipatory powers of Persian literary humanism. It is on that invisible line that I intend to locate this meditation on what precisely is literary about humanism.

Poets, Palaces, and Battlefields

The encounter between Ferdowsi and three Ghaznavid court poets is the apocryphal narrative of a very critical point in the history of Iran in the aftermath of the Muslim invasion. One uncompromising poet spending a lifetime collecting courage, material, and imagination to sit down for 30 years, as he said so himself proverbially, to write the magnificent epic of a people, made into "a people" precisely by virtue of that singular act of poetic genius. Ferdowsi was no typical court poet, nor was he a product of court poetry—precisely the opposite: the very raison d'être of all the subsequent courts and their poets was the product of his poetic imagination. He was an outsider, and in his epic achievement he remained the deus ex machina of a literary heritage that dwelled in

the twilight zone of an optical illusion that can be seen in two diametrically opposed ways: serving and subverting the dynastic court at one
and the same time.

Ferdowsi coming to the Ghaznavid court to solicit support for his
monumental project marks the Turkish dynasty as the historical epicenter of a critical point in the rise of Persian literary humanism. Ferdowsi's work on his epic poem, *Shahnameh*, had started earlier, during
the Samanid period (819–1005), and then came to full fruition during
the Ghaznavids (977–1186). Between the Samanids and the Ghaznavids
ruling successively for a couple of decades shy of two centuries over a
vast territory from Transoxiana to the greater Khurasan and what today is Afghanistan, the eastern territories of the Abbasid empire were
the site of a cultural renaissance unprecedented in its history. The epicenter of resistance to the Arab and Muslim conquest of Iran was always the greater Khurasan in the northeast, diametrically in the opposite direction from the Abbasid caliphate now centered in Baghdad.

The establishment of the Tahirid dynasty (821–873) in the eastern
region is usually considered the first dynastic basis of territorial autonomy from the central Abbasid caliphate. Taher ibn Husain, the founder
of the Tahirids, was initially a general in Caliph al-Ma'mun's (r. 813–833)
army, who soon rebelled against the caliph and established an autonomous dynasty in greater Khurasan. From Khurasan in the east to Azerbaijan in the west, a vast territory always remained in a state of rebellion
and autonomy against Islamic and Arab imperialism. Between these
two poles, the Caspian coast lands of Gilan and Tabarestan were equally
important as the sites of fiercely autonomous dynasties that were never
completely conquered by the invading Arab armies. A succession of local and regional dynasties ruled in the Alborz mountain range from
this early period all the way down to the time of the Safavids in the
sixteenth century. Among these northern dynasties, particularly noteworthy are the Bawandids (665–1349) in Azerbaijan, the Mosaferids
(916–1090) in Daylam and Azerbaijan, the Rawwadids (ca. 900–1071)
in Azerbaijan, the Shaddadids (951–1174) in Arran and eastern Armenia, the Ziarids (931–1090) in Tabarestan and Gorgan, and above all,
the Buyids (934–1055) in much of northeastern Iran and all the way
down to Iraq and even Syria. These were not mere political dynasties
resisting Arab imperialism. These were bona fide sites for the cultivation of Persian language and literature as the modus operandi of the

court culture, and as the most pronounced cultural constitution of resisting Arabic literary imperialism.

The eastern territories under the control of these either concurrent or successive empires, all either Iranian in lineage (such as the Saffarids, the Samanids, or the Buyids) or else heavily Persianized in courtly language and culture (such as the Ghaznavids and later the Seljuqids), extended from Khurasan as the epicenter, north into central Asia and Transoxiana, south into Sistan and down to the Persian Gulf coast lands. The Buyids would in fact stretch the boundaries from north even further eastward all the way down to the Persian Gulf and Iraq, including the capital Baghdad, and Mahmoud the Ghaznavid would pull the edge eastward as far as the Indian subcontinent. The central Arab caliphate in Baghdad had no political or moral authority over these dynasties. Leaders like Ya'qub bin Laith as-Saffar, the founder of the Saffarids dynasty, would wage war against the caliphate, in this instance Caliph al-Mu'tamid (r. 870–892), and boldly challenge their authority. The Buyid Sultan Adud al-Dawlah (r. 949–983) conquered Baghdad, subjugated the reigning caliph, and extended his reign all the way to Syria. Under the reign of these Iranian and/or Persianate dynasties the central Abbasid caliphate had no power over Iranian territories and were in fact sitting upon their shaky thrones entirely at the mercy of the Buyids, the Ghaznavids, or even more so in later years, the Seljuqids. Constant in the court and customs of these vast empires as they territorially rose and fell remained Persian language and literature, both prose and poetry. Persian by this time had arisen as the lingua franca of a counter-imperial drive, checking Arabic and balancing its power—one pushing toward a centralized and centripetal domination, the other pulling by divergent and centrifugal resistance to that domination.

Persian literary humanism was the crowning achievement of this period of resistance and triumph, particularly in Khurasan and at the court of the Samanids, where the first extant translations from Arabic and original compositions in Persian took place, where poets like Rudaki (858–941) and Daqiqi (ca. 935–980) flourished, and where Ferdowsi first conceived of his monumental project. Hailing from the village of Saman near Samarqand, and Zoroastrian in origin, the Samanids ruled for nearly a century in Khurasan and Transoxiana. Led by such deeply cultivated monarchs as Nasr ibn Ahmad and Nuh ibn Nasr, the Samanids were chiefly responsible for advancing Persian language and literature in their court and throughout their realm. But, and this is the crucial context of the rise of Persian literary humanism, by no means was their patronage of the arts and sciences limited to Persian. We have it from the pen of none other than the great medieval Iranian philosopher Ibn Sina (Avicenna, 980–1037), when he was a young man of no more than eighteen, that he visited the library of Nuh ibn Mansur and found room after room filled with the widest range of books, from Arabic philology to Greek philosophy.[2] The legendary physician and scientist of the period Abu Bakr al-Razi (Rhazes, 865–925) wrote his Arabic treatise on medicine, *al-Kitab al-Mansuri*, for yet another Samanid king. The cosmopolitan worldliness of the Samanids, in which Persian literary humanism found a rich and fulfilling habitat, had a much wider frame of reference for itself.

The larger frame of this cosmopolitan worldliness was not limited to the Samanids. From the Tahirids to the Ghaznavids, these royal courts attended to Persian literature with the same open-minded liberality that they did to anything that was happening in arts and sciences in Arabic or even Greek. Perhaps the greatest medieval philosopher-scientist Abu Rayhan al-Biruni (Alberuni, 973–1048) flourished at the court of Sultan Mahmoud the Ghaznavid (997–1030) and his son Sultan Mas'ud. Al-Biruni had solid command of Persian, Arabic, Khwarezmian, Greek, Sanskrit, Syriac, and perhaps even Berber. How could he learn all these languages, were it not for the multilingual cosmopolitanism of the Transoxiana of his birth and breeding under the Samanids and the Ghaznavids? Another luminary philosopher-physician of this age, Ibn Sina was also a product of this environment, as was Ibn Miskawayh (932–1030), who flourished during the reign of the Buyid Sultan Adud al-Dawlah. Despite their Iranian lineage and reports of their even being Zoroastrian (Daqiqi) or Mazdian (Ibn Miskawayh), these prominent philosophers and scientists wrote most of their work in the dominant lingua franca of their age, namely Arabic, and that very fact informs and enriches the production of Persian literary humanism in that very cosmopolitan environment.

The formation of Iranian and Persianate dynastic courts in the eastern provinces was the political bedrock of the rise of Persian literary humanism. These dynasties needed moral and imaginative legitimacy, and Persian literature was there to provide it—always with a subversive twist, a Ferdowsi standing in the presence of court poets, one foot inside their gathering, as it were, the other out—never sure if he was joining or leaving them.

Locus Classicus of Persian Literary Humanism

Perhaps a singular indication of the political autonomy of these Iranian and Persianate dynasties and the confident environment they had created over a vast geographical territory is the production of their own theories of government, irreducible either to Islamic doctrines theorized by such contemporary Muslim jurists as al-Mawardi (Alboacen, 972–1058) in his famous treatise *Al-Ahkam al-Sultaniyyah* (*The Ordinances of Government*),[3] or the pre-Islamic Arab tribalism that both informed the Umayyads and ultimately led to the decline and demise of the Abbasids. The primary example of these treatises, which are usually categorized as "Persian Mirrors for Princes," is the text *Qabusnameh* (composed ca. 1080), written by Amir Unsur al-Ma'ali Keikavus ibn Iskandar ibn Qabus ibn Vushmgir ibn al-Ziyar for the benefit of his son Gilanshah on his marriage to a daughter of Sultan Mamoud of the Ghaznavids. This was matched during the Seljuqids period by the *Siasatnameh* of Nezam al-Molk al-Tusi (1018–1092) and the *Nasihat al-Muluk* of the great al-Ghazali (1058–1111), and Khwajah Nasir al-Din al-Tusi's (1201–1274) *Akhlaq-e Naseri* in the wake of the Mongol destruction of the Abbasid empire in 1258—all of them written originally in Persian.[4] What is crucial about these Persian texts and the genre of Mirrors for Princes they represent is that from the onset of the Arab conquest of Iran down to the Mongol invasion and the end of the Abbasid empire there is a sustained and elaborate body of theoretical and pragmatic literature about the nature and function of government that was specifically written for and in the context of a Persianate world that was deliberately neither written in Arabic nor (except for occasional gestures of piety) Islamic. They are all, in varied degrees, either directly rooted in a retrieval of pre-Islamic, Sassanid theories of kingship, or else pragmatic instructions as to how to run an empire. But, and there is the rub, there is more to this genre of political thought than just teaching a prince how to rule a realm properly.

Both the *theoretical* aspects of these Persian Mirrors for Princes and their *pragmatic* dimensions have been explored in understanding the medieval Persian political culture as something distinct within (or adjacent to) Islamic political culture.[5] But equally important are their *literary* dimensions. Particularly evident in Amir Unsur al-Ma'ali's *Qabusnameh*, which was produced in this crucial and nascent moment, is the fact that its author is fully conscious of performing a *literary* act, a *political* act, and a *pragmatic* fatherly duty all at one and the same time. The whole narrative power of the text resides in its having the authorial voice of a father addressing his son directly and telling him in writing what he thinks is the best manner of not just ruling a realm but in fact living a life. Of the forty-four chapters of the book, the overwhelming majority are on ordinary matters of a life well lived, with only three chapters on vizierate, commanding an army, and kingship, all within the context of a much larger frame of *Bildung* appropriate to a young man and how he should lead a fair, balanced, happy, and judicious life. The text of *Qabusnameh* is in fact the best example of the sort of literature that posits *Adab* (literary humanism) as the defining moment of an aesthetic conception of a self-disciplined life beyond the metaphysical mandates of any revealed religion or its legalized mandates.

What exactly are the instructions of Amir Unsur al-Ma'ali to his son Gilanshah in *Qabusnameh?* The prince teaches his son to be prayerful to God, respectful to his prophets, and reverential to his own parents, all almost in the same breath. Then he instructs his young prince to pursue knowledge and wisdom, learn the etiquette of how to eat food properly, how to drink wine in moderation, how to host a banquet with elegance and flair, how to joke properly with his friends, and how to play chess. He seems to have imagined his son going through life as a full-bodied human being, at once enjoying it and yet having a sense of dignity and propriety about him. He leaves no stone unturned. He even teaches his son the proper manner of making love and having sex ("go with boys in summer and with women in winter,"[6] avoid sex in extreme weather, on a full stomach, or while taking a bath). But above all among his concerns is the proper diction and demeanor that his son must observe most punctiliously. Almost in the same manner, he teaches his son how to take a bath, how to sleep and rest, how to hunt, how to play polo, how to wage war, how to accumulate wealth, how to be a trustworthy person, how to buy slaves, how to conduct business, how to buy horses, how to find a good wife, how to be a good parent, how to be a good friend, how to be afraid of one's enemies ("He who has no enemy his enemies have succeeded"[7]), how to punish proportionate to the crime committed, how to seek knowledge, and how to conduct commerce. He

gives him preliminary instruction in the sciences of medicine and astronomy and tells him how to recognize good poetry and have a knowledge of good musicianship, and then he goes on to advise him on how to
be a good companion to a king, or else even the confidant of a good king,
how to be a good scribe to a king, how to be a vizier or an army chief or,
ultimately, a king, and then at the end how to be a proper *dehghan*
(farmer, landed gentry) or any other professional. He concludes by telling
him how to be a chivalrous man (*javanmard*).

Paramount in the *Qabusnameh* narrative is a balanced reach for the
Aristotelian "golden mean"—avoiding extremities of anything, good or
bad, one way or another. This wisdom is delivered through what always remains a basically literary act, a prose with grace and panache.
Through the thicket of the narrative, the literary disposition pulls
everything together in its own unique way. There is no other way of
categorizing the narrative—religious or secular, Islamic or anti-
Islamic. It is what it is: it is in Persian and has the whole world at its
disposal—Islamic or non-Islamic, Arab or Greek, contemporary or ancient, anecdotal or canonical. Even the appellation "Mirrors for Princes"
(*specula principium*) is something that European Orientalists have as-
cribed to the genre, extending from its European models (which culminated in Machiavelli's *The Prince* [1513]), with a certain degree of justi-
fication, but not completely so. *Ketab-e pand-ha* (*The Book of Advice*) is
what the author calls his own work, written from the vantage point of
what he calls "*shart-e pedari*" (fatherly duty), and he says from the very
outset that he is not so hopeful that his son will actually listen to the
father's advice.

There are indications from the text that the royal father had no
expectation that his son will in fact ascend the throne one day, and that
this epistolary set of advice is just a narrative device. Be that as it may,
in his book Amir Unsur al-Ma'ali assures his son of his noble lineage
and reminds him of his duty to honor that lineage, which goes back to
pre-Islamic Persian kings and monarchs. That royal lineage gives a certain aura of antiquity to the recently minted (in relative terms) Persian
prose. In the active process of that prose, *Qabusnameh* crafts its own narrative, quotes from the Qur'an and the Hadith on one page and from
Persian and Greek wisdom literature on another, with a personal anec-
dote about being out on campaign dropped in on the next. The final
result is a text that can be read almost a millennium after it was written

with delight and deference at one and the same time, a sense of antiquity framing its immediacy and humanity almost 1,000 years ago when it was composed, and yet fiercely insightful even today, without demanding any leap of faith from its readers.

Perhaps the single most important reason for the timelessness of *Qabusnameh* is that in it there is the idea that good government emanates from a sense of a good life, a worldly, self-conscious life. The Islamic metaphysics, the whole Qur'anic revelation, and the sense of the transcendence that is coterminous with it is here stripped of its metaphysical immanence (embedded in the Latinate Arabic in which the Muslim Holy Book was revealed), and a mode of being is posited that is not just within human reach, but is in fact the only plausible design evident in its worldly reality. Islam as a whole revelatory production is here not so much as opposed or challenged as it is assimilated, digested, into a more fragile and tangible and contingent meditation on the very materiality of life, a materiality that can only yield to a meaningful life embedded in its immediate worldliness. The very prose of that kind of worldliness detranscendentalizes the transcendence. After reading *Qabusnameh*, and without the book having anything but reverence for the Qur'an, you may wonder with a book like this why would anyone need a divine revelation about how to conduct one's life fairly and squarely. To be sure, the author does not posit his book in juxtaposition against the Muslim holy book, nor does he privilege it with extrajudicial authority over the mandates of a civilized life. In and of itself, *Qabusnameh* is a perfectly decent book to regulate a noble and purposeful life. Certainly there are aspects of it that may offend later readers, for example, chapters on slavery and its treatment of women as mere sexual objects at the disposal of the primacy of the masculinist sexuality. But you can easily alter, disregard, or altogether change them, or substitute other ideas that supersede them, all without much metaphysical commotion in the universe. It is not as if you are touching God's words! The author of the book was no god—just a man, a self-consciously fallible father, writing words of advice to his son, or daughter for that matter, not even sure his child will listen to what he has to say. That's all.

In *Qabusnameh* the Persian poet and the Persianate court have finally come together to produce a political prose that theorizes power in the public domain of the literary. Ferdowsi attending the Ghaznavid royal poets both awaits and departs from the political formation of the Persianate court at one and the same time. In the figure of Amir Unsur al-Ma'ali Keikavus ibn Vushmgir and his *Qabusnameh*, Persian literary humanism becomes a reality sui generis, gracing the Persianate court at will and withdrawing that grace by virtue of its cultivated literary sovereignty.

Literary Worldliness

The related domains of political power and patronage of arts and science of these Iranian and Persianate dynasties was not limited to the eastern territories and extended well into the heartland of the Abbasid empire in Baghdad. The Buyids in particular excelled in this regard. Adud al-Dawlah (936–983), the Buyid prince, ruled Iraq with an iron fist, sponsored Shi'i scholars and causes against the will of the Sunni caliphate, and promoted arts and sciences in every field. In the words of one leading literary historian of Arabic literature, Adud al-Dawlah "built a great hospital in Baghdad, the Bimaristan al-Adudi [even the name of the hospital is in Persian], which was long famous as a school of medicine. The Viziers of the Buwayhid [Buyid] family contributed in a quite unusual degree to its literary renown. . . . The academy which he [another dignitary of the Buyid dynasty, Sabur ibn Ardashir, the prime minister of Abu Nasr Baha'u 'l-Dawla] founded at Baghdad, in the Karkh quarter, and generously endowed, was the favorite haunt of literary men, and its members seem to have enjoyed pretty much the same privileges as belong to the Fellows of an Oxford or Cambridge College."[8] The result of such cosmopolitan disposition of the Buyids was that the great Arab poets like al-Mutanabbi (915–965) praised their princes.[9] These princes did not think of themselves as ruling a province. They thought they were ruling the world—and that worldliness was evident in the literary humanism they promoted.

These dynasties were mostly heterodox and even proto-Zoroastrian in contradistinction to central caliphal Sunni orthodoxy—but the cause and course of Persian literary humanism was irreducible to either orthodox or heterodox sectarianism. Persian literature remained a reality sui generis, rooted in a culture of resistance to Arab imperialism and Sunni orthodox scholasticism, informed and enriched by the ecumenical cosmopolitanism in which it was embedded. The same was not true about Arabic literary humanism, which remained canonical in its commitment to the imperially imposed language of the Arab conquerors and their tribal racism. The relation between Arabic and Persian remained categorically imperial. You would rarely find a Persian poet who did not know and even excel in his knowledge of Arabic language and literature, but you would rarely find an Arab poet who had reasons to command a superior Persian. This was in the logic of imperial domination and had nothing to do with a people's aptitude for learning a foreign language. To this day, there are staunch Arab nationalists who believe Persian to be the language of "soft *ghazals*" and "poetry" and not suitable for "hard sciences" and "scholastic learning." This is a heritage of a once-imperial masculinity attributed to a tribal constitution of the Arab caliphate of the Umayyad (in its ascendency) and even of the Abbasid era (in its decline). With the same logic, it is as unlikely today that a literate American, British, or Frenchman will know an "Oriental" language, yet it is common for people from around the world to know at least some English, or even French, and in fact at times—such as Indian authors who write in English—having massively contributed to its enrichment. Arabic was the lingua franca of a vast imperial project, in the same way that English was to the British Empire or Spanish was to Spanish imperialism. A Persian poet (namely any poet from India to central Asia to Asia Minor whose literary language was Persian, meaning "Persian" as an actual linguistic and cultural designation and not as a nonexistent racial or ethnic marker) had to know Arabic, for the prosody and poetics of his very craft depended on it. But the same was not true of an Arab poet, who had no material or imaginative reasons to know anything other than Arabic or to produce knowledge about the conquered peoples in any language other than Arabic (the "Orientalism" of their time). This made Arabic the triumphant language of an empire (just like English, French, or Spanish at the height of British, French, or Spanish imperialism), rich and powerful in its imperial self-image, and Persian the cosmopolitan language of people revolting against that imperialism, and in time even crafting their own empires—from the Samanids and Buyids to the Ghaznavids and the Seljuqids, and ultimately the Il-Khanid branch of the Mongols. Arabic, Persian, and later Turkish thus emerged as three imperial languages, serving multiple empires—but while Arabic had its roots in the revelatory language of the Qur'an and the triumphant discourse of Islamic scholasticism and Arabic literary humanism, Persian had its roots in the culture of resistance to that imperialism, and Turkish, from the Timurid period forward and culminating in the Ottoman Empire, in turn rebelled against the imperial hubris of Persian.

The literary worldliness of Persian humanism was rooted in this culture of resistance to Arab imperialism and Islamic scholasticism alike. The fact that there were many Iranians among the leading Arab poets (such as the great Abu Nuwas and Bashar ibn Burd) or that the leading Muslim theologians and jurists were also of Iranian origin are among the solid evidences that Persian literary humanism was a global literary movement beyond any ethnic origins—for from this very early period the triumph of *logos* over *ethnos* was definitive to Persian literary imagination. This literature, this humanism, belonged to no ethnicity, but to the language and literary imagination in which it was produced. From India to central Asia to Iran to Asia Minor, poets and prose stylists had equal, identical, legitimate claims to it. It was a literature of resistance to Arab literary imperialism and Islamic scholasticism alike—the two dominant ideological apparatuses of Muslim conquest. The "nationalization" of Persian language and literature in the aftermath of colonial modernity, and its exclusive and flawed claim by contemporary Iranians in the face of its factual transnational disposition are chiefly responsible for this confusion of the illusion of *ethnos* over the fact of *logos* in the making of Persian literary humanism. From Tajikistan to Afghanistan to Iran to India, Persian-speaking communities have an identical claim to this literary heritage within the context of multiple colonially manufactured nation-states. Poets and literati from India to central Asia to the Ottoman territories spoke and wrote in Persian not because they were ethnically "Persian" or that they could prove lineage to a "client" of any "Persian tribe" (a nonexistent category)—but because Persian language and literature were the professional and emotive domains of their imaginative competence.

To understand the worldly disposition of this literary humanism of resistance, we must understand the racialized disposition of the empire that the invading Arab army had crafted. The relation of domination between Arab warlords and their conquered lands was racially coded: Arabs over non-Arabs ("Ajam," meaning mainly "Persians," literally "dumb" or "barbarian"). In many ways what Edward Said observes about English literature in its colonial context is in fact entirely applicable to Arabic literary humanism at the moment of its imperial and triumphalist identification with Arab imperialism of the early Islamic period. If indeed "the pen is mightier than the sword," the pens of Arab and Arabized poets and prose stylists were entirely coterminous with the rise of Arab territorial imperialism, to which Islamic scholasticism of the Sunni schools and Arab literary humanism were institutionally subservient. As Edward Said demonstrated extensively in his *Culture and Imperialism* (1994) the most powerful modus operandi of European colonialism was in fact literary in character and disposition. These literary productions were indeed weapons of conquest, bought and paid for by both the Umayyad and Abbasid caliphates, against which Persian literary humanism was among the strongest voices of resistance (before it became itself a similar vehicle for Persianate empires). The very fact of the survival of this non-Arabic language, let alone the production of a thriving literature in it, remained a supreme sign of resistance to imperial Arabism leading to imperial Persianism. Poets and literary giants like al-Jahiz (781–869) and Ibn Durayd (838–933) were the Jane Austens (1775–1817) and Rudyard Kiplings (1865–1936) of their times. Just as Said's critical reading of nineteenth-century European masterpieces in connection to European imperialism does not diminish their literary significance, and in fact finds a renewed meaning in them, what I suggest here in no shape or form diminishes the literary greatness of al-Jahiz or even Arabized literary masters like Ibn Qutaybah, al-Baladhuri, or al-Zamakhshari, who were in fact deeply Arabized Iranians anyway. What we are witnessing here is the triumph of Arab literary imperialism as the modus operandi of the dominant ideology of conquest. The more that hegemonic claim was universal, the more Persian literary humanist resistance to it became worldly.

"My basic point being," Edward Said says in his *Culture and Imperialism,* "that stories are at the heart of what explorers and novelists say about strange regions of the world."[10] He singles out Carlyle and Ruskin, "even Dickens and Thackeray," and is deeply disappointed that other critics before him have not paid attention to their ideas about "colonial expansion, inferior races, or 'niggers.' "[11] From geographers and historians to poets and prose stylists, Arab literati were instrumental in fashioning "the Persians" as the supreme site of their alterity, their central trope of inferiority and corruption, which confirmed them in their own sense of superiority, of being (literally) God's gift to humanity. There were many derogatory terms for Iranians in this period—al-Majus, al-Gabr, and above all al-Zindiq (plural Zanadiqa) chief among them. The Zanadiqa were the nightmare of Arab imperialists and Sunni theologians alike. Rooted in the Persian word *Zend*—meaning commentary and referring to Middle Persian commentaries on the individual Avestan books—the Arabized word *Zanadiqa* became a racialized slur dismissing Iranians as licentious, dissolute, profligate, wicked, shameless, and just plain morally corrupt. Caliph al-Mahdi (775–785) had appointed a Chief Inquisitor in charge of the *Zanadiqa* to hunt them down and force them to repent or else to crucify them and destroy their books.[12]

Said complained, and rightly so, that "most professional humanists . . . are unable to make the connection between the prolonged and sordid cruelty of practices such as slavery, colonialists and racial oppression, and imperial subjection on the one hand, and the poetry, fiction, philosophy of the society that engages in these practices on the other."[13] Said spoke of a "difficult truth" he discovered in terms of his favorite writers never taking objection to the racialized inferiority to which colonial subjects were treated "in India or Algeria." The same is true of those subjects in every land that came under Arab imperial conquest from the middle of the seventh century to the destruction of Baghdad by Mongols in the middle of the thirteenth century. The racialized ideas of the great Arab literary giant al-Jahiz and others were not any less vicious and dehumanizing about non-Arabs, especially Iranians. "The coming of the white man," Edward Said notes in his *Culture and Imperialism*, "brought forth some sort of resistance."[14] Persian literary humanism, the historical record of a similar resistance, is charged by the sustained memories of these nascent, formative traumas.

The constitution of "the Persian" as the morally corrupt alterity of "the Arab" was definitive to the medieval imperial caliphate. When the conquering Arab generals were not busy pacifying Iranians who dared to put up a resistance to their imperialism, or else hanging slave plates around the neck of their peasantry to make sure they paid all their taxes, their poets and literati were actively engaged in "accusing" them of being soft and effeminate and having polluted the manly Arab virtues with "soft Persian femininity." In his groundbreaking *Desiring Arabs* (2007), Joseph Massad has provided a thorough genealogy of this train of thought and traces this Arab penchant for feminizing Persians (as a negative attribute) and "accusing" them of being the source of "feminine qualities," and in fact the singular site of "homosexual perversion," to the height of Arab nationalism, and from there he traces this attitude to immediate Orientalist influences, but obviously back to the sources of European Orientalism, namely the primary Arabic sources of the late Umayyad–early Abbasid period. Salah al-Din al-Munajjid, for example, a leading Arab liberal nationalist, believed that "there is no doubt that Arabized Persians had a big influence in the spread of sodomy [*lawat*] and the love of youthful boys."[15] Sodomy and sapphism, in the estimation of these leading figures in Arab modernity, were "sexual deviance that had originated from the Persians." In doing so, Massad believes, al-Munajjid wanted to "safeguard Islamic civilization against the Persian-derived 'deviations of the Abbasid era.'"[16]

Massad seeks to explain this formative racism informing the homophobia at the heart of Arab nationalist modernity by way of "the Shah's alliance with Israel against Arab nationalism,"[17] which of course flies in the face of an entire gamut of anticolonial nationalism and Third World socialism in the Iranian political culture of the Shah's period, with which Arab nationalism of this vintage could—but did not— identify.[18] Many other leading Arab nationalists, including the great literary figure Taha Husayn, shared this penchant for projecting their homophobic and misogynist anxieties onto "Persians." Shawqi Dayf, a major literary historian, had identical thoughts. "Dayf's nationalism," Massad says, "got the better of him when he discussed other [early Arab] poets accused of 'bawdiness and *zandaqah*' and attributed their entire tradition to Persian origins."[19] Muhammad Ali al-Barr, a naturalized Saudi of Egyptian origins and an Islamist physician, believed that "the habit of sodomy moved from the Greeks to the Persians and Romans."[20] Massad traces such Arab modernist thinkers' harboring such racist homophobia back to their European Orientalist sources.[21] But the cultural consequences of colonial heteronormativity notwithstanding, European Orientalists did not manufacture such assumptions from thin air, and Arab modernists had direct and unmitigated access to Arab poets and literati of the Umayyad and Abbasid periods—luminaries like al-Jahiz and al-Baladhuri—long before Orientalists knew which way to read Arabic. What was being cast into a renewed anti-Persian racism in the course of Arab modernism, admirably documented by Joseph Massad, was in fact a very old trope dominant early in the Islamic period, in which "Persian feminine" attributes were believed to have corrupted "Arab manliness."

The racialized trope of "the Persians," however, assumes an even more convoluted pedigree when we turn from a critical take on homophobic layers of Arab nationalist modernity to Arab feminism. Leila Ahmed, a leading feminist scholar, in her pioneering work *Women and Gender in Islam: Historical Roots of a Modern Debate* (1992), categorically blames "Persians" for the patriarchal traits of heterosexual polygamy and harems full of concubines. "Sasanian society, which prevailed in the Iran-Iraq region," Leila Ahmed believes,

> is particularly important . . . in that Muslim conquered its people and directly inherited its culture and institutions. The mores of the incoming Arabs and the existing society fused after the conquest, and the new Muslim society that arose in Iraq played a key role in defining Muslim law and institutions, including many which are still in place today. Customs of the Persian royalty at the time of the first Persian conquest of Mesopotamia continued to be practiced and became even more elaborate under the Sasanians. Harems grew vastly larger and were kept by the elite as well as by royalty, their size reflecting the owner's wealth and power. . . . During the Sasanian period Zoroastrianism grew in power and influence and eventually became the state religion, establishing the regulations that governed male-female relationships among the upper-classes. The patriarchal family, as endorsed by this church (at least in this period of its history), demanded the wife's total obedience to her husband.[22]

So not just modern Arab society but in fact the medieval Islamic legal institutions were all, in Leila Ahmed's view, influenced by the Persian penchant for heterosexual philandering, and in fact Muslim Arabs were borrowing from Zoroastrian Persians when it came to demanding and exacting "total obedience" from their wives and concubines. Not just the innocent Arabs, but in fact the equally innocent Greeks and the Byzantines, all took their patriarchal, polygamous, insatiable appetites for concubines from these Persians. "Not uncommonly," Leila Ahmed believes, "students of Byzantine society attribute the oppressive custom toward women to 'oriental influences.' Indeed the Greeks and Byzantines did borrow some such customs from the Persians, for example, Alexander's decision to keep a harem the same size as that of the Persian king he had conquered."[23] Arabs, in Leila Ahmed's reading of early

Islamic history, got all their bad habits of having concubines and multiple wives from these philandering Persians. "Most of the Persian upper class not killed in the wars of Arab conquest," she believes, "converted from Zoroastrianism to Islam, the new state religion; they and their descendants retained their upper-class status and became the bureaucrats of the new state. Surely, it is the accents and assumption of that heritage—in which kings traditionally had concubines by the thousands and proclaimed far and wide the specifications of women to be sent to them—that are most evident in the advice a courtier now offered al-'Abbas."[24]

The moral of the story here is that when we look at the modern Arab take on medieval Islamic history through the combined critical perspectives of Joseph Massad and Leila Ahmed, we cannot be quite sure if these "Persians" were sex-crazed, heterosexual philanderers with thousands of concubines to their names who infiltrated the innocent Arab and Muslim (as well as the Greek and the Byzantine) communities and corrupted them, or alternatively, if the very same Persians were in fact homosexual pederasts who introduced their homosexuality all the way from Khurasan to the selfsame innocent, heterosexual, monogamous Arabs. The Arab masculinist nationalism and Arab feminism could not quite figure out which one of these two contradictory tropes was to be affixed to "the Persians." Common to both assessments, however, remains the trope of "the Persian" as the epiphany of sexual perversion—one way or another, as it were. In this hermetic tribalized fantasy, the Arabs emerge as innocent bystanders, who if left to their own devices would have been law-abiding, monogamous, heterosexuals who loved and respected their wives and treated them like equals—pretty much a Victorian fantasy that through British colonialism was offered Arab masculinist (or evidently even feminist) nationalism.

While the modern versions of anti-Iranian Arab sentiments indeed have their roots in European colonial heteronormativity and globalized capitalism, their medieval vintage (informing this modern take) was rooted in the imperial hubris of an empire that branded, ridiculed, and sought to humiliate any culture of resistance to its domination. The thriving effervescence of Persian literary humanism is the historical evidence of a literature of resistance that in its transmutation to its courtly garb and decorum became the cosmopolitan site of a universal claim on being-in-the-world.

Genres of Poetry, Modes of Being

Contrary to its Arabic counterpart, Persian literary humanism began not as the triumphant language and literature of a conquering empire, but as one among other modes of resisting it in revolutionary uprisings and eventually in dynastic formations. Persian literary humanism thus emerged as the collective possession of vast and diversified peoples— Iranian, Turk, Mongol, Indian, or central Asian in their origin. But embedded in both Arabic and Persian literary humanism, once these differing points of origin are bracketed, was their identical services to two sets of imperial projects—a service always compromised by the innate literary proclivity to turn against its own patronage. Persian literary humanism continued with this paradox well into the Mongol invasion and until the dawn of the Safavid empire in the sixteenth century, when (as we will see) something structurally destabilizing happened to it, which started its historic exit from the court altogether and its entry into the public domain of the ordinary people, whom it in fact helped to define and constitute.

By the common consensus of literary historians, this early period was the golden age of Persian poetry, when its major forms, genres, and principle prosodies were established and consolidated, beginning with the monumental work of "the father of Persian poetry," as he is honorifically known, Abu Abdullah Jafar ibn Mohammad Rudaki Samarqandi (858–941), and culminating with the crowning achievement of Persian epic poetry, written by one of the most beloved figures in the entire gamut of Persian literary humanism, Hakim Abu al-Qasim Ferdowsi Tusi (940–1020). The most obvious reason for this golden age of Persian poetry is the fact that the Samanid and Ghaznavid monarchs paid these poets generously, although ironically Ferdowsi never received the reward for the composition of his *Shahnameh* that he was promised by the Ghaznavid Sultan Mahmoud. Poets were by and large very wealthy, and being a court poet was a lucrative profession, in part because these courts in the east were emulating Baghdad or else were ceremoniously appealing to the memories of the Sassanid court, on the imperial model of which even the central Abbasid caliphate was modeling itself. This period of Persian prose and poetry was marked by the presence of very few Arabic words, not out of any deliberate intention to avoid them, but because the natural growth of the Persian language in the Islamic period was far more inclined toward Persian words than to Arabic, although many leading Iranian scholars (scholastics in particular) composed their work in the Arabic that was sacerdotal to Islam. Poetry of this period was a mirror of courtly life—of archetypes of love, valor, banquets, pageantry, chivalry, and nobility. The best form of poetry that corresponded to all these was panegyrics, or *madiheh-sara'i*, from which both *ghazal* (lyricism) and even *hamaseh* (epic) would be the natural outcomes. Onsori (d. 1040), Farrokhi Sistani (d. 1037), and Manouchehri Damghani (d. 1040) were the prominent poets who praised Mahmoud and Mas'ud, the Ghaznavid monarchs, and established the normative elegance of Persian poetic imagination for generations to come.

While the roots of Persian poetic imagination are grounded in political resistance to the central caliphate, it soon begins to branch out as the ideological apparatus of the eastern courts, which became the political beneficiaries of that anti-imperial spirit, as is best evident in the first, most successful form of its historical record—the rise of Persian panegyrics.[25] As it emerged in Khurasan between the tenth and twelfth centuries, Persian court poetry put itself at the disposal of the Samanids and the Ghaznavids, who (positing themselves against the central caliphate) consciously fashioned their reigns after the enduring memories of the Sassanid empire. Rudaki, who was a blind poet close to the Samanid court, to Nasr ibn Ahmad ibn Isma'il in particular, was very productive in his career and composed thousands of lines of poetry. He also turned "Kelileh and Dimnah" (a redaction of *Panchatantra*) into poetry. As Rudaki, Farrokhi, and Manouchehri, among scores of others, marked the particular characteristics of Persian panegyric poetry, tropes of chivalry and warfare, as symbolics of banquets and feasts, found their way into the operative repertoire of Persian aesthetics.[26] Perhaps the most striking aspect of this poetry, best exemplified by Rudaki's pictorial representations of nature, Farrokhi's penchant for exquisite physical details, and Manuchehri's festive celebration of nature and particularly his joyous descriptions of wine and wine drinking, is its worldly imagination, which has an unmitigated, direct, and spontaneous contact with the physicality of being. Thus, although Persian panegyrics developed into a highly stylized courtly form, its imageries and historical consciousness represent a wide spectrum of aesthetic and material sensibilities.

Embedded in the thriving panegyrics of this period is a sustained celebration of physical love. The nature of love for a poet like Shahid Balkhi, another major figure of this period who reflected on the differences between physical and spiritual pleasure, even had philosophical dimensions. This is the commencement of figurative and metaphoric readings of the physical and spiritual body, the world, and pleasure in Persian poetry, pulling and pushing the centrality of mortal man in a vast and endless universe. There were many other poets who during this early period used poetry for philosophical reflections (*hekmat*) and/or worldly advice (*va'z*). These philosophically inclined reflections on this-worldly and otherworldly matters eventually pave the way for the introduction of *mysticism* into Persian poetry. The appearance of Abu Sa'id Abi al-Khayr (967–1049) in this early period in Persian literary effervescence is particularly noteworthy, because in him we have one of the earliest extant sources of mysticism, which is at once integral to Islamic metaphysics and yet subversive of it, not in the least because it is in Persian and not in Arabic. The location of mystical poetry in the Persian literary imagination opens up a whole new vista on the autonomy and sovereignty of the literary act. Abu Sa'id Abi al-Khayr was a famous Persian Sufi who was globally celebrated more than a century after he passed away by virtue of the book *Asrar al-Tawhid*, which Mohammad ibn Monavvar, one of his grandsons, wrote about him some 130 years after his death. Born in Khurasan, and raised and educated in the arts and sciences of his time, Abu Sa'id abi al-Khayr was eventually drawn to Sufism and became a world-renowned mystic. His lyrical poetry provides the earliest extant evidence of the transmutation of physical into spiritual love.

The appearance of the first woman poet in this period is immediately connected to the transmutation of the ideas of physical and spiritual love into each other. Rabe'eh Qozdari (also known as Rabe'eh Balkhi) was a mystic poet who composed her poetry in both Persian and Arabic and had a reputation for being promiscuous. She was a contemporary of Rudaki, and she is also later remembered as a mystic by such luminary masters of Persian mysticism as Abu Sa'id, Attar, and Abd al-Rahman Jami. She is the first recorded Persian woman poet. She is reported to have descended from an Arab family that immigrated to Khurasan after the Muslim conquest. She eventually became a semi-legendary figure who putatively wrote her last poems with her blood on the prison walls of the jail in which she had been incarcerated because of her love for a slave named Baktash.[27] A number of enduring tropes gather here about the figure of Rabe'eh—the fact that she was the first woman poet among a predominantly male pantheon, that she was a Persianized Arab who wrote in Persian, that she was a polyglot, that she was an historical figure who eventually became legendary, that she was a lyricist who later developed a reputation as a mystic, and that her conception of physical love increasingly became metaphoric and spiritual.

From this point forward the interface between Persian literary humanism and mysticism becomes a poetically versatile and hermeneutically veritable zone—at once dangerous and exciting, metamorphic and perilous. Mysticism in this zone takes full advantage of Persian poetic disposition to advance its own cause, and yet at the same time it inevitably yields its metaphysical authority and narrative autonomy (and thus, I daresay, its very claim to Islamicity) to the contingency of the poetic act. In this zone, mysticism poetically compromises its mystical metaphors when it embraces the poetic contingency of the real—of the metaphors of the real. The mystics may mean divine beauty as a metaphysical referent, but once they have submitted it to the open-ended semiosis of Persian poetic metaphors, they must admit, and they will admit, that this beauty is in the eye of the beholder and the face of the beheld. The wedding between the two—the poetic and the mystical—has been auspicious and fruitful, but not without its sporadic metamorphic crises. Obviously, in the capable hands of a Rumi, that fusion and union is delightful to behold and euphoric to embrace, but in less capable hands it becomes merely pious and pedantic.

The presence of mysticism in the fold of Persian literary humanism at this very early stage will have to be balanced with the equally, if not even more crucial, prevalence of epic poetry or *hamaseh-sara'i*.[28] In the tradition of Persian epic poetry, the rewriting of *Shahnameh* in prose or poetry in the modern Persian that emerged in the aftermath of the Arab invasion seems to have been a particularly poignant idea that attracted many poets and prose stylists in the Samanid period. In addition to Abu Mansur Abd al-Razzaq's prose *Shahnameh*, to which Ferdowsi had access, at least two other poets—Mas'udi Marvazi and Abu al-Mo'ayyed Balkhi (both from the Samanid period)—had begun composing their own versions of *Shahnameh* before Ferdowsi. But it is to Daqiqi, another major poet of the Samanid period, that Ferdowsi himself refers as the pioneering poet who had begun composing the *Shahnameh* and finished 1,000 verses of it before he was murdered. Daqiqi was a Zoroastrian. He was killed by a slave at a very young age, and Ferdowsi has a cryptic reference to his murder being because of his *"khu-ye bad"* (bad habit)— perhaps a veiled allusion to Daghighi being a "homosexual."[29]

Rooted in the same political context of resisting an imperial domination, Persian epic poetry came to its fullest and aesthetically most sustained and fulfilling manifestation in Ferdowsi's *Shahnameh* (composed ca. 1000). Composed in some fifty thousand couplets over a period of 30 years, *Shahnameh* is a singular heroic narrative of a people's mythical, legendary, and historical memories. In *Shahnameh*, Ferdowsi brings the diverse and scattered memories of a people he deliberately identifies as "Iranians" into the sustained imaginative force of a single poetic event. *Shahnameh* is self-consciously heroic, from its metrics to its diction, from its majestic narrative poise to its grand poetic ambitions.[30] It is a singular act of poetic genius, rooted squarely in a much longer tradition of epic poetry, from which Ferdowsi freely derives to build his own unique monument. Ferdowsi's epic narrative describes the heroic deeds of Rostam, the treacheries of Zahhak, the innocence of Seyavash, the bedeviling attraction of Sudabeh, the tragedies of Sohrab and Esfandiar, the love stories of Bizhan and Manizheh, Zal and Rudabeh. What holds these stories together is Ferdowsi's self-conscious presence, his periodic interruptions of the epic narrative to dwell on the nature of human beings and their destiny, his unfailing moral gaze at the glories and atrocities of human existence. Ferdowsi tells old stories with an unmistakably moral verve that exudes from the heart of the towering imagination of a self-confident poet, fully conscious of composing an epic narrative for the posterity of a people.[31]

These genres of poetry are modes of aesthetic attendance upon the time that produced them, manners of being-in-the world—and the self-conscious cosmopolitanism they thus entailed is worldly, this-worldly, physical, moral, imaginative, trustworthy. They constituted a people, a culture, a state of being, by providing them with the very horizons of their emotive universe, teaching and telling them who and what they were.

What Is Human?

What sort of human emerges from Persian literary humanism, so early in its formative period? In response to the question "What is Man?" that Antonio Gramsci posed to himself while in prison (from 1926 to 1937), he readily offered that the answer to this seminal question ought to be known "now," or more precisely "in the given conditions of the present," and about "the daily life" of man and "not about any life and about any man."[32] He then proceeds to suggest that "the most important of these patterns is the 'religious' one and a given religious one— Catholicism." Before that proposition can create confusion, Gramsci qualifies his statement by adding that if a Catholic were to do all that was demanded of him as a Catholic, "his life would appear as a monster." The point of Gramsci's argument is that no one individual, Catholic or otherwise, belongs to one thing and that one thing alone, that individuals are connected to one another, and "the individual does not enter into relations with other men in opposition to them but through an organic unity with them," and thereby he or she becomes part of "social organisms of all kinds from the simplest to the most complex."[33]

What Gramsci is discovering in the solitude of his prison cell as his country is going through the Fascist frenzy is that "the number of societies in which an individual can participate are very great (more than one thinks)."[34] Gramsci must have recognized that between the immense possibility of belonging to multiple societies and the atomized individuals fabricated under Fascism was a long and vast difference. "It is essential," he writes in his prison notes, "to evolve a theory in which all these relationships are seen as active and in motion, establishing clearly that the source of this activity is man's individual consciousness which knows, wills, strives, creates because he already knows, desires, strives, creates, etc. and conceives of himself not as an isolated individual but rich in potentialities offered by other men and by the society of things of which he must have some knowledge."[35]

What Gramsci in effect was contemplating here was more than what the German sociologist Georg Simmel (1858–1918) had discovered at the same time, or perhaps even earlier, in his essay "The Web of Group-Affiliations" (1922), probably entirely unbeknownst to Gramsci. Simmel had also observed that the formation of the social person is contingent on the web of group affiliations that is naturally cast around a person in the course of varied sociations. What Gramsci is offering here is in fact "the world" that the individual occupies by virtue of a conscious awareness of these sociations that at once form and inform social persons of their worldly whereabouts. "The most satisfying answer," Gramsci says, "is that 'human nature' is a 'complex of human relationships' because this answer includes the idea of 'becoming' (man becomes, changes himself continually with the changing of social relations)."[36] The course of that "becoming" is where humans qua humans find the world that inhabits them.

More than the fact of those social relations, the *creative consciousness* of being aware of them is what matters in the formative constitution of a culture. What is ordinarily lost in literary historical narratives is the world in which poets and prose stylists become the architects of a moral and imaginative universe by virtue of which they "world" the world they inhabit, as they welcome that world to inhabit them—thus uplifting it to become conscious of itself. At the heart of Persian literary humanism stretches a consistently self-creative world, a self-conscious world that is aware of and transcending itself, flaunts and celebrates itself. The creative effervescence of the fragile *Adami* (human) we encounter later in Sa'di's moral imagination is now taking shape here in the nascent period of Persian literature. In this world is posited an "I" that is already implicated inside the narrator's story, compromised by it, its subjection always already metamorphic. The fragility of that *Adami* is entirely independent of the God/man binary at the heart of Islamic metaphysics. Kings, heroes, lovers, contemplative saints—they all come together to posit a *homo poeticus* that regenerates itself in multiple terrains. Thus posited, this *homo poeticus* moves toward a metaphoric conquest of the earth, having abandoned "the other world" to speculative scholasticism and opting for this visible, tangible, material world— seeking poetically its invisibilities, intangibilities, and immaterialities. There is a metaphoric urge in this conquest, as if after the Arab conquest of their homeland, these poets and literati wanted to claim the earth poetically, to universalize its particulars, to transcend and ascertain it, deliberately celebrating its ephemerality.

In claiming and constituting that worldly self-awareness, transcending and ascertaining it at one and the same time, Persian panegyrics had a central role to play at this early period of Persian literary humanism. In a typical panegyric poem by its master practitioner Manouchehri

Damghani, which consists of thirty to fifty lines, about half of them are devoted to a vivid and exceedingly visual and even "cinematic" description of nature and the other half to the praise of the reigning monarch, which in his case is mostly the Ghaznavid ruler Sultan Mas'ud. The tableau that Manouchehri "draws" is so vividly visual, musical, and sensual that one oscillates between seeing, listening, and smelling it. It is like a short film, a vignette, and a recital. The musical sound of words, the visual effects of the imageries, the aromatic sense of flowers and herbs all gather to entice and appease the senses. It is fair to say that this is the phase in Persian poetic parlance in which the very disposition of the senses is poetically constituted. In one very famous panegyric that begins with the famous line,

> Abr-e Azari bar-amad az karan kuhsar,
> Bad Farvardin bejonbid az miyan marghzar . . .
> The spring clouds are rising from the mountain,
> The April winds are blowing over the prairie. . . .[37]

Manouchehri begins by describing an early spring scene in which the pregnant clouds are appearing and a gentle breeze is blowing upon a vast and beautiful prairie. Every hemistich now begins to act like a camera shot—in one we see moving white clouds, in the next a gentle breeze crossing over green grass, in the third we see colorful flowers budding at the foot of a mountain, just before we cut to a close-up of a few red roses growing upon the background of grass. The camera moves in close-ups and medium- and long-range shots before Manouchehri informs his audience of the aroma of flowers, the sound of the flowing rivers, the music that the leaves of trees play to the dancing of other leaves on adjacent bushes. Manuchehri's camera then takes a close-up of a tulip with drops of rain, and another shot of a daffodil and anemone embracing each other. These descriptions and depictions continue leisurely, rhythmically, melodiously, and then ever so gently they transmute toward the king, the monarch, Khosrow-e Adel (the Just King), whose teacher is the Archangel Gabriel (just like the Prophet Muhammad but without saying so), the monarch whom God Almighty has anointed and appointed. God and Gabriel have selected this king because of his justice and have taught him nothing "except goodness and justice." Beyond God and Gabriel, the heavens and the stars now enter the scene, acknowledging the king's good fortune of long life and a vast empire. Here the monarch—so praised for his valor and power in battle—is placed over all other kings from east and west of his realm. Then at some opportune moment, the poet mentions the name of the monarch by playing on the meaning of it—"Mas'ud," meaning "the lucky one." And then eventually, slowly, and gracefully, the poet sings the praise of the monarch's valor and taste for banquets before closing his poem.

What is the human in Persian literary humanism? Humans are the microcosm of the world they inhabit and the world that thereby inhabits them. Appeasing the king may be the immediate point of the poem, but the text and texture of it claim and constitute nature as the landscape of a world that the poet poetically appropriates for a much larger audience who has yet to encounter his poetry. The extended audience of Persian poetry (though composed in and for the court) is posterity, the world that is being crafted and history will soon people. That audience, humanity at large, is always present in the poet's mind, even (or particularly) when addressing the king. "The King," in fact, becomes the principal protagonist of the unfolding history, of Man as such, humanity at large, personified, incorporated. The body of the king has already become the body of the world politics he incorporates and upon which he projects his power. Perhaps precisely in the same manner that a Bach cantata may have been played to the glory of God, or a Mozart concerto for the appeasing of a monarch, Manuchehri's panegyric becomes a reality sui generis, the form and fabric of a world that will inhabit the soul of multitudes yet to be born into a nation, a people precisely by virtue of that poetry. The panoramic claiming of the earth in its earthly beauties and sublimity is at the heart of that emerging world that therefore transcends itself. The pleasures of the earth are the constituent forces of that world, its senses and sensibilities, while the king might emerge as the extension of the elegance and grace that sustains the earth. The claim of the poet on earth is the claim on the real, the physical, the evident. The king is a divine dispensation, precisely as nature and earth are the larger, more universal domain of that dispensation and dominion. The poetic claim is on earth, its seasons and wonders and fruits, thus poeticizing the politics of kingship and thereby crafting a world, an earthly domain upon which resides humanity, is integral to its worldliness.

A key element in constituting this self-conscious worldliness is the consistent awareness of an emerging *tradition* in one's poetic profession

(profession in the sense of a calling—the German *Beruf*). As were all his other contemporaries, Manouchehri was very much a self-conscious poet and fully aware of the tradition of great poets and literati from which he had descended and to which he was responding and paying homage. Referring with love and admiration to both Arab and Persian masters before him, Manouchehri honors "the master of all masters of our time Onsori," as he says in one poem.[38] There are references to many other poets, including Ibn al-Rumi (836–896), who was born to a Persian mother and a half-Greek father and became prominent at the court of the Abbasid caliph al-Mu'tamid. Ibn al-Asma'i (ca. 740–828), a prominent Arab scholar, and Sibawayh (ca. 760–797), a celebrated Persian grammarian of the Arabic language, are among many other masters to whom Manouchehri refers with respect and admiration. While these are indications of the liberality of his education in both Persian and Arabic literatures, they also point to the existence, so very early in the history of Persian poetry, of a literary worldliness that was conscious of its own traditions and through that awareness had reached for a literary transcendence.

The selfsame worldly consciousness, predicated on a deep sense of tragedy, is equally evident in the writing of the epic masterpiece of the period, Ferdowsi's *Shahnameh*. In one crucial example, the story of Rostam and Esfandiar is one of the most powerful episodes of the entire *Shahnameh* and arguably one of the greatest tragedies in the entire cycle of Iranian national epics. Esfandiar is the son of Goshtasp and the prince to his crown. Goshtasp is reluctant to let go of his throne and keeps sending his son on dangerous missions in faraway lands, from all of which Esfandiar returns victorious. Finally, Goshtasp sends Esfandiar on an impossible mission: to arrest and handcuff the Iranian national hero Rostam and bring him to his court, knowing full well of a prediction that his son Esfandiar is destined to be killed by Rostam. The encounter between Rostam and Esfandiar is one of the most moving and powerful episodes of the entire *Shahnameh*. Esfandiar loves Rostam and hates to subject him to this damned humiliation but must do as his father commands, for he wants to become the king. Rostam loves the young prince in return and will do anything to help him ascend that throne, even going with him to the court, walking while the prince is mounted on his horse, as the sign of his submission to his will, but handcuffed he will not be, even for Esfandiar. The tragic setup is now complete. The two heroes, the two doomed protagonists, finally meet in battle. Rostam did not know that Esfandiar was immortal because he had swum in the sea of immortality. He is almost defeated when he asks for a respite, during which he discovers Esfandiar's secret—he is immortal, except for his eyes, which he had closed when he swam in that sea of immortality. So Rostam devises a special arrow, with a feather of the legendary bird Simurgh and a twig of a tamarisk tree. They resume the battle, and Rostam aims that arrow at Esfandiar's eyes and kills him.[39]

The enduring power of Ferdowsi's *Shahnameh*, rooted in such stories as Rostam and Esfandiar, is in introducing an ennobling sense of tragedy into the emergent Persian poetry—and thus poetically marking the precious fragility of being human into Persian literary humanism. The world as we know it, and wish to trust it, succumbs under the piercing gaze of the *Shahnameh* tragedies, in which taking sides between opposing heroes is difficult and dwelling in the world is perilous. What is human? Human is worldly, the world that resides in humans, reflecting the world in which this human lives—and this world is precarious, self-contradictory, morally meandered.

—————

3

The Prose and Poetry of the World

The Rise of Literary Humanism in the
Seljuqid Empire (1038–1194)

"SOME for the pleasures here below," says Omar Khayyam (1048–1131) in a famous quatrain,

> Others yearn for The Prophet's Paradise to come;
> Ah, take the cash and let the credit go,
> Nor heed the rumble of a distant drum.

The certain fragility of the world of here and now has never been so palpably preferred over the dead certainties of the world of there and then, of the world to come. The habitual Orientalist reading of "The pleasures here below," predicated on an escape from disciplined Victorian austerity, amounts to a hedonism that is a limited and limiting reading of this and all other quatrains of Omar Khayyam. The point of preference is neither hedonistic nor anti-ethical. The point is counterethical, marking the fragility of being, a philosophical pause that dismantles any theology of being that seeks to dominate it by way of explaining it. "The Prophet's Paradise," reduced poetically to a "rumble of a distant drum," is not as much doubted here as it is sidestepped. The quatrain is a celebration of certainty, the only certainty, the certainty of the moment, of here and now—now sublated into a countermetaphysics of its own, a detranscendentalized sense of transcendence, a material intuition of the sublime.

Is this intuition of the sublime also what the Nietzschean aphorism "the world as a work of art that gives birth to itself" could mean? Perhaps. The aphorism is ordinarily read as a sign of Nietzsche's aestheticism.[1] But more than anything else on this and other occasions when Nietzsche reflected on the link between art and the world, the world assumes a reality sui generis, irreducible to the metaphysics that habitually lay a claim on it, and as such the world is ordinarily lost to itself, and it comes to self-recognition in and through works of art. Socratic transcendence for Nietzsche was "the Prophet's Paradise" for Omar Khayyam. In that context we might think of Persian literary humanism as both—and there is the rub—the offspring and the parent of the world it conceived and made possible. That people who speak and sing Persian today have a world at all is the gift of that paradoxical parenting and birthing, when a world is born unto itself, an "immaculate conception"—in which the Madonna is the language and the Child is the world that her literary imagination has made possible.

The Will to World

"Take the cash and let the credit go" celebrates the world without in a face-off with the promise of the otherworld, and the poetic occasion itself, the whisperish quatrain, amounts to its own assurances—for it offers no other. "The world as a work of art that gives birth to itself" punctuates the moment when the world becomes (periodically) aesthetically conscious of itself, aware of its whereabouts, delivered from transcendental illusions to evident materiality via the power of poetic allusions. Worlds change and alter their whereabouts by virtue of poetic rediscovery of themselves, by way of aesthetically giving birth to themselves— art as the erotogenics of body-politic.

How does the body-politic, in the age of empires, become aware of itself—of the pleasures of its power and the power of its illusions? When we move from one dynasty to another, from the Samanids to the Ghaznavids and now down to the Seljuqids, we are traversing through the alternating and altering worlds that these dynastic and imperial adventures have crafted as the riverbed of their time and being, upon which the world flows and becomes (repeatedly) aware of itself. Empires breed meaning and significance, opposition and resistance, whereby the world becomes contrapuntally posited for what it is—the summation of forces that have occasioned it, even (or particularly) when negating it. The will to world is embedded in any imperial project to own (up to) it.

The Ghaznavids, just like the Samanids, ended with a whimper, not a bang. The Persianate Turkic empire of the Seljuqids (1038–1194) emerged in their stead with verve and panache to stretch from the east to the west of the known and civilized world—from China to the Mediterranean—and on this vast expanse the epochal European Crusades were but minor border skirmishes. Even at its height, the Abbasid empire was nowhere near the territorial expanse and might of the Seljuqids.[2] From 1037 to 1157, during the height of the Seljuqid empire, namely for more than a century, the dynasty ruled over a vast territory, subjugated the Abbasid caliphate in Baghdad, controlled the Fatimids in Egypt, warded off the European Crusaders in Anatolia, and furthered Persian language, culture, art, architecture, and literature, all of which experienced one of their most glorious episodes in medieval history. Whether they served the Seljuqid empire or opposed it, Persian poets and literati expanded the emptive universe of Persian literary humanism beyond anything previously achieved.

Four mighty Seljuqid warlords in particular are noteworthy for the longevity of their reigns, the vastness of their empires, and their patronage of the arts and sciences: Tugrul I (Tugrul Beg, r. 1037–1063), Alp Arslan bin Chaghri (r. 1063–1072), Jalal al-Dawlah Malik Shah I (r. 1072–1092), and Sultan Sanjar (governor of Khurasan 1096–1117 and sovereign of the Seljuqid empire 1117–1157). The capital of the Seljuqids was initially Isfahan and then Hamadhan, and then during the reign of Sanjar it was moved farther east to Marv. From Tugrul to Sanjar, the period known as "the Great Saljuqs," the dynasty ruled from China to the Mediterranean, and after the zenith of the empire, there were still more minor Seljuqid dynasties in Kerman, Syria, and Anatolia, where they ruled until the rise of the Ottomans in the late thirteenth century through the early fourteenth century.

The Seljuqid warlords were masters of courage and imagination— and territorial conquest seems to have been as natural to them as breathing. The Seljuqids descended upon the Ghaznavids and ultimately the Abbasids with the force and ferocity of nomadic verve and fury overcoming sedentary urbanism and decadent court life.[3] The origin of the Seljuqids goes back to central Asia, from which they eventually crossed the Volga River into the Black Sea steppes sometime in the ninth century. The house of Seljuqs was a branch of Oghuz Turks who dwelled north of the Caspian and Aral seas, and they were recruited by the Samanids in their central Asian domains. In the tenth century the Seljuqs migrated into Khurasan, where they became heavily Persianized and eventually rose to prominence during the Ghaznavids and were strong enough to pose a constant threat to Ghaznavid control of central Asia. With the renewal of every rising dynasty and the formation of a new empire, Persian language and literature, art and architecture, and the whole cause and course of Persian literary humanism, adjacent to Islamic scholasticism, received renewed power and purpose. The Seljuqid was the vastest empire after the Sassanid to have ruled the Iranian territories, and Persian literary imagination began to reconnect to that imperial imagining, in concordance or in defiance.

The Seljuqids conquered the Muslim world from one end to another and expanded it to unprecedented territories, and with that expansion Persian literary humanism received renewed global confidence and audacity. That emerging confidence was coterminous with the fate of the Seljuqids who conquered Muslim lands with the force of a destiny. It was Tugrul Beg who initially moved south from central Asia and conquered Gorgan, Tabarestan, Khwarizm, Rey, and Hamadhan in 1041 and received the blessing of the Abbasid caliph. By 1055, Tugrul was in Baghdad, with Caliph al-Qa'im's blessings. By 1062, the Seljuqid warlord had married al-Qa'im's daughter, having already married his own niece to the caliph. Before his death on September 4, 1063, Tugrul had consolidated the Seljuqid dynasty as a major force, with vast territorial claims over Muslim lands and beyond. Central to the imperial conquest and administrative apparatus of Tugrul was his Persian vizier, Amid al-Molk Abu Nasr Mansur ibn Muhammad al-Kondori (served 1055–1063). Less gifted as a statesman than his chief rival Khwajah Nezam al-Molk al-Tusi (1018–1092), al-Kondori nevertheless did serve Tugrul competently, leaving the more illustrious achievements for his chief rival, who served for three decades not just as the political intelligence behind the reign of two Seljuqid warlords—Alp Arslan and Jalal al-Dawlah Malik Shah I—but in fact as the most powerful political theorist of medieval Islamic history. In Nezam al-Molk al-Tusi the Seljuqid empire found its most powerful vizier, Islamic political thought its most illustrious theorist, and Niccolò Machiavelli (1469–1527) his Iranian counterpart almost half a millennium before he was born in Florence.

Nezam al-Molk's greatest political challenge was the renewed rise of revolutionary Isma'ili uprisings, to which he ultimately lost his life. The Isma'ili Shi'i revolt, led by Hassan Sabbah (ca. 1050–1124), was by far the most powerful and widespread revolutionary uprising to threaten the reign of the Seljuqids from within the empire, for which Nezam al-Molk was in charge of internal stability and external expansions.[4] When Alp Arslan succeeded Tugrul, he appointed Nezam al-Molk as his vizier, and the first thing they did was to kill al-Kondori and clean the slate for a new era of Seljuqid ascendency. Aided by the astonishing political thinking of Nezam al-Molk, Alp Arslan extended the domain of the Seljuqid empire from the Mediterranean to central Asia, including Armenia and Georgia. The Seljuqids came to ascendency as the Isma'ilis Fatimids were in power in Egypt, and during the reign of Malik Shah the renewed Isma'ili uprising in Iran that was led by Hassan Sabbah shattered the foundations of both the Abbasid and Seljuqid rule.[5] Two intellectual and political giants of the time rose to the defense of the Sunni orthodoxy of the Abbasids and the Seljuqids—Nezam al-Molk al-Tusi and the great philosopher-theologian-mystic Abu Hamid Muhammad ibn Muhammad al-Ghazali (1058–1111). The Isma'ili assassins disturbed the peaceful dreams of the Seljuqid empire and even managed to assassinate its central command and control intelligence, Nezam al-Molk, in 1063. The Seljuqid warlord Malik Shah died the same year. The Isma'ili uprising notwithstanding, under Malik Shah the Seljuqid empire extended from China to Mediterranean Sea. After the death of Malik Shah the empire began to tremble and fall until the ascendency of the last Seljuqid warlord, Sultan Sanjar.

Formation and ascendency of the Persianate Seljuqid empire was a critical turning point in the systematic and incessant overcoming of the presumed *ethnos* of various peoples under their dynastic power by the enabling *logos* of Persian literary humanism, which reached unprecedented heights during their more-than-a-century reign. It is precisely during the span of their empire—from the ninth to the sixteenth century—that we see more than ever Iranian, Turkic, and soon Mongol dynasties embracing Persian literary humanism as the modus operandi of their empires and thus facilitating the cosmopolitan worldliness that became its transnational and deracialized hallmark. Inventing and consistently re-inscribing a global worldliness for itself, Persian literary humanism became the aesthetic imagination with and through which this worldliness self-worlded itself against the de-worlding will of Arab and Muslim political conquest. By "worlding" I mean to signal the creative consciousness through which a people posit themselves in and over their world, map and mold it in their collective self-image—and thus by "de-worlding" I mean the violent imposition of any imperial imagination that must by defintion wipe out the existing maps that ipso facto, just by being there, contest that imperial hegemony. At this critical juncture, Persian literary humanism was made possible by contesting one empire (Abbasid) and serving another (Seljuqids)—and that paradox remained definitive to it until its fateful encounter with European colonial modernity. The indomitable will to world the world was embedded in the vast empire the Seljuqids built and in the arts and sciences they made possible—and Persian literary humanism became its crowning achievement. The imperial will to world the world amounted to the Seljuqid empire owning up to it, politically embodying the world and making it possible for a literary imagination both to project and to reflect it.

Where in the World?

The world that successive Iranian and Persianate empires made (possible) projected the horizon of linguisticality within which Persian literary humanism took place. "Language is not just one of man's possessions in the world," observes Hans-Georg Gadamer, the German hermeneutician, in his *Truth and Method* (1960), "but on it depends the fact that man has a world at all."[6] The constitution of Persian language as the lingua franca of cultural resistance to Arab imperialism was coterminous with the formation of Persian literary humanism as the emerging collective consciousness of multiple peoples who claimed and called that language their own. "Language," as Gadamer posits, "has no independent life apart from the world that comes to language within it. Not only is the world 'world' only in so far as it comes into language, but language, too, has its real being only in the fact that the world is re-presented within it. Thus the original humanity of language means at the same time the fundamental linguistic quality of man's being-in-the-world."[7] The representation of the world in the language and the linguistic horizon of the world come together to make the worldly disposition of a language self-conscious. Persian language made the Persianate world possible, and the making of that world was the political disposition of successive empires that had laid claims on the poets and the literati who represented and furthered their legitimacy. The making of those worlds was the handiwork of the linguisticality of the project at the heart of Persian literary humanism.

Running the World

Mapping the world by way of conquering it was the combined effect of successive imperial projects claiming it and the literary imagination that went along owning up to its wonders. The world was giving birth to itself in imperially mapping it out by world-conquering monarchs and by aesthetically imagining it in literary acts of narrating the idea for the present absentee, for posterity, for humanity to come. Thus running the world—how to run the empire that was thus conceived—became the *condito sine qua non* of the rise of a brand of political theory specific to the Seljuqid empire in which pre-Islamic and non-Islamic traits began to rethink Islamic imperialism in ever-expansive, renewed, and worldly ways. That this genre of political thought was written specifically in Persian was the key operative force of these Persianate empires. The political thinking embedded in this genre of writing became the theoretical backbone of the empire they in/formed.

Two of the masterpieces of prose narrative from the Seljuqid period are directly related to the imperial imagining of the political order that kept that massive empire together: Khwajah Nezam al-Molk's *Siasatnameh* (composed ca. 1086) and Abu Hamid Muhammad al-Ghazali's *Nasihat al-Moluk* (composed ca. 1109). These two texts are the direct descendents of Amir Unsur al-Ma'ali Keikavus ibn Vushmgir ibn al-Ziyar's *Qabusnameh* (ca. 1080), although with a vastly different imperial self-confidence, point, and purpose to them. Written by the specific command of mighty Seljuqid warlords for their immediate benefits, these political tracts by Nezam al-Molk and al-Ghazali are the most solid evidence of a Persian political imagination that was the bedrock of the literary humanism that had grown naturally on its fertile soil. In other words, the theoretical vertebrae of the Persianate empire of the Seljuqids was narrated in a manner that consciously assimilated it into the universalizing imagination of a decidedly Persian political parlance, thereby giving the Seljuqid empire a distinctly Persianate royal idiomaticity.

Nezam al-Molk composed *Siasatnameh* in fifty chapters of simple and elegant prose that to this day reads with marvelous precision and impeccable political poignancy. *Siasatnameh* is one of the most significant medieval texts in Persian political thought, and yet it is written in an eloquent prose that marks it as a masterpiece of its genre. It does not have the fatherly affection or the paternal finesse of *Qabusnameh*, for which it compensates with precise and uncompromising political potency. *Siasatnameh* was composed at the specific instruction of Malik Shah, one of the two powerful Saljuq warlords whom Nezam al-Molk had served over three decades. The great Seljuqid vizier had originally composed his book in thirty-nine chapters, which he presented to Malik Shah; he then added to it, as the monarch had liked it and asked his vizier to expand it.[8] As Nezam a-Molk says in his own introduction, Malik Shah had asked him to compose this book so that the monarch could learn from the example of previous kings as to how to run his empire. Predicated on a multifaceted, global, and worldly consciousness of empires and dynasties, the text is pointedly pragmatic in its recommendations. By the time of the writing of *Siasatnameh*, Seljuqid imperial thought becomes distinctly Persianate in its diction and disposition.

At the center of Nezam al-Molk's political theory stands the figure of the King/*Padeshah*, whom he believes is divinely ordained, but who remains in power by virtue of dispensing justice, which is in gratitude of that divine gift he has received.

> In every age and time God (be He exalted) chooses one member of the human race and, having adorned and endowed him with kingly virtues, entrusts him with the interests of the world and the well-being of his servants; He charges that person to close the doors of corruption, confusion and discord, and He imparts to him such dignity and majesty in the eyes and hearts of men, that under his just rule they live their lives in constant security and ever wish for his reign to continue.[9]

The verticality of authority here comes down from God Almighty/*Izad-e Ta'ala* down to the King/*Padeshah*, and reaches the People/*Khalq*. God is the One who chooses one among his creatures and thus anoints him to be His Shadow/Zill on earth, and thus adorns him with Royal Virtues/*Honarha-ye Padeshahaneh* so that he can rule with grace and authority. The physical domain of this authority is the expanse of the World/*Jahan*, and more specifically the Interests of the World/*Masaleh-e Jahan*. The theory of authority connects from divinity to humanity, through the intermediary of the body of the King, and thus with the text of Nezam al-Molk's *Siasatnameh* the Persian *Homo politicus* is in effect made possible.

The initial preoccupation with the source and the format of legitimate authority, however, is only the metaphysical foregrounding of royal authority, beyond which the king must rely on a system of intelligence-gathering to know the details of his realm. No kingdom is possible without judges (*qaziyan*), propaganda officers (*khatib*), and police officers (*muhtasib*). Nezam al-Molk then proceeds with giving specific advice, ranging from how to send special envoys from the court on various missions to appointing spies for different parts of the kingdom. It is imperative that the king consults with the elders of his realm. His instructions for a healthy and steady operation of an empire are so detailed that he even gives the king the specifics of how to plan for way stations for materiel and resources on his way to a battlefield. He gives him advice on drinking parties at his court, attending to the needs of the military officers, and appreciating and rewarding those who have served him well. He then devotes a whole section to revolutionary uprisings that might and do indeed threaten an empire and how to effectively deal with them.

The result of Nezam al-Molk's political thought is not entirely political. From *Siasatnameh* emerges a solid societal framing of an ideal of *humanitas*, as a mode of pragmatic thinking and being that posits the political person as an operative unit in an empire of order and virtue, of legitimate violence and imperial weal. There is a moral universe within which Nezam al-Molk is operating that is neither dogmatically Islamic nor exclusively Iranian. It is a worldly disposition rooted in a sense of *humanitas* that is born out of the imperial context of his thinking and writing. Without that imperial order that makes this *humanitas* possible, Nezam al-Molk sees the abyss.

In al-Ghazali's *Nasihat al-Moluk*, he addresses the king directly and simply warns him that God Almighty has granted him many favors, chief among them authority over the worldly matters of his created beings.[10] After a long prolegomena, which is a short treatise on legitimate authority in and of itself, al-Ghazali divides his book into seven chapters: On Justice of Kings, On Politics of Viziers, On Art of Scribes, On Might of Monarchs, On Wisdom of Philosophers, On Dignity of Reason, and, finally, On the Good and Evil of Women. Each one of these chapters deals with an aspect and a prospect of an imperial order, beginning with justice, which is the very raison d'être of political order, down to the necessity for reason in running worldly matters.[11] In al-

Ghazali's text the figure of the king in effect emerges as the ideal-type of *humanitas*, something of a prototype for humanity as such, in his exemplary virtuosity in ruling his own kingdom.

In al-Ghazali's estimation, God Almighty has anointed two particular groups of leaders: one the prophets and the other the kings. Prophets are sent to call people toward him, while kings are appointed to keep people from harming one another. Kings are the "Shadow of God on Earth." The key concept here for al-Ghazali is kingship/*padeshahi* predicated on the idea of divine grace/*farr-e izadi*—and people "must love" (it is their duty) the king who is thus anointed. *Farr-e izadi* is a specifically pre-Islamic, Iranian idea that al-Ghazali uses in his theory of legitimate authority. To buttress his theory of authority, al-Ghazali then resorts to the Qur'anic phrase: "O ye who believe! Obey Allah, and obey the messenger and those of you who are in authority; and if ye have a dispute concerning any matter, refer it to Allah and the messenger if ye are (in truth) believers in Allah and the Last Day. That is better and more seemly in the end" (4:58). He further uses another Qur'anic phrase that expands on this basis of legitimacy: "Say, 'O Allah, Owner of Sovereignty, You give sovereignty to whom You will and You take sovereignty away from whom You will. You honor whom You will and You humble whom You will. In Your hand is [all] good. Indeed, You are over all things competent" (3:26).[12] Al-Ghazali is in effect manufacturing consent to the king's authority predicated on such theories of legitimate authority, but by the same token he is educating and obligating the king to a divine mandate by way of casting him as the prototype of humanity as such.

Because *Nasihat al-Moluk* consists of two parts—a long prolegomena and seven chapters—the late prominent Iranian scholar Jalal Homa'i, who edited the critical edition of the text, believes the first part was composed for Sultan Muhammad and the second part for Sultan Sanjar.[13] Homa'i, however, ultimately concludes that *Nasihat al-Moluk* was written at the request of Sanjar, as indeed *Siasatnameh* was written at the specific request of Malik Shah. Three major Seljuqid emperors, as a result, were the direct beneficiaries of these two seminal texts, which both imagined and guided them in ruling their empires. Nezam al-Molk was not just any old vizier, nor was al-Ghazali any old advisor to the reigning Sultan. One was the greatest political thinker of his time, and the other was a major intellectual force of medieval Islam.[14] Between three emperors and two philosopher-viziers the Seljuqid empire gave birth to a world through and beyond its imagination.[15]

Both Nezam al-Molk and al-Ghazali pay particular attention to women, in part because during the Seljuqid empire there were a number of very powerful and influential women, such as Malik Shah's wife Tarkan Khatun, who in fact competed and outmaneuvered Nezam al-Molk on the crucial question of succession to Malik Shah. The concern and particular attention of both thinkers indicate the paradoxical fact that women like Tarkan Khatun were exceedingly powerful figures in the Seljuqid court and yet (or thus) they were the subjects of the most vicious gender profiling, especially by Nezam al-Molk, who considered them paradoxically to have "incomplete intelligence" and yet to be remarkably manipulative. It is crucial to keep in mind that much of these discussions about women are inspired by abstract announcements in "wisdom literature" and courtly life, and in the case of Nezam al-Molk specific hostilities and rivalries between him and Malik Shah's wife Tarkan Khatun, whom he thought had too much power and influence over the sultan.[16]

What are the qualities of women that Nezam al-Molk and al-Ghazali praise? To be able to bring children, to be pretty, and not to require too much dowry: these are the qualities to be sought in women. *Parsa'i* (virtuous) is the key attribute to be sought in them. But there is a fundamental difference between the two thinkers regarding women. Nezam al-Molk is bitterly angry with women and wants to have nothing to do with them in politics or in any other matter, while al-Ghazali is mostly interested in finding a balanced way of a virtuous and harmonious marital life. Most of the anecdotal examples that al-Ghazali gives are those of successful marriages based on the virtues of both husbands and wives, while most of the examples that Nezam al-Molk gives are about the treacheries of women. Nezam al-Molk categorically counsels avoidance of any dealing with women, while al-Ghazali recommends gentility with them for they are "weak and short in intelligence." For Nezam al-Molk it is order and longevity of the empire that matters and that must be protected against the follies of women, while for al-Ghazali bliss and happiness are the key objectives of a worldly life. In fact many of al-Ghazali's ideas are taken from his other Persian text, *Kimiya-ye Sa'adat* (*The Alchemy of Happiness*), specifically on striking a balance of a fair and fruitful life. But ultimately for both Nezam al-Molk and al-Ghazali what they mean by "women" ("the veiled ones" or just "*zanan*") is just a metaphor, an abstraction, a trope, a thing, a sign, completely devoid of humanity, character, identity. What will remain troubling about the entire gamut of Persian literary humanism in its medieval texture is the fact that women, in the plurality of who and what they are, might be, might become, are not fit to become the prototype of *humanitas*, of a perfect and complete person, an "*Insan-e Kamel*," until well into the encounter with European colonialism, when not just women, but humanity at large, will have a renewed rendezvous with the historicity of being-in-the-world.

In their overall political theories, both Nezam al-Molk and al-Ghazali are extending the Iranian, pre-Islamic, theories of kingship to the Seljuqid empire, the former with less and the latter with more attempt at incorporating them into Islamic material. The imperial disposition of the Seljuqids had obviously invoked the pre-Islamic (Sassanid in particular) notions of kingship, and yet attempts are made to justify them in Islamic (Qur'anic) terms as well, especially on the part of al-Ghazali. In both their cases, however, the balance is between the divinely ordained *farr-e izadi* and the socially justified factor of justice. Sources of active political imagination for both Nezam al-Molk and al-Ghazali are pre-Islamic Iranian and Arab material, as well as non-Islamic Greek and a variety of mystical and wisdom literatures. In addition, al-Ghazali also uses Nezam al-Molk's *Siasatnameh* as a source, acknowledging the authority of the grand vizier as a political theorist. The worldly disposition of these texts gives them not a categorically pre-Islamic, Iranian, or Iranshahri/Persopolitan character,[17] as suggested by the distinguished intellectual historian Seyyed Javad Tabataba'i, but in fact a Jahanshahri/ Cosmopolitan outlook, as evident in the transcultural disposition of their intellectual pedigree. The cosmopolitan worldliness of this political culture, in which both Nezam al-Molk and al-Ghazali freely and naturally partake, informed the imperial order that had occasioned and celebrated them. They both politically imagined the world that the Seljuqids were to rule—and it is precisely the worldliness of that world, in which literary masterpieces were conceived and delivered, that in the course of colonial modernity the imaginative geography of the West has both repressed and overdrawn. For in that imaginative geography, to be *human* is to be Western European.

Resisting the Empire

Neither elaborate political theories in Persian or Arabic nor indeed the mighty reign of the Seljuqid warlords could have prevented massive revolutionary uprisings against their power and authority. Persian humanism was not all in literary terms or performed paradoxically at the court of tyrants. People revolted, took up arms against tyranny, and in doing so restored the dignity of their humanity, which had been compromised by the might and majesty of those who sought to use, abuse, and rule them. Battlefields of revolt against tyrannous empires were also the sites of Persian humanism—in action.

The dominant theories of political authority were categorically cast in the feudal context of the excessive abuse of the impoverished peasantry and the urban poor to enrich the treasury of the Arab caliphate and the Seljuqid warlords in order to finance their imperial conquests. The medieval history is inundated with accounts of ungodly abuse of the peasantry and the urban poor, which inevitably resulted in various modes of rebellion—mobilized by Islamic sectarian or else non-Islamic syncretic (proto-Zoroastrian) ideas. Those who benefited from the caliphate's racialized sense of superiority were not all Arabs, and there were many Iranian nobles and Turkic warlords among them; those who were disenfranchised were not all non-Arabs and included many Arab peasants and the urban poor.[18]

Many revolutionary uprisings in this period assumed understandable communalistic dispositions, denouncing private property and advocating the communal possession of things. The Carmatians—an Isma'ili splinter group that established a utopian community in 899 in eastern Arabia—staged one of the most radical revolutionary uprisings resisting Sunni scholasticism and Seljuqid feudalism alike. As did all other proto-Shi'i revolutionary movements, the Carmatians opposed the imperial pedigree of the ruling empires and opted for a proto-communalistic option during their revolt. The abused and impoverished peasantry and the urban poor were the natural recruiting ground of these revolutionary movements, while the artisans and merchants were the natural members of the guilds with Sufi inclinations. Both Mahmoud and Mas'ud of Ghazna sought to confront the Carmatians, as did the Abbasids and the Seljuqids. After the Carmatians, other militant Isma'ilis were active against the Ghaznavids and the Seljuqids, opposing their feudalism with their communalistic practices and beliefs, their dogmatic scholasticism with iconoclastic philosophy and mysticism, and their Sunni orthodoxy with Shi'i heterodoxy—at one and the same time.[19] The Isma'ili movement ultimately resulted in the establishment of the Fatimid dynasty (909–1171) in Egypt and the rest of North Africa, which ruled for some 270 years, during which time the Fatimids obviously lost their revolutionary disposition and became as repressive and abusive as any other dynasty. But the defiant disposition of Shi'ism as religion of protest soon picked up its revolutionary agenda in Iran under the leadership of Hasan Sabbah (1034–1124). There were times that the Sunni caliphate could easily have fallen to the Fatimids, such as during the revolt of Arsalan al-Basasiri (d. 1059) who dethroned the Abbasid caliph and declared the Fatimid caliph as ruler, but the Seljuqids soon defeated al-Basasiri and restored the Abbasid caliphate for their own purposes and benefit.

Under whatever banner they took place, revolutionary resistances to the Abbasid and Seljuqid empires were acts of political, moral, and intellectual defiance—acts that in and of themselves restored people's trust in their own humanity. From that trust emerged renewed engagements with Persian literary humanism outside, and in fact in opposition to, courtly environs. Revolutionary resistances to the Abbasid and Seljuqid empires, of whatever sort, further worlded the imperial gathering of their historic momentum by positing their potential alterities in not just political or doctrinal but in literary and imaginative terms. These were revolutionary resistances with ideological components and cultural consequences—chief among them literary modes of imaginative restitutions of "the world as a work of art that gives birth to itself."

Dissident Poets and Philosophers

The Isma'ilis were the principal source of menace for the Seljuqids throughout their reign, and they ultimately assassinated the Seljuqids' major political theorist Nezam al-Molk. While Nezam al-Molk and al-Ghazali were on the side of the Seljuqid and Abbasid political power and Sunni scholastic orthodoxy, Avicenna (980–1037) and Naser Khosrow (1004–1088), two major intellectual luminaries of their time, were on the Isma'ili side—though one more by implication and the other far more overtly. This was a battle between Sunni orthodoxy and its juridical scholasticism on one side and revolutionary reason of Shi'ism on the other. Avicenna's project remained basically philosophical and scientific (medical) and his contribution to Persian humanism was limited to writing a number of the earliest philosophical tracts in the language.[20] But Nasir Khosrow was a moral and intellectual force of an entirely different caliber, not just in the history of Shi'ism, but even more so in bringing out for a full display the defiant character of Persian literary humanism.

Hakim Naser ibn Khosrow ibn Hares, al-Qubadyani, al-Balkhi, al-Marvazi, commonly known as Nasir Khosrow, was an Isma'ili political activist (*Da'i*), philosopher, and poet of unsurpassed moral rectitude and intellectual audacity.[21] The combined effect of Nasir Khosrow's work makes it impossible to identify him only as a poet or a philosopher or a prose stylist author of a major travelogue or a political activist. He was all of those at one and the same time, and as such he was a monumental figure in Persian literary humanism. It is, as a result, mostly as a literary humanist that he would make sense in the eloquence of his philosophical diction, the precision of his observations in his travelogue, and then in the power and brilliance of his poetry—all of them coming together to present one of the most magnificent manifestations of Persian prose and poetry of the time.

Above all it is the catholicity of Nasir Khosrow's learning that is the decisive disposition of his character and culture. He had comfortable command of both Persian and Arabic languages and literatures, prose and poetry, and a vastly cultivated knowledge of Greek and Islamic theology and philosophy, as well as an astonishing eye for sociological details when writing his travelogue, which covered the Seljuqid empire from one end to another. While he was alive his Arabic and Persian poetry was widely known and celebrated. In his philosophical treatises—*Goshayesh wa Rahayesh* (*Emancipation and Liberation*), *Zad al-Mosaferin* (*Provisions for Travelers*), *Wajh-e Din* (*Countenance of Faith*), and *Jami' al-Hekmatayn* (*Summa Philosophica*)—Nasir Khosrow writes one of the earliest and most eloquent Persian philosophical prose extant, in fact far superior to the little that Avicenna managed to write. Not until a generation later in the writings of Shahab al-Din Yahya Suhrawardi and then Khwajah Nasir al-Din al-Tusi will we encounter such a robust and powerful Persian philosophical prose. That philosophical prose, and the vast erudition that informs it, becomes definitive to the nature and disposition of Persian literary humanism.

Equally important in the prose and poetry that Nasir Khosrow commanded was his worldly cosmopolitanism, the globality of the vision that informed his encounters with the world. Most of Nasir Khosrow's work was written either while he was traveling around the Muslim and non-Muslim world or while he was in exile in Yamgan. This fact gives his literary diction and intellectual disposition an innately peripatetic, exilic, but above all cosmopolitan character. Khurasan for him was home, and he always missed his homeland, and yet the figurative power of his thinking and writing were categorically formed while he was absent from his homeland. The catholicity of Nasir Khosrow's learning is at once astonishing to behold and yet representative of the range of knowledge available to an intellectual activist of his stature and determination. He easily moves from Islamic scholasticism to Greek philosophy to Arabic and Persian literature and displays an encyclopedic knowledge of master Arab and Persian poets.

Should we call the Persian poet humanist a "renaissance man" and thus claim the Renaissance for its more southern climes? He was, among other things, an accomplished painter, and while in Arabia he in fact made a living by painting portraits and murals. His knowledge of astronomy, mathematics, and trigonometry was equally noteworthy. He traveled with his books—his library being carried on the back of his camel, while he walked alongside them. He is believed to have traveled all the way to India in search of knowledge and certainty. He was an earthly man, consistently committed to a confessional prose, marking his tumultuous moral meanderings. Before he had a dream and converted to Isma'ilism at the proverbial age of forty, he confesses he indulged excessively in drinking and sex, having completely abandoned the hope of ascertaining any truth beyond the limits of his flesh. Ultimately, his attraction to Isma'ilism was because of his own restless soul and its revolutionary disposition against the Abbasid and Seljuqid scholastic orthodoxy and imperial hubris—and not vice versa. He was attracted to Isma'ilism because he was a restless revolutionary; he was not a restless revolutionary because he was an Isma'ili. These are two vastly different readings of Nasir Khosrow. The evidence of this claim is in his work, particularly in his poetry, in which he is first and foremost a moral voice of defiance against tyranny and hypocrisy. In one of his legendary poems he has a line that has become proverbial to his poetic and political disposition.

Man anam keh dar pay-e khukan narizam
Mar in qeimati dorr lafaz dary ra—

I will never throw the precious pearl
Of Persian poetry to the feet of pigs.[22]

Before coming to this conclusion, the poem begins with admonishing those who blame their fate and the stars for their worldly lot and tells them to assume responsibility for their lives and actions. Then he tells his readers to seek knowledge and be fruitful. He then denounces those poets who join a royal court and thus demean themselves to the level of the monarch's entertainers. He denounces the poets who exaggerate in their praise of the monarch just to earn a lucrative living:

For how long are you going to compare [the figure of the king]
To a tall boxwood tree or [his face] to a tulip?
Or else compare [his countenance] to the moon and
The fragrance of his hair to ambergris?
You praise for knowledge and virtue
The person who has nothing but ignorance and vice—
You keep composing poems [full] of lies and greed, yet
Lies are the source of dishonesty—
Is it fair for Onsori to praise and compare Mahmud [the Ghaznavid]
With Ammar and Abu Dharr?[23]

The defiant spirit of Persian literary humanism is rarely on display more poignantly than in Nasir Khosrow's poetry. In his work, he embodies the revolutionary origins of the language and literature that he best commanded. The transformative power of Persian poetry as well as the restless disposition of the poet are both here to mark a crucial character of Persian literary humanism at the heart of the Seljuqid empire. A rebellious poet, a daring philosopher, and a defiant activist committed to the most emancipatory intellectual and political movement of his time all come together in marking Nasir Khosrow as the defining moment of Persian literary humanism of his period.

Nasir Khosrow was not of course the sole prominent representative of this defiant disposition of Persian humanism. Between the death of Nasir Khosrow in 1088 and the birth of Suhrawardi in 1155 there is the span of almost a century. But what links them together is a deeply rooted philosophical penchant that brought the iconoclastic Persian prose to narrative perfection. Suhrawardi was more than just a philosopher. He was, like Nasir Khosrow, a phenomenon, though of a different sort—far more defiant in his philosophical soul than in any palpably political terms. Today we remember Shahab al-Din Yahya ibn Habash al-Suhrawardi (1155–1191) mostly as a precocious philosopher who despite his young age and short life turned the received history of Greek and Islamic philosophy around, wedded it to an astonishing resurrection of pre-Islamic Iranian philosophical thinking, and founded the Ishraqi (Illuminationist) school of philosophy.[24] He drew freely and creatively on Islamic, Zoroastrian, and Platonic ideas to master a syncretic mode of critical thinking in Persian that would surpass anything achieved before or (some would even say) after it.

The honorific titles of Shaykh al-Ishraq/The Master of Illumination, or Shaykh al-Maqtul/The Murdered Master (for he was executed on charge of heresy by Salah al-Din's son al-Malik al-Zahir Ghazi [1172–1216]) are the most immediate indices of his significance as a philosopher who radically altered the course of Islamic philosophy and paid for it with his life, for the juridical scholasticism of his environment had no patience or capacity for such radical thoughts. But it is his significance as a master prose stylist that secures his significance in Persian literary humanism—his writing philosophy as a work of art, as a literary act, particularly because of his penchant for fables and allegories. His philosophy is deeply iconoclastic, transformative, and transgressively bordercrossing in resuscitating repressed or forgotten Iranian elements and pre-Islamic tropes, and posits a theory of light and visuality, thereby projecting a deeply ocularcentric force in Islamic philosophical thinking. In 1186, at the age of thirty-two, he completed his magnum opus, *Hikmat al-Ishraq* (*The Philosophy of Illumination*), and with it established an entirely new course in philosophical thinking that would find its way as far east as India. In his work, Suhrawardi offers a unique philosophical interpretation of the same stories, plots, and characters that appear in Ferdowsi's *Shahnameh* in which he uses such figures as Fereydun, Zahhak, Kay Khosrow, or Jamshid as allegorical references to what might be considered a semiological philosophy of light. Throughout his works, he uses Zoroastrian symbolism to put forward a highly allegorical philosophy of light.

His philosophical masterpieces aside, Suhrawardi has a number of shorter treatises in the figurative form of "visionary recitals," or *Resaleh*, that enriched Persian prose and injected into it an allegorical language rarely encountered with such power and poise in the long history of the language. The allegorical prose of Suhrawardi in these treatises is self-propelling, self-referential, poised, and purposeful in diction and disposition. Cast in the form of allegorical parables, these narratives at one and the same time mount and dismantle themselves, and thus the knowing subject who narrates them becomes suspended in dis/belief. The art of allegorical philosophy reaches an unprecedented height in Suhrawardi's work.

In one of these allegories, "Risalah al-Tayr" ("Treatise of the Bird")," Suhrawardi tells the story of a group of bird hunters who come to a prairie and set their traps. Soon a flock of birds appears.[25] The birds are attracted to the seeds used to lure them down, descend upon them, and get caught in the trap. They initially try to set themselves free, but they fail and thus settle down to their fate. What is remarkable about this story is that the narrator, "Suhrawardi," is one of the birds thus fooled and trapped, and the story is uttered in the first-person narrative— initially by "Suhrawardi" himself, then his voice is transmuted to one of "the birds," and finally back to "Suhrawardi himself." The allegory begins with Suhrawardi speaking in his own voice. As soon as he introduces the flock of birds flying over the prairie, he matter-of-factly says, *"va man mian-e galleh-ye morghan mi-amadam* [and I was flying in the midst of the birds]." From then on, "Suhrawardi" speaks as one of the birds until the very last moments of the narrative, when he resumes his initial voice.

He (Suhrawardi the Bird) soon notices that a group of birds have managed to free themselves from the trap, and yet they cannot fly away because some remnants of the trap are still clinging to them. He asks the partially freed birds to help him release himself too. They do. He asks them to get rid of the remaining trappings they all have on their feet. They say they cannot, otherwise they would have done so for those still hanging on themselves. So the relatively emancipated birds decide to go and find someone who will help them in their predicament. They fly over long and desolate lands and over seven mountains, and finally land on the eighth summit where they are told that "the King" will address their wish. They approach the majesty and glory of the King. The King tells them however that the only person who can set them free is the one who entrapped them in the first place—but he says he will send a messenger along with them so that person will set them free. "So now we are on our way back," Suhrawardi the Bird reports to his friends, "accompanied by the King's emissary."

Upon finishing his allegory, Suhrawardi exits his persona as one of those birds, resumes his "ordinary" (publicly rational) voice, and says that upon hearing this account some of his friends have questioned his sanity and told him that he has gone mad, that people don't fly like birds, and that he should seek professional help and get some rest. The more his friends talk, Suhrawardi says, the less he listens to them, and he concludes by assuring them that they are indeed ignorant (*na-dan*).

The birds are an allegory for humans, attracted to and trapped in material living. A few of them start thinking and exit that trap, but that is not enough. They need something beyond reason to set them free, a mode of suprarational thought. A philosophical or mystical gathering points to a higher mode of intelligence, which must be extracted from the material life and reason itself. That is, perhaps, one way of interpreting Suhrawardi's allegory. But no interpretation exhausts the open-ended suggestiveness of the allegory or answers the question "Why opt for the allegorical language in the first place?" These allegorical narratives occur in the constitutionally transgressive landscape of the Persian language, and as such they uplift the metaphoric into the transcendent. The assured power of the allegorically outlandish dismantles the publicly (compromised) reason embedded above all in the Sunni legalism in the scholastic traditions. The allegorical realism that results, however, is at once self-constitutive and self-deconstructive. So it does not run away from scholasticism to be trapped in a metaphysically assured reason/*aql*. It defies reason too and opts for an open-ended semiosis. The consequence of the allegory is thus categorically transgressive. If Arab imperial domination, the feudal mode of economic production, and Islamic scholasticism (law in particular) were to be considered as three interrelated modes of subjection (empowered modes of transforming human beings into subjects), Suhrawardi's philosophical project in general and his allegorical writings in particular suspend all such modes of subjection by transgressing the accepted and practiced modus operandi of discursive formations in the dominant institutions of theology, jurisprudence, or even philosophy. That ultimately is the enduring power of these allegories. They at once say and do not say anything that posits a definable (and trapped) subject.

Beyond his Illuminationist philosophy and allegorical language, Suhrawardi in effect discovers a new literary mode of being that is at once *fictive* and *phenomenal*. This counternarrative, as a result, is ipso facto confrontational with power, which is precisely the reason why the dogmatists could not tolerate Suhrawardi, even if (or particularly because) they did not understand what he was saying. It was ultimately the combined conspiracy of political power (Salah al-Din's son as governor of Aleppo) and scholastic power (the clerical establishment, which accused him of Batini, meaning Isma'ili, tendencies, a stock accusation amounting to charges of heresy). These modes of subjection—in feudal, scholastic, and political terms—were institutions of violence, which could not tolerate Suhrawardi's narrative defiance of their modality of power as modes of subjection—and thus they conspired and killed him. And precisely for that reason, his allegorical prose in particular (as the most subversive) is instrumental in any understanding of Persian literary humanism, for precisely this allegorical language suspended the subjection of that humanity on precarious and unchartered territories. If the power of these three institutions—political, economic, and juridical— was *transversal*, meaning it traveled from one to another, the creative mode of resisting them in literary humanism was ipso facto *transgressive*— allowing for that transversalism to be registered and yet evading it by deluding it.

With a poet like Baba Taher Oryan (fl. ca. 1055 in Hamadhan), who was a contemporary of Tugrul Beg, the transgressive power of Persian literary humanism reaches wider than mere political or philosophical domains. Baba Taher is an iconoclastic figure in a number of ways, beginning with the political but not limited to it. Legends have it that he in fact met with Tugrul, and the Seljuqid warlord asked for his blessing in his empire-building project, upon which request Baba Taher famously gave him the handle of a jar from which he had been doing his ritual ablutions before his prayers all his life and told him to rule justly and kindly. Tugrul is reported to have asked Baba Taher to ask him for a favor, and the ascetic poet told him to just please get out of the way so the sun could shine on him![26]

This hagiographical account, repeatedly cited by subsequent admirers of Baba Taher, is only one aspect of his iconoclastic significance as a poet who emerged and flourished entirely outside any royal court and has remained endearingly closest to the hearts and minds of his readers. Precisely because his poetry was not meant to appease any monarch, many of Baba Taher's quatrains are in fact composed in the Lori dialect of western Iran, which was far from the accepted official Persian of the courtly life. Equally important about his poetic legacy is his preference for the subversive genre of the quatrain, which is simple, gentle, and whisperish, compared to the long, at times even burdensome, pomposity of the panegyrics. Every one of his quatrains is an epiphany of beauty and elegance. Here is one example:

> Nasimi kaz bon on kakol ayo
> Mara khoshtar ze bu-ye sonbol ayo
> Cho sho girom khialesh ro dar aghush
> Sahar az bestarom buy gol ayo

> The breathe that comes from that perfumed hair
> Is sweeter to me than the fragrance of hyacinth;
> Once I embrace the thought of her at night,
> In the morning my bed smells like [a] flower.

Along the same lines as Baba Taher's poetry, but with much more global appreciation, is the magnificent subversion of Islamic scholasticism (and the successive empires that have accessed and benefited from it) as best evident in the work of Omar Khayyam (1048–1131)—mathematician, astronomer, philosopher, and above all iconoclastic poet.[27] In addition to his reputation as such, Omar Khayyam also wrote treatises on mechanics, geography, and music. He was born and raised in Neishabur and forever gave global significance to his place of birth and upbringing and final resting place. His character has become legendary, associated with Avicenna as his student, conversant with al-Ghazali as his philosophical interlocutor, and even made into a classmate of Hassan Sabbah and Nezam al-Molk! But above all he is remembered as a mathematician, astronomer, philosopher, and a poet only by avocation.

There is nothing particularly wrong or flawed with the hedonistic image of Omar Khayyam as it has been promulgated by the exquisite translations of Edward FitzGerald (1809–1883) in the heat of the Victorian morality—asceticism and discipline—projecting an erotic and even riotous balance onto it.[28] But in the context of Persian literary humanism proper, Omar Khayyam is a far more radical thinker, poet, and philosopher who categorically dismantles Islamic scholastic surety and posits a far more suspended fragility for human existence, or even more radically for the un/knowing subject.

Central to Omar Khayyam's philosophical disposition, as best evident in his poetry, is the fragility and tragic pointlessness of being. The moon will shine many nights, and we will not be here anymore; there is no beginning or end to this world, and no one knows what we are doing here—theologians, philosophers, mystics, and scientists all sing their own amusing tunes. The clerical establishment in particular obviously did not like these ideas, nor did he care for them, and there are reports that he in fact would go out of his way to scandalize their hypocrisy. If there is a wonder, amazement, and metaphysics left to mortal humanity, it is embedded in the dusty disposition of being, of the fact that every speck of dust we see upon the earth is in reality the beautiful countenance of a once-beautiful person. So be careful when you wipe your face, for all the dust you are cleaning is in fact the remnants of other human beings. And that is the reason why:

> Here with a Loaf of Bread beneath the Bough,
> A Flask of Wine, a Book of Verse—and Thou
> Beside me singing in the Wilderness—And
> Wilderness is Paradise enow.

If poetic brevity and a celebration of the fragile disposition of life and knowing were the soul of Khayyam's humanism, a philosophical fixation with the nature of writing is what defined Ayn al-Qudat al-Hamadhani (1098–1131) and his lasting significance in medieval Persian literary imagination. One of the most remarkable figures in medieval intellectual history, Ayn al-Qudat offers yet another case of transgressive writing that is definitive to Persian literary humanism.[29] Ayn al-Qudat is ordinarily considered a Sufi master, and his ideas are studied in the context of Islamic mysticism. That context is of course a perfectly legitimate but not sufficient or exhaustive frame of reference to understand his ideas. The nature of his writing is such that it demands an expansive and nondenominational attention. To be sure, he was both a mystic and a philosopher. But in his writing he also achieved a level of literary distinction that was above and beyond any ordinary philosophical or mystical frame of reference. Most of Ayn al-Qudat's writings were in Persian. He had a highly productive though short life, and his unusually creative imagination was brought to an abrupt end when he was brutally executed at the age of thirty-three in his native Hamadhan, where he had spent much of his adult life under the reign of Mughith al-Din Mahmud (r. 1118–1131), a minor Seljuqid prince whose higher aspirations were aborted by his more powerful uncle, Sultan Sanjar (r. 1117–1157). Ayn al-Qudat's first most significant book was *Zubdat al-Haqa'iq* (*Choice Truth*) (1122). But his *Makatib* (*Letters*) (1123–1131) is most representative of his thinking, as indeed is his *Tamhidat* (*Preludes*) (1127). His *Shakwa' al-Gharib* (*Apologia*) (1131) is his last defense against charges of heresy and was written in Arabic. Both his *Letters* and his *Preludes* thrive on an intoxicated prose, in which his philosophical and gnostic ideas are sublated into a conversational prose.

In his work, the very nature of writing (in and of itself) becomes an issue for Ayn al-Qudat—the fact that there was "an ebb and flow" to a person's heart, that there are times he would write relentlessly and lecture extensively on various issues and yet there are times that for months on end he cannot as much as write a sentence or deliver a single lecture.[30]

> God knows I have no idea if writing as I do is the cause of my salvation or damnation; and since I don't know then I wish I had become completely ignorant and be set free . . . whatever I write disappoints me. If I write on prophethood I seek refuge in God Almighty, and if I write about lovers it is not appropriate, and if I write about philosophers it is not appropriate either, and whatever else I write is not appropriate, and it would not be appropriate if I were not to write anything at all; if I were to talk about it, it would not be appropriate either, nor would it be right if I were to be completely silent; this very thing I said is not appropriate for me to say it, nor would it be right if I were not to say it at all either.[31]

That degree and depth of self-consciousness in a writer about the very act of writing deeply planted any assumption of "truth" in the narrative that inevitably embraced it. This was no ordinary challenge to the dogmatic and doctrinal foundations of a scholasticism that had cornered the market on how to interpret the sacred, revelatory, language of the Arabic Qur'an. This Persian language was itself revelatory, in a subversive expository manner in which the act of writing itself becomes the issue, exposing the fact that before there was *theology* or *philosophy* or even *mysticism* there were "writings," the strange, overpowering, self-subversive act of writing. What will remain after this exposition? Certainly not scholasticism or any of its divergent branches. All that will remain is *writing*, the self-revelatory, incessant, self-propelling, act of writing— writing like dancing, to an ethereal melody, without any prize or purpose, before it is politically, too politically, interpreted. Dissident poets and philosophers performing in Persian literary humanism subverted more than just the dominant scholasticism and the empires they served. They narratively undermined any truth-claim—playfully. The world that they thus revealed, enabled, mapped out, and animated was its own alterity, *via negativa*.

Discovery of the Inner World

The Seljuqid period witnessed one of the highest peaks of Persian Sufi prose and poetry—with such pioneering master practitioners and theoreticians gracing it as Abu Sa'id abi al-Khayr (967–1049), Abu al-Qasem al-Qushairi (986–1074), Ali ibn Othman al-Hujwiri (990–1077), Shaykh Abu Ali al-Farmadi (d. 1084), Khwajah Abdollah Ansari (1006–1088), Shaykh Ahmad al-Ghazali (ca. 1061–1126), Shaykh Najm al-Din Razi (also known as Dayah, 1177–1256), and many other towering figures. Sufism as a mode of thinking, feeling, believing, and being developed its ascetic exercises and gnostic ideas in dialectical opposition to the outlandish wealth of the ruling caliphate and sultanate, as well as to the excessive nomocentricism of Islamic law, and then in turn against the combative logocentricism of Islamic philosophy—both of which soon lost connection with the common, lived, experiential fears and aspirations of ordinary human beings, upon which Sufism built its homocentric edifice. Practical (*Erfan-e Amali*) and theoretical (*Erfan-e Nazri*) gnosticism have historically acted upon each other to produce both a veritable social force and a potent mystical discourse.

As both a movement and as a discourse, Sufism is the narrative transmutation of the fear of God, embedded in Islamic scholasticism, into the love of God—and thus the potent and enduring theoerotic hallmark of Sufism. In addition to a mode of being, and a rich and diversified prose and poetry, Sufism was a social force, predicated upon communal formations of various Sufi groups (*ferqeh*) and orders (*selseleh*). Because of their social presence and communal power, Sufis had a politically viable following, both in urban and in rural settings, but by the same token they were also subject to excessive hostility and persecution by the clerical (juridical) establishment, which was wary of their popular appeal and potential political might. Jurists by coveting political power and mystics by denouncing it, Sufis became both implicated in and integral to the political culture of their time.

The political power of the Sufis was predicated on their iconoclastic subversion of the scholastic juridicalism and theological orthodoxy of Sunnism. Doctrinally, Sufism eventually developed the notion of the Unity of Being/*Wahdat al-Wujud*, doing away with the fearful distance between humanity and God, drawing upon an overriding conception of Love/*Ishq*, wishing to do away with various Veils/*Hejab* that separated humanity from divinity. In doing so, some Sufis went overboard with their ecstatic pronouncements/*shathiyyat*—such as Hallaj's famous phrase, *Ana al-Haq*/I am the Truth—while others remained sober and precise, and even punctilious in their mandatory religious (ritual) observances.

Because poetic prose and ecstatic poetry were the primary manner in which Sufism propagated its ideals and doctrines, the movement had a profound impact on Persian literary humanism. The allegorical dimension of Sufi narratives, predicated on the idea of the Unity of Being/*Wahdat al-Wujud* made their work particularly appealing to those with literary tastes—as perhaps best evident in Farid al-Din Attar's *Manteq al-Tayr* (*Conference of the Birds*). With master poets like Attar it is hard to say (and ultimately it makes no difference) if they are great poets with a penchant for mysticism or great mystics with a gift for poetic precision in their thoughts. Though Sufism (*Tasawwuf*) as an institution and a discourse has a reality sui generis, and as such it remains irreducible to a merely literary act, it compounds Persian literary humanism by virtue of carving out a potent narrative spot in Persian linguistic and cultural registers, thereby enriching Persian prose and poetry beyond anything achieved before. The fact is that Persian prose and poetry could not do without Sufism, nor could Sufism thrive as it did without Persian prose and poetry. It was a perfect match—and they both benefited happily ever after. But even beyond that narrative disposition, Persian Sufism has a profoundly humanist dimension to it by virtue of the experiential knowledge and the feeling intellect that points above and beyond *logos* of philosophy and *nomos* of law—against both of which it deliberately posits its *homocentric* disposition.

The allegorical dimension of Persian mysticism as a language is of course immediately, and perfectly legitimately, interpreted in a manner that is conducive to institutional Sufism, but the fact is that it remains narratively open-ended and multisignificatory. Consider Farid al-Din Attar's *The Conference of the Birds*, one of the masterpieces of this period, which is (just like Suhrawardi's allegory) about a journey by a group of cantankerous birds, led by a mostly persuasive hoopoe, in search of a king for their dominion.[32] One by one, many of the birds find an excuse and refuse to move on to their final destination with the hoopoe, and ultimately only thirty of the birds make it to the end of the journey. Ordinarily, and perfectly justifiably, this classic of Persian poetry is interpreted as an allegory for a Sufi master leading his disciples to unity with divinity, after overcoming many material and worldly distractions and excuses. But that interpretation and canonization neither exhausts the exegetical possibilities of the text nor preempts its consideration as a cornerstone of Persian literary humanism. In fact quite to the contrary: the poetic allegory, as a work of art, *The Conference of Birds* remains entirely open-ended and transcends its canonical legislation into Persian Sufism.

Consider, for example, Attar's ingenious wordplay with the word *Simurgh*, which in Persian is both the name of a mythical bird for which the birds are searching and, when as a compound word decomposed, literally means "Thirty Birds" (*Si Morgh*). The fact that only thirty (*si*) birds (*morgh*) finally make it to Mount Qaf, and all they see awaiting them after this difficult journey are their own reflections in a mirror—thirty birds—is the final punch line of the poem. But what does that exactly mean? Well it *exactly* means nothing, but metaphorically it means many things—including, but not exclusively, that truth is just the mirror image of the collective consciousness of those who search for it, an expression of their collective will. Almost 800 years after its composition, the poem continues to inspire artists and performers with no or very little connection to Islamic mysticism. Not just the literary but also the visual and performing aspects of *The Conference of Birds* have historically attracted many interpretations.[33] No one of these interpretations precludes others. Not just the literary act, but the act of multiple interpretations of it is only human—all too human.

But even beyond these multisignificatory allegories, the inner world that Persian mystics discovered and embellished sculpted a whole new topography of human experiences, of being human, mapped out and peopled outside the purview of the opulent and powerful courtly life—and Persian literary humanism became further enriched by it, for in it *being human* was the site of discovering the divinity. Persian Sufism humanized the divine experience, and de-institutionalized salvation from its entrapment within scholastic mandates.[34]

Romancing the World

The world that the mystics discovered and embellished within was mixed and matched with the world that the masters of romance literature crafted and celebrated without. If epic poetry appealed to the heroic aspirations of the changing monarchies, a particular aspect of it, romance, catered to finer sensibilities of love and adventure. By the time Nezami Ganjavi (1141–1209) composed his famous *Khamseh* (*Quintet*), the Persian romance tradition was already rich and diversified. Written about 1050, Fakhr al-Din As'ad Gorgani's (d. ca. 1058) *Vis and Ramin* borrowed from pre-Islamic Iranian themes and constructed the first and most successful example of this genre. Composed during the reign of Tugrul I (1037–1063), Gorgani's *Vis and Ramin* is one of the most exciting and adventurous examples of Persian narrative poetry, one in which pre-Islamic stories are retrieved with powerful poetic imagination. The origin of *Vis and Ramin* has been traced back to the Sassanid (224–651) or even the Arsacid (250 B.C.E.–224 C.E.) period. Gorgani reports that he found the Pahlavi version of this story in Isfahan and, following the orders of Abu al-Fath Mozaffar al-Nishaburi, a local dignitary, rewrote it in poetic Persian with particular attention to the dramatic rhetoric of storytelling.[35]

In producing his version, Gorgani took advantage of both written and oral accounts of the story, but he embellished it with particular attention to the details of dramatic delivery, a trademark of Persian narrative poetry. Adopting a number of Pahlavi words in his poetic rendition, Gorgani writes a clear narrative with a stunning simplicity as its moving energy. The illicit love affair between Vis and her brother-in-law Ramin, while she is betrothed to Ramin's brother King Mobed, gives Gorgani ample opportunity to produce one of the most passionate love stories in Persian literature. Despite the brilliance of its poetic composition, *Vis and Ramin* experienced a period of eclipse when its uncompromising celebration of physical and passionate love offended Islamic sensibilities. Nevertheless, *Vis and Ramin* had a profound impact on subsequent Persian romances, not least on the master of Persian romance narrative, Nezami Ganjavi (1141–1209).

Nezami's achievement in *Khamseh* brought the Persian romance tradition to a height comparable to that of Ferdowsi's achievement in epic poetry.[36] In a masterful construction of a dramatic narrative, Nezami, always personally present in his tales, constructs a literary humanism resting on nothing but the dramatic movement of his own power of storytelling. *Khamseh* consists of five narratives, each revolving around a thematic treatment of love and adventure. As is evident in such stories as "Khosrow and Shirin" and "Leili and Majnun," Nezami took full advantage of dramatic techniques to develop particularly haunting stories of love and adventure.[37] Just as in Gorgani's masterpiece, pre-Islamic sources are freely evident in Nezami's work, though here they are equally conversant with works of Arabic origins and are combined with a story of world conquerors, the elements of which come together to create a worldly disposition for love and adventure in his *Khamseh*. These stories carve out a vast panorama for romance, in which love becomes a supreme virtue—love in a real, tangible, mundane, and material sense, shorn of all manners of metaphysics and mysticism, such as the love of Khosrow and Shirin, or the longing of Majnun for Leili. This world is as, if not more, powerful as the mystical love conceived and cultivated by Sufi poets, and in fact lent support for a mystical interpretation of physical love, and, indeed, for a physical passion exuding mystical love. The unabashed materiality of the love celebrated in romance literature has a catalytic impact on mystical love, so that the two mirror and magnify each other. No one could now conceive of physical love without detecting in it a superior sense of being, nor could anyone speak of spiritual love without a material reference.

The romance genre brought to full fruition by Gorgani and Nezami soon unfolded into a rich tradition to which such gifted poets as Amir Khosrow Dehlavi (1280–1325), Khwaju Kermani (1280–1352), and Abd al-Rahman Jami (1414–1492) added dimension and brilliance, qualities never again to reach the height of the masters of the genre here during the Seljuqid period. Romance was a genre that exposed the expansive universe of imperial conquests, and spoke of a confidence and a trust in the world that afforded such adventures both within and without a human soul, into the vastest terrains of human folly.

Poetry, Poetics, Folklore

As the masterpieces of romance literature clearly indicate, the predominance of subversive literature during the Seljuqid period, such as the works of Naser Khosrow, Suhrawardi, Omar Khayyam, or Ayn al-Qudat, does not imply the absence of court-affiliated poetry and prose. Such great poets as Anvari (1126–1189) were the master practitioners of panegyrics, eulogies, and satire in this period. Anvari's panegyric in honor of Sultan Sanjar (1117–1157) won him many royal favors and allowed him to benefit from the patronage of other Seljuqid monarchs. In part because of the prominence of classical, court-affiliated poetry in the periods leading up to the Seljuqids, we eventually get such prominent literary critics as the eleventh-century pioneer theorist Mohammad ibn Omar al-Raduyani, whose *Tarjoman al-Balaghah* (*Guide to Eloquence*), informed by both Persian and Arabic sources on eloquence, was among the first texts of the genre. The eventual emergence of this body of critical reflections on the nature and function of poetry gives Persian literary humanism a level of unprecedented theoretical self-consciousness that is exceedingly crucial in its narrative autonomy from the court. The commencement of these theoretical reflections of course predates the appearance of Raduyani's treatise and are already evident in the body of the works of such poets as Ferdowsi, Attar, and Nasir Khosrow, who invariably reflect on the nature of their craft. At the end of *The Conference of the Birds*, for example, Attar has a whole section in which he reflects on the nature of poetry.[38] But with Raduyani such scattered reflections finally find an extended, autonomous, and self-confident theoretical domain.

After Raduyani, Rashid al-Din Vatvat (d. 1177) wrote his *Hada'eq al-Sehr fi Dagha'egh al-She'r* (*Enchanted Gardens on Delicacies of Poetry*), which was written following Raduyani's text and as a kind of critical take on it. The tradition then continued with Nezami Aruzi's *Chahar Maqaleh* (*Four Treatises*) (composed 1156–1157), which is in four chapters—*Dabiri/* Being a Scribe, *Sha'eri/*Poetry, *Teb/*Medicine, and *Nojum/*Astronomy. Nezami Aruzi also has an extensive discussion of the nature of poetry in his book, which begins with certain pragmatics and extends into a full theoretical disquisition. Finally, Shams al-Din Muhammad ibn Qays al-Razi's *al-Mu'jam fi Ma'a'ir Ash'ar Ajam* (*Compendium on the Principles of Persian Poetry*) (composed after 1232) became the summation of all previous critical reflections on poetry. The writing of these seminal texts on the particular parameters of Persian poetics uplifts the practice of poetry in or out of the court to a new theoretical register. This intensive level of theorization, which has nothing to do with the court and is concerned only with the art and craft of poetry in and of itself, is a clear indication that Persian poetic imagination had by this time reached a narrative self-consciousness, a discursive self-confidence, beyond the courtly practices of poets.

Equally outside the purview of the court and entirely from the midst of common people, we have the earliest records of a vast and fantastic folkloric tradition from this and preceding ages, as perhaps best represented in *Samak Ayyar* (composed sometime in the twelfth century), which is sometimes anachronistically considered one of the earliest versions of "novels" in Persian, but more accurately it is in the tradition of *Qesseh*/Story or *Dastan*/Narrative, variations on the idea and practice of storytelling.[39] A man named Faramarz ibn Khordad ibn Abdollah al-Kateb al-Arjani recorded *Samak Ayyar* as it was told by a master story-teller named Sadaqeh Abolqasem Shirazi. The writer of *Samak Ayyar* repeatedly mentions the fact that he has collected this story, or transcribed it, from the actual storyteller. So the text that we now have is indeed directly from the oral tradition of storytelling; it had been known and recited in public and some of it had even been put into poetry by un-known poets. The fact that it is from the oral tradition, that it was per-formed in public, is even evident from the text itself, where we hear the storyteller asking for donations and contributions from the audience.[40]

The primary location for these storytellers was such public places as tea- or coffeehouses, street corners, crowded bazaars, or even cemeteries. Both urban and rural areas are believed to have been witness to these popular storytellers.[41] Tales of heroic romance, fantastic stories about brave princes and their worldly conquests, wrestling or fighting matches with mighty enemies that included such supernatural things as jinns and paris. The principal protagonists of these stories are the *ayyars*, young and valiant men who dared the elements, challenged and tricked the authorities, won the heart of beautiful princesses, and were always on the side of ordinary people. The genre soon produced many other examples similar to *Samak Ayyar*, including such classics as *Darabnameh*, *Iskandarnameh*, and *Amir Hamza*.[42] All these romances shared common features: public space of performance, folkloric themes, popular heroes, oral traditions, creative and spontaneous arts and crafts of storytelling, or improvisations on established themes. *Samak Ayyar* and other similar stories are filled with astonishing details of ordinary people's lives, fears, hopes, aspirations, and expectations from their imaginative heroes. Both the oral tradition and the written record of these sources are crucial in seeing Persian literary humanism in action outside the royal courts. That someone in the early twelfth century went to the trouble of writing down the oral performances of these stories by a master storyteller is a clear indication that transmitting them had become a matter of literary importance. That oral tradition was deeply informed but not bound by the literary—and precisely in that mode it extended Persian literary humanism far and wide into the daily fictions and fantasy of an entire people whose language it spoke.

Narrating the World

The Seljuqid period also witnessed the height of Persian historiography—the most spectacular achievement of which by the end of the Seljuqid period was Abu al-Fazl Bayhaqi's (995–1077) *Ta'rikh-e Bayhaqi*. Born and raised in Khurasan, Bayhaqi wrote prose that is today considered something of a literary treasure both for the precision of its emotive universe and the depth of its historical imagination. As a historian, Bayhaqi was a deeply cultivated man, educated in Neishabur and employed at the court of Sultan Mahmud, the Ghaznavid monarch.[43] Bayhaqi's magnum opus, *Tarikh-e Mas'udi*, also known as *Ta'rikh-e Bayhaqi*, is not only the most reliable source of factual information about the Ghaznavid period, with references to pre-Ghaznavid dynasties as well, but is also written in a beautiful and eloquent Persian prose that set the standard for generations to come.[44] Never after Bayhaqi will accuracy of historical accounts, precision of historical thinking, and beauty and eloquence of Persian prose come together so graciously and effortlessly as they do in his *History*.[45] The book is in fact the summation of a lifetime of thinking about history. Bayhaqi began writing his book when he was forty-three and spent twenty-two years completing it in thirty volumes, of which only five volumes and half of the sixth have survived. He spent the remaining nineteen years of his life augmenting his *History*. What we read in Bayhaqi's book—particularly in such stories as that of Hasanak the Vizier, the royal minister to Mahmud, whom his son Mas'ud murdered on suspicion of being an Isma'ili—is the elevation of the craft of historiography to the art of a literary work. In Bayhaqi's *History* one might suggest that history as such (not just Ghaznavid history) finds a literary consciousness. Persian literary humanism from this text forward commands, ipso facto, a historical depth akin to its poetic disposition—a feat that will mark a depth of field to its worldly disposition that will remain its hallmark for the rest of its history.

Worlds Give Birth to Themselves

Successive empires—from the Saffarids to the Seljuqids, resisting from the Umayyads to the Abbasids—*embody* the world they conquer and coin their names in political terms that tally with their literary subconscious, giving their poets and literati something to sing and signify. These empires are the extended shadow of world-conquerors who by conquering the world earned the power to map it. By mapping the world these empires were ipso facto inventing it, willing it, naming it. That willing the world created a counter-will—and both the willing and the counter-willing posit their concomitant literary imagination, both to dominate and yet paradoxically also to liberate the world. In both willing and mapping, counter-willing and remapping the world, empires make possible and impossible at one and the same time a world that becomes the wide spectrum of a literary imagination in which humanity is made possible—sculpted, multifaceted, intuitive, counterintuitive, human, all too human: peopling the world, as it were, as a work of art that gives (repeatedly) birth to itself.

4

The Triumph of the Word

The Perils and Promises of the Mongol Empire (1256–1353)

THE MONGOLS descended upon the world like a sudden thunder, a storm, a tsunami—and took the sedentary, sedate, civilized, and corrupted empires of the Seljuqids and the Abbasids, and beyond them the known and the unknowing world, by their throats. The Mongols hit like a vengeance—and in the fertile soil of blood and booty they shed and plundered and the ruins and fears they left behind, grew flowers— colorful, aromatic, deeply rooted, robust, and plentiful—of life and love and liberty and revolt and a renewed pact with humanity all before they had descended from their horses. *Amadand o kandand o sukhtand o ko-shtand o bordand o raftand* (*they came, they uprooted, they burned, they killed, they plundered, and they left*)—historians would recount for generations to come, but there was much more to the world the Mongols had mapped than those mere words could convey.[1]

Writing a Global Empire

By the time the Mongols descended upon the Persianate and Muslim world, the primacy of *ethnos* in ascertaining communal imagination had completely given way to that of *logos* as the *nexus classicus* of Persian literary humanism. Moving from the early Iranian dynasties of the Saffarids and the Samanids, to the Turkic dynasties of the Ghaznavids and the Seljuqids, and now yielding to the Mongols, Persian literary humanism no longer needed to fabricate any ethnic lineage for itself with respect to a pre-Islamic Iranian heritage. It was in the Persian language—and people from four corners of the world had contributed to its making—that this literary humanism deepened its imaginative and emotive roots. Persian literary humanism by now had become a reality sui generis, celebrating the language that it had uplifted—spoken and written by poets and literati from northern, southern, eastern, and western climes and sustaining ever-larger imperial projects. The empires it served were ever more expanding and global, and so was the literary imagination it harbored, and so were the poets and literati who joined ranks with it. No "ethnicity" had any exclusive claim on this language. The language claimed and characterized any and all who spoke, wrote, and enriched it. "Persian" was now a completely linguistic mark, not a marker of ethnicity—which in the vast Iranian context meant nothing. Khurasan, not the Fars province (a mis-appellation for Persian language) was the locus classicus of the rise of new Persian, with Turkic and Indic extensions of the site of the spoken and written language. What made Persian language global was indeed the globality of people who spoke it, and the global disposition of empires (all of them non-Iranian) that employed it.

All other empires that were home to Persian literary humanism paled in comparison to the Mongol Empire. Combining the Mongol and Turkic tribes under the leadership of one mighty Genghis Khan (ca. 1162–1227), who was proclaimed ruler of the land in 1206, the Mongol Empire expanded to rule over almost a quarter of the total land mass of the earth for two—thirteenth and fourteenth—centuries. Beginning in the central Asian steppes, the empire eventually stretched to the heart of Europe to its west and the Sea of Japan to its east, included Siberia to its north, and extended southward into the Indian subcontinent and then all the way to the eastern coasts of the Mediterranean. It was the largest contiguous empire on planet earth in history.[2]

The branch of the Mongol Empire that ruled over Iran and the rest of the Muslim world was known as the Il-Khanids (1256–1353). Hulagu, the brother of Emperor Möngke Khan (r. 1251–1259), was entrusted with the task of consolidating the imperial conquests to the south of the Oxus River. Hulagu defeated the Isma'ilis in 1256, conquered Baghdad in 1258, and was only stopped by the Mamluk dynasty in Ayn Jalut in Palestine in 1260. So in less than 5 years he had consolidated his rule over much of the Muslim world. The Il-Khanids ran a tight ship, and once they settled they became great patrons of the arts and sciences. They were ecumenical and multifaceted in the ideological foregrounding of their empire. Hulagu's wife, Doquz Khatun, was a devout Christian, and under their reign both Christianity and Buddhism were as important and honored as was Islam. The great warlord Mahmud Ghazan (r. 1295–1304), heavily Persianized, converted to Islam. Until their eventual decline in the mid-fourteenth century, the Il-Khanids were the hallmark of imperial conquest and their courts a haven for poets, literati, scientists, artists, and architects. Abu Said (r. 1317–1335) was the last great khan of the dynasty and soon after him began the eventual decline of the Il-Khanids until the rise of Timur (Tamerlane, 1336–1405), the founder of the Timurid empire (1370–1506) in central Asia.

Persian literary humanism achieved its absolute and final zenith during the course of the Mongol Empire in more than one sense, a level of normative, aesthetic, and moral imagination never to be matched again in its long and illustrious history. A planetary, universal, and cosmic imagining of the physical and metaphysical worlds became the pinnacle of a literary humanism that would remain definitive of it for millennia to come. If we look at the history of the region from the period of the minor dynasties of the Samanids, the Taherids, and the Saffarids to the major dynasties of the Ghaznavids and the Seljuqids, ultimately yielding to the planetary Mongol Empire, there is a decidedly ever more expansive imperial domain, and a corresponding literary imagination that had sought to fathom those successively expansive worlds. With that imperial world now historicized, it soon found its regal replicas in other areas and domains—of mind and soul, of philosophy, mysticism, arts, sciences, poetry, and architecture. What Iranian ethnocentric nationalism remembers as its literary heritage is in fact constitutionally flawed—for all these empires had to abandon any sense of ethnic identity in order for the Persian literary imagination to become global, universal, and, with the Mongols, even planetary. It is a matter of historical fact that we must think of medieval history not in "national" but in transnational and decidedly imperial terms, and of Persian literary achievement not in ethnocentric but in linguistic terms.

That literary imagination found its deepest manifestation first and foremost in historiographical narratives. One must simply thumb through the pages of *Ta'rikh-e Jahan-gusha* (*History of the World Conqueror*) by the preeminent Mongol historian Ala'eddin Ata-Malik al-Jovayni (1226–1283) to grasp the immense power and reach of Persian language at the height of its narrative might. *Ta'rikh-e Jahan-gusha* is a monument in Persian historiography without which the world at large would be deprived of the most detailed accounts of early Mongol history. Ata-Malik Jovayni was born and raised in Juvain in Khurasan in a learned Iranian family, rose in the ranks of the court officials, and visited the Mongol capital of Karakorum twice before he commenced on or about 1252 the writing of his magnum opus.[3] Al-Jovayni accompanied Hulagu in 1256 when he captured the Isma'ili fortress Alamut, and then proceeded to march with the Mongol warlord in his conquest and sacking of Baghdad in 1258, and even for a while functioned as a governor of Baghdad and environs. Juvayni's brother Shams al-Din was also a high-ranking functionary in the Mongol Empire.

The particular features of al-Jovayni's history are all embedded in the power of its authoritative narrative—it is based on his own personal observations, research, travels, and affiliation with the Mongol warlords, in all of which he was a participant observer. Al-Jovayni traveled to Mongolia, where he had access to the famous text of *The Secret History of the Mongols*, which was composed some time after Genghis Khan's death in 1227, originally in the Uyghur script. *Ta'rikh-e Jahan-gusha* is not just about the political history of the Mongols. It offers much information about the social, economic, and religious dimension of the epochs and eras that it covers. The first volume of *Ta'rikh-e Jahan-gusha* is on the rise of Genghis Khan and his descendents; the second volume is on the history of the Khwarezmshahid dynasty (1077–1231), which ruled central Asia at the time of the Mongol invasion, up to the rise of Hulagu; and the third volume covers the period from the rise of Hulagu to the conquest of Alamut and the destruction of Baghdad. Some editions of *Ta'rikh-e Jahan-gusha* have an addendum by the great Persian philosopher and scientist Khwajah Nasir al-Din al-Tusi (1201–1274) about the conquest of Baghdad. Al-Jovayni lived for a long time after he had completed his history of the Mongols, but he did not add anything to it. He was very courageous in his account of his patrons, whom he praised profusely while reporting on their atrocities.

Al-Jovayni's prose has a literary flair, and citations from such poets as Ferdowsi and Mas'ud Sad Salman regularly adorn it. He knew personally such prominent poets as Sa'di Shirazi, which means he kept a literary company despite his active political position. Reading *Ta'rikh-e Jahan-gusha* is a lesson in learning the mastery of powerful Persian prose put squarely at the service of a vast historical imagination. The narrative soon takes over from the narrator and becomes a reality sui generis, as if writing itself for a posterity known and unknown at one and the same time. At the heart of al-Jovayni's narrative dwells a persistent quest for a vast historical canvas of human folly and imperial conquest at one and the same time.

The next great historian of the period who complemented al-Jovayni's work was Rashid al-Din Fazlullah Hamadhani (1250–1317), who was born to a prominent family of Jewish physicians in Hamadhan. He subsequently converted to (Sunni) Islam to facilitate his rising fortune in the Il-Khanid court and eventually became the personal physician to Abaqa Khan (r. 1265–1282). But the health and well-being of the Mongol warlord was more a minor task of his career as a leading member of the literati at the service of the empire. Rashid al-Din Fazlullah was one of the most prominent and powerful viziers in the service of the Mongol Empire, devoting his time between matters of state and his literary and historiographical preoccupations. He served successive Mongol emperors with audacity and panache, but he was finally murdered at the instigation of his rivals at the age of seventy-three.

Rashid al-Din Fazlullah's *Jame' al-Tawarikh* (*Compendium of Histories*) was an even more ambitious project than al-Jovayni's *Ta'rikh-e Jahan-gusha*. *Jame' al-Tawarikh* is a unique and concerted effort to bring to perfection a universal history not just of the Mongols but of all the known peoples of earth. Legends and religion to history, anthropology, mythology, and rituals are the subjects of Rashid al-Din Fazlullah's universal history, ranging from pre-Islamic and non-Islamic history to the history of prophets from Adam to Muhammad. *Jame' al-Tawarikh* is not just a history, for it includes extensive chapters on geography and topography, seeking in effect to narrate a complete account of humanity and its habitat. Rashid al-Din Fazlullah began writing his magnum opus at the order and during the reign of Ghazan Khan (r. 1295–1304) and finished and dedicated it to Uljytu (r. 1303–1316).[4] It took him 10 years to write (1300–1310), and he did so with such purposeful determination that to this day it reads with the royal confidence of the empire for which it was conceived and delivered. Rashid al-Din Fazlullah's history is the best source of information about the later Mongol period, complementing al-Jovayni's account, which is particularly good for the early Mongol period, so that between the two of them they cover the entire Mongol imperial expanse.

As its title suggests, *Jame' al-Tawarikh* is a compendium of other histories. It includes a complete history of the Turkic dynasties leading up to the Mongol Empire, narrated around the conquests of Genghis Khan. Iranian history is included, from the very beginning to the fall of the Sassanids, as well as the history of Muslim conquests up to the Ghaznavids and the Seljuqids and the Mongols. The book also covers the history of Europe, including the histories of the popes and the caesars. The final volume is dedicated to geography and what today we might call "cultural anthropology." In preparation for writing this book, the Mongol warlord Ghazan Khan had put all the imperial documents at the disposal of Rashid al-Din Fazlullah and had commanded the elders of the tribe to give Fazlullah as much information as he needed. This great historian was conscious of the fact that he was writing a comprehensive world history occasioned by the Mongol Empire. While comfortably flaunting his command of Turkish, Mongol, and Arabic words, Rashid al-Din Fazlullah wrote his history in a confident, robust, and purposeful Persian prose, very much aware of its power of narrative.

Reading al-Jovayni and Rashid al-Din Fazlullah back to back, one is made immediately aware of the vastness of their historical imagination, the audacity of their Persian prose, and the panache and poise with which they give momentum to their worldly account of the Mongol Empire. What is also evident in these accounts is how the final collapse of Baghdad in 1258, while destructive in and of itself, also liberated Muslims from pre-Islamic tribal thinking and domination. The *logos* overcoming *ethnos* in Persian literary humanism had now gone positively global and planetary with al-Jovayni and Rashid al-Din Fazlullah's historical imaginations trying to come to terms with the empire they simultaneously administered and narrated.

The fact that the Mongol Empire was narrated by two major historians during their own time did not of course mean that everyone in their realm bought into those imperial accounts of the reign, which were delivered from a position of power. As did any other vast empire, the Mongols produced their own deeply rooted despair and destitution and consequent revolt among the impoverished peasantry and the urban poor. The more mighty and vast the empire, the more domestic abuse of the weakest strata of the lands they rule. Medieval historians—Rashid al-Din Fazlullah chief among them—report extensively on "the menace of thieves and bandits" that plagued the Mongol Empire. It is only through the painstaking work of modern scholarship that we know these "thieves and bandits" were in fact runaway peasants and urban poor who had resorted to revolutionary uprisings against their Mongol rulers. By far the most significant of these revolutionaries were known as the *Sarbedars* (literally, "head on gallows," meaning they were ready to die for their cause), who, like previous revolutionaries during the Muslim conquest, had gathered around a proto-Shi'i mystical ideology to assert their opposition to the Sunni orthodoxy that informed the Iranian and Muslim realms of the Mongol Empire, as well as the *Yasa* (code of law) of Genghis Khan, the principal law of the Mongol Empire.[5] The Sarbedars revolted and ruled over part of western Khurasan from 1335 to 1386 in the midst of the disintegration of the Il-Khanids that began in the mid-fourteenth century. From their capital in Sabzevar, the Sarbedars were a combination of local and minor landlords and the rural and urban poor, who obviously harbored a much more radical agenda. The Sarbedars were ultimately defeated by Timur (Tamerlane).

The Philosopher as Humanist

From the narratives of triumphant domination to the battlefields of revolt, the Mongol Empire was the site of a vast historical imagination unprecedented in its magnitude and dimensions, overwhelming whatever memory of the pre-Islamic empires Iranians and non-Iranians had. The magnitude of that historical imagination reconvened the idea of the human for history. The vast territory of the Mongol Empire generated a correspondingly cosmic historical imagination in Persian, which in turn normatively expanded Persian literary humanism and consolidated its logocentricity, for now Persian literary imagination was far beyond any ethnicity or ethnic nativism. It had been consolidated by a Mongol Empire picked up from two previous Turkic empires, which were predicated on a number of minor Iranian dynasties—the Tahirids, the Saffarids, and the Samanids among them. This historical imagination was self-confident and even more importantly self-conscious, which in turn made Persian literary humanism worldly and cosmopolitan in its literary imagination. Both al-Jovayni and Fazlullah depended not only on previous historians like Bal'ami and Bayhaqi, but more importantly on Persian literary prose to write their universal histories of the Mongol Empire from the confident constitution of Persian literary imagination.

This vast historical panorama of time and space was aptly reflected in the intellectual output and particularly the philosophical imagination of the age, where we witness the rise of a rainbow of syncretic philosophical thinking in Persian, entirely unprecedented in the mostly Arabic parlance of Islamic philosophy, and with a close discursive tie to Persian literary humanism. To be sure, philosophers like Nasir Khosrow and Suhrawardi had produced major works of philosophy in Persian during the preceding centuries, and they had used that remissive space adjacent to Islamic scholasticism to dare to think the impermissible, the inaudible, the whisperish, in their mother tongue. But the magnitude of what happens during the Mongol period, particularly in the production of a liminal philosophical space, is entirely unprecedented both in range and in diction.

Philosopher-poet-mystics like Sadr al-Din Qunawi (d. 1274), Amir Khosrow Dehlavi (1253–1325), and Shaykh Mahmud Shabestari (1288–1340), among many others, defined an entire spectrum of creative thinking that crossed many scholastic borders and broke many doctrinal taboos. A text like Shaykh Mahmud Shabestari's *Golshan Raz* (*Garden of Secrets*) is a prime example of how poetry, philosophy, and gnosticism came together into the body of the Persian language to form a unique diction reducible to none of the three and transcending them all. Primacy here was given to the language, the universe of its imaginative possibilities. Discourses were accidental to it. Here in this diction, the poetic presides and the philosophical and the mystic yield to form a hidden layer of meaning otherwise impossible to imagine. Although thinkers like Shabestari are habitually assimilated into institutional discourses, doctrines, and practices, the narrative fact of their writing transcends all categorization. There is always a hermeneutic surplus evident in these texts that is embedded in their poetic registers and is never totally exhausted either logically or metaphysically. As such, these thinkers are the unrecognized and implicit masters of Persian literary humanism with their oeuvre systematically read and assimilated into the context of the established, canonical, and repressive discourses of their and subsequent generations of interpreters.[6]

Consider the case of Afdal al-Din Kashani (d. 1214) who produced a vast and expansive body of work that precisely because it is conducted and performed in Persian, posits a discursive universe not entirely assimilable to Islamic scholasticism, and in fact is doctrinally and emotively inimical to it. The key defining moment of this patently literary philosophical tradition, picking up from Nasir Khosrow, Suhrawardi, and Omar Khayyam, is the fusion of poetry and philosophy, from there merging with the gnostic tradition in mysticism to posit a syncretic language that crosses discourses, disciplines, and schools to reach for a different mood of thinking-as-being. It is important to recognize this full-bodied language as distinctly different from the established schools of philosophy of, say, Neo-Platonism or Aristotelianism, as best represented by Alfarabi and Avicenna, which were performed almost entirely in Arabic. In the syncretic liminality that Persian language and by extension Persian literary humanism made possible, these philosopher-poets crafted an inner space, immune and immortal, in which human thinking beyond the scholastic borders was made possible, self-evident, and even inevitable.

It is thus in Afdal al-Din Kashani (also known as Baba Afdal al-Din Kashani, or affectionately just as Baba Afdal) that we must look for the soul of Persian literary humanism in this period. A philosopher-gnostic-poet who effortlessly combined literary, poetic, philosophical, and mystical thinking, Baba Afdal produced a unique literary prose in Persian that projected an irreducible mode of thinking that demanded to be read poetically, in a literary register. This prose was as much definitive to Persian literary humanism as it was alien to the courtly life and scholastic institutions alike. Though not much is known about his life, what little is known characterizes Baba Afdal as someone entirely ill-disposed toward political power, and even subject to a term in prison on charges of engaging in *sehr* (magic), an accusation that in and of itself shows how troubled and disturbed the scholastic establishment must have been by his ideas.[7]

Baba Afdal brought together a unique combination of Suhrawardi's philosophical penchant and Khayyam's preference for quatrains to reach for a different mood of philosophical thinking—at once poetic and metaphysical, and yet reducible to neither. He is known for his astonishing ability to craft a powerful Persian philosophical prose, at times even superior to what Suhrawardi or before him, on a much more limited scale, Avicenna had done. The result is a prose that is at once poetically musical from a literary perspective and yet philosophically probing and precise. His poetic proclivity undoubtedly had an impact on the formation of his prose. Baba Afdal's prose is irreducible to any sectarian disposition in philosophical thinking and is entirely his own, informed by philosophy, theology, and mysticism but reducible to none of them. It has been rightly suggested "that he was a careful stylist in his philosophical works as is shown by his letters, which are written less formally and show a preponderance of Arabic words."[8] The stylistic formalism reveals his consciousness of the literary disposition of his philosophical project. Though he is not a Sufi in the specific sense of the term, a mystical/visionary disposition does inform and animate his philosophical thinking.

The result of all these characteristics is that Baba Afdal's philosophy is entirely homocentric, and farthest from the theocentricity of much of Islamic scholasticism in general and even Islamic philosophy, which remained at its roots theo-ontological. This is not to say that God has no place in his philosophy of self. He does. But it is ultimately the *mardom* (people) or *insan* (human) that chiefly concerns and preoccupies him. His philosophy is entirely geared toward the perfection and happiness of the humanity that he thus constitutes and defines in his homocentric philosophy. As William Chittick rightly summarizes Baba Afdal's philosophy:

> Philosophy is valuable because people who meditate upon its truths will look within themselves and come to understand that they already possess everything they seek. "Man has no need of anything but himself." . . . By classifying the kinds of knowledge and existents, philosophy awakens human souls from forgetfulness and incites them to reach the perfection of existence. . . . It prepares man for death by allowing him to undergo a cognitive separation from the body before it dies.[9]

Baba Afdal is the supreme humanist philosopher and one of the pinnacles of Persian literary humanism, in fact the very architect of the human soul, beyond anything achieved in Islamic philosophy proper— and as such formed and articulated entirely outside both orthodox scholasticism and the royal court. He has been falsely assimilated into "Islamic" philosophy—just because he was a Muslim and a philosopher does not make him an "Islamic philosopher," in the technical sense of the term, for his moral and metaphysical preoccupations were of an entirely unique disposition and the fact that he wrote in Persian was neither accidental nor inconsequential to his philosophy. Chittick has rightly suggested that Baba Afdal subsequently influenced many Muslim philosophers and that the great Shi'i philosopher of the Safavid era Molla Sadra Shirazi (1571–1641) extensively reproduced his ideas without citing him. But even that does not make Baba Afdal into an Islamic philosopher in the strict and technical sense of the term.

Afdal al-Din Kashani's magnum opus is a book called *Aradnameh* (*On Human Attributes*), which is devoted entirely to the manners of the perfection of the human soul—beginning with the corporeal bodies (*ajsam*), upon which act subjects (*konandegan*) through the intermediary function of concepts (*danesteh-ha*) and the agency of those who know them (*danandegan*). The astonishing simplicity of these Persian words at one and the same time demystifies their Arabic counterparts and posits the vast array of possibilities in Persian philosophizing. In this and almost all his other works, Afdal al-Din Kashani is chiefly concerned about the elevation of the human soul to full self-knowledge and the liberation that is contingent upon it. In *Madarej al-Kamal* (*Stages of Perfection*), Baba Afdal dwells on the notion of human perfection, or *Kamal*, in contradistinction to human fallibility or imperfection, or *Noqsan*, and the passage through *Noqsan* to achieve *Kamal*, and how to recognize it once we have gained it. He dwells in this essay on the benefits of self-knowledge in achieving *Kamal*. His *Rah-anjam-nameh* (*On Destination*) is about the nature of human "self" and the benefit of knowledge (*elm*) and awareness (*agahi*) in elevating that self toward perfection and ultimately "self-knowledge" as the way to achieve *Kamal*. *Saz-o Pira-ye Shahan Por Mayeh* (*On the Adornments of Majestic Kings*) is delivered in the guise of a Mirror for Princes but is in fact a treatise on ordinary human beings and how they can achieve superiority over other human beings by way of self-knowledge. *Javdan-nameh (On the Everlasting)* is basically on the purpose of life, wherefore and whereto this purpose is also contingent on achieving knowledge about the purpose of this life on earth. His entire philosophical project is in fact on human reason saving humanity from darkness descending upon the soul. His philosophy can be summarized in this short and precise quatrain in his *divan*:

> Ay ankeh to taleb-e Khoda'i beh khod a!
>
> You who seek God get to know your self!
> Begin with your self, for God is not apart from your self.
> First know thy self for if you know thy self, I swear by God
> You will also confess to the Godness of God.[10]

It is useful to compare Baba Afdal's homocentricism with a more theocentric mystic of this era, another luminary philosopher-mystic-poet, Ala' al-Dowlah Semnani (1261–1336).[11] Initially employed at the court of the Mongol warlord Abaqa Khan (1234–1282) at a very young age, Semnani eventually abandoned his official positions and became a moderate mystic who made a reputation for himself by opposing the radical mysticism of the great Andalusian mystic Muhy al-Din Ibn Arabi (1165–1240). In addition to his critical position against Ibn Arabi, Semnani was equally if not more traumatized by the presence of Buddhist monks in the Il-Khanid court and engaged in prolonged disputations with them. Throughout his writings he tried to cultivate a disciplined spiritual quest within the confinements of Shari'ah.[12] The sobriety of his prose, and the fact that he first excelled in and then altogether abandoned politics reveal a spiritual serenity about him and his work. In one of his major treatises, *Al-Urwah li-Ahl al-Khilwah wa al-Jilwah* (*The Pillar for the People of Solitude and Epiphany*), he tried to bring theology, theo-ontology, prophetology, and the spiritual authority of saints (*Velayat*) together into a solid and stable narrative.[13] By and large, Semnani remains a pivotal figure in modest and measured mysticism, sustaining the theo-centricity of Islamic scholasticism against what he considers to be the excesses of a more radical mysticism.

The disciplined theocentricity of Semnani's gnosticism is compromised only by the supplementary poetic disposition of his work, which simultaneously enriches and qualifies it. What is far more consequential in implicating his conservative scholasticism is the delayed defiance in his teaching that soon emerges in his devoted disciple Khwaju Kermani (1280–1352), one of the most prominent poets of this era, who pushes the erotic boundaries of romance poetry, which had been perfected by Nezami earlier and was later matched by Amir Khosrow Dehlavi (1253–1325), and brings it to a height that only a generation later Nur al-Din Abd al-Rahman Jami (1414–1492) can match during the Timurid period (1370–1506). Semnani heavily influenced the great poet Khwaju Kermani, who is in fact believed to have compiled his master's collection of poetry. Khwaju Kermani thus in effect actualizes the poetic potentials of Semnani as a form of deferred defiance and his famous *Khamseh* (*Quintet*) achieves a renewed pact with romance poetry. In Kermani's *Quintet*, deeply influenced by Nezami, the two romances of "Homay and Homa-yun," a love story between a Syrian prince and a Chinese princess, and

"Gol and Noruz," another love story between Prince Noruz and a Roman princess named Gol, become the masterpieces of the genre during the Il-Khanid period. The other three parts of the *Quintet*, "Rowdah al-Anwar" ("Garden of Lights"), "Kamal-nameh" ("Book of Perfection"), and "Goharnameh" ("Book of Jewels"), are all mystical narratives. In this *Quintet*, as a result, we are witness, following the model of Nezami, to physical and mystical love narratively intertwined.[14]

Central to this genre of poetic gnosticism is its irreducible force of supplementarity. The poetic supplement initially suggests itself as mere *accretion* but may (and does) in fact become a *substitution*—in other words the supplement may appear just to augment but in effect surreptitiously supplants the metaphysical underpinning of the totalizing gnostic project. Here the poetic is the supplement that makes the totalizing discourses of mysticism at once (and paradoxically) possible and suspect—it enables that discourse precisely at the moment that, like a Trojan horse, it subverts and supplants it. Mysticism could not do without the poetic, and the poetic at one and the same time supplemented and supplanted the mystical. The Persian mystics' love for Persian poetry was their Achilles heel, entirely (perhaps) unbeknownst to themselves.

The poetic supplementarity of gnosticism in this period is further augmented by the universalizing proclivity of such monumental figures as Khwajah Nasir al-Din al-Tusi—philosopher, scientist, scholastic, and statesman par excellence. In his massive and multifaceted output, Khwajah Nasir al-Din al-Tusi reflects the imperial imagining of the Il-Khanid dynasty, which he wholeheartedly served. In the astonishing range of his moral, philosophical, scientific, and scholastic imagination he invested a global vision that had lasting consequences for the normative universe of Persian literary humanism. In fields ranging from astronomy to biology, chemistry, physics, logic, mathematics, theology, philosophy, literary criticism, and ethics, al-Tusi constructed an edifice of learning that defined the intellectual contours of his age.[15] It is particularly in his writings on ethics—*Akhlaq-e Mohtashami* (*Mohtashami Ethics*) and *Akhlaq-e Naseri* (*Naserian Ethics*)—that he posited the figure of a philosopher-vizier.[16] Throughout his writings, Khwajah Nasir al-Din al-Tusi is syncretic in his language, planetary in his imagination, and universal in the range of his sentiments. He is a major figure in multiple fields, particularly in astrophysics, philosophy, and theology.[17] But it is his work on ethics that should be considered his lasting influence on Persian literary humanism. What is of particular interest in his *Akhlaq-e Naseri* is not merely the vast moral imagination that informs it but the moral self-consciousness of the ethicist who writes with a universal claim to his positions. Al-Tusi combined Iranian, Islamic, and Greek sources and heritages to reflect widely on individual, communal, and political ethics. He completed the text while he was still in the service of the Isma'ilis and then revised it when the Isma'ilis fell under Hulagu. So in effect he combines the daring imagination of the Isma'ilis and the global conquest of the Mongols in mastering a moral imagination that can address a universal humanity. Al-Tusi borrowed freely from Greek and Muslim thinkers before him but cast the result in a confident and engrossing Persian prose.

The Mystic Triumvirate

Philosopher-poets like Baba Afdal unapologetically concerned themselves with the self-knowledge of the fragility of humanity as the only reliable sense and site of getting to know the divinity. By narratively positing the human, Baba Afdal had philosophically deferred the divine. But even beyond Baba Afdal, who was decidedly homocentric, when we come to theocentric philosophers like Ala' al-Dowlah Semnani, their penchant for poetry posits a supplementarity for their philosophy that at one and the same time sustains and supplants the philosophical text with a markedly human contingency. In the case of Semnani we even have a deferred defiance in him that is later materialized in his student Khwaju Kermani, who became a great poet of romance, inflecting the canonized manner of reading philosophical or gnostic, or altogether metaphysical, texts and doctrines. The literary and poetic supplementarity of the text defies all the assured certainties of such narratives and their institutional canonization. The symbolic here defies the institutional and discursive legislation of the text and thus creates an open-ended space for Persian literary humanism.

The organic link, simultaneous in its creation, between Islamic mysticism (Sufism) and Persian poetry went far beyond these erudite and yet limited circles and reached for much wider domains. Neither the romantic nor the lyrical possibilities of Persian poetry escaped the attention of Persian mystics. Devoted to a particular doctrinal reading of the Qur'an and of the Muhammadan message, the Persian Sufis joined their Arab, Turkish, and Indian brethren in a massive mystification of the physical world. Finalized in the doctrine of *Wahdat al-Wujud (the Unity of Being)*, the Sufis collectively engaged in a radical sublation of both the literary act and of physical love to reach for a richer, and more humanely palpable, reading of their faith. Persian lyrical poetry in particular proved most appropriate for such a grand act of purposeful piety. Three successive poets, Sana'i (d. 1131), Attar (1145–1221), and Rumi (1207–1273), are chiefly recognized as the master-builders of Persian mystical poetry.

In the character and poetic demeanor of Sana'i, we witness the decline of the royal court as the patron of Persian poetry and the rise of religious sentiments to substitute the physical beauties that principally informed the imaginative repertoire of Persian poetry. The substantial overmystification of Sana'i by later Sufis is not borne out by the actual presence of religious sensibilities in his poetry. Sana'i professed that his worldly poetics did not in any significant way promote his station in life, and that consequently he decided to devote his talent to religious sentiments and mystical poetry. He blamed his contemporaries, a vague reference to his liaisons with the Ghaznavid court, for not having appreciated his poetry. He seems to have felt particularly humiliated by submitting his poetic gift to the brute taste of his patrons. He was the master of the world of words, he thought, and yet a servile slave to his brute masters—and this bothered him. As a result, he informs us, he abandons worldly poetry and turns his attention to religious matters. But the conversion is not so dramatic as to abandon poetry altogether. He simply decides to attend to religious matters poetically. "My poetry shall be a commentary on Religion and Law / The only reasonable path for a poet is this." Despite his Shi'i sentiments, Sana'i equally praised the first three caliphs, indicating a less than zealous religiosity.[18] Nevertheless, later Sufis took full advantage of this "conversion" and imagined fantastic stories about it, allowing for the dominant discourse of Sufism to turn Sana'i into a full-fledged Sufi. As a poet, Sana'i remained singularly attached to religious sentiments, a fact best represented not only in his poetry but also in his pilgrimage to Mecca, which he undertook from Khurasan.[19] But the poetic attendance to his religious concerns was a reality unto itself—nor should his turn to piety be categorically cast to the entirety of his career as a poet. *Karnamah-ye Balkh*, a *mathnavi*, thought to be Sana'i's earliest poetic composition, is in an entirely worldly and humorous mode, and was composed for the Ghaznavid ruler Mas'ud ibn Ibrahim.

After his pilgrimage to Mecca, a friend of Sana'i, a man named Khwajah Ahmad ibn Mas'ud, provided him with a home and daily sustenance and asked Sana'i to collect his poems and prepare a *divan*. Sana'i spent the rest of his life in this house in Ghaznin and compiled his collected works, including his masterpiece *Hadiqat al-Haqiqah*. Sana'i's *divan*, masterfully edited in more than thirteen thousand verses by the great Iranian literary scholar Modarres Razavi, is a compendium of his worldly and religious sensibilities. His *madayeh* (panegyric praises) demonstrate Sana'i's mastery of the genre and are clear indications of a boastful awareness of his poetic gifts. *Hadiqat al-Haqiqah va Shari'at al-Tariqah/The Garden of Truth and the Path of the Right Passage* (also known as *Ilahi-nameh/Theosophy*) is by far the most significant work of Sana'i, which he composed between 1129 and 1130 in ten thousand verses. He dedicated this *mathnavi* couplet to the Ghaznavid warlord Bahramshah (r. 1118–1152). *Hadiqat* begins with conventional salutations to God and the Prophet and his companions and then proceeds to perform poetic discourses on reason, knowledge, wisdom, and love. In his original version, something must have been in Sana'i's *Hadiqat* that caused the anger of contemporary religious authorities. He sent a copy of it to a prominent religious authority, Bohran al-Din Abu al-Hasan Ali ibn Nasir al-Ghaznavi, in Baghdad and asked him to issue an edict in its support. In his letter, composed in the form of a poem, Sana'i went so far as to identify *Hadiqat* as "the Qur'an in Persian," a phrase that has been used for other texts as well, particularly by Jami in reference to Rumi's *Mathnavi*. Immediately after the death of Sana'i, there was no complete version of *Hadiqat* extant. Muhammad ibn Ali al-Raffa', a Sufi to judge by his introduction, prepared an edition of the text. *Karnamah-ye Balkh/The Balkh Account* is full of praises for the nobility and poetic dialogues with his contemporary poets. *Sayr al-Ibad ila al-Ma'ad/The Passage of the Pious towards the Destined Return, Tariq al-Tahqiq/The Path of Certainty,* and *Ishq-namab/Love Story* are three of Sana'i's other *mathnavis*.[20]

There is an organic continuity in mystical imagination between Sana'i and Attar, the next major Sufi poet to come after him and who also excelled in the genre of *mathnavi*. Attar's *Manteq al-Tayr* (*Conference of the Birds*), among his numerous other *mathnavis*, has been persistently read as a mystical allegory, foretelling Rumi's masterpiece, which categorically (and rightly) claimed the whole genre and is simply known as *The Mathnavi*. But before that feat, Attar had so vastly popularized the *mathnavi* genre that in addition to his own compositions, numerous others were composed and attributed to him. In addition to *Manteq al-Tayr,* the other *mathnavis* that have been verified to have been from Attar's own pen are *Asrar-nameh* (*Book of Secrets*), *Ilahi-Nameh* (*Book of Theology*), and *Mosibat-Nameh* (*Book of Calamities*). In addition to these *mathnavis,* Attar is also the author of *Tazkirat al-Awlia,* a masterpiece on the lives and miraculous deeds of the early Sufis. In *Ilahi-Nameh,* Attar extols the superiority of love over intellect in understanding the nature of being.[21] In the seven categories that Attar posits in stages of being, *insan* (humanity) comes fifth, after *arkan* (elements), *ma'aden* (minerals), *nabat* (vegetal), and *heyvan* (animal), and just before "prophets" and ultimately "Muhammad." Muhammad as the Prophet of Islam is here the iconic gathering of *Insan-e Kamel* (*The Perfect Humanity*). The key to Attar's homocentric mysticism is the fact that the fragile figure of the human is in fact the final site of the recognition of the divine—and Muhammad as the supreme site of that recognition is in fact humanity par excellence.

Sana'i and Attar's experimentation with didactic *mathnavi* narrative for suggestion of mystical allegories ultimately reached Mawlana Jalal al-Din Rumi, in whose hands Persian mystical poetry achieves its highest and most prolific summits. Rumi's *Mathnavi,* dubbed "the Qur'an in Persian" by Jami, is the highest achievement and the meta-logical conclusion of Persian mystical poetry. With slight poetic modifications in conceptual and aesthetic sensibilities, Rumi gave full expression to a mystical narrative that posited an all-loving God presiding over the worldly manifestation of his omnipresence. Man (degendered) in Rumi's narrative became a Man-God potentially endowed with the realization of all divine attributes. Rumi's journey became a passionate quest inward, toward the realization of God within.[22] Rumi conquers a vast empire within, matching and upping the ante on the empire of the Mongols without. He sat there, like God, Man incarnate, divine, sublime, supreme, serene, unbeknownst to himself, speaking with a divine voice, writing with a divine pen—drawing a circle around humanity and siting it for what and where it was and there, right there, it was God, having descended upon humanity. Invisible, invincible, sonorous, *sokhan kashti-o ma'ni hamcho darya* (speech like a vessel), and meaning like a sea, and he sailed that boat upon that sea. Rumi is the Bach of Persian poetry: majestic, calm, quiet, confident, trembling with certainty, conviction, the expanse of an infinity the domain of his assurances and vastly evident on and about his countenance. He is here and nowhere, atemporal, amorphous. He is not outside. He calls God not to him, but to Himself.[23]

Rumi's *Mathnavi* is like a sea—vast, welcoming, warm, vertiginous, life-affirming.[24] Stories, woven into stories—telling it like it is: Moses was once walking through a landscape and chanced upon a shepherd who was happily singing his heart out to God. Oh God, the shepherd was singing, how much I love you. I wish you were here so I could comb your hair, mend your clothes, massage your feet, be your most obedient servant. What nonsense is this, Moses admonished the poor shepherd, upon hearing him sing his blasphemy. God is not a human being to get tired and be in need of your massaging his feet, or combing his hair, or mending his suit. Repent you idiot and be quiet. The poor shepherd was properly reprimanded and became quiet and went his way. What Rumi now does is on the borderline of blasphemy. He sits Moses, the great prophet, down, and begins to talk down to him like God. God begins talking to Moses through Rumi—thriving on the audacity of his poetic conviction. Why did you do that? God (speaking through Rumi) asks Moses. Why did you alienate my friend from me? By what authority, and who gave you that authority? I have sent you down to bring my friends closer to me, not to alienate them from me. How dare you? It's none of your business what language my friends use to talk to me. To every people I have given a language appropriate to them in coming close to me. Indians praise me in their own language, Chinese in theirs. Go back and apologize to him—and Moses does as he is commanded.[25]

Take Rumi out of Islam, Bach out of Christianity, Maimonides out of Judaism—and something definitive will be lacking. Rumi performs the divinity—in the human language. The human becomes sublime, while earthly, in Rumi.

Persian mystics excelled in all kinds of poetry, but it is in *mathnavi* that they found their ways. What *mathnavi* does is allow for narrating the divine thriving in human, temporal, terms. It posits the divine in narrative terms, which is inevitably, as Paul Ricoeur noted, in timely tonality. In *mathnavi*, the a/historical time becomes human, temporal, time, for as Ricoeur says, "narrative attains its full significance when it becomes a condition of temporal existence."[26] *Mathnavi* inevitably demarcates, and thus narrativizes, and thus humanizes, the divinity, whereas it has been constitutionally read as sanctifying the human. In his *Mathnavi,* Rumi, and before him Attar and Sana'i, reverse that order. The innate and sublated humanity of the narrative has been systematically denied, repressed, and disguised in sacred terms, and thus the narrative energy is systematically sapped to sustain the presumption of a divinity at the costly expense of dehumanizing the narrative. The very proposition of Persian literary humanism allows for the retrieval and resuscitation of that human agency, by way of casting the necessity of a humanist look at a literary history that has been overtly (and violently) theocentricized.

For the Love of Life

Whereas epic, romance, and *mathnavi* forms demanded longer attention spans, the brevity of lyrical poetry tested the power of the Persian poets for the economy of their wording and the precision of their sentiments. From its origins in amorous occasions in the panegyric, epic, and romance poetries, lyrical poetry eventually emerged and found its most successful and enduring form in the Persian *ghazal.* The *ghazal* became the functional equivalent of musical sonatas in Persian poetry. With sustained and implacable economy of wording and precision of sentiments, masters of Persian lyrics—principally Rumi, Sa'di (circa 1209–1291), and Hafez (1325–1390)—shed all extra-poetic functions of poetry and created perhaps the most artistically successful experiment in the whole spectrum of Persian literature. The *ghazal* is the aesthetic challenge of brevity, the formal occasion of poetic mastery, a short space in which the mosaics of words, sensibilities, and imageries demand the best in aesthetic creativity that a poet can command. Master lyricists like Rumi, Sa'di, and Hafez raised the form to such a perfect pitch that the *ghazal* became the defining moment of Persian literary imagination.

Although the origins of the *ghazal* go back to such masterful practitioners as Sana'i and Nezami, it is with Sa'di that the composition of these miniature lyrics came to its most brilliant fruition.[27] Sa'di's *ghazals* are the very picture of beauty and subtlety. Rarely has a Persian poet had such a perfect, almost magical, command over words, with flawless harmony in their sound effects. The sheer musicality of Sa'di's *ghazals* defies description. His *ghazals* read and sound like a Chopinesque nocturne: crisp, clear, concise, brevity the very soul of their amorous movements. Sa'di's works portray a human, physical, perfectly tangible love that registers with unfailing impact. The whole spectrum of Persian poetic repertoire, having come to perfection by the thirteenth century, is at the disposal of Sa'di. Never after Sa'di did the classical Persian *ghazal* benefit from the ingenious powers of a word magician with such an expansive embrace. Rumi and Hafez took the form in different directions. But Sa'di had already fathomed the field and registered its aesthetic manners and measures. Sa'di's lyrical humanism is arguably the zenith of Persian poetry and all its worldly possibilities. Sa'di's *ghazals* thrive on the subtlety of their sentiments, the swift precision of his turns of phrase, and the fastidious courage of his imagination. He has made an art of poetic license for exaggeration. But those exaggerations do not sound outlandish, for they are natural habitats of his teaching modesty.

Sa'di is in love. His *ghazals* are the pastures of his amorous reflections on what it means to be in love. A whole caravan of sugar, he says in one *ghazal*, is on its way from Egypt to Shiraz, should his beloved return to his hometown. Being in love runs out of ways of manifesting itself before Sa'di runs out of metaphors for describing it.

Man agar nazar haram ast basi gonah daram

If looking is a sin, I have much sinned,
What can I do I cannot keep my eyes to myself.
Who is doing this injustice, which I must endure—
Neither can I bear my wound, nor a moment to sigh,
Neither the peace to rest, nor the patience to leave,
Neither a place to stand, nor a haven to run to,
Neither would she cast a kind glance at me if I were to sit,
Nor if I were to run away I will have a refuge elsewhere.
People's approval and good name I am done with—
When I have given up my head what use do I have for a hat!
My body a sacrifice to your soul, I make, my head upon your doorsteps
I lay—what better than being a pauper when you're the king?
When with your majesty you step so righteously,
It would be wrong of me to darken my vision.
What a night is tonight, Almighty God—that with the rise of just
    one star
I have no desire for the sun, nor a yearning for the moon!
Oh those who suffer, stop complaining from separation—
For I have this beautiful morning from that dark night!
Beholding a beautiful face is not a sin to Sa'di—
Yes you guessed right, I have committed that sin![28]

Sa'di was worldly. Rumi was otherworldly—resting on this one to make the other one palpable, leading from the physical to the translucent, from the tactile to the imperceptible, from the visible to the indiscernible, made discernible in and through his poetry. Rumi incorporated the Persian *ghazal* into an overpowering, transformative, universe—of his own making. In Rumi content becomes form, form becomes word, words become color, shape, patterns, rhythms: dancing. Rumi is drunk in some ethereal sense: a whirlwind in motion, with grace and panache. Words matter to him not—he just spins them up and out from the fountain of his poetic soul and (lo and behold) meaning descends upon them, like a revelation, the dawning of the sun, the rise of a moon upon a desert, a sea, all made of words that he splashes on his pages, just as Jackson Pollock did with paint on canvas. Rumi throws the words up and the forms chase after them, carrying their meanings with them, not knowing where Rumi is taking them, until it dawns on them they are it: the world in words.

The best one can do is to try to follow Rumi through a *ghazal* that begins, you will note, simply and inconspicuously with the easy assertion that when he (Rumi, the poet) fell in love, or followed the path of getting to know truth, he had no idea what he was getting himself into, for how could I, he asks rhetorically, know that this venture (*soda*) would have turned me so mad, turned my heart into a hellish fire, my eyes like the river Jeyhoun, swelling with tears, how could I know that a flood would suddenly steal me, and just like a ship throw me into an ocean of blood, and then a wave would rise and hit that ship so hard that it would split into a thousand pieces, and every piece would be cast upon multiple whirlpools, and then a whale would surface and drink the water of that sea, so that vast sea would become dry like a desert—and when all these changes happened, neither that sea remained nor that desert, and I have no idea how and what happened, for howness was now drowned in no-howness, and there are many such have-no-ideas, for I just had a mouthful of narcotics from that sea.

That is Rumi: operatic, dramatic, phantasmagoric, colossal, magnificent, forgiving, playful, dwarfing you—before he, once again, pulls you together, lifts you up, and makes you believe that you, yes you, personally, are God's gift to humanity. If Rumi were a European composer he would be a shade between Richard Wagner and Richard Strauss, with a

touch of Giacomo Puccini. If he were a Japanese filmmaker he would be
a cut between Akira Kurosawa and Yasujirō Ozu, and a bit of Kenji
Mizoguchi on the side. He is a universe—and in that universe, he dismantles you, all lovingly, plays with you, pulls you in, turns you around,
takes you for a ride for every concealed idea that you might have, and
then strips you naked of them all and tells you that everything depends
on the preposition you have used! Baffled? Good! Now you go away
and be happy. How does he do it? Here is how he does it. Listen to this
strange, astonishing *ghazal*: in this translation I have opted not to try to
render the rhyme and meter of the original, but instead approximate the
loving, playful, disarming, intimacy of the diction that ultimately makes
Rumi what he is:

> Man gholam-e qamaram gheyr-e qamar hich magu
> Pish-e man joz sokhan sham'-o shekar hich magu. . . .

> I am the most obedient servant of that beautiful moon
> You see up there—
> So don't talk to me about anything except about that moon—
> And when you are with me,
> Would you please don't talk to me about anything
> Except candlelight and sweets—would you?
> Don't talk to me about pain,
> In fact don't talk to me about anything but of treasures—
> And if you know nothing about treasures,
> Then please don't bother and just say nothing at all!
> You see, yesterday I was just completely mad,
> And I ran into Love and it said to me:
> "Be quiet now, I am on my way, don't you kick and scream,
> Don't tear your clothes off, don't make a scene—
> Don't say a thing!"
> I said: "Love, I am afraid of something else!"
> Love said: "That something else is no longer,
> But don't you say a thing."
> "I will whisper into your ears a few secret words,
> But you just shake your head in approval and don't say anything
> Except nodding with your head!"
> I said: "Is this the face of an angel or of a human being?"
> Love said: "This is different from angel and human being—
> But you just keep quiet and don't say a thing!"
> I said: "What is this, please tell me, or it'll ruin me!"
> Love said: "That's just fine, you be ruined and don't say anything."

"I tell you what: you have been sitting in this house full of forms
and figures,
You just get up and pack and leave this house, and do not utter
a thing!"
I said: "My Sweet Heart, be a good Father, isn't this the very description
of God?"
"Yes, it is," he said, "but by your father's life do not say a thing!"[29]

Rumi has been *there* and he has come back. Not Hafez though: Hafez
is here—wondering. With Hafez, who happens a generation later during
the Timurid period, but who ought to be considered here for comparative
reasons, the Persian *ghazal* becomes sublimity manifest. Plaintive, probing, impatient, Hafez became the voice of the hidden treasure that was
him. His *ghazals* made him, as he made his *ghazals*—the intertwining of a
pair of twins, of form and phantasm, measured revolt and untapped sentiments. Hafez is wise, wondrous, naked in his sentiments, stripping you
of yours, decorous in his delivery. Words, words, words—Hafez is a word-
smith: he plays with them, like with marvelous marbles, throws them up
and grabs hold of them again in midair of their meanings and then again
lets them go . . . and magic they mean again. They mean any which way
Hafez throws them. Hafez is a formalist of the matter of the words, the
miniaturist of their sublimity, otherwise hidden even to themselves, particularly to themselves, before Hafez grabbed hold of them. Hafez rein-
vented Persian humanism anew, once again reassuring the world what it
means to be human, happy, ponderous, sad, defiant, assertive, assured.
In this *ghazal*, the playful wording of it is beyond the reach of translation,
I hope to get the strangely plaintive defiance of it through in English.

Yari andar kas nemibinim yaran ra cheh shod . . .
Sincerity I cannot detect in anyone, what happened to friendship?
When did camaraderie come to an end, where did all the lovers go?
The water of life is polluted, where is the auspicious Khidr?
Blood is dripping from the stem of the rose, where is the vernal breeze?
No one speaks of the rights of friends and friendship anymore,
What happened to gratitude, where are the friends?
Not a single gem has been excavated from the mine of friendship,
What happened to the sunshine, where are the efforts of winds and
rains?
This used to be the city of lovers and the abode of the kind,
When did kindness come to an end, what happened to princes?
The ball of dignity and triumph is cast into the court,

No one enters the playing field, what happened to the cavalries?
One hundred thousand flowers bloomed and not a single note from
   a bird,
What happened to the sparrows, where are the nightingales?
Venus has not played a melodious music, has its lute been burned?
No one has the joy of drunkenness anymore, what happened to the
   revelers?
Hafez no one knows the Divine secrets, be quiet—
Whom are you asking what happened in the spheres of time?[30]

With Hafez Persian lyrical poetry reached a new height, the refreshing space of a whole new poetic way of thinking. Hafez's poetic purpose, the physical beauty of his verses, is above and beyond anything achieved before or after in Persian lyrics.[31] In Hafez's poetry dwells an unrelenting engagement with the physical presence of life, with the stunning irreducibility of being. He comes after both Sa'di and Rumi, and in a remarkable way weds the worldliness of one to the passionate intensity of the other. Hafez's *ghazals* defy the assured temptations of Rumi's mysticism, confront the world directly, and shift Sa'di's worldliness to a new, aesthetically more compelling, philosophically more pensive, engagement with being. The overriding sentiments of Hafez's lyricism are the pivotal primacy of physical love necessitated by an existentially ironic and paradoxical conception of being. The two crosscutting senses of paradox and irony give Hafez's conception of love a critical sense of urgency:

Seize the moment, you and I here together,
Once the short trip is over, and we shall never meet again.

And as for the promises of knowledge and wisdom to mediate any conception of being:

Thank God, just like us, no faith no fidelity
Was in he who was called the wise, the trustworthy!

Thus with the appearance of Hafez soon after the Mongol period, another archetypal triumvirate appears in the Persian *ghazal*: Rumi, Sa'di, and Hafez. Rumi is paradisial certainty, Sa'di is earthly and worldly, and Hafez is purgatorial doubt and thrives on oscillation. Rumi takes the sublime for the assured beautiful, Sa'di takes sentiments for the transformative form, while Hafez plays with words for uncertain and fragile emotions. Heaven, earth, and the passage in between—Rumi, Sa'di, and

Hafez gave Persian literary humanism a universe—a paradise to imagine, an earth to behold, and a purgatory to navigate, in which to live, to breathe, to wonder, and to be: human. The active, consistent, and irreversible canonization of the three master poets has completed the panorama of Persian literary humanism and thus sealed upon itself its transversal epitome. This triumvirate leads to full universality and self-consciousness, in which the beloved, whether divine and ethereal or earthly and real, is, above all, *formal*. It has achieved and it exudes self-conscious universality. The knowing subject here has become a lyrical, loving target, and love has replaced fear as the modus operandi of humanity. In lyrical poetry, as opposed to quatrains, it is no longer the settled fragility of the doubtful human that narrates the world but the trusting confidence of the loving person that wholeheartedly embraces it and makes it trustworthy—and that is the central significance of lyricism in Persian literary humanism.

Sensus Moralitus

Arguably the grandest achievements of Persian literary humanism during the Mongol era were two books, both by one poet and master prose stylist, both celebrated ever since as the hallmarks of a universal sense of morality beyond their age and circumstances. Sa'di's *Bustan* (1257) and *Golestan (Rose-Garden)* (1259) remain, to this day, beyond any dispute, two of the greatest literary masterpieces of the entire spectrum of Persian literary imagination. In their poise, precision, elegance, and audacity, *Bustan* and *Golestan* are the twin summits of a literary imagination that could never excel beyond these two master texts. The vast moral imagination of Sa'di in conceiving and delivering these two cornerstones is rooted in the vast imperial imagination of the Mongol Empire. Not just the fact that Sa'di could travel from his hometown of Shiraz to North Africa in one direction and to India in another, but that he could have fathomed and imagined the vast globality of his habitat, of the humanity that embraced him, are intertwined with the moral imagination that conceived these two texts. In his *Bustan* and *Golestan*, Sa'di is the supreme universalizer of Persian literary humanism. Persian prose and poetry never hit a higher, subtler, or nobler note, the fact and the act of the literary never flaunted its grace more forcefully—and humanism was never staged more convincingly.

Sa'di evidently wrote *Bustan* while he was traveling around the world, although it is not quite clear if all these travels are actual or if at times they were literary metaphors, and thus effectively a combination of both. Sa'di is proverbial because of his love of traveling. He was a peripatetic humanist—his worldliness literally embedded in the fact that he had seen the world. But in his narratives he also relies on a heavy dose of traveling metaphors that assume narrative and allegorical dimensions. *Bustan* is composed as a *mathnavi* and in the meter conventionally used for epic form, which Sa'di puts squarely to his humanist purposes.

Bustan is divided into ten chapters, amounting to some four thousand couplets.[32] Each chapter is devoted to a key humanist ideal: Justice, Magnanimity, Love, Humility, Contentment, Remembrance, Cultivation of Good Character, Gratitude, Repentance, Supplication, and Conclusion of the Book. What makes *Bustan* a supreme humanist text is also its peculiar challenge: the book is so poetically beautiful that the composition in and of itself keeps attracting attention to itself and distracting attention from the content of the poetry. One never knows if one is drawn to the formal elegance of the poetry or to the exquisite ideas that are being communicated. But after a while that apparent binary dissipates, and the reader is drawn and tucked away into an entirely different domain irreducible either to form or to content.[33]

In *Bustan*, Sa'di builds his entire moral edifice on the virtue of silence—the tabula rasa of his eloquence. Story after story in the Seventh Chapter are strung together under the rubric of "Fazilat Khamushi" ("On the Virtue of Silence"). Be like a seashell, Sa'di suggests, and open your mouth only for pearls, otherwise be quiet—his metaphors thrive with vivid and sharp similes. A king kept a secret for one year to himself, and as soon as he divulged it to his "confidants," within a day it was all over his realm. Another wise man in Egypt had a great following until he finally opened his mouth and threw a monkey wrench among his admirers and detractors. The late Gholam Hussein Yusefi, the distinguished Sa'di scholar, considers *Bustan* Sa'di's "utopia."[34] This utopia is worldly. Even when he praises God he thanks him for the beauty of this world. He turns God into a good and trustworthy friend, a confidant of humanity. Justice is paramount for Sa'di—in life, in politics, in friendship, it is a balance that holds everything together. He gives particular attention to wise men as the cornerstones of a civilized society. But central and paramount in *Bustan* remains *insan*, human, and the best quality of this *insan* is *hamdardi*, sympathy. Nothing disturbs the balance of life more than tyranny: "Mayazar muri keh daneh kesh ast / Keh jan darad-o Jan shirin khosh ast [Don't bother even an ant / For it too has life, and sweet life is precious!]" The balance of this world dwells in this world—not anywhere else. Paramount in *Bustan* is love that is the glue holding all of humanity together. This love extends from the love of one person for another to the love of God for humanity—and includes the very essence of what makes the world turn around.

While *Bustan* is entirely in poetry, *Golestan* is in an exquisite combination of prose and poetry, in both Persian and Arabic, yet again a graceful mixing of both, to a point that the distinction becomes impossible, irrelevant, imperceptive—the prose is poetic, the poetry reads as easily as conversational prose.[35] *Golestan* consists of an introduction and eight chapters: "On the Attributes of Kings," "On the Disposition of Dervishes," "On the Virtue of Contentment," "On Benefits of Silence," "On Love and Youth," "On Weakness and Aging," "On the Influence of Education," "On the Proper Etiquette of Companionship."[36] *Golestan* is not the fruit of a bookish author arguing against other authors, but the virtuoso performance of a worldly man, reporting with wit and wisdom on his worldly observations. Sa'di is an eyewitness—either in reality or else narratively—and his poetic persona is definitive to his writing character. He is a social psychologist. He typifies, identifies, describes, diagnoses, prognosticates, and then concludes. He says how he was once unhappy because he did not have shoes, until he saw a man who had no legs. His punch lines catch you completely off guard and plant a bouquet of joy in your heart. *Golestan* is full of people from different walks of life: kings, beggars, philosophers, mystics, poets, blacksmiths, sportsmen, ascetics, rich people, poor people, powerful people, prostitutes, police officers, merchants, thieves, highway bandits, good women, terrible women, young and handsome boys, frail and repentant old sinners. Gholam Hussein Yusefi believes that *Bustan* is Sa'di's ideal, but *Golestan* an expression of reality. He quotes approvingly from Abdolhossein Zarrinkub, another major literary scholar, that "Sa'di portrays humanity as it is, not as it should be."[37] To which one may add that Sa'di ultimately detects, or bestows, a fair balance to what he sees.

Ever since their composition in the thirteenth century, *Bustan* and *Golestan* have been canonized and studied as the model of eloquence and propriety, of *Adab*, and an entire academy of humanistic education has been built upon them by generations of people from one end of the Persian-speaking world to the other. These two texts are in effect a curriculum of learning, of *Bildung*, of cultivation of decency, humility, justice, reasonableness—virtues by which an entire humanity can (and must) live. In effect, they are a mirror but not for princes, for ordinary people, for humanity at large.

The Making of a Geographical Imagination

Sa'di made Shiraz world-famous. But Shiraz was not the only metropolis in the Persianate world. After the Mongol invasion, Tabriz emerged as the major cosmopolitan capital of the Il-Khanids, chosen by Abaqa Khan, and after him Ghazan Khan, as the administrative capital of their empires, now stretching from Egypt to the Oxus River, from the Caucasus to the Indian Ocean. At this point Tabriz was the intellectual, artistic, and commercial capital of the empire. Tabriz, Shiraz, Balkh, Samarqand, Bokhara, Herat, Isfahan, Hamadhan, and Tus were chief among the major cosmopolitan capitals of successive empires from the Ghaznavids to the Seljuqids to the Il-Khanids. These were seats of power, cultural and commercial capitals of vast empires to which were brought the riches of the world and the opulence of the conquests, all evident in magnificent architectural monuments, courtly demeanor, literary imagination, artistic achievements, and commercial wealth. These capitals were the worldly cosmopolises that reflected the planetary imagination of the empires that had built and turned them into the epicenters of their global claims on power, on the world. The "human" in the Persian literary humanism was a universal call—paradoxical by virtue of the power that this humanism at once posited and challenged. A poet could come from the remotest village in the empire—but in these epicenters of the universe poets became humanists.

Dominant in these major cities was a highly cultivated geographical imagination that by the time of the Mongol Empire was already evident in, indeed made possible through, a rich literature that had made the inhabitants of this and preceding empires highly conscious of lands and cultures beyond their own immediate horizons and yet informing their knowledge of their place in the world. This geographical imagination was the cosmopolitan horizon of Persian literary humanism. In other words, Persian literary humanism (as a craft) was performed within the expansive horizons of this geographical imagination.

It is impossible to exaggerate the fascination of Muslim geographers and travelers—writing in both Arabic and Persian, and as such identically informing Persian literary humanism—with exploring and mapping out the geographical and cultural diversities of the world. From Ibn Khurdadbah's *al-Masalik wa al-Mamalik* (composed in 864), to Qudamah ibn Ja'far's *Kitab al-Khiraj* (composed in 880), to al-Ya'qubi's *al-Buldan* (composed in 891), to Ibn Rustah's *al-A'laq al-Nafisah* (composed in 903), to Ibn al-Faqih's *Mukhtasar Kitab al-Buldan* (composed in 903), a solid foundation was laid in the ninth century for a phenomenally rich and vastly diversified body of literature on world geography and cultures. By the time al-Mas'udi composed his *al-Tanbih wa al-Ashraf* in 956, a cosmic/cosmopolitan conception of being had been thoroughly established for his generation of scholars, geographers, and historians. Al-Mas'udi (893–956) composed *al-Tanbih wa al-Ashraf* toward the end of his life and in it is evident a geographical imagination in which cosmology, astronomy, geography, history, cultural anthropology, and moral and political philosophy all come together in a self-sustained and enabling narrative.[38] A contemporary of al-Mas'udi, Abu Ishaq Ibrahim ibn Muhammad al-Farsi al-Istakhri's (d. 957) *al-Masalik wa al-Mamalik* (composed in 951) began to extend the boundaries of cultural anthropology into a study of comparative religion, in which Islam and its various sects became just one among a number of other *masalik* (plural of *maslak*, "path people traverse"). Al-Istakhri's *Masalik wa al-Mamalik* was based on Abu Zayd al-Balkhi's (d. 934) *Suwar al-Aqalim. Masalik wa al-Mamalik* was soon translated into Persian but was falsely attributed to Khwajah Nasir al-Din al-Tusi.[39] Although al-Istakhri commences his geographical division of the world with Arabia, "because God's House is located there," and pays particular attention to his homeland, because "there is no land which is more civilized, more complete, more beautiful than the Iranian kingdoms," he still proceeds to consider the Roman (Europe), the Chinese, and the Indian cultural worlds in a vast and comparative context.[40] He was narratively mapping the world, remapping it from those from whom he had inherited it.

Ibn Wadih al-Ya'qubi (fl. 864) is usually considered the father of geographical literature in Arabic and subsequently in Persian.[41] He was not only a geographer and historian, but also a student of astronomy and a poet—namely an exemplary model of a literary humanist. A native of Isfahan, al-Ya'qubi wrote extensively on the geography of the Byzantine Empire, on the African conquest by Muslims, a book on Byzantine emperors (composed by 873), as well as a treatise on "The History of Ancient People." Probably composed by 892, his *al-Buldan* has not reached us in its entirety, and yet what has survived shows its author's global conception of the world in which he lived. With designated sections on Armenia, the Byzantine Empire, India, and China, *al-Buldan* is the earliest record of a thriving literature on world geography. Books such as *al-Buldan* indicate a vastly inquisitive mind, restless in a permanent quest to know about the world and its natural and cultural variations, and above all a disciplined mode of knowledge production in geography. The material basis of that inquiry was obviously evident in the military and commercial expansion of initially the Abbasid and subsequently the Ghaznavid and Seljuqid empires, and the fact that by virtue of their conquests they had made a worldly imagination possible.

Two other significant geographical texts, Ibn Hawqal's *Surat al-Ard* (composed in 978) and al-Maqdisi's *Ahsan al-Taqasim* (composed in 983) mark the tenth century as one of the richest in the expansion and effervescence of the geographical imagination. By the time that Ibn Hawqal (fl. 977) wrote his *Surat al-Ard*, there already had been multiple mappings of his inherited universe by generations of geographers, so much so that in its introduction he confides to his readers that "from my youth I was always fascinated by books on lands and cultures (*Masalik wa Mamalik*). I wished to know [other] people's various customs, habits, [forms of] knowledge, sciences, and religions."[42] Ibn Hawqal composed his *Surat al-Ard* because he was not fully satisfied with the existing literature. By 982, the geographical literature was already rich enough for the unknown author of *Hudud al-Alam min al-Mashriq ila al-Maghrib* to compose a book on "the frontiers of the world from the East to the West."[43] When one reads *Hudud al-Alam min al-Mashriq ila al-Maghrib* today, one cannot but marvel at the range of its author's global interests, not only in matters geographical but also those that were scientific and cultural. A general introduction to the habitable quarters of the earth and its seas, islands, mountains, rivers, deserts, and climates is succeeded by chapters on China, India, Tibet, Mongolia, Transoxiana, Iran, Armenia, Syria, Egypt, Andalusia, Russia, Europe, and Africa. A global conception of the world (the author of *Hudud al-Alam min al-Mashriq ila al-Maghrib* knew that the earth was round, "The earth is round, just like a ball, and the heavens surround it. It turns on two poles, one called the North Pole, the other the South Pole")[44] is evident in the minutiae of details provided in this text.

In the early fourteenth century the *Taqwim al-Buldan* of Abu al-Fida' (1273–1331) is a remarkable example of a most detailed geographical study, again on a global scale.[45] Abu al-Fida' writes a full introductory section to his book on the science of geography. *Taqwim al-Buldan* provides the most detailed geographical information on every civilized corner of the world, with a language at once precise and sympathetic. From China, India, Transoxiana, Europe, and Armenia to Iran, Arabia, Syria, Andalusia, and Africa, Abu al-Fida' covers such issues as the precise geographical location of a place, bibliographical sources on that region, and a description of its history, architectural sites, agricultural products, commercial centers, etc. What is particularly remarkable about his introduction to the text is his full awareness of a rich geographical literature on which he draws, and yet none of which fully satisfies his objective, and he therefore sets out to write a new book. What matters in these repeated takes is the fact that the geographical imagination that feeds this genre is constantly remapping and reinventing itself. Successive empires, from the Abbasids down to the Mongols, come and conquer the world, as the geographical imagination that sustains Persian literary humanism keeps remapping itself on a globe that it thus claims and characterizes.

The geographical part of *Nuzhat al-Qolub*, composed by Hamdollah al-Mawstawfi, the author of the celebrated *Ta'rikh-e Gozideh*, in 1340, demonstrates how when authors set out to write the geography of one particular land and culture, in this case Iran, they did so with a thorough attention to global geography.[46] Mawstawfi's book on Iranian geography includes sections on Arabia, Asia Minor, Armenia, and lands to the east, west, north, and south of the Iranian plateau, plus a concluding section on Tibet, central Asia, Georgia, China, Bulgaria, India, Mongolia, Russia, down to Andalusia, and Africa. Geography was no mere act of defining a place on planet earth; it was to center one's consciousness in a planetary vision of history.

This trend was richly sustained from the ninth through the fourteenth centuries and was augmented with travel narratives. In 1047,

Naser Khosrow in his *Safarnameh*, and in 1355, Ibn Battuta in his *Rihla*, made extensive observations of social, political, religious, and literary life into a rich and fulfilling narrative on the cultural history of lands from the borders of China, into the Indian subcontinent, central Asia, Asia Minor, the Iranian plateau, the Arabian peninsula, and through North Africa. Toward the middle of the fourteenth century, the Moroccan traveler Ibn Battuta (1304–1368) produced one of the most celebrated travelogues of the medieval period. Starting his journey from Morocco, he traveled to Egypt, Syria, Arabia, Iran, Asia Minor, the eastern part of Europe, Transoxiana, the Indian subcontinent, China, and back to some parts of Africa.[47] At the age of twenty-two, in the year 1324–25, Ibn Battuta left his hometown, with no intention of entering into an almost 30-year-long journey. But a passion of unbelievable intensity led him from one spot to another, not letting him come home until 1352. The travelogue that Ibn Battuta produced upon his return became one of the most popular and influential texts in an already highly developed travel literature. Whence this interest, and to what purpose this remarkable curiosity about other lands and cultures? From the heart of Africa to the frontiers of China became the subject of Ibn Battuta's penetrating insights, elements of a global conception of communities, societies, polities, cultures, and civilizations, constitutionally irreducible to any particular faith or doctrine, and informed by the sheer power of imagination to have and hold a planetary conception of the world. Such a global conception of the world is constitutionally anti-dogmatic, humanist in the most life-affirming sense of the term, and precisely in those terms informed the poets and the literati who imagined themselves in the worlds thus repeatedly mapped and overmapped.

An inquisitive mind of relentless curiosity and an unending attraction to a cosmic and global conception of human existence inform every page of this remarkably rich literature on world geography, which in reality is more a descriptive "cultural anthropology," if we were to name it with a contemporary disciplinary designation, than a mere description of lands, mountains, rivers, and cities. Ibn Rustah, a geographer from Isfahan, in his *al-A'laq al-Nafisah*, for example, gives the most detailed description of Constantinople, its cathedral, the huge organ in that cathedral, and the pomp and ceremony of Byzantium.[48] This body of literature is not a mere description of lands beyond "the Islamic world." It represents a cosmos vision of reality that is not subsumed by "Islam," but embraces it. Persian literary humanism was the direct beneficiary of that cosmic vision, that worlding of the world by overmapping it.

Palimpsestic Maps

The Mongol world mapped the world and owned (up to) it—so that the thriving cosmopolitanism that was embedded in Persian literary humanism had a territorial claim on a worldly self-consciousness. Centuries later, the self-universalizing autonormativity of "the West" became an overriding map that erased all previous maps so that it could powerfully remember itself. But the recognition of alternative worlds—the maps that have existed, and in which "the West" has only been the most recent incident—is the *condito sine qua non* of coming to terms with the worldliness of cultural productions domestic to these universes, thus resisting their narration to the periphery of a "Western" imagination.

The geographical imagination of the age was not even limited to earth. It extended well into the extraterrestrial spheres. Consider the Maragheh observatory that Khwajah Nasir al-Din al-Tusi established in northwestern Iran under the patronage of the Mongol warlord Hulagu, to which he invited scientists, astronomers, and mathematicians from as far as India and China and as close as Baghdad and Damascus to form the most significant scientific center of the time.[49] Under the guidance of Khwajah Nasir al-Din al-Tusi, aided by his capable student Qotb al-Din Shirazi, these scientists were mapping not just the planet earth, but in their astronomy and astrophysics they were mapping the farthest reaches of the universe.

Retrieving the multiple global maps that in their palimpsestic juxtapositions have repeatedly and even concurrently made and remade the multiple worlds we have inherited is the only assured framing of the cultural landscape of literary production. In anticipation of the evolving world we live in today and in which our parallel histories are still pregnant, the cosmopolitan worldliness of Persian literary humanism will only make sense if it is read in the worlds that enabled it, and that it in turn envisioned. To that end, what we need is active scholarly imagination to retrieve those worlds—of the sort we see, for example, in what John Darwin has capably done in *After Tamerlane: The Rise and Fall of Global Empires 1400–2000* (2008), or Stewart Gordon in *When Asia Was the World* (2008), or Tamim Ansary in his *Destiny Disrupted: A History of the*

World through Islamic Eyes (2009)—admirable and competent attempts at retrieving those multiple maps and the cultures they have entailed. Against the grain of a systematic concealing of the multiple maps of multivariate worlds humanity has inhabited, retrieving the manifold worlds the planet has produced is the anchored and assured manner of reading its varying cultures, its lived experiences—otherwise these maps become systematically erased as they are coded as "areas that general official histories have marginalized,"[50] and thus we would be condemned to the vertiginous repetition of a history of the always already vanishing present.

5

The Lure and Lyrics of a Literature

The Center and Periphery of the
Timurid Empire (1370–1506)

NIZAM al-Din Amir Alishir Nava'i (1441–1501) was a very learned man, a deeply cultivated man, a man of letters, and a man of unsurpassed caring intellect, a powerful patron for artists, the literati, and the scientists of his time. Amir Alishir Nava'i had a generous and gracious company. He was a humanist par excellence—poet, painter, prose stylist, vastly learned in his contemporary intellectual traditions, and a statesman of exceptional courage, tenacity, and imagination. Imagine his contemporary Lorenzo de' Medici, Lorenzo the Magnificent (1449–1492), if you must, turning the Florentine republic into the epicenter of the Italian Renaissance, and you come close to Amir Alishir Nava'i's significance at the helm of the vast Timurid Empire, as a wise and judicious vizier, patron of scholars, artists, architects, and poets. Born and raised in Herat, the city that later under his judicious and generous care would have made Florence of the time look like a small town way station, Amir Alishir Nava'i was ambidextrous in his own poetic and literary capabilities and wrote both in his native Chagatai Turkish and also in Persian, the lingua franca of learned cultivation in the Timurid (as all other previous) Empire, particularly in Mashhad, Herat, and Samarqand—three vast imperial cosmopolises enriched with the wealth and abuzz with the gifts and talents of the expansive empire.

With the rise of the Timurid Empire, reclaiming what was left of the Mongol Empire and recasting it for a renewed imperial dispensation, the center of Persian literary humanism moved further eastward to Samarqand and Herat, two of the most magnificent cosmopolises of the time. If we were to give a nationalistic account of Persian literary humanism, modern-day Tajikistan and Afghanistan would have uncontested claim over the entirety of this period—linking it directly all the way back to the Ghaznavid dynasty. But transnational empires, not ethnicized nations— Tajiks, Afghans, Iranians, Arabs, Turks, Indians, etc—were the modus operandi of political order and cultural production in this and other periods. From the ninth to the sixteenth century, from the Tahirids (821– 873) to the Timurid (1370–1506) dynasty, Persian literary humanism witnessed the systematic triumph of its defining *logos* over any exclusive *ethnos*, when Iranian, Turkic, and Mongol dynasties all become Persianate in their cosmopolitan worldliness by virtue of the primacy of the language they celebrated and enriched, and not by the divisive factor of ethnic origins, which would have deeply alienated and separated them. All these empires were in dire need of imperial legitimation, which is precisely what Persian language and culture, and by extension and in effect Persian literary humanism, provided. If the ruling elite were to claim rightful authority through ethnic origin, they would have never succeeded in projecting an aura of imperial legitimacy. Amir Alishir Nava'i was of Turko-Mongol descent. The Turkish language was native and natural to him. He is in fact considered the founding father of Turkic literature—its Chaucer or Dante, as it were. But Persian was the language of the high court and high culture *Bildung*—and he had mastered it and commanded it, and it was as much his as anyone else's.

Persian language and culture had by now, and as it did previously, a vast imperial heritage embedded in its texture and disposition—a claim on a heritage and a vision of its posterity, anteriority, and emotive universe. The Timurid era was not just the concluding moment of the complete transmutation of the *ethnos* into *logos* of Persian literary humanism. It was also the inaugural moment of the internal dynamics of this humanism working itself toward a more advanced stage of its historical self-consciousness, predicated on both its domestic developments and its eventual encounter with European colonial modernity— the dialectical results of which would unfold over the next half-millennium. The Timurid Empire was the scene of the very last stage of the classical age of Persian literary imagination.

Amir Timur

Amir Alishir Nava'i's name and reputation as a wise, judicious, and deeply cultivated statesman and patron of arts are coterminous with the Timurid Empire. Founded by the warrior Amir Timur Gurkani (also known as Timur-e Lang or Timur the Lame, or by the Latin distortion Tamerlane, 1336–1405), through a series of swift campaigns, conquests, and shaky but brutal consolidations of territories initially conducted between 1363 and 1370, the Timurids were a heavily Persianate Turko-Mongol empire that eventually ruled over a vast territory extending from central Asia and the Caucasus to modern Uzbekistan, Tajikistan, Turkmenistan, Afghanistan, Iran, Pakistan, northern India, and then west, contending with the Ottomans in Mesopotamia and Anatolia. Timur's conquest of Khwarizm (1371), Mongolia (1374), Khurasan (1380), Mazandaran (1384), India (1398), and Anatolia (1401) defined the contours of his expansive empire. Before his death on February 18, 1405, as he was getting ready to launch a major campaign to invade China, Timur had single-handedly led an army of swift vengeance upon hapless domains ready and ripe for his conquests. Three consecutive campaigns—known as 3-year, 5-year, and 7-year campaigns—very much define the single-minded determination of Timur to flatten the earth under his sword and vanity. Timur achieved his empire by the power of his sword, a tint of mysticism, a proverbial brutality, and a penchant for a college of scribes and historians in his retinue. His edifices of power and glory and high culture were predicated on the slaughter and plunder of the people and the lands he conquered. He was a visionary conqueror, with a singularly enchanting sight of Samarqand as a mega-cosmopolis—and he plundered the world to build the city of his dreams.[1]

After Timur, his son Mo'in al-Din Shahrokh (r. 1405–1447) is usually considered the grandest monarch of the Timurid period and the king under whose reign arts and sciences greatly advanced. Shahrokh had solid command over Iran and Mesopotamia and nominal suzerainty over China and India. Historians remember him fondly for being temperate, moderate, generous, and a liberal patron of poets, scholars, and scientists. He was also a poet and a good calligrapher. Herat achieved its status as a grand cosmopolis under his reign. His wife Gowharshad Agha was also a great patron of art and architecture. Her mosque in Mashhad is still famous (as a child I used to play in this mosque during our summer visits to Mashhad). Shahrokh's son Ulugh Beg (r. 1447–1449) is remembered as a major patron of sciences who was greatly interested in astronomy. Sultan Husayn Bayqara (r. 1470–1506) was the last and most culturally influential grand monarch of the dynasty. His reign coincided with some of the greatest achievements of the Timurid period in the arts and sciences. He was also responsible for transforming Herat into the magnificent cosmopolitan capital of his time, aided by his capable friend and vizier Amir Alishir Nava'i.

With the establishment of the Timurid era, we have entered the age of Muslim encounter with European colonial modernity. The initial contacts of Europeans with the Timurid court—and later with Aq Qoyunlu (also called White Sheep Turcoman, r. 1378–1508) and Qara Qoyunlu (also called Black Sheep Turcoman, r. 1375–1468) who ruled in eastern Anatolia and western Iran—was mostly because of their fear and hostility toward the Ottomans. Henry IV of England (r. 1366–1413) and Henry III of Castile (r. 1379–1406) were both in communication with Timur regarding his campaigns against the Ottoman Sultan Bayezid I (r. 1389–1402). The more serious and enduring contacts, however, were to take place on the Indian subcontinent. Well into the establishment of the Timurid dynasty in the fourteenth century, the Timurid prince Babur (1483–1531), who claimed to be descended from Timur on his father's side and Genghis on his mother's, invaded North India and founded the Mughal Empire, which ruled North India until 1858, when it was overcome by the British Raj (1858–1947). Both the internal developments within the Timurid dynasty and the fateful encounter with European colonialism would have lasting consequences for the dramatic unfolding of Persian literary humanism.

Historical Poiêsis

Timur was very particular about the meticulous recording of his name and reputation and deeds and adventures for posterity, and he paid close attention to the historians who would record the tenor and timbre of his time. He and his son Shahrokh would employ professional historians and put at their disposal a vast body of official documents for the minutest details of their conquests. The Timurid period, as a result, witnessed the height of Persian literary historiography—namely a kind of history writing with a particular penchant for an elegant and poetic prose. Such prime examples of historiography in this period as Muhammad ibn Fazlullah Musavi's *Asahh al-Tawarikh* (from creation of the world to the time of Timur), Hafez Abru's *Majma' al-Tawarikh* (covering world history to the year 1426), Nezam al-Din Shami's *Zafarnameh* (with detailed knowledge of Timur's conquests up to the year 1403), Ahmad ibn Jalal al-Din Muhammad's *Mojmal Fasihi* (covering the pre-Islamic to Islamic periods up to the year 1441) all reveal the predominance of poetic prose in conveying the historical events of the time for the posterity. The trend continued well into the latter part of the Timurid period and into the early Mughal and Safavid periods, with such prime examples as Kamal al-Din Abd al-Razzaq Samarqandi's (1413–1482) *Matla' al-Sa'dain*, Fazlullah ibn Ruzbahan's *Alam-ara-ye Amini*, Mir Khwand's (d. 1497) *Rawda al-Safa*, and Gheyath al-Din Khwand Mir's (1475–1525) *Habib al-Seyar*. Prominent historians of Persian prose and poetry have paid particular attention to this genre of literary historiography, which, independent of its content, advanced the narrative of literary prose.[2]

One of the best examples of this genre and one of the most detailed sources of information about Timur and his conquests is Mawlana Sharaf al-Din Ali Yazdi's *Zafarnameh* (*Book of Victories*) (completed 1424).[3] As his name suggests, Sharaf al-Din Ali Yazdi (d. 1454) was born and raised in the central Iranian city of Yazd, where he was closely associated with the Timurid royalties. Yazdi had intended his book as a trilogy on Timur, his son Shahrokh, and then the historian's own patron, Ibrahim Mirza. But because his patron died, he abandoned the whole project. He used massive documentation and eyewitness accounts and had a penchant for detail in his description of military conquests. The great literary scholar Malik al-Sho'ara Mohammad Taqi Bahar (1884–1951) thought *Zafarnameh* was one of the best (most literary) examples of historical prose after Juvayni's *Jahangosha* and the work of one of the very last masters of classical Persian prose. Sharaf al-Din Ali Yazdi's *Zafarnameh* was the source of detailed information for many subsequent historians. One of the masterpieces of historiography, it covers a vast geographical domain— from India to Afghanistan, central Asia, Iran, Georgia, Armenia, the Caucasus, Russia, Asia Minor, and Mesopotamia down to the Persian Gulf areas. It is as much a social as it is a political history, brilliant in its literary style, adorned with poetry, and punctuated with historical wisdom for posterity.

Sharaf al-Din Ali Yazdi begins his *Zafarnameh* by praising God Almighty and continues with a long poetic composition in praise of Timur—the auspicious sultan.[4] The poem itself, composed in the rhythm and meter of Ferdowsi's *Shahnameh,* begins yet again with the praise of God and all his magnificent creation, his prophet Muhammad and his virtues, and from there the author proceeds to praise Timur, whom he compares in his blessings and attributes to the Prophet Muhammad. In this poetic prolegomena Sharaf al-Din Ali Yazdi in fact gives a full summary of Timur's conquests "from the boundaries of China to the end of Rum [Asia Minor]/Including Egypt, Syria, and India/Iran, Turan (central Asia), and all the seas and lands, . . ." Timur conquered all these lands in his own person, with his wisdom and perspicacity, whether with magnanimity or in rage. Once he conquered the whole world he established justice and spread Islam.

Sharaf al-Din Ali Yazdi continues in this triumphant and celebratory praise of his patron king to the end of this poetic composition, and then he ends the poem and begins his history proper with a description of Timur's auspicious birth.[5] After a full and vastly festive treatment of Timur's birth, Yazdi turns his attention to a brief discussion of what distinguishes his book from other histories of the period. There are three factors that specifically characterize his book, he says: (1) his reflections on strange events and his delicate observations, which will help the readers sharpen their wits and intelligence about history, and this is particularly useful because Yazdi will cover the reign of Timur from the very beginning to the very end, and thus will have much to teach future generations of kings; (2) his attention to the minutest details, including those that other historians have left out because of the fear of incredulity on the part of their readers; and (3) his commitment to truth, the whole truth, without the slightest prevarication. Elaborating on the third virtue of his book, Sharaf al-Din Ali Yazdi describes how there was always a literary and scholarly entourage in Timur's company who would write down, in prose and poetry, in Persian and in Turkish, his daily deeds and conquests, and he had left very specific instructions that his deeds were not to be exaggerated, nor a very floral language used in describing what he did. Timur would then have these accounts read back to him, and he would ask for revisions and emendations if he did not like some exaggeration in the scribes' accounts. After a full description of this procedure, Yazdi adds, "no exaggerations were to be made in phrasings so that the prose would not be unnecessarily elongated . . . except for poetry, which I have kept to a minimum."[6]

Though indeed kept to a minimum, poetry still plays a major role in Sharaf al-Din Ali Yazdi's *Zafarnameh,* as indeed in the rest of the Timurid historiography, which might thus be described as a kind of "poetic historiography," in which anything from a line to a panegyric regularly punctuates the prose of the narrative and thus effectively severs the implied link between the time of the event and the narrative of the prose. For example, when describing the conquest of the fortress of Tikrit in Iraq, Yazdi tells his readers in prose that after the conquest of Baghdad, some travelers and merchants told Timur there was a magnificent fortress nearby that a group of highway bandits had occupied and used to attack caravans and lead a life of rebellion and menace to the region, harassing the caravans traveling between Egypt and Syria. Here Yazdi breaks his prose and turns to a poem:

> It is a fortress made of mountainsides,
> Groups of highway bandits dwell in it.
> No catapult can cut a path to it,
> Nor does it have fear of any other siege engine.
> All day and night they attack the caravans,
> The evildoers cut down people's lives.

After this short poetic interlude he again resumes his prose, in which he says how Timur in fact proceeded to conquer that fortress by way of helping the caravans conduct their routine business and people were saved from those highway bandits.[7] The poetic interlude, here and elsewhere, interjects an emotive implosion that shifts the time of the narrative from an immanent past to a transcendent latitude—and thus sculpts a full-bodied story.

These sorts of poetic implosions are not incidental to Yazdi's manner of historiography. They are definitive of it.[8] The decidedly literary disposition of Yazdi's *Zafarnameh,* whether in poetry or in poetic prose, and precisely considering the manner in which it was subsequently canonized, points to the significance of poetic historiography that comes to a canonical height in the Timurid period. In the making of that historiography, prose reveals itself as a matter of fact, while poetry is at once supplementary to that prose and yet alluding to a suspenseful interlude (in the mood, for example, of Ferdowsi's epic) that thus charges the historical prose. The resulting historical narrative does not become atemporal; it becomes detemporalized. The prose of history (not just the one that Yazdi had received) is excessively temporal, chronically imminent, while the poetic interlude is entirely transcendent, superseding the time and narrative that it punctuates. The two parts—poetry and prose—confront and suspend (not subvert) each other and thus detemporalize the narrative encounter with history. Historiography as a result, framing the author who is writing this kind of history, always stops short of becoming a *discourse*—for it does not posit, nor does it need, a solid, knowing subject. The knowing subject is conflicted. The poetic prose confuses, disrupts, and thus preempts any all-knowing subject. But the peculiar thing is that it does not dismiss history; it embraces and poeticizes it and posits and deposits it.

The possibility and practice of a poetic historiography that suspends the evident and posits the plausible points toward the formation of a narrative *poiêsis* in Persian literary humanism that makes the writing and the conception of history akin to each other. Thus conceived, the evident *poiêsis* at once transforms and makes the world conceivable. It disrupts the link between time and narrative to posit a link between the human (made contingent) and the world (made trustworthy), thus making the evident worldliness of both possible. In the positing of the *poiêsis*, we are witness to both the writing and the making of history as a human act beyond the span of mortality and into the domain of manmade morality. This *poiêsis* thinks of history as creation in physical, metaphysical, and a fortiori moral terms. It brings-forth (Heidegger's term) by way of a potentiality gushing into actuality. During the Timurid period, the writing of history, long in the making, finally achieves this condition of *poiêsis* by way of the matter of history giving birth to its manner, its reality breeding ideality.[9] *History* here finally becomes what it always was: what is remembered, not what is made. The poet-historian was a warrior here—at one and the same time positioning and effacing *the human* whose illusions made history real.

The Literary Subconscious

The triumph of the Timurids as a dynasty, descending from warring tribes in central Asia that traced their origin back to the Mongol conquest, was entirely indebted to their complete adaptation to the Persianate royal administrative apparatus and their adoption of Persian literary humanism. While the Turko-Mongolian military apparatus of the empire was maintained along the lines of the Seljuqids and the Mongols, the empire's administrative apparatus and its emerging ideological foregrounding were heavily Persianized. Timur himself was deeply immersed in Persian language and culture. The literary imagination of the age, continuing from the Mongol Empire, remained and thrived in Persian, as Samarqand and Herat emerged as the administrative, intellectual, and artistic centers of the new age. The vast consequences of the height of Persian literary humanism attained during the Timurids was such that its resonance extended for centuries, well into the Mughal dynasty in India and the Safavid period in Iran, the founders of these two empires—Babur and Isma'il (1487–1524)—being deeply cultivated poet-conquerors.

The might and majesty of the Timurid court is forever identified with the legendary figure of Nizam al-Din Amir Alishir Nava'i, the renowned vizier of Sultan Hussein Bayqara (r. 1470–1506). Amir Alishir was a classmate of Sultan Husayn Bayqara and a close friend of the mighty poet of the time Abd al-Rahman Jami (1414–1492). As an administrator, Amir Alishir was not only responsible for the education of a whole generation of Timurid princes and the construction and/or restoration of countless mosques, madrasas, libraries, hospitals, caravanserais, and other public buildings, but was also a poet and prose stylist of uncommon brilliance and a close confidant of the ruling elite of an empire that would have lasting influences on a number of other empires that emerged from its political and imaginative bosom. A humanist par excellence, a musician, calligrapher, painter, and above all a poet of extraordinary power, Amir Alishir left an indelible mark on the Timurids and their reputation as a vastly cultivated and opulent empire. Amir Alishir was at once a deeply cultivated man and a vastly generous patron—having made his own personal collection of manuscripts a public library for the use of poets, literati, scholars, and scientists. Amir Alishir was instrumental in the propagation of Persian literary humanism not only in the Timurid realm but in fact deep into the Indian subcontinent, where Babur, the founder of the Mughal Empire, cites him as an inspiration in his autobiographical epic *Baburnama*. In the figure of Amir Alishir Nava'i we in fact see the inaugural moment of the spread of Persian literary humanism into four emerging empires: the Ottomans

(1281–1924), the Safavids (1501–1732), the Mughals (1526–1858), and the Russian (1721–1917). While in the Safavid and Mughal realms this continuity was mostly in Persian visual and literary humanism, in the Ottoman and central Asian domains of the Russian empire this was in Chagatai Turkic.[10]

All his achievements aside, Amir Alishir Nava'i was above all a bilingual humanist, composing prose and poetry in both Persian and Chagatai Turkic, and for this reason he was in fact known as *Zu-lesanayn* (*Bilingual*). He believed that Turkish was in fact a superior language to Persian, and yet he was a singularly accomplished poet in Persian too. This is not a contradiction, because as a high-ranking imperial vizier he could not afford not knowing or even flaunting his command of Persian. But his love, admiration, and devotion to Turkish emerged from the cosmopolitan multilingualism of a region and age he superbly personified. Amir Alishir Nava'i was instrumental not just in promoting Persian literary humanism but in laying the foundation of Chagatai Turkic literature. He is rightly considered to have done what Geoffrey Chaucer (ca. 1343–1400) did for English or Dante Alighieri (ca. 1265–1321) did for Italian. His voluminous work in Chagatai may in fact be considered as the inaugural moment of *Turkish* literary humanism.[11]

Performing Persian Humanism

Nur al-Din Abu al-Barakat Abd al-Rahman ibn Nizam al-Din Ahmad ibn Muhammad Jami (1414–1492), was the greatest literary figure of the Timurid period. A poet of exquisite taste, a prose stylist of precise and balanced cadences, a mystic of delicate balance and insight (influenced by Muhy al-Din Ibn Arabi [1165–1240]), Jami has been known as Khatem al-Sho'ra (the Seal of the Poets). He was the paramount urban intellectual of his time, whose name is coterminous with the cultured magnificence of the city of Herat. He studied in Herat, he came to magnificent moral and intellectual fruition in Herat, and he was chiefly responsible for making Herat the cultural capital of the Timurid Empire. Jami was Persian literary humanism incarnate. His poetry and his sagacious wisdom and saintly disposition were vastly popular from central Asia to Asia Minor to the Indian subcontinent.[12]

Jami was a poet of grand ideas and composed his poems with astonishing facility and ease, with a remarkable command of the language, which he put squarely at the service of his complete devotion to mystical ideas—formed and enriched over a lifetime. Jami was born in Kharjerd in Khurasan to a family that was originally from Isfahan. His family moved to Herat soon after his birth, and he received his vastly erudite and thorough education there. After his early education, he studied with all the major mystic masters of his time, who in turn thought very highly of him and praised his poetic and intellectual gifts. His prodigious mind, subject of many legends, was the product of Herat and Samarqand. All his life Jami was very particular about meeting with and benefiting from the sagacious company of Sufi saints and masters, and they in fact sought his company. He was particularly attached to the Naqshbandi Sufi order, which was very much attracted to Ibn Arabi's ideas. Jami was instrumental in promoting Persian Sufism, in which he assumed a saintly disposition among his admirers, though he declined to lead any group of devoted followers.[13] In addition to being a leading Sufi, Jami was also a devout Sunni, quite critical of Shi'ism, a fact that got him into trouble when he visited Baghdad.[14] This sectarian aspect of his intellectual disposition foretells the rise of the Shi'i Safavid dynasty soon after the demise of the Timurids. This ideological scholasticism of the poet thickly frames his literary interests. After traveling around the Muslim world he returned to Herat, where he was associated with the Sultan Bayqara's court, and where he died at the age of 81. The sultan and Amir Alishir attended his funeral. As Zabihollah Safa puts it, "he was the luckiest Iranian poet and writer . . . he lived in bliss and he died in bliss," with his good name and reputation extending from Anatolia to India.[15]

Jami was highly conscious of his literary output and legacy. Following a model established by Amir Khosrow (1253–1325), the master Persian poet-musician from India, he collected his poetry into three categories: Youth, Middle Age, and Final Years. Jami also collected his *mathnavis* into his *Haft Awrang* (*Seven Thrones*): (1) "Selselatu al-Dhahab" ("Chain of Gold"), a series of didactic poems on the general theme of mysticism; (2) "Salaman va Absal" ("Salaman and Absal"), a new rendering of an old romance initially turned into mystical narrative by Avicenna in his *al-Isharat wa al-Tanbihat* and later explained by Khwajah Nasir al-Din al-Tusi in his commentary on Avicenna; (3) "Tohfatu al-Ahrar" ("A Gift for the Free"), again a didactic poem; (4) "Sobhatu al-Abrar" ("A Rosary for the Pious"), another didactic poem made of anecdotes on the mystical path; (5) "Yusuf and Zoleikha" (Joseph and

Zoleikha"), based on the Qur'an with Nezami's story of "Khosrow and Shirin" as his model; (6) "Leili va Majnun" ("Leili and Majnun"), again following Nezami's model; and (7) "Iskandarnameh" ("Alexander Romance"), expounding on Greek wisdom literature. In every stage and in every detail of his poetic legacy, Jami projects the image of an exquisite connoisseur, an aficionado of good manner and cultivated and judicious taste.

More than anything else, Jami had put his exquisite command of Persian poetry and prose almost entirely at the service of Islamic mysticism, giving it, perhaps, its most sustained and enduring Persian rendition. The act had a double entendre effect. It mystified Persian humanism as it equally humanized the divine dispensation at the heart of Islamic mysticism. In prose, Jami's masterpiece is *Baharestan* (*Where the Spring Blooms*), which he composed on the model of Sa'di's *Golestan* (*Rose-Garden*) for the benefit of his own son and dedicated it to Sultan Husayn Bayqara. His other important book is *Nafahat al-Uns* (*Breaths of Companionship*) on Sufi masters and their *karamat* (blessings), which he composed following Amir Alishir Nava'i's suggestion. His *Lavayeh* (*Shafts of Light*) is also on mysticism. His other book is *Asha'at al-Lama'at* (*Sparkles of Fire*), a commentary on Fakhr al-Din Iraqi's (1213–1289) *al-Lama'at* (*Divine Flashes*), which was itself based on Ahmad Ghazali's *Sawanih* (*Incidents*). Jami's *Naqd al-Nusus fi Sharh Naqd al-Fusus* (*Critique of the Texts as a Commentary on the Patterns of Bezels*) is a commentary on Ibn Arabi's *Fusus al-Hikam* (*Bezels of Wisdom*). Because of this extended body of work, Jami can be read as much (if not more) in the context of intellectual history as for his gifted talents in prose and poetry.

As "the Seal of Poets," Jami has a terminal significance as not just the end of an era but also as the opening gate of a new age. As perhaps best evident in his *Baharestan*, Jami was very particular in simplifying Persian prose, and for that reason his prose might be considered the inaugural move in rendering classical Persian literary humanism more accessible to a wider reading public. That Jami had composed this text for his own son assumes further symbolic significance, as if he were in fact writing for the birthing of a new generation of literary imagination that needed to leave the classical phase behind and move on to wider and greener pastures. Consider this: *Baharestan* is composed of eight "gardens"—the first on Sufi masters, the second on wisdom, the third on just governance, the fourth on magnanimity, the fifth on love, the sixth on pleasant anecdotes, the seventh on the nature and function of poetry, and the eighth on animal fables. The text is in effect the very summation of Persian literary humanism, composed by a master practitioner, a farewell gift from all the foregone masters, summing up all that had been done well before and dispatching it to the unfolding, uncharted, future.[16]

As best evident in his lifetime literary and poetic achievements, Jami was first and foremost a deeply cultivated mystic, with a vast knowledge of Islamic philosophy and mysticism, and yet with a natural penchant and manifest facility for poetry. Above all a mystic saint, Jami staged Persian poetry like a virtuoso performer, a master musician. His compositions are above all performative, putting his astonishing poetic abilities at the service of Persian mysticism. This staging and performing of Persian literary humanism was as much the final bravura of the classical period as it was the inaugural moment of it marching toward uncharted territories. Classical Persian literary humanism had now reached a zenith, performed to perfection—epistemically exhausted at the supreme moment of its visionary recitals, the very last summit of its own emotive sublation into something else.

In Praise of Folly

The Timurid period is also known for perhaps the greatest satirist in classical Persian literature. Nezam al-Din Obeydollah Zakani, known affectionately only as Obeid Zakani, or just Obeid (d. ca. 1370) was from the city of Qazvin. He was educated in Shiraz but returned to his hometown, where he flourished as an uproarious satirist. His political satire is the testimony of his age. His *Resaleh-ye Delgosha* (*The Pleasant Treatise*), as well as *Akhlaq al-Ashraf* (*The Ethics of Aristocrats*), and his major political satire, which he composed as a fable, *Mush-o-Gorbeh* (*Mouse and Cat*) have made him immortal.[17] It is impossible to exaggerate the singular significance of Obeid Zakani as a political satirist, a social critic, a rambunctious wise man, and a defiant rabble-rouser, embarrassing the polite company of Persian literati, as they try to control and conceal their chuckles. He was a gifted poet, a learned essayist, and a counter-moralist. If he were alive today he would be a stand-up comedian, a George Carlin

(1937–2008) or a Richard Pryor (1940–2005). Zakani does not shy away from using obscenities—he in fact thrives on them. His virtuoso tomfoolery flaunts a chastising voice, deadly serious in his satirical depiction of his time, merciless against political corruption, moral depravity, hypocrisy, duplicity. Injustice deeply troubles him. He is worldly, wise, principled, and witty—he is a man of the streets, boisterous in his demeanor, restless in his poignant observations. Zakani celebrates no ideals, but nor is he dark and foreboding. He is lewd, insatiably sexual, like a distant uncle of the Persian literary family—when he is paying a visit, adults ought to be forewarned, children sent away. He has a wet sense of humor.[18]

Zakani is best known for his staccato anecdotes—short, witty, pithy, punchy, lewd, and lascivious. Reading Zakani is like looking at a Pieter Brueghel the Elder (ca. 1525–1569) painting: crowded, noisy, raucous, rough and rowdy, rude and unruly, vastly populated, urbane, transgressive. Here in this corner we see a man who has just married. Going to his wife for the first time, he notices that her pubic hair is not shaven, and when he starts having sex with her she farts. "You keep what you must let go," he objects to his newlywed bride, "and you let go what you should keep." There, in that corner we see another man having sex with his wife at home. In her excitement she is gently slapping her husband's neck. A beggar is knocking at their door asking for a handout. The woman tells him to go away, they don't have anything to offer. "Please give me whatever it is you are having." "I am having a dick and my husband a slap." The beggar runs away aghast, "No thank you very much!"[19] There in that corner we see a Shi'i entering a mosque. He notices the name of the first three caliphs and spits at them, but the spit sits on the name of Ali. "Well it serves you right," the Shi'i says, addressing Ali's name, "that's what happens to you when you sit next to them."[20] The tableau is crowded with men having sex with boys, boys having sex with animals, women cheating on their husbands, neighbors prancing to jump on their neighbor's wives. People of Obeid Zakani's hometown Qazvin are strewn all over the canvas, mingling with Turks and other characters. His racialization of levity, however, does not stereotype. A Turk can be both a pretty boy who while drunk is taken advantage of by a pederast, or a robust sexual predator who has sex with a boy and his mother at the same time. "Will you remember him if you were to see him again?" the mother asks her son. "No mother, but you should. He was facing you when he was fucking you." Wives who covet other men are lurking behind doors here and there, as are men who yearn for young boys. Obeid Zakani sees everything—the unseen, hidden, the forbidden, the denied, the repressed.[21]

Zakani is the poet and prose stylist of the forbidden zones, the banished words, the transgressive gestures—factual and real but banned from polite companies. He disturbs those polite companies. As a satirist, he almost single-handedly constitutes frivolity as the laughing subject of a subterranean world, subversive to the very core of its satirical being. Although there is a long tradition of satire and anecdotal merriment in Persian literature, what happens in Zakani is something different.[22] He brings forth the subversive dimension of Persian literary humanism for a full frontal display. Obscenity here reaches an art form, and literary imagination finally exposes its underbelly. Unabashed sexuality, erotic encounters, pornographic detail, homoerotic and heterosexual sex lives—reality is naked here. Old women, young men, vaginal intercourse, anal sex—deeds done abundantly with words that were effaced, verbs that were censored, all come out in Zakani for a parade, a pageant. Obeid Zakani's prose and poetry is the repressed vocabulary, sentiments, and rambunctious frivolity of Persian literary humanism coming up to breathe. It is a carnival, a remissive occasion, when things ordinarily not permitted are performed. Zakani's pages are a burlesque—pornographic, peeping into the bedroom of Persian literary humanism. A subversive pleasure excites Obeid Zakani's work. As the distinguished literary critic Gholam Hossein Yusefi notes, a crucial aspect of Zakani's satire, "in which regard he is matchless in classical [Persian] literature," is his recognition of contradictions and paradoxes in his people's lives. Yusefi cites Zakani as a demonstration of this point: A man was admonishing his disobedient son, "Do as I say," the concerned father points out, "learn some tricks, a few somersaults perhaps, jumping dogs through hoops, or walking a trapeze, so you'll be successful in life, or else I swear by God I will send you to school so you become a scholar and spend the rest of your life in misery and destitution."[23] In Zakani, Persian literary humanism exits the courts and comes into the streets—subversive, erotic, crowded, revelatory, debauched, real, and above all human, all too human.

Letterists and Pointillists

The most powerful revolutionary movement of the Timurid period, challenging both the ruling monarchy and the Sunni scholastic orthodoxy of
their empire, was the Hurufiyyah (Letterists) movement, launched by
the mystic visionary Fazlullah Astarabadi, also known as Fazlullah Hurufi (1340–1394), as a typically proto-Shi'ite doctrinal challenge to the
clerical establishment and their royal patronage. Fazlullah Hurufi began
his visionary mission as an interpreter of dreams.[24] The launching site of
the Hurufiyyah movement was Khurasan, where it was vastly popular
among the urban poor and some of the leading intellectual elite.[25] Fazlullah Hurufi had converted some of the leading Timurid elite to his
ideas, which were deeply rooted in Persian Sufism, but having failed to
win Timur himself over, he was executed by Timur's son Miranshah in
1394. In 1426, a Hurufi activist named Ahmad Lor tried to assassinate
Shahrokh, the Timurid prince. Ahmad Lor had connections to some
high-ranking member of the Timurid elite. The movement that Fazlullah
Hurufi had launched, however, survived in various guises in central Asia
for a long time, including within the Baktashi Sufi order.[26]

As their names imply, the Hurufis had a particular penchant for the
mystical connotations of the 32 letters of the Persian alphabet, considering them the sum total of divine manifestation. In *Javidan-nameh-ye
Kabir* (in prose) and *Arsh-nameh* (in poetry), Fazlullah Hurufi expanded
on his mystical ideas, narrated around the central mystical potency of
Persian letters and their numerical weights. He believed in reincarna-
tion, and his proto-Shi'i thoughts was predicated upon the rise of the
Isma'ilis during the Seljuqid period and anticipated the Babis during the
Qajar period.[27] He reduced existence to the 32 Persian letters, considering them a manifestation of divine grace, by virtue of which the form,
norm, and the nominal disposition of worldly existence was made possible. The Hurufiyyah were in effect radical cabalists who thought all
existence was conceivable and possible only through and by virtue of
the letters of the alphabet.[28] In their estimation, the letters of the alphabet were the building blocks of existence that in their combinations
posited not just meaning of words but also essence of things. The Hurufis believed that the human figure was the perfect manifestation of divinity and that even God appeared as man to the angels when he told
them to prostrate themselves to Adam. Prophets were also specific hu-

man manifestations of this divinity, as indeed was Fazlullah Hurufi him-self. This radical divinism was in effect a radical humanism. As B. S. Amoretti points out, "although this concentration of interest on the hu-man figure as representing completely the ultramundane mystery is its closest link with Isma'ilism, Hurufism differs from the latter in its recog-nition of the reallocation of the Haqiqa in the substance of the letters rather than in the person of the imam."[29]

An offshoot of the Hurufiyyah movement became known as the Noqtavis, or the Pointillists. Mahmud Pasikhani Gilani, the founder of the Pointillists in the year 1397, was initially a follower of Fazlullah Hurufi. But he eventually founded his own movement, in which he went even further than his master and believed that everything was in fact represented in the diacritical dots of the Arabic and Persian alpha-bets, identifying the absolute dot with earth as the primal matter of everything else. Amoretti explains the relationship of the Pointillists to the Letterists as an extension of their inherent humanism: "Its rela-tionship to the accepted Hurufi theory that man is the starting-point for any form of superhuman knowledge is clear. For the Noqtavi deity, man does not represent an object of activity, and it is man himself who, through self-knowledge, can raise himself up to the divine sphere."[30]

The common features of these revolutionary movements during the Timurid period is that they were directed immediately and force-fully against the empire, that they were rebellious in their politics, icono-clastic in their doctrinal challenges to Sunni scholastic orthodoxy, vastly popular among the urban and rural poor, humanist in their philoso-phy, and in these cases not just Letterists but in fact Pointillists—namely, a radical *reductionism* is definitive of their doctrines. In these two related and powerful movements, ideas and sanctities were reduced ad infini-tum to words, words to letters, and even letters to points and dots—to which divine attributes were then affixed and from which humanity emerged as the modus operandi of the universe. That these ideas were the mobilizing thoughts behind some of the most radical revolutionary uprisings of the period marks the manner in which the vast edifice of Sunni scholastic orthodoxy was reduced to scattered and disparate let-ters and dots, to get them ready for a new revolutionary and revelatory dispensation. Man becomes the measure of everything here—a man that, as Fazlullah Hurufi saw it, was not just the manifestation of divin-ity but in fact the prototype of divinity itself. This radical humanism,

rooted as it was in an iconoclastic Shi'i disposition that came to full fruition in the Hurufi and Noqtavi movements, would have vastly emancipatory consequences for generations to come.

The Making of a Polyfocal Imagination

Between the death of Shahrokh in 1447 and the commencement of
Sultan Husayn Bayqara's reign in 1470, a period of suspenseful confusion reigned in the Timurid realm. The dissipated synergy of these two-
and-a-half decades, however, was blown with full force into the next
magnificent 36-year reign of Bayqara, which now, in addition to the
great patrons of arts and sciences like Amir Alishir Nava'i and poets
like Abd al-Rahman Jami, boasted of the presence of the glorious
painter Kamal al-Din Behzad (ca. 1450–1535), a legendary artist and
head of the royal ateliers in Herat and Tabriz from the late Timurid period into the early Safavid period. In his life and career Behzad linked
the two empires together. He was born and raised and began his illustrious career in Herat under the Timurids and then continued in Tabriz
under the Safavids. He was a protégé of the prominent painter Mirak
Naqqash, and Amir Alishir Nava'i was his principal patron. Sultan Husayn Bayqara was his chief royal patron under the Timurids, after
which Shah Isma'il I employed him at the Safavid court. The last great
Timurid and the founding monarch of the Safavids are thus linked in
the person and artistic production of Behzad.

The principal and primary function of the court painter was to il-
lustrate the manuscripts prepared in the royal atelier by way of marking the monarch's ascendence to power. One of the first things that
Amir Alishir Nava'i did for Sultan Bayqara was to compose a *Zafarnameh* for him that linked him to Timur and was lavishly illustrated by
Behzad. The visual depictions in this manuscript

> illustrate Timur's accession, four decisive battles, and the building of
> the mosque of Samarqand. The choice of subjects suggests that the pa-
> tron wished the manuscript to underscore his direct descent from
> Timur, who founded the dynasty. . . . There can be no doubt that the
> manuscript was created in anticipation of Husayn Bayqara's victorious
> campaigns in Khurasan and the establishment of the capital in Herat. It
> later became a symbol of Timurid legitimacy, as it too was taken to the

Mughal court in India, where it became a prized possession of the emperors Akbar, Jahangir, and Shahjahan.[31]

In Sultan Bayqara's court, Behzad "was placed in charge of librarians, calligraphers, painters, gilders, marginal draftsmen, gold-mixers, and lapis lazuli washers."[32] He thrived in this capacity, not only in leading a major artistic adventure, but also in inaugurating a transformative realism in the art and craft of Persian manuscript illustration. "The figures," in Behzad's work, art historians report, "are lively, often humorous, and engage in such everyday activities as building, eating, and drinking. Actions are depicted more realistically than in earlier paintings. . . . They are no longer types, but individualized personalities."[33] This is in 1488—namely the period of High Renaissance art in Italy (1475–1525), when Leonardo da Vinci (1452–1519) and Michelangelo (1475–1564) were busy defining the contours of European visual modernity. Painters like Behzad were at the very same time engaged in no less drastic alterations in Persian visual humanism. Although the origin of the School of Herat goes back to the time of Shahrokh, it is during the time of Bayqara that it reached its highest achievement and produced Behzad as its most illustrious and crowning achievement. The School of Herat subsequently went both to the Mughal court in India and to the Safavid empire in Iran, where it yielded to the School of Isfahan (Makteb-e Isfahan), in which Reza Abbasi (ca. 1565–1635) became the great artistic descendent of Behzad.

One of the masterpieces of Behzad, according to leading art historians, is his "Seduction of Yusuf," from the so-called Cairo *Bustan*. This painting depicts the famous story of Joseph and Zoleikha (Potiphar's wife) as initially (for Muslims) depicted in Chapter 12 of the Qur'an, but later expanded by Jami. Zoleikha is passionately in love with Joseph and attempts to seduce him by having him come to her private quarters, where she shows him erotic murals of the two of them together. In Behzad's rendition we see the highly aroused Zoleikha reaching for Joseph as he runs away. The painting is depicted "as in all Persian manuscript painting, in contemporary terms."[34] The literal sense of the story and its more mystical interpretations are combined here via "the perfectly executed combination of the decorative and the realistic."[35]

A number of key conceptual and compositional factors come together in Behzad's paintings, and the School of Herat associated with him that will have a lasting influence on Persian literary humanism. Poetry, prose, painting, mysticism, and above all architectural design all come together to define Behzad's works, moving them, formally and narratively, toward a *polyfocal* architectonics of signs that push the boundaries of Persian humanism beyond anything previously achieved. As the eye of the beholder is gently forced to move from one register to another in these works, so is the forming subject equally gently guided to dance with the spectacle. In this compositional edifice we move from the formal to the narrative, from the semiotic to the symbolic, from the painterly to the poetic, the realistic to the mystical—all in one flowing gesture, like a well-choreographed dance. The result is the revelation of a corporeal physiognomy, positing a transcendental pattern of apperception reducible to none of its composite forces. This is not just poetry, it is also painting, not just a painting, but also an act of mystical piety, a philosophical meditation in pictorial registers, an edifice that invites you in and gives you a strange sense of homeliness. Visual categories become pure form, positing their own schemata, while the borderline between the poetic and the pictorial fade into each other and form a sublated plateau of its own. Behzad in effect is inventing a narrative flow, framed within a structural composition at once formal and mannered, verbal and yet ocularcentric. The pictures thrive on their cosmopolitan flamboyance, with a variety of people depicted in elusive or busy positions, while everything is framed in a poetic mood that arrests and wrests your attention from the mundane toward a transcendence of its own making. Figures have distinct individuality, even psychological depth and realism, helping Behzad depict his story with narrative creativity—and yet the aura of a poetic encounter gives the experience an almost metaphysical domain to fill with memory. Sufi allusions and something of a *Farbenlehre* come together to form unique allegorical registers. This was the art of manuscript illumination at its absolute height, where a flowing organicity on the surfacing narrative is framed within a decidedly architectonic angularity.

Through the pages of these manuscripts, with these sorts of edifices, the *logos* of Persian literary humanism now goes through a transformative metamorphosis, and its deep-rooted grammatology is absolved into a semiosis, whereby the *logos* retreats to being a constellation of signs, and signs in turn are released toward an open-ended semiosis. It is no longer the *language* that matters and means—it is the emotive constellation of *signs* and the *ethos/hanjar* they reveal that does. But the tension between the legislative semantics of meaning and the open-ended semiosis of signs is sustained on these pages and not resolved in one way or another (which resolution will remain for a later stage in Persian literary humanism when this *ethos/hanjar* becomes *chaos/ashub*). Instead, a sustained dialogue between the visual text and the textual caption occurs. Persian literary humanism is semiotically imploded on these pages, and rushes toward an ocularcentric cascade. This transmutation of the *poiêsis* into *semiosis* is taking place way ahead of the fateful encounter of Persian literary humanism with colonial modernity in India. By bringing poetry and painting and mysticism and architecture closer together, Behzad and the School of Herat are responsible for this semiotic implosion of the sign in Persian literary humanism, upon which is then contingent the transformation of a polyfocal subject.

What we are witnessing in the School of Herat, and in Behzad in particular, is not merely the achievement of Persian visual humanism, but the appearance of the more universal horizon of a *metalingual* humanism, in which prose and poetry, painting and architecture, mysticism and realism, formalism and narrativity, all come together to posit a paralingual symbiosis. It is right here, in this paralingual fusion of the verbal and the visual, that the *logos/sokhan* of Persian literary humanism finally yields to the rise of an *ethos/hanjar* from within its own historic consciousness. The *logos/sokhan* trespasses the borderline of visuality, fuses the verbal and the visual, the poetic and the pictorial, the painterly and the architectural, the formal and the narrative, to project a new metalingual idiomaticity. On that borderline, the *logos/sokhan* of Persian literary humanism finally yields to a superior metalingual parlance that in its polyfocal idiomaticity gives birth to its *ethos*. This polyfocality, as best evident perhaps on Behzad's *Yusuf and Zoleikha*, projects not just one but multiple focal points that bring and hold the picture together, making the visual subject at one and the same time present in more than one focal point of the painting. The result is the creative formation of a polyfocal semiotics that thrives on a paralingual imagination that shifts the ocularcentricism that has emerged from the heart of Persian literary humanism toward the active formation of the sovereignty of an aesthetic judgment. This happened, and we need to mark it here, right at the heart of Persian literary humanism and right at the height of the Timurid Empire in the fourteenth century.

The Un/knowing Subject

By the time of the Timurids the transmutation of *ethnos* into *logos* in the making of Persian literary humanism had come to full fruition. It had already achieved its highest manifestations in the Mongol period, when Persian poetry and prose hit its highest summits within a vastly transnational empire. No great poet or prose stylist, no height of literary or moral imagination, appeared in the Timurid Empire (which was equally transnational) that surpassed or even matched those already achieved during the Mongol Empire. During the Timurid period, Persian literary humanism was fully in charge of providing the basis of a civilized and cultured life, as is best evident in the two major cosmopolitan capitals of the reign, Herat and Samarqand. During the Timurid era, Persian literary humanism was more *practiced*, than *produced*. All the major and minor tunes and tropes of the tradition had all been produced in earlier generations—from the Samanids to the Mongols. The Timurids were the beneficiaries of this tradition in performing Persian literary humanism, very much like a great musician who performs Beethoven or Mozart but does not compose like them. Yes, Hafez (1325–1390) is nominally from very early in this period (Timur was just ascending to power when Hafez died), but in letter and in spirit he is in the league of Rumi and Sa'di in the previous period. Abd al-Rahman Jami, representing a vast array of great poets and humanists, is far more representative of this age and he is, above all, a virtuoso performer of Persian prose and poetry but not a groundbreaking or transformative discoverer of any new domain. The Timurid period as a result is the highest manifestation of the sort of civilized life that Persian literary humanism could have imagined, achieved, and made possible—but it was not the launchpad of any new discovery. The Timurid period lacked that sense of historic trauma that would be conducive to groundbreaking creativity in still-classical terms.

The significance of the Timurid age for Persian literary humanism is in something entirely different: not in what literary or poetic masterpieces it produced but in what aesthetic possibilities were envisioned and enabled. The world was changing, and the Timurid era was crucial in preparing the passage into the multiple imperial ventures emerging in its stead. The year of Jami's death, 1492, has of course an uncanny resonance in the rest of the world, the world outside Herat and Samarqand and beyond the horizons of the Timurid Empire. The year of the Spanish Reconquista and the year of Columbus's "discovery" of the New World inaugurated modern history and the rise of a new age of European imperialism that left no corner of the world untouched. European imperialism would soon come into direct contact with the Ottomans, the Safavids, and the Mughals—the three Muslim empires that inherited the Timurid Empire. The rest of the Muslim territories would be absorbed into the Russian empire in central Asia. These four empires will have their respective and fateful encounters with the escalating European imperialism. The fate of Persian literary humanism was now about to be cast fast and steady onto these emerging maps— military and emotive at one and the same time.

As I argued at the outset of this study, at the heart of contemporary philosophical antihumanism remains the enduring crisis of the all-knowing (European) subject, a crisis that by simply multiplying the sites of humanism, as Edward Said has suggested, in multiple literary directions, we are not resolving but in fact exacerbating it. The literary answer to that philosophical crisis must be sought in manners of dissolving that all-knowing subject or retrieving its irresolution in varied literary traditions. It is the precarious disposition and multiple subject positions of the literary act, in and of itself, that are the defining modes of Persian literary humanism, and it is in those terms that literature qua literature does not face the cul de sac of philosophical antihumanism. Throughout its long and varied history, Persian literary humanism was an epiphenomenon precisely because no false authorizing subject, partaking in the absolute alterity of any viable God-term as its absolutist transcendence (the way Islamic scholasticism had worked), had authorized its formative *nomos*—for it had claim to none. Instead of that *nomos,* it had, in literary terms, uplifted the inaugural moment of an *ethnos* initially into *logos* and from there worked itself toward the authorizing voice of an *ethos* in sustaining the literary act. The term "modernity," which much of the world received as "colonial modernity" and as such posited against a generic "tradition," is far too limited a proposition to be at once universally applicable and specifically insightful. But if we were to cast the history of Persian (or any other) literary humanism, barring historicity, this successive transmutation of *ethnos* into *logos* into *ethos* and ultimately *chaos* is a far more overarching and endemic thrust than a mere "modernity."

The Timurid Empire had summed up from the seventh to the fifteenth centuries the entire course of the transmutation of *ethnos* of Persian literary humanism into *logos*, and the classical period thus came to closure and a commencement with the combined figures of Timur, Amir Alishir Nava'i, Jami, and Behzad. In the Timurid historiography we are witness to the formation of a historical *poiêsis*, while in Amir Alishir Nava'i a poetic *subconscious* produces Turkish literary humanism from its Persian and Arabic bedrock. The modus operandi of all these humanisms of course remains imperial—from the Timurid Persian to the Ottoman Turkish to the Mughal Persian. But by now the creative force of *logos* had sublated into the *ethos* of translinguality. Jami's *performing* Persian literary humanism was the final bravura of classical period, as it was the inaugural moment of its transcendence toward uncharted territories. In Obeid Zakani the Persian *senses satiricus* finds its highest and most perfect public performance, whereby Persian literary humanism exits its decorous courts and enters the rambunctious streets. In the Hurufi and Noqtavi movements we see the revolutionary manifestations of the Letterists and the Pointillists splitting the atom of Islamic scholasticism in deeply subversive and radically literary terms. In Behzad, the *logos* of Persian literary humanism finally yields to a superior metalingual parlance that leads the ocularcentricism that emerged from the heart of Persian literary humanism toward the active formation of the sovereignty of an aesthetic judgment. All these forces came together to move the *logos/sokhan* upward to the *ethos/hanjar* and then beyond toward the creative *chaos/ashub* that will define the moment of encounter in India between Persian literary humanism and European colonial modernity. Whatever it lacked in *matter* of literary creativity, the Timurid period overcompensated for with the *formal* outburst of vast and untapped possibilities in pushing Persian literary humanism beyond its poetic and aesthetic ruptures.

The eventual transformation of the *ethnos/nezhad* into *logos/sokhan* finally came to a radical closure in the Timurid period when the un/ knowing subject at the heart of Persian literary humanism went through an extensive transmutation and was dissolved into a sweeping and pervasive semiosis. Every dimension of Persian literary humanism during the Timurid period worked toward the transmutation of the subject from *ethnos/nezhad* to *logos/sokhan* to *ethos/hanjar*—through a historical *poiêsis* that was soon reflected on a visual semiosis. The successive splitting of the Persian literary subject was taking place right here before any encounter with colonial modernity and was then exacerbated, which led to its transmutation toward *ethos/hanjar*, while it kept the seeds of *chaos/ashub* within itself. It is a combination of *semiosis* (defiant signs becoming suggestive beyond their legislative semiotics) and *poiêsis* (the poetic paucity in the making/writing of history) in particular that paves the way for the transmutation of *logos* into *ethos* when Persian literary humanism moves even further east and encounters British colonial modernity in India. The combination of this *semiosis* and *poiêsis*, as evident and on display on a page of Behzad's illustrated manuscript, has a tendency toward *chaos/ashub*. But the overriding paradox that is ultimately posited between this *chaos* and the *cosmos* of the cosmopolis resists and thwarts the paradox of individualization and totalization of the forthcoming modern state on its colonial frontiers.

The fundamental paradox of any disciplinary subject formation, as Foucault discovered, is that the *individualizing* and *totalizing* power of any discourse go hand in hand. This indeed is a bizarre paradox that a literary tradition is made of individualizing tropes and totalizing narratives that both come together to posit and entrap subjectness—resulting in the irony that we get to *know* by way of *distortion* and *identify* by way of *alienations*. But what we are witnessing in the case of Persian literary humanism unfolding in its long and sinuous history, is the locomotion of a certain narrative "motility" (Julia Kristeva's term, based on Lacan's psychoanalytic) that calibrates the creation of the (always) impending subject, which ipso facto interrupts the totalizing regime that seeks to claim it, while allowing for an enabling agency. This is particularly the case when we remember the formation of Persian literary humanism in the immediate vicinity of Islamic (both Sunni and Shi'i) absolutist scholasticism. Because of this motility, the unstable subject is always on the move, spontaneously and actively, within an evolving tradition, as if through a multicellular organicity. This locomotion, thus set in motion, is what we detect in the transmutation of the un/knowing subject in Persian literary humanism from its inaugural *ethnos* to its formative *logos* and then to its transformative *ethos* and ultimately working its way toward an open-ended *chaos*. The impending experience of the literary subject, thus defined, always already places it outside the attempted enclosures of its habitually individualizing tropes precisely because it is unstable, and therefore destabilizing its own totalizing proclivities. In the case of Persian literary humanism, then, this successive moving from *ethnos* to *logos* to *ethnos* and ultimately *chaos* leads toward the making of an aesthetic will to resist power via the implication of an always already un/knowing subject.

6

The Contours of a Literary Cosmopolitanism

Treading over Multiple Empires (1501–1732)

THE LEGACY of Persian literary humanism was delivered from the Timurids to no less than four imperial projects in the sixteenth century: the Safavids (1501–1722), the Mughals (1526–1858), the Ottomans (1281–1924), and the Russians (1721–1917)—and it was in the context of yet another, a fifth imperial venture, the European imperialism in general that descended upon them all, that Persian *Adab* would find a renewed historical relevance for itself. Treading over four empires and facing a fifth was the fate and unfolding path of Persian literary humanism between the sixteenth and the eighteenth centuries. Historically, this period is a vastly variegated expanse that covers some 250 years, a quarter of a millennium, beginning with the reign of the Safavid monarch Shah Isma'il in 1501 and ending, or at least symbolically so, with the commencement of the official British rule over India in 1857. Geographically, the domain of this literature extended from China's borders to the Indian subcontinent, through the Safavid mainland and Russian southern provinces, all the way to the Ottoman territories and the Balkan borders of Europe. This is a literary phenomenon at once multifaceted and polyvocal, global in its reach and universal in its appeal, cosmopolitan in its texture, and worldly in its material rootedness. Equally crucial in the making of this literary cosmopolitanism are the vast resources of its archival evidence, of which we only have a very general and schematic awareness, almost a century after its monumental works of scholarship were created. Persian literary humanism assumed a decidedly cosmopolitan character and spread far and wide beyond the Safavid dynasty—which consolidated itself by way of assuming Shi'ism as its state religion—and became definitive to the courtly cultures of the Mughals, the Safavids, and the Ottomans, while at the central Asian peripheries of the fourth, the Russian empire, it began to cultivate seeds of literary dissent that would soon come to fruition at the dawn of colonial modernity.

Power and Poetry

In this era, the heartbeat of Persian literary humanism moved further east toward India, for the birthplace of Ferdowsi, Nezami, Sa'di, and Hafez was now fully in the grip of a vast Shi'i empire. The Safavid era was marked by two major monarchs, Shah Isma'il (r. 1502–1524) and Shah Abbas I (r. 1587–1629), and its remnants were picked up later by the founder of the Afsharid dynasty, Nader Shah Afshar (r. 1736–1747), two Shi'i monarchs and one anti-Shi'i monarch, the three of them, in one way or another, exacerbating the fusion of the medieval spirit of messianic Shi'ism with the body politics of the Safavid empire and its aftermath—a fact and a phenomenon that left very little space for the Persian poets and prose stylists, who had to seek their fortune in the greener pastures of the Mughal territories.[1] Although Shah Isma'il (1487–1524) died at a very young age, the military foundation and the scholastic Shi'ism that he had managed to establish as the ideological foregrounding of his empire sustained the reign of his son Shah Tahmasp I (r. 1524–1576) for over half a century, thus consolidating the territorial foundations and ideological foregrounding of the Safavid dynasty. Shah Tahmasp I had no use or patience for Persian poets (or, for that matter, painters, toward whom he was quite tight-fisted), and yet he was exceedingly attentive to such Shi'i clerics as Muhaqqiq al-Karaki (1465–1533), a leading jurist from southern Lebanon who had come to his court. It was during the reign of Shah Tahmasp I that Ottoman Sultan Suleiman the Magnificent (r. 1520–1566) invaded northern Iran and thus sustained a course of sectarian binary between Sunnism and Shi'ism that pushed the Safavids even deeper into their sectarian convictions. These internecine rivalries between the Ottomans and the Safavids continued well into the middle of the sixteenth century.[2]

The Safavids were on much friendlier terms with the Mughals. The second Mughal emperor Humayun (r. 1530–1540 and 1555–1556), the son of Babur (r. 1526–1530) who founded the Mughal dynasty, in fact spent a year in the Safavid court after he lost his throne to Shir Shah Afghan, and it was the Safavids who helped him regain his throne. While in Iran, Humayun became deeply versed in Persian poetry and painting, and upon his return to his own court he took along many Iranian poets, painters, and prose stylists, and later invited even more to his court. Humayun's son Akbar (r. 1556–1605) became the greatest patron of Persian letters in India. On another occasion, Shah Isma'il relieved Babur's sister from custody with the Uzbeks and sent her back to Babur, a royal kindness that Babur never forgot.[3] It was not until the time of Nader Shah (r. 1736–1747) that an Iranian monarch invaded and plundered India. Throughout the Safavid period, the Mughal-Safavid relationship was an exemplary model of regional alliance in political, commercial, and cultural terms. This neighborly relationship proved crucial, for it resulted in a constant flow of poets and literati from Safavid realms to the Mughal courts in search of patronage and hospitality. As the Safavids imported Shi'i jurists and theologians from the Shi'i regions of the Ottoman Empire, they exported poets and prose stylists to the Mughal courts.

The reign of Shah Tahmasp I was followed by a decade of utter chaos and brutality until the commencement of the reign of Shah Abbas I. Barely sixteen when he ascended the Safavid throne, Shah Abbas brutally eliminated all the local and regional warlords who challenged his central authority; then he concluded a peace treaty with the Ottomans in the west so he could turn his attention to quell the menace of the Uzbeks. Having done this, he recruited two British brothers, Sir Robert and Sir Anthony Shirley, to assist him in modernizing his army and headed westward to take back the territories he had conceded to the Ottomans. Soon after he cleared all his northern borders, Shah Abbas turned south, and after decades of confronting the Portuguese early in the seventeenth century, he managed to establish complete control over the Persian Gulf by 1624.[4]

Not much happened politically after the end of the Shah Abbas I era, and the Safavid dynasty effectively collapsed into a succession of incompetent and useless monarchs. The decline of Safavid central power meant resumed territorial conquests by the Ottomans from the west, the Afghans from the east, the Russians from the north, and the renewed colonial rivalries between the British and the Portuguese in the Persian Gulf region. The Russian emperor Peter I (Peter the Great, r. 1682–1725) was particularly zealous in taking advantage of the post–Abbas I chaos and trying to gain access to the Persian Gulf. Even the affable Mughals took advantage of the Safavid weakness and invaded Afghanistan and renewed their claim on Kandahar during the time of Shah Jahan (reign 1628–1658).[5]

The three paramount preoccupations of Shah Safi I (1629–1642) pretty much sum up what the post–Shah Abbas empire looked like and what expedited the decline and fall of the Safavid empire: insatiable lust for female companions, flowing wine cups, and unending disputations of Islamic *fiqh*. The collapse of the Safavid empire after the Afghan invasion and conquest of their territories (1722–1730) was so traumatic that literary historians compare it to the downfall of the Sassanid empire after the Arab invasion. "The victory of the Afghans over Isfahan took place with the same ease that the Arabs conquered Ctesiphon."[6] Be that as it may, the fall of the Safavid empire was due less to the rise of Mahmoud of Afghan and his son Ashraf of Afghan, the two Afghan warlords who temporarily got hold of the Safavid capital, and far more to pressures from the Ottoman and Russian empires, which effectively divided the northern and western territories between their respective spheres of influence.

The far more hospitable domain for Persian literary humanism in this period was the Mughal Empire. The founder of the dynasty, Zahir al-Din Muhammad Babur was a contemporary of Shah Isma'il. Descendents of the Timurids, the Mughal monarchs were deeply immersed in Persian language and literature. From the commencement of the reign of Babur to beginning of Aurangzeb (r. 1658–1707), the Mughal Empire was the sublime site of a renewed flourishing of Persian *Adab*. Although the origin of Persian literature and culture in the Indian subcontinent in fact predates the rise of the Mughals, it was under this rich and opulent dynasty that Persian literary humanism found one of its most glorious and enduring literary ranges and cultivated unsurpassed poetic elegance. To be sure, Persian poets at the court of the Mughals did not match those hosted by previous empires from the Samanids and the Ghaznavids to the Seljuqs and the Mongols or produce any Ferdowsi, Nezami, Sa'di, or Hafez. But they followed and performed the poetic elegance of these masters with a perfection that rivaled the very last master of that pantheon, Abd al-Rahman Jami. They did not stray from the territories that these masters had already charted, but within that space they discovered many precious niches.

It was not until Nader Shah's invasion of India, when he conquered Kandahar in 1738, and subsequently defeated the Mughal army at the Battle of Karnal in 1739 and entered Delhi, that the Afsharid conqueror weakened the Mughal dynasty and thus inadvertently paved the way for the subsequent British conquest of India. Both Humayun, who actually spent some time in Iran, and Akbar were particularly known for their active patronage of Persian *Adab*. Precisely at the time when the monarchs of the Safavid realm were more inclined to substitute Shi'ism for Persian literary humanism at their court and in their country, Persian language and literature in India began its command over the Mughal court with the very Persian names of its princes and monarchs (Humayun, Jahangir, Shah Jahan, Dara Shikoh, Aurangzeb), and extended it to their preference for the Persian calendar to record their epic deeds. In the sixteenth century Mughal India was the primary home of Persian literary humanism, and Safavid Iran was a hotbed of scholastic Shi'ism.[7]

The Sunni-Shi'i hostility was very much the *condito sine qua non* of the Ottomans too. The hostility of the Ottomans toward the Safavids and their protracted warfare were by and large religiously tuned and territorially inclined. They fought in ostensibly sectarian (Sunni-Shi'i) terms, but effectively for territorial gains. In the Battle of Chaldoran, on August 23, 1514, which ended with a decisive victory for the Ottoman Empire over the Safavids, the Ottomans gained control over the northwestern part of the Iranian territories. The Ottoman rulers were even more successful in their other battles in the Arab world, North Africa, and Europe—and during the reign of Selim I (r. 1512–1520) they began to be recognized as "caliphs," endowed with the power and authority of the early Muslim caliphate of the Umayyad and Abbasid periods in early Islamic history. The presence of Persian language and literature in what would later become Ottoman territories of course goes back at least to the time of Mawlana Jalal al-Din Rumi (1207–1273), namely before the establishment of the Ottomans. But the imperial gathering of wealth and power during the zenith of the Ottoman Empire resulted not only in magnificent libraries and centers of learning in Istanbul, but the natural attraction of Persian literati to the Ottoman courts, whereby the presence of Persian literature was extended all the way to the heart of Europe. But at the Ottoman court, Persian literary imagination lived vicariously through its transmutation into Ottoman Turkish *Adab*, picking up in Anatolia in the sixteenth century what Amir Alishir Nava'i had started in central Asia in the fourteenth.[8]

The amicable relationship of the Safavids with the Mughals was not replicated between the Safavids and their northern neighbors. The Safavid-Russian relationship was more like the Safavid-Ottoman encounters, though this one more on a Muslim-Christian axis rather than a Sunni-Shi'i disputation. The Safavids never had the control of the Timurid Empire over central Asian territories. Shah Tahmasp's repeated invasions of Georgia during his reign, other than its catastrophic consequences for the local inhabitants, speaks of the commercial, political, and cultural contacts that existed between the Safavids and the southern provinces of the Russian empire. From 1555 to 1747, Georgia was very much under the control of the Safavids and heavily Persianized in its culture but was later incorporated into the Russian empire. The predominance of Persian language and culture never dwindled in central Asia—no matter who ruled over the vast territories from the borders of China to those of Russia, from Afghanistan up to Kazakhstan, Kyrgyzstan, Tajikistan, Turkmenistan, and Uzbekistan.[9]

But whatever the political circumstances, the territorial domains of Persian literary humanism extended well into northern climes of the three Muslim empires, right into the bosom of Muslim realms of the Russian empire in central Asia. Again, Persian language and literature were not new in these regions, and as early as the Samanid dynasty (819–1005) they were integral to the Persianate literary and artistic world, and in fact instrumental in the rise of Persian literature in the aftermath of the Arab invasion of the seventh century. Just before the rise of the Safavids and the aggressive Shi'ification of their domain, central Asia was part of the Timurid Empire and after that empire broke into smaller Turkic dynasties, it was eventually incorporated into the Russian empire in the nineteenth century and into the Soviet Union soon after the Russian revolution of 1917, reemerging as liberated republics after the collapse of the Soviet Union in 1991.

While Russia's imperial interest in its southern neighbors had a logic of its own—at once commercial and strategic—European imperialism appeared at the doors of Ottoman, Safavid, and Mughal empires as part of far mightier colonial interests and urges. While Persian literary cosmopolitanism resurfaced and trod over the four adjacent empires, all of them were eventually at the mercy of the mighty forces of European imperialism—the British, the French, the Spanish, the Dutch, and the Portuguese in particular. The decline of the Safavid empire and its adjacent empires was coterminous with the expansion of European colonial interest in the very same region. When Mahmoud of Afghan was laying siege to Isfahan, the Safavid authorities approached both the Dutch and the British colonial interests in the region for military assistance and they received none. The Dutch and British had bigger fish to fry in the Indian subcontinent.

More direct and extended contact with Europe intensified during the reign of the two tribal dynasties of Qara Qoyunlu (also called Black Sheep Turcoman, 1375–1468) and Aq Qoyunlu, (also called White Sheep Turcoman, 1378–1508), who ruled over parts of eastern Turkey, Armenia, Azerbaijan, northern Iraq, and western Iran. The origins of these sorts of military and diplomatic contacts go back to the Timurid era (1370–1506), with the easternmost parts of Muslim territories. Further south, Alfonso de Albuquerque (1453–1515), the Portuguese naval genius, had the entire Indian Ocean, Arabian Sea, and Persian Gulf under his control. Portuguese advances, for a combination of economic and geopolitical reasons, soon spurred the naval and military might of other European forces—the British and the Spanish in particular—to enter the southern scene. The three Muslim empires—the Mughals, the Safavids, and the Ottomans—were now completely drawn into the colonial rivalries between the tired and old Russian empire to their north and the robust and mighty European imperial projects to their south. Under these conditions, the Persian literary imagination in its old and outdated provisions would wither away in its own dusty libraries and those of emerging European Orientalist museums or else it would resurrect itself in newer and bolder strokes.

In 1622, Abbas I used British naval power to defeat the Portuguese and expel them from Hormuz and Qishm in the Persian Gulf in exchange for certain commercial concessions to the British. The occasion was properly celebrated by a couple of epic poems composed by court poet Qadari.[10] The commercial and diplomatic relations with England continued apace with the delegation that Anthony Jenkinson (1529–1611), a British naval officer, led to the Safavid court initially on behalf of the Muscovy Company and later for the British crown. He also met

Ivan the Terrible (1530–1584) several times during his trips to Moscow and Russia. The British, the Dutch, and the French were at this point competing for commercial favors at the Safavid court. In addition to commercial and diplomatic contacts, this era is also the period when the region was inundated by Christian missionaries and European Orientalists. Another major reason for European interests in Ottoman, Safavid, and (to a lesser extent) Mughal courts was to turn them against one another, so that the Ottomans in particular would be preoccupied with their eastern neighbors and leave their western frontiers open for European consolidation of a Christian front. The increasing presence of Europeans in Persian environs inevitably led to the emergence of the word *Farang* (for Frank, meaning European in general) in Persian poetry and letters: Mirza Jalal Asir says in a poem, referring to the green eyes of his beloved: "A Farangi pair of eyes have stricken me, place a green candle upon my grave!"[11] That was indeed a lethargic tune for a much mightier battle ahead in which Persian literary humanism would have to march to the beat of an entirely different drummer.

Literary Imperium

The spread of Persian literature from the Timurid into the Mughal, Safavid, Ottoman, and Russian empires was not something entirely unprecedented and was quite obviously predicated on the earlier presence of Persianate cultures in these regions. With the consolidation of the Shi'i disposition of the Safavid empire, a sizable population of the Persian poets and literati sought their fortunes in the greener pastures in the surrounding empires, particularly in India. Both the Ottomans and the Mughals, as indeed all great Muslim empires before them going back to the Abbasids, appealed to the Sassanid empire (224–651) as their imperial model, and thus were drawn to Persian literary traditions as the modus operandi of their respective imperial imagination, particularly in its epic, panegyric, and even lyrical dimensions. Both *razmi* (epic) and *bazmi* (romance) poetry appealed to all these courts at various stages of their power. Precisely because scholastic Shi'ism (from jurisprudence and theology to philosophy and mysticism) supplanted Persian literary humanism (almost completely) in this period as the ideological foregrounding of the Safavid imperial imagination, Persian prose and poetry was forced out of the Safavid court and let loose upon the fertile soils of three other empires that immediately (and the European empires that by the logic of their colonial extensions distantly) surrounded and defined its emerging sensibilities. Persian literary humanism was perforce being globalized in multiple and concurrent cosmopolitan empires, in each in a different imaginative register, but nowhere more potently than in the Mughal courts.

Not just in its immediate and distant contexts, but even in Europe and the Americas too, this was the beginning of the period when their emerging romanticism (which originated in the second half of the eighteenth century), transcendentalism (especially in the 1830s and 1840s), and what Raymond Schwab called the "Oriental Renaissance" (1680–1880), encouraged Europeans to pay closer attention to Persian literature.[12] As early as 1634, Andre du Ryer translated Sa'di's *Golestan* into French. Soon after, German translations were to follow. In 1651 a Latin translation appeared in Amsterdam, done by the German Orientalist George Gentz (1618–1687), which was in turn read by a subsequent generation of Orientalists that included Sir William Jones, Johann Gottfried von Herder, and Johann Wolfgang von Goethe (1749–1832), who then used these and other translations for inspiration when he wrote his *West-östlicher Divan* (1814–1819).[13] One might even argue that European romanticism and Orientalism, as well as American transcendentalism, were in fact the extended takes on Persian literature, on the same template that the Mughals and Ottomans also had their own take on Persian literature, so much so that when Montesquieu (1689–1755), for example, or Johann Wolfgang von Goethe began to adapt Persian literature for their own reasons, it was not just that they put an Orientalist or romanticist spin on Persian literary heritage but Persian literature put a spin on the European imagination—on the model that Raymond Schwab proposes in *The Oriental Renaissance: Europe's Discovery of India and the East, 1836–1886,* rather than the one criticized by Edward Said. It is crucial to keep in mind at this very juncture that contrary to a major train of thought in postcolonial thinking, it is not only "Western" humanism that is capable of globally worlding itself. Multiple literary humanisms—including Persian, Turkish, and Arabic—have at various times done precisely that. The sustained course of translation of Persian literary humanism in European and American contexts becomes particularly significant later in the eighteenth through the twentieth centuries when Persian literary imagination begins to recast itself in the globalized culture of European empires.

What is crucial to keep in mind in this period is that three Muslim empires—the Ottomans, the Safavids, and the Mughals—consciously modeled themselves after the Sassanid empire and gave three different expressions to an ancient imperial model in which the Persian *Adab* that had emerged after the Muslim conquest had various degrees of significance. But two non-Muslim empires—the Russian and the European imperialisms in general (the French and the British in particular)—were also fertile ground for Persian literature, although one in the original (central Asian domains of the Russian empire) and the other in its European translations. Meanwhile, the consolidation of Shi'ism in Safavid Iran exacerbated already racialized and sectarian tensions and provided opportunities for Europeans to abuse Muslim dynasties to further their own ends. So far as the Sunni inhabitants of the Safavid realms were concerned, there were even grander designs they had in mind for the Ottomans to take over the Safavids: a certain Khwajah Isfahani has a poem addressed to Selim I in which the poet pleads with the Ottoman Sultan to kill Isma'il and add Iran to Ottoman territories. Referring to Shi'i Iranians as "Zoroastrians, infidels, and animals," Khwajah Isfahani pleads with Selim that just as Alexander the Great had added Persia to his kingdom, Selim too should add the Safavid territories to Rum (Asia Minor extending to Europe—namely the Ottoman territories).[14]

The consolidation of these three Muslim empires—adjacent to the Russian empire and beginning to be squeezed by European imperialism—also meant that the expanding economic growth, predicated on the already globalized European imperialism, had initially made them key partners (and not colonial subjects) of European imperial projects.[15] The combined power of the Ottomans, the Safavids, and the Mughals, in both political and economic terms, was more than a match for Russian and European imperialism.[16] The Ottomans in particular were a major contender in the Mediterranean scene from the fifteenth through the eighteenth centuries. The combined preoccupations of Europe during the Thirty Years' War (1618–1648) in the Holy Roman Empire and the Eighty Years' War (1568–1648) between Spain and the Dutch republic coincides with the height of not just the Ottoman Empire but also the Safavid and Mughal empires. It is only after the Peace of Westphalia

(1648) that European powers begin to face up to the Ottoman might; and it was not really until the Crimean War (October 1853 to February 1856) that the French and the British empires became major contenders in Anatolia and beyond. These empires in effect divided into competing forces the British, Portuguese, and Spanish imperialisms. Both in terms of economic growth and scientific discoveries, Muslim lands were in a position of competition with European powers and not subjugation to them.[17] With the same token that adoption of Shi'ism by the Safavids as their state religion gives the revolutionary faith an imperial momentum to universalize itself, Persian literary imagination was now let loose into the realm of multiple empires to rehabituate itself in even more global terms.

Over the expanse of these multiple empires, Persian literary humanism was now set to recast itself in a renewed cosmopolitan configuration. It was no longer confined even within the wide boundaries of the Timurid Empire, the very last Muslim empire that claimed still-classical Persian literary humanism exclusively for itself, celebrating its *logos* as the defining trope of its creative imagination. Facing these multiple empires, Persian *Adab* was transcending that *logos* to discover and cultivate the *ethos* that would now carry it forward into uncharted territories.

The Making of a Cosmopolitan Humanism

The origin of Persian literary humanism in the Indian subcontinent does not begin with the Mughals—it culminates and reaches its zenith with them. Beginning with the Bahmani sultanate (1347–1527) of the Deccan in southern India, who believed themselves to have been the descendents of the legendary king Bahman, and extending to other dynasties, such as the Adilshahi sultanate (1490–1686) of Bijapur in the western area of the Deccan region, Persian prose and poetry had spawned illustrious progeny in India.[18]

But the real champions and the star-studded cast of patrons promoting Persian literary humanism in this era are the Mughals—with such now, legendary kings as Babur, Humayun, Akbar, Jahangir (r. 1605–1627), Shah Jahan (r. 1628–1658), and with the exception of Aurangzeb (r. 1658–1707).[19] To the list of these great patrons of arts and sciences, and of Persian *Adab* in particular, must also be added the name of Prince Dara Shikoh (1615–1659), eldest son and the heir apparent of Shah

Jahan and his wife Mumtaz Mahal, who was defeated and outmaneuvered by his younger brother Aurangzeb. This dynasty richly deserves
the epithet of poet-warriors. They were great patrons of the arts, their
court a lavish abode of cultivated poets and literati, but they were themselves deeply cultivated and practicing poets. The only exception seems
to have been Aurangzeb, who in his rush of hostility and rivalry with his
brother Dara Shikoh; reversed everything that his dynasty was known
for and became a belligerent Sunni and denounced poetry, very much
the same way that before him Shah Tahmasp had denounced painting at
the Safavid court. The golden age of the Mughals, one might argue, culminated with Dara Shikoh, who was committed to cultivating a common language between Islam and Hinduism, for which purpose he
translated portions of the Upanishads from Sanskrit into Persian (1657)
so they could be studied by Muslims. A painter, a poet, prose stylist, and
a great patron of architects, Dara Shikoh was the perfect model of a
learned and benevolent monarch. In his writings he was determined to
think through the possibilities of a syncretic religion that would bring
Islam and Hinduism together toward a third, common faith. He gave his
life for that effort. In the course of bitter and bloody succession feuds
with his brother Aurangzeb, Dara Shikoh was assassinated on August
30, 1659.[20]

One of the most salient features of Persian literature in this period,
precisely because it was traveling far and wide, was the appearance of a
number of classical dictionaries and encyclopedias, particularly in the
Indian subcontinent, where Persian literary tradition was being reimag-
ined in a new imperial context. Persian literature was now in mostly
fresh and uncultivated territories—in royal courts of multicultural settings that needed a reinvention of its idiomaticity. A whole new courtly
constituency was attracted to the history and practice of Persian *Adab*.
They needed to have authoritative access to what words meant, signified, entailed, and especially the poetic weight and connotations that
they carried. These dictionaries more than anything else functioned as
the manual of style for the emerging poets in the Mughal territories. As
Mawlana Mahmoud (1488–1517), the author of *Tohfat al-Sa'adah* (also
known as *Farhang-e Sekandari*), says in the preface to his dictionary, he
prepared the book for some novice poets who wanted to become familiar with the best examples of old poetry "and particularly understand
the difficult words in eloquent poems."[21] Classical Persian poets—

particularly Ferdowsi, Sana'i, Nezami, Sa'di, and Hafez—provided the authors of these dictionaries with authoritative texts on which they were in effect writing glossaries for the benefit of the new poets, such as in the case of Mohammad Lad's *Moayyed al-Fozala* (composed ca. 1519), which is evidently the first Persian dictionary that explains difficult Persian, Arabic, and Turkish words solely on the basis of their occurrences in classical Persian poetry.[22]

The rise and flourishing Persian *Adab* in the Mughal Empire was very much (but not entirely) the consequence of its demise under the Safavids, for whom Shi'ism now had ideological primacy. Not just Sunnis or unruly poets, but even the Shi'is of non-Twelve-Imami sects (such as the Isma'ilis) or the Sufis of rival orders were equally unwelcome in the Safavid courts and realms. Their presence in the Mughal Empire, however, meant a closer ecumenical encounter with Hinduism, working toward a syncretic harmony—both narratively and pragmatically, among various communities. Persian literary humanism in both prose and poetry becomes a conduit of facilitating a conversation among Muslim-Hindu segments of the empire. At the height of the Mughal empire, Persian *Adab* was hard at work, particularly through the valiant efforts of Dara Shikoh, to put forward a syncretic literary imagination in which the divergent and hostile sectarian trends of the subcontinent would have come together—and yet precisely at that moment, British colonialism entered the scene and did precisely the opposite—using the old Roman law of *divide et impera* (divide and conquer) to facilitate their own domination. As Gauri Vishwanathan has demonstrated, the teaching of English literature was established in India long before its institutionalization in England and was in fact used as a strategy of colonial control. The teaching of English literature was in effect used in the British Raj to manufacture an Indian elite that would facilitate the British domination, precisely in the opposite direction of Persian literary humanism, which was working to bring disparate components of the Mughal realm together.[23]

A typical example of the Persian literati of this period (both a poet and a prose stylist) would be Shah Taher Dakani (d. 1545) who ran away from Shah Isma'il, went to Deccan, and became a very prominent writer.[24] He specialized in royal correspondence between Deccan sultans and the Safavids. Dakani was an Isma'ili activist who became very prominent under the Safavids, and Shah Isma'il ordered him executed.

He escaped to India, where he went to the court of Borhan Nezam Shah (1508–1553), the monarch of Ahmednagar in the state of Maharashtra. He was prominent in both the Nizam Shahi dynasty that ruled the sultanate of Ahmednagar and the Adil Shahi dynasty that ruled Bijapur in the western area of the Deccan. His prominence had a lot to do with his poetic and literary capability to strike a balanced ideological foregrounding for his patron princes.

Perhaps the grandest humanist of them all in this era was Mohammad Dara Shikoh, the favorite son of Shah Jahan and his wife Arjomand Banu, known as Mumtaz Mahal, the daughter of Yamin al-Dowleh Asef Khan Muhammad Tehrani. Dara Shikoh was a deeply cultivated man, a poet, prose stylist, and calligrapher, who had studied with both Muslim mystics and Hindu masters and had a singular commitment to bring the Muslim and Hindu components of his realm together. His partial translation of the Upanishads is a clear indication of his untiring ecumenical attempts at bridging the sectarian gaps dividing his homeland. His brother Aurangzeb accused him of blasphemy and had him murdered (August 30, 1659). Dara Shikoh was the author of many books that speak to his interest as a comparatist, syncretic humanist. His *Safinah al-Awlia* on Sufi masters, and *Sakineh al-Awlia*, on Qaderi masters, his own Sufi order, are typical examples of his preoccupations. He wrote his *Resaleh Haq-nameh* thinking of it as complementing Ibn Arabi's two seminal texts of *Futuhat al-Makiyyah* and *Fusus al-Hikam*, as well as Shaykh Ahmad al-Ghazali's *Sawanih al-Ishq*. In his *Hasanat al-Arefin*, Dara Shikoh turned his attention to the *shathiyyat* of Sufi masters. His *Sirr al-Akbar* (or *Sirr al-Asrar*) is a translation of fifty Upanishads from Sanskrit to Persian.[25] His most famous book, however, is *Majma' al-Bahrain*, which is an attempt to bring together the teaching of Muslim mystics and Hindu masters.[26] In this book he offers the Upanishads as in fact mystical commentaries on Qur'anic verses and tries to compose a syntactical mystical prose of his own to facilitate a comprehension of that proposal. Dara Shikoh was ultimately murdered by his brother for political reasons, though his ecumenical and comparative disposition must have offended fanatics on both sides of the sectarian divide. What is central to his significance as a humanist is the language that he found in Persian literary humanism as a site of the syncretic sentiments he wanted to establish in his realm—as, perhaps, a kind of humanist-king. Fate did not allow that to come to pass. There are reasons to believe that the history of the Indian subcontinent would have been much different during and in the aftermath of British colonialism had he succeeded in realizing his dream.

To be sure, the Safavid realm was not entirely bereft of great and celebrated poets such as Vahshi Bafqi (d. 1566) who became prominent in Yazd, and who never left for Mughal India but managed to survive by praising his local princes. Vahshi Bafqi is celebrated for, among other works, his romance of *Farhad and Shirin*, which he composed after Nezami's masterpiece but did not finish—it was left for two other poets to complete after his death. There were other poets such as Mohtasham Kashani (d. 1587) who praised both Safavids and Mughals. But following Shah Tahmasp's repentance, Kashani composed religious poetry for him, mostly in praise of Shi'i Imams.[27] Others such as Orfi Shirazi (1555–1590) began their careers in the Safavid realm but moved to India to the court of Akbar, a place where Shirazi became a seminal figure during the height of Persian *Adab* in India. As the case of Mirza Mohammad Ali Sa'eb Tabrizi (1601–1677) clearly indicates, some poets went to the Mughal court just for work. Sa'eb's father went to Agra and asked him to come back after seven years at the Mughal court. While in India, Persian poetic vocabulary was obviously influenced by its new environment. Kalim Kashani (ca. 1581–1651) is known for the beauty and elegance of his *ghazals*, but also for having incorporated into his poetry Hindi words from his life at the court of Shah Jahan. He went to Kashmir and remained one of Shah Jahan's favorite poets.[28]

We must also adopt a more flexible definition of Persian literary humanism in this period—allowing for poets who traveled between the multiple empires. With a figure such as Mirza Mohammad Hossein Naziri Neishaburi (d. 1612), we encounter another significant category of poets who were peripatetic merchant-poets—they began and continued in their careers as merchants, traveling from one imperial domain to another, attending to their business and yet cultivating their taste for poetry.[29] Mirza Mohammad Hossein Naziri Nishaburi was born and raised in Khurasan and with his poetic disposition carried on the legacy of his fertile birthplace. He was a young merchant when he began traveling around the Safavid and Ottoman territories. During his travels he met with other poets, composed his own poems, and expanded his knowledge of poetry from other places and cultures. He eventually went to India and approached the Mughal court and found his way to Jalal al-Din Akbar. Once highway bandits robbed him while he was making a Hajj pilgrimage, and he appealed to a Mughal royal who also was on his way to Mecca, praised him in a poem, received some money in exchange, and proceeded to finish his journey. Upon his return to Ahmadabad in Gujarat he evidently was so successful as a merchant that his home became a salon for other poets, who praised him in exchange for his hospitality. But when Jahangir became the Mughal emperor, al-Din Akbar attended to his court and praised him lavishly. Naziri Neishaburi died in Ahmadabad in 1612 and is buried there and has a mausoleum.[30]

At the Safavid court, there were also prominent Shi'i scholastic philosophers like Shaykh Baha al-Din Amili (1547–1621), known as Shaykh Baha'i, who had a poetic proclivity and would occasionally try their hand at the craft. He was an eminent Shi'i jurist and theologian who had accompanied his father to the Safavid court as a young boy. Shaykh Baha'i became prominent mostly because of his scholastic achievements during the reign of Shah Abbas. He is in fact the perfect example of the dearth of poetic imagination in the Safavid period and the fact that the best and the most talented in the realm were attracted to philosophical scholasticism rather than *Adab*. What is perhaps most remarkable about Shaykh Baha'i is a letter that his father wrote to him in which he said, "if you want to be successful in this world go to India, if you want to be saved in the next world come to Arabia; and if you care neither for this world nor for the next just stay in Iran."[31]

One of the brightest stars of Persian poetry in the Mughal era was Mawlana Abu al-Ma'ani Mirza Abd al-Qader Bidel, also known as Bidel Azim-abadi and Bidel Dehlavi (1642–1720). A prolific composer of *ghazal* and quatrain, a deeply cultivated man, and a vastly tolerant humanist, he is the crowning achievement of the Mughal era and his name and reputation is synonymous with the so-called *Sabk-e Hendi* (Indian Style). His significance recently resurrected in Iran after a pioneering work on him by the eminent Iranian literary critic Mohammad-Reza Shafi'i-Kadkani, Bidel has been widely influential on subsequent poets of both the subcontinent and central Asia, especially Mirza Ghaleb (1797–1869) and Muhammad Iqbal Lahuri (1877–1938). Bidel's poetry is loved and admired today from Afghanistan to Tajikistan, Pakistan, and India.[32] Although his work was until very recently, and before the scholarship of Mohammad-Reza Shafi'i-Kadkani, scarcely known in Iran, the significance and influence of his poetry in central Asia is of an entirely different proportion. As the Czech literary historian Jiri Becka reports, something of a "bedil cult came into being under the name of 'bedilkhoni', the poet's verses and philosophical writings were read and analysed at weekly meetings."[33] In Iran too, Shafi'i-Kadkani's work has sparked an unprecedented interest in Bidel's poetry. After a detailed study of Bidel's work, Shafi'i-Kadkani proposed the second hemistich (*misra'*) of Bidel's lines (*bayt*) as the key to his poems—characterizing them as both exquisite and yet at times very convoluted. Shafi'i-Kadkani is at once highly appreciative of Bidel's poetry and yet critical of the puzzling wordplays that characterize his poetic diction—at one point even not hesitating to say that "this sort of work is not poetry, but stupidity."[34]

Mohammad-Reza Shafi'i-Kadkani's critical assessment of certain aspects of Bidel's poetry points to a vexing controversy surrounding the so-called Indian Style. For entirely wrong and misbegotten reasons, the term *Sabk-e Hendi* has become a deeply contentious appellation, some having used it as a derogatory designation to dismiss, diminish, or altogether denigrate the aesthetic qualities of the poetry produced mostly (but not entirely) in the Indian subcontinent and mostly (but not entirely) during the Mughal period, while others quite obviously get offended by this abuse and defend the work of that place and period adamantly.[35] Something of a feud between Iranians and Indians (both expounding a national/ist historiography and aesthetics) has thus emerged—one saying it is not beautiful, the other saying that it is, both evaluating its aesthetics predicated on nonaesthetic (national/ist) frames of references. As the prominent Pakistani literary critic, a leading authority on the subject, Shamsur Rahman Faruqi puts it quite succinctly:

> Although almost always viewed with disfavor and disdain by the modern Iranian literati and their Indian followers (whose number has tended to increase since the nineteenth century), sabk-e hendi has loomed large enough in the historical consciousness of the Iranian as well as the Indo-Muslim literary community for several speculations to be made about its origin which has invariably been found to have been in a place or area other than India. . . . A case has been made out even for as early a poet as Khaqani Sharvani . . . who wrote very few ghazals and is recognized as a master of the qasida while sabk-e hendi is associated overwhelmingly with the ghazal.[36]

The crux of the controversy, as Shamsur Rahman Faruqi summarizes it, is this: "The Iranians' disapproval of the Indian Style betrays a certain puzzled anxiety—for the poetry, though occasionally bristling with uncomfortably high imaginative flourishes and unusual images and unconventional constructs has yet a potency, vigor and éclat which mainline Iranian poetry would be hard put to match," and thus he concludes, "One reason for the Iranian eagerness to find a non-Indian place of origin for the Indian Style could lie in the fact that some of the major Iranian poets of that style never went to India: the names of Shafi'i Mashhadi (d. 1613), Mirza Jalal Asir (d. 1630/31), Shaukat Bukhari (d. 1695/99) and Mir Tahir Vahid (d. 1708) come instantly to mind. If native, untraveled Iranians too wrote in the Indian Style, this was a matter for further anxiety unless a non-Indian, Iranian origin could be found for the style."[37] Obvious and evident in this very assessment is the ahistorical *nationalization* of Persian literary heritage and the entirely flawed division suggested between "mainline Iranian poetry" and Indian Style poetry—a deeply defective categorization of Persian poetic traditions along postcolonial national boundaries that did not exist, nor did they decide literary and poetic tastes, at the time of the Mughal Empire. The literary and poetic heritage of the Mughal era is entirely integral to Persian *Adab*, not an appendage to it, and these sorts of assessments, prevalent on both Indian and Iranian sides of the debate are false postcolonial anxieties with little to no relevance to the body of poetic evidence they address.

Mohammad-Reza Shafi'i-Kadkani's take on the Indian Style, meanwhile, is entirely, well, stylistic—and quite rightly so. He has provided, over a lifetime of exquisite scholarship, a carefully argued periodization of Persian poetry that begins with the Samanid period and comes forward to his own time, and which he describes in terms of aesthetic "norms" established in one period and "deviation/*enheraf*" from those "norms" in the subsequent period, which in turn creates its own "norms," awaiting the next round of "deviations."[38] He describes these "norms" in terms of the frequency of certain poetic and stylistic usages that are prevalent in every period. He considers the Indian Style as nothing different from any other "deviation from the norms" as, in this case, those "norms" were established in the Timurid period. He then offers a number of stylistic frequencies peculiar to the Indian Style, which include: "paradoxical images, synaesthesia, personification, and abstraction."[39]

The problem with Shafi'i-Kadkani's assessment is precisely this structural-functional tendency to *normalize* every period and consider the next stage as *aberration*—thus attributing to pathbreaking moments in Persian poetry a certain *pathological* proclivity. Its pathological demeanor set aside, and its mechanical rendition of the Hegelian dialectic disregarded, this is a simple, if not simplistic, manner of periodization, but it at least remains true to the poetic evidence itself and does not reduce it to historically national/ist terms. The great advantage of Shafi'i-Kadkani's assessment as a result is that it stays mostly clear of anachronistic historiography and aesthetics and reads the Indian Style in stylistic terms, with which periodization other literary critics may differ but they will have to do so in precisely stylistic and not national/ist terms. This indeed is a vast improvement from futile contests between Iranian and Indian national/ist literary historiographers reading the Indian Style anachronistically in one way or another. But even Shafi'i-Kadkani still describes the period after the Timurids initially as that of the Safavids, which is accurate, before he too proceeds to divide the Safavid period into Indian (best exemplified in Bidel) and Iranian (best exemplified in Sa'eb) branches, which again takes us back to national identitarian divisions that are entirely ahistorical and inimical to the timing of the Safavid and Mughal dynasties, which were contemporaneous with each other and in cultural productions in obviously imperial (cross-national) terms.

Shafi'i-Kadkani's partially insightful intervention notwithstanding, the problem with all these characterizations ("Indians" did this and "Iranians" thought that) is a patently false and anachronistic (but prevalent) "nationalization" of literary traditions, tastes, and styles that in their origin and disposition were in fact formed in *imperial* contexts and in dynastic courts that were by nature "transnational" or even more accurately "non-national." If a poet like Sa'eb was from Tabriz, it does not mean that at the time his poetic style was "Iranian," as opposed to Bidel, whose style was "Indian." If they appealed to the Safavid or Mughal court, their poetry was obviously influenced by the poetic and aesthetic disposition of their patrons, the emperors, empresses, princes, and other royals to whom they catered. The term "Indian Style" was indeed coined as a derogatory term, because it emanated from a nationalist distortion of the legacy of Persian literary humanism by literary historians like Muhammad Taqi Bahar (1886–1951) at the height of Reza Shah's ethnic nationalism, itself predicated on an Orientalist literary historiography, best represented by the eminent British Orientalist Edward G. Browne (1862–1926), who along with other European Orientalists had already cast Persian literary history on an ethnic nationalist grid, entirely disregarding the inner dynamics of its historical unfolding. As a designation of a poetic formation, the Indian Style alludes to a period in Persian poetic imagination and practice that (like all other periods) reflected the particular tastes and flavor of its time (and here Mohammad-Reza Shafi'i-Kadkani's aesthetic, or *stylistic* as he calls it, characterizations are perfectly plausible, albeit incomplete and perhaps even a bit abstruse and recondite).

The fact is that the whole designation of the Indian Style is a deeply flawed appellation, distorting the particular aspects of Persian literary humanism in the Mughal period by both denigrating *and* nationalizing it, when in its original formation it was and it remains both perfectly legitimate and uplifting and an entirely *imperial* product, like every other phase of Persian literary traditions. In both prose and poetry, and there is no reason to privilege one over the other as the Indian Style does, and perhaps that false privileging is the culprit in this confusion, Persian *Adab* of this period and clime was formed during the heyday of the Mughal empire. Whether the poets and the prose stylists went to the Mughal realms, came from areas today located in India/Pakistan, Afghanistan, central Asia, Asia Minor, or Iran, at the time these locations were divided into the Safavid, Mughal, and the Ottoman empires. This was literally hundreds of years before the collapse of these empires and the rise of European (British in particular) colonial dominations that later resulted in the emergence of contemporary, postcolonial, nation-states. It is not just politically foolhardy but in fact sheer historical distortion to accuse and brand, or else to defend and dismiss, literary forms that emerged in entirely different imperial contexts for anachronistic nationalistic rivalries of the postcolonial period.

If we were to take the actual poetry of Bidel as the best manifestation of Persian literary humanism of the Mughal period, and we certainly can, instead of anachronistically branding (denigrating or celebrating) it as Indian Style, we read in his astonishingly beautiful and elegant *ghazals* the playful and ecumenical diction and the working of a vastly learned mind, a humanist who is traversing the distance between *kofr* (disbelief) and *din* (faith), navigating a more universal union between humanity and being-in-the-world, to map out a different mood of being-toward-life. Paramount in Bidel's poetry is a full consciousness of the distance between *ma'ni* (meaning) and *alafz* (words), which he stages in order to posit a new meaningful worldly union with words. He finds the playful embracing of *lafz* (word) and *mazmun* (content) troublesome, not coming together comfortably. Humans in Bidel's poetry become manifestations of the divine, as he wills them poetically, while at the same time oscillating between *heyrat* (wonder) and *tars* (fear). He can easily summon his readers to turn the tomorrow (the day after) of resurrection into yesterday, today—what then?—or else to abandon the search for this or the next world for the key to here and now.[40] By transcending transcendence he turns his poetry into an intuition of transcendence in and of itself. But above all, the melodious vocalization of words that he turns into poems read and sound as if they were deliberately composed as musical compositions and for vocal accompaniment to musical performances. He is as much a musician as he is a poet—and he knows and flaunts it.[41]

Persian literary humanism, in both prose and poetry, realized one of its most crucial and enduring aspects at the Mughal court.[42] The melodious and floral aspects of this phase of Persian *Adab* are the perfectly logical manifestations of its environmental affinity with painting and particularly with music within the Mughal context—as it continued to reverberate in the formation of Indian classical and Qawwali music.[43] The key to the Persian poetry of this period is the factor of musicality. Many poets in the Mughal court were also musicians and performers, singers and songwriters—a fact that is also evident in their poetry.[44] We may thus suggest that Persian literary humanism finally found its *melos* in the Mughal Empire. The closest thing to which we may in fact compare this particular phase of Persian literary humanism, by way of demystifying it and underlining its principal historic trope, is with the Symbolist movement in European poetry, whereby both Sa'eb and Bidel become the Stéphane Mallarmé (1842–1898) and Charles Baudelaire (1821–1867) of Persian literary humanism, containing in their poetry the music of Claude Debussy (1862–1918) and Franz Liszt (1811–1886).[45] As David Michael Hertz, a scholar of the Symbolist movement puts it, "the Symbolist moved language away from the task of journalist, away from the emotive excess of the romantic, and toward an ideal realm where the poet, freed from the necessity to describe reality, could create language that referred to itself, poetry chiefly about poetry."[46] One might argue that this is also precisely what the Persian poetry of the Mughal period achieved—particularly in the works of such master poets as Bidel or Sa'eb. The predominance of *melos*, in which words in effect become musical notations, will then have a phenomenal formal force and impact on the future of Persian poetry of the twentieth century, when in the context of his encounter with European romanticism and symbolism Nima Yushij (1896–1960) proposes to restore to Persian poetry its "natural music."

The Mughal Empire was instrumental in the making of a syncretic cosmopolitan humanism with enduring consequences for the rest of Persian *Adab* in the eighteenth through the twenty-first centuries. The prose and poetry of the Mughal period were definitive in crafting the literary subconscious of a people, beyond their sectarian divisions and toward the crafting of a common literary universe, a task that was ultimately defeated by British colonialism underlining and exacerbating those divisions in their own immediate interest by investing in them and effectively discarding Persian literary humanism and substituting it with English literature, as articulated in the Minute on Education by Thomas Babington Macaulay (1835), in which we read:

> I have no knowledge of either Sanscrit or Arabic. But I have done what I could to form a correct estimate of their value. I have read translations of the most celebrated Arabic and Sanscrit works. I have conversed, both here and at home, with men distinguished by their proficiency in the Eastern tongues. I am quite ready to take the oriental learning at the valuation of the orientalists themselves. I have never found one among them who could deny that a single shelf of a good European library was worth the whole native literature of India and Arabia. The intrinsic superiority of the Western literature is indeed fully admitted by those members of the committee who support the oriental plan of education.[47]

Macaulay's project was successful and to this day the leading Indian intellectuals have scarcely any knowledge of Persian (or Arabic) and do most of their literary and theoretical work in English and in fact pride themselves in being "Europeanists." "We must at present do our best," Macaulay insisted and delivered, "to form a class who may be interpreters between us and the millions whom we govern—a class of persons Indian in blood and color, but English in tastes, in opinions, in morals and in intellect."[48]

The Art of the Book

Around the year 1000 on Muslim calendar, 1591 on the Christian calendar, a certain Qazi Mir Ahmad Qomi wrote the first draft of a book
on history of calligraphy, paintings, and other manuscript-related arts
and called it *Golestan Honar* (*The Rose Garden of Art*) (1591–1597). Qazi
Mir Ahmad continued to work on and revise his book for several more
years until he produced the final version of the book we now have in its
critical edition with notes and commentaries.[49] Qazi Mir Ahmad was a
typical humanist of his time. His writings include historical narratives
as well as a biographical dictionary of poets. But it is precisely for this
Golestan Honar that he is best remembered now. This book consists of an
introduction on the creation of the pen, four chapters that consist of one
on creation of writing, two on the lives of famous calligraphers, a final
chapter on prominent painters, and a conclusion on various arts per-
taining to manuscript ornamentations. The text is written in a simple
and elegant prose and as such is the best link we have between Persian
literary humanism and the magisterial rise of art during the Safavid
period.

Halfway through *Golestan Honar* we read about an accomplished
Safavid painter named Mir Mosavver who was very prominent at the
court of the Safavid monarch Shah Tahmasp, but the Mughal emperor
Sultan Babur saw his work when he was visiting the Safavids and became so enamored by him that asked his Safavid counterpart Shah
Tahmasp to send him to his court in exchange for the sum of one thousand tumans. Shah Tahmasp agreed, and before Mir Mosavver left for
India, his son, Mir Seyyed Ali, "who was even a superior artist than his
father," according to Qazi Mir Ahmad, went to India. Soon the father
joined his son—and on the occasion of relating this story Qazi Mir Ahmad, reflecting the general mood of the time, composes this poem:

> I am leaving for India for there
> Artists have a good life—
> Here, however, magnanimity and generosity
> Have sunk into the black earth.[50]

What the Safavids lacked in prose and poetry they overcompensated for in art and architecture. Many poets, painters, and architects
traveled back and forth between the Safavid and the Mughal empires,

but by and large Persian poets were far better off with the Mughals than with the Safavids, while Persian painters and architects had much to do and accomplish at the Safavid courts. The Safavids did not produce any Ferdowsi, Nezami, Sa'di, Rumi, or Hafez—but they did produce a Reza Abbasi, a Mo'in Mosavver, and a Mohammad Zaman, and by extension they gave birth and breeding to what art historians call the *Maktab-e Isfahan* (School of Isfahan), named after the Safavid capital, in painting—and that added to and extended the visual and artistic aspects and dimensions of Persian literary humanism.[51] Extending the literary into the visual, the poetic into the painterly, the Safavid realm was witness to a magnificent extension and extrapolation of Persian *Adab* by the appearance of the masterpieces of Persian literature—Ferdowsi's *Shahnameh* and Nezami's *Khamseh* in particular—in the form of illustrated manuscripts. Words on these manuscripts transmuted into images, shapes, forms, colors, and pushed even further toward the polyfocal architectonics of signs that had its inaugural heights during the Timurid period. The active transmutation of words into signs through the celebrated art of calligraphy now added myth and momentum to the paralingual semiosis of Persian literary humanism that had achieved astounding vintages with Behzad in the previous generation.

The universally celebrated masterpiece of this period is the illustrated *Shahnameh* known as either "Shah Tahmasp *Shahnameh*," named after the Safavid monarch Shah Tahmasp I, who ordered its production, or else as the "Houghton *Shahnameh*," named after Arthur A. Houghton Jr. (1910–1993), the American art dealer who vandalized and destroyed it when it was in his possession.[52]

Art historians consider the Shah Tahmasp *Shahnameh* a masterpiece of the genre, "an enormous project" made of 742 large folios with "258 large illustrations grace[ing] the text."[53] Only one of the paintings is dated (1527), but the whole manuscript is believed to have been produced in the decade 1525–1535. Sheila Blair and Jonathan Bloom, two eminent Islamic art historians, also say that the only manuscript of this magnitude dates back to another *Shahnameh* that was produced during the Mongol period. Upon its completion, the book was sent in 1568 "as an accession present-cum-peace offering to the Ottoman Sultan Selim II."[54] It remained in the Ottoman royal collection until 1801. By 1903 it was sold to the collection of Baron Edward de Rothschild. His family sold it to Arthur A. Houghton Jr. in 1959—and "then the manuscript, which had survived intact for four hundred years, was subsequently dismembered. Individual folios were sold at auction like so many slices of pizza, and the integrity of one of the masterpieces of Islamic art was ignominiously destroyed."[55]

What we are witnessing in the singular production of this and many other manuscripts is a visual celebration of poetry, staging the words of such masters as Ferdowsi or Nezami, with their stirring stories and ideas inspiring ingenious painters, calligraphers, and other artists busy in the exquisite art of manuscript illustration to come together to imagine these stories and ideas in rich and powerful imageries. Though the history of manuscript illustration is much older than the Safavid period, the art reaches its formal and technical zenith here at the School of Isfahan. In one such tableau depicted in the "Shah Tahmasp *Shahn-ameh*," the legendary king Gayomarth is depicted at the inaugural moment of the world, the birth of humanity from the *mythos* of a people, and not from any divine intervention or will. The viewership of these royal manuscripts, to be sure, remained very limited until the appearance of coffeehouse painting in the Qajar period (1789–1926), when works of art exited the palace and entered the public sphere. But in the safety and luxury of the Safavid court ateliers, painters, calligraphers, and other artists were still dreaming of a humanity beyond the reaches of Shi'i jurists or any other Muslim scholastics. The jurists as doctors of Islamic law had forbidden paintings. Painters were the visual poets of precisely those forbidden dreams—right under the blinded insights of the grand metaphysicians of the sacred.

The grandest painter of this period, the Michelangelo (1475–1564) of the Safavids, was Reza Abbasi (1565–1635). He was closely associated with Shah Abbas, and thus his sobriquet. The significance of Abbasi is in having been instrumental in (1) a historic transformation of Persian visual culture from a collective craftsmanship into an individual artistic creation, and (2) the equally groundbreaking rise of autonomous subjects of painting independent of manuscript illustrations. In this period, "the importance of the book as a collective work of art by several artists," art historians report, "was increasingly supplanted by the single page as a product of one individual."[56] In this respect, what is remarkable about Reza Abbasi's career is that he began at the court of Shah Tahmasp as an artist working on manuscripts, but when the monarch suddenly renounced the whole act of painting, Reza Abbasi moved to Mashhad and began a career as an artist of nonroyal painters. He had by now exited the court (as painting had exited the manuscript)—not just physically, but emotively, professionally, and, eventually, even stylistically. Of course in a work like *Young Man in a Blue Coat* (1587) he continued with "the features of court painting in the 1570s and 1580s."[57] Formal changes, however, soon began to appear in his work when "his standard subject matter expanded from courtly youth to include workers and mystics."[58] But this was not all: "Shortly after 1603 he appears to have undergone a mid-life crisis, for contemporary chroniclers state that he took up with low-life characters and ceased painting court figures."[59] In other words, he had become an artist of the real people, ordinary folks, indeed "low-life characters" to the art historian still behind the closed doors of the royal ateliers.

These associations with so-called low-life characters are precisely what alters the moral imagination of the artist and was soon reflected in the formal and stylistic aspects of Reza Abbasi's work. The painting *Nashmi the Archer* (1622) might indeed depict, as Sheila Blair and Jonathan Bloom suggest, "one of the low companions" of Reza's middle years. But it also depicts a far more realistic character—"a pot-bellied slipshod slob smoking an opium pipe. His appearance would have affronted the refined sensibilities of the court."[60] But precisely in depicting "a pot-bellied slipshod slob smoking an opium pipe," Reza Abbasi had entered a public sphere far beyond the reach of the Safavid court and its royal entourage. The move, to be sure, must have had its formal and aesthetic appeal to the artist. But precisely in that move also dwells the emotive, normative, and moral expansion—exponentially—of Persian humanism: not just from the verbal to the visual, from the book to the page, from the written story to the untold history, but also from the limited court to the expansive public. The depiction of *Nashmi the Archer* also reflects something else in the Safavid realm. As Sheila Blair and Jonathan Bloom point out, this work "ironically alludes to the momentous change in Safavid society brought about by Abbas's reorganization of the army along functional, rather than tribal, lines and by the acceptance of firearms. A traditional archer, such as Nashmi, became superfluous in an army of musketeers, and this pensioner would have sought solace in puffs of his opium pipe."[61] Be that as it may, the change of subject also marks the transformation of the royal army, and by extension the society from which it was drawn, from *mechanical* to *organic* solidarity (Durkheim's concepts). This is an exceedingly crucial development for the marking of the emerging organicity of the public sphere to which these paintings were now responding, and for which obviously there was a public audience. The transformation of *logos* into *ethos* in Persian literary humanism, now enabled via the formation of a paralingual semiosis of signs, and further facilitated by this expansively polyfocal architectonics of signs, now will have a far wider public sphere to embrace and address.

The extraordinary achievements of Reza Abbasi are carried forward by one of his chief students Mo'in Mosavver (1617–1708), who extended the innovation of single-page composition of his master to new and more daring directions. His *Tiger Attacking a Youth* (1672) is a document of unsurpassed significance for the history of Persian humanism in many groundbreaking, surprising, and delightful ways. What is absolutely astonishing about this drawing is that Mo'in Mosavver has written a long description on it, in which he gives not only the harrowing story of how this tiger he had drawn had just attacked a young grocer, but also adds some exceedingly unusual details. He first gives a complete weather report about heavy snow—"eighteen heavy snowfalls of such magnitude that the trouble of shoveling snow has exasperated people"—that had made regular life in the city impossible. Then he gives an account of the economic difficulties people were facing in this weather. "The price of most goods has gone up and firewood, one *man* at four *bisti*, and kindling one *man* at six *bisti*, were still unobtainable."[62] He continues to write about other basic material shortages. As Sheila Blair and Jonathan Bloom point out: "such immediacy of drawing and specificity of reference are unique in Persian painting and can be explained by Mu'in's unusual choice of subject."[63] What is remarkable here is that instead of classics of Persian poetry being visually complemented, a mundane (albeit dramatic) occurrence is illustrated ex nihilo. Drawing and painting, in that very simple drawing, are in fact liberated from the classical texts, and the daily realities of ordinary people (a young assistant grocers) are given the dignity of time and place, of a court painter's attention. The development, to be sure, was gradual. In the course of his own lifetime, Mo'in began his career illustrating the *Shahnameh* and *Khamseh*, but eventually he proceeded to represent events "in his own lifetime. Such representations have the immediacy of photojournalism and did not belong to any established genre; they needed captions to explain their subject."[64] This innovation also signifies the growing autonomy of the artists, the fact that because of the heavy snow he was homebound, he had to watch his budget, he could not afford to keep himself warm. "This location confirms the growing independence of seventeenth-century painters from royal patronage and court atelier."[65] As it is also evident in Mo'in's painting of his teacher Reza Abbasi (1673), the individuality of the artist and a full consciousness of his craft are now on full display.

By the time we get to the work of Mo'in Mossaver's contemporary Mohammad Zaman (fl. 1649–1704), the artist's exiting of the royal court and entering the wider public sphere extends all the way to exposure to Europe and European art, for Zaman's "work includes figures in European dress and even Biblical scenes based on Flemish and Italian prints, which circulated widely in Safavid Iran, and emphasize such foreign elements as atmosphere, night scenes, and shadow."[66] This expansion and exposure was bound to have formal consequences. "Muhammad Zaman's Europeanizing composition differs from traditional Persian manuscript painting in the use of single-point perspective to create a sense of space and focus attention on the figure of the ruler [focally centered in the painting]."[67] If it had become dominant, this reduction of the deeply cultivated polyfocality of Persian painting to a unifocal perspective could have had catastrophic consequences for the development of the free-floating subjection in the formation of Persian literary *ethos* and could have deeply compromised its transmutation into *chaos* in the nineteenth and twentieth centuries. But the fact that Mohammad Zaman was operating within a still very powerful tradition of multiple settings, and that polyfocality therefore prevailed in many other locations, sustained the course of tropic developments in Persian humanism.[68] What is significant about Mohammad Zaman is his having taken the Persian visual humanism even one step further and allowed it to experiment with even wider public spheres.

Thus as the *logos* of Persian literary humanism moved to Mughal India and discovered and heightened the melodious disposition of its formal diction, its *melos*, at the Safavid court it sublated in the further development of a *paralingual semiosis* through the work of such spectacular artists as Reza Abbasi, Mo'in Mosavver, and Mohammad Zaman, and ultimately the founding of the School of Isfahan. Painting was of course not the only art form that thrived in this period, and the panorama of fine arts extended well into calligraphy and other book-related arts in one direction, and architecture, urban design, and a conscious and ambitious expansion of the public sphere in another.[69] In this Safavid context, painting finally exited the manuscript and received and canonized narratives, as artists exited the court, and as poets started traveling between courts and climes, on their ways expanding the public domain of their crafts. In the Mughal context, the logocentricism of Persian *Adab* turned toward a full recognition of its *melos*, matching the Safavid mutation toward a paralingual semiosis, where in the privacy of royal manuscripts all letters and signifiers melt into signs, signs begin to signate, and all subjection starts dancing like particles of dusty light. Soon these private gestations go public, not just when artists like Reza Abbasi and his students leave the court, but even more pronouncedly and visibly in the magnificence of Safavid architecture and urban design.

Meanwhile in the Ottoman Empire, Persian literary humanism had given rise and momentum to Ottoman Turkish literature and through it had a vicarious life of its own and thus helped pave the way for a cosmopolitan disposition evident in and around the Ottoman territories, thereby the *logos* of Persian *Adab* recognized the *cosmos* of its worldliness. A similar development soon took place in the Indian subcontinent when Persian *Adab* became instrumental in the formation of Urdu language and poetry, with figures like Mirza Asadullah Khan Ghaleb (1796–1869) or Sir Muhammad Iqbal (1877–1938) as two of the most accomplished bilingual poets of their time. As in the case of Ottoman Turkish, in Urdu too, Persian literary imagination has a historic rendezvous with and through another language. The same catalytic effect of Persian literary humanism can be detected in the formation of Judeo-Persian literature. Mawlana Yusuf Yahudi (1688–1755) and his famous *Mokhammas* in praise of Moses is one of the hallmarks of this literary tradition that developed mostly in central Asia.[70] These developments are all critical aspects of the cosmopolitan manifestations of Persian literary worldliness. At the same time, in the southern territories of the Russian empire, in central Asia, Persian literature thrived apace and its *logos* found a multivariate reading of the urbanity, the *polis*, that it had always harbored. It is in central Asia that "beginning in the 15th century, representatives of the middle classes, individual craftsmen, wandering singers, etc., were entering the literary world" and thus gave rise to what Jiri Becka rightly calls "poetry of the town craftsmen."[71]

The atom of *logocentricism* of Persian literary humanism was split open, as it were, in the Timurid period and paved the way over the next centuries and in the context of four empires facing a rising fifth toward a paralingual semiosis in which the literary act of subjection became entirely amorphous, like the dancing particles of dusty light, meeting the eye and sparkling with motion and yet nowhere to be had or held. The *melos* of the Mughals, the semiosis of the Safavids, the *cosmos* of the Ottomans in Anatolia (echoed in Urdu in South Asia and Judeo-Persian in central Asia), and the polis of central Asia—four different sedimentations in four imperial contexts ultimately paved the way for the fateful formation and encounter of Persian literary *ethos* with European imperial experiences. The more this *logos* explodes in multiple gestations, the more Persian literary humanism becomes cosmopolitan, and the more the *subject* becomes amorphous, so that when it enters its historic encounter with European colonialism in the eighteenth through twentieth centuries, the European phenomenon of "modernity" becomes entirely tangential and incidental to it. What I am suggesting here is not a theory of *alternative modernity*—it is an *alternative theory* to modernity, both in its European vintage and in its colonial extensions.

Persian as a Worldly Literature

Appearing on the horizons of multiple imperial settings—in both historical and geographical extensions—Persian literary humanism was on full view as the mighty edifice of a *worldly* (not a "world") literature. This, as for any other worldly literature, has nothing to do with the idea of "world literature," as the proposition is manufactured in western European and North American literary parlance—for the very assumption of "world literature" (understood in Eurocentric terms) in fact means nonworldly literature, local literature, subsidiary, tangential, non-Western (as they say) literatures, and as such the designation robs, denies, and conceals the worldly character of literary traditions beyond the reach of their horizons. Throughout the sixteenth century, the multiple—historical and geographical—worlding of Persian literature implanted itself in four adjacent and concurrent empires, from their centers to their peripheries, and thus constituted a literary cosmopolitanism that fed on these empires' claim to globality but by virtue of its inner drive and confidence transcended them all. The millenarian eschatology at the heart of the Safavid empire gave it a universal determinism that combined its imperial imagination (which it borrowed from the Sassanids) with Islamic metaphysical universalism (which it invested in Shi'ism). From the time of Sheikh Safi al-Din Ardabili, the eponym of the Safavid order and dynasty, there was a mass populist appeal to their claim to divine authority. The same was happening in the Ottoman Empire, which now saw itself as the direct descendent of the early, universal, Muslim empires. The Mughals had a syncretic, cross-cultural, trans-sectarian claim to universality. But at the very same time Persian literary humanism projected a far more global imaginary that extended into four adjacent empires as they were awaiting their fateful encounter with a mightier, fifth, European imperialism.

During the transformative Timurid era, when the classical age of Persian literary humanism comes to an end and we are headed toward an encounter with European imperialism, the inaugural *ethnos/nezhad* of Persian literary humanism had completely sublated and yielded to a performative *logos/sokhan*, while the un/knowing subject at the unsettling heart of its imagination had also imploded in two complementary directions: a *poiêsis* that had made history poetically memorial and a semiosis that had liberated all manner of signs and signing from any legislated semantics. On the magnificent pages of Behzad, signs went dancing—freed from the incarcerated semantics of one grammatology or another. This disquieting liberation made all acts of signification predicated on a retrieval of their signs such that they would sing and dance to unending tunes of their own. From the sixteenth century forward, as the Safavid-Ottoman imperial rivalries drew them both into a Sunni-Shi'i sectarian divide, and as indeed the Russian-Ottoman encounter became a Christian-Muslim conflict, Persian literary humanism had far richer and more fertile ground in which to thrive. It is right here that the transformed imperial dominions of Persian *Adab* reach a full spectacle—so that we have the complete *Aufgehoben* of Persian *logos/sokhan* into *ethos/ hanjar*—readied for the fateful encounter with European imperialism that will be the context in which the final transformation of the central tropes of subjection at the heart of Persian literary humanism will take place and blossom into *chaos/ashub*. That global encounter with European imperialism was initially facilitated, we might suggest, in the context of the Russian empire, where Persian literary imagination in central Asia had to contend with the rise of the mighty Russian literature.

Persian *Adab* was always a literary decoy, a trap for the monarchs, a ruse, a counterdiscourse that opposed, ipso facto, all other discourses of power and subjection, including or perhaps particularly the political, subverting while serving it. It thrived on its own playful frivolity, uncertainty, iconoclastic literariness. Even in its *ethnos* and *logos* phases, it played with words, took them out for happy sojourns with the world—and that, ipso facto, made the doctors of law, custodians of the sacred, and scholastics of absolute certainties nervous; rulers of realms uneasy; and courtiers wondering, suspicious, alert to conspiracies with their swords drawn. The poet was a rebel, even when he was at court, subservient—for he was a magician, words the tricks of his trade. He appeased, he angered, he soothed, he assured—he incriminated. The eventual formation of the *ethos/hanjar* as the central trope of Persian *Adab* was a combination of internal combustion of the un/knowing subject, initially through *poiêsis* and semiosis cultivated in the Timurid period, and then in a choral rise of a paralingual semiosis that spread across four empires, bracing for a fateful encounter with the aterritorial imperialism coming from Europe, which led to the complete staging of its *ethos/ hanjar*. In effect, Persian literary humanism exited its classical phase in the Persianate courts and faced the aterritorial European imperialism, and thereby its transformative *ethos/hanjar* reached for a renewed cosmopolitanism in a much more expansive public sphere, now globally wider. In the European imperial context, the inner dynamic of Persian literary humanism from *ethnos* to *logos* to *ethos* to the brink of *chaos* remained valid, operative, and enduring through and beyond the false consciousness of colonial modernity, which was doubly alienating in its colonized climes: (1) for being *colonial* and robbing the people it colonized of their agency and (2) for becoming a subterfuge concealing the internal dynamics of Persian literary humanism. The battle was fateful, and the historic course of Persian literary imagination was triumphant in its further unfolding in the larger context of European empires and the specific locality of postcolonial nation-states.

Persian literary humanism sustained itself as the variegated site of an autotransformative semblance of subject formation. It remained reproductive in its material intercourse with the changing and successive worlds that historically embraced it. Its autonormativity has never been in insularity, and thus what we are beholding in it is an open-ended reproductive heterotransformativity that is always already transcending itself, always already a semblance of subjectivity, acting as, and thus being, the real thing. As a literary act it is always overcoming itself. This open-ended transference of subject-formation shapes its own iteration in positing agential autonomy. There is not even a *will* here to overcome, let alone replace, any metaphysics. This was a gift to and from Persian literary humanism for a lifetime of more than a 1,000 years having been, having flourished, outside Islamic scholasticism, even if it had to seek temporary refuge from the clerical mosque at the royal court. There is not even a hint of any "transvaluation of values" here (Nietzsche's term for *ressentiment*, for the sour grapes complex). The unending play of *Adab* as both *literature* and *humanity* signifies mimetically and moves on to the next game—leaving no marks, no metaphysics of certainty, behind. Persian literary humanism never had any will to power, only an innate proclivity to play one power against another. In between there were plenty of songs to sing, pictures to paint, poems to recite, dramas to unfold. There was no divinized humanity in Persian literary humanism—for the human moved here as it remained polyfocal, polyvocal, polylocal, mimetically transitory—always—fragile, meandering, mortal. Being here was let be, in Persian literary humanism, and with that being it played hide-and-seek. But it stopped short of what the European project of *modernity* would later call *nihilism*. It had no metaphysics to overcome. But it always mattered. It always cared. It always signified—for art's sake.

7

The Dawn of New Empires

Literary Humanism in Search of Itself (1736–1924)

IN THE eighteenth and the nineteenth centuries, Persian literary humanism perforce exited its habitual home at royal courts and found its bearing in the context of a new imperial setting—something that it had always done, from its very conception during the Saffarid and Samanid periods in the eighth and ninth centuries down to its spread over four adjacent empires in the sixteenth and seventeenth centuries. The only significant and traumatizing difference this time around, which turned out to be the liberating ordeal of Persian literary humanism, was the fact that Persian literati were now facing an *aterritorial* empire that had descended upon them, as if from nowhere. To Persian literati, European imperialism was an immaterial empire at whose epicenter—its cosmopolis, its London, Paris, or Madrid (instead of its Isfahan, Herat, Delhi, or Istanbul)—they were not welcome, for Persian literary humanism was no longer the lingua franca of the imperial imagination. In fact far from it, Persian was not the language of this new imperial conquest: it was, quite to the contrary, the language of its vanquished—and that very fact was precisely the defining moment, the liberating trauma, of what would finally resolve the inner paradox at the heart of Persian literary humanism. It is precisely because of this *aterritorial* estrangement that quite a number of leading members of the literati, either from India or from Iran, traveled to European capitals and wrote extensive travelogues in which they tried to come to terms with this new imaginative geography—and thus gave rise to an extensive travel literature. But even when in Paris or in London for short or even longer periods of time, the language barrier prevented any meaningful entry into the royal courts of the ruling monarchies—except as occasional ambassadors or else as *objets de curiosité*. They would return home and their account would further alienate the literati from what had descended upon them and push them en masse out of the royal court altogether and widely (and in bewilderment) into what would now be eventually recognized and cultivated as a public sphere—in which Persian literary humanism would finally resolve its constitutional and historic paradox—and the defining trope of its *humanitas* would be resolutely transformed from the normalizing *ethos/hanjar* into emancipatory *chaos/ashub*.

Exiting the Court

This historic dislocation of Persian literary humanism from its habitual setting at the helm of reigning empires to the periphery of imperial projects that had their own corresponding culture of imperialism[1] became the defining trauma that gave historic momentum to Persian literary humanism's own internal developments from the Timurid era on, causing and conditioning the transmutation of the *ethos/hanjar* at the heart of Persian literary imagination finally to transmute into *chaos/ashub*. This transmutation, to be sure, was thematically internal to the logic of Persian literary humanism, pushing it forward from within its paralingual semiosis starting in the Timurid period. But the new imperial project that descended upon Persian humanism externalized and exacerbated that internal development. The encounter of Persian literary humanism with European imperialism was thus similar to its initial shell-shocked reaction to the Arab conquest, in which Persian was not the language of conquest and domination but the language of the conquered and vanquished. But this time around Persian literary tradition had more than a 1,000-year history of having been an imperial language, and having grown from its originary *ethnos/nezhad*, as its defining trope, initially to *logos/sokhan* and then to *ethos/hanjar* as the selftransformative moments of its claims to a worldly literature. Predicated on internal developments of its own formative tropes within multiple empires, and now exposed to an imperial onslaught over which it had no discursive control, the *ethos* of Persian literary imagination now sublated, perforce, toward *chaos/ashub*.

Placed by the forces of history outside the ruling European courts of the new imperial projects, Persian literary imagination finally came to its conclusive liberation from its innate epistemic paradox by reversing its habitual *will to power* to a corresponding *will to resist power*—facing European colonialism at its receiving end, where it was now integral to a poetics and politics of defiance, where *semblance* meant immanent apparition, the specter that haunted Europe. It is precisely at this point that European Orientalists enter the scene and effectively pacify and silence the inner dynamic and force of Persian literary humanism, as they give it voice in their own English, French, or German diction. Persian literary humanism was now recast to and for a European audience in a new imperial context. By virtue of the imperial power of that diction, the Persian literary historiography *in toto* began to internalize that pacifying trope, precisely (and paradoxically) at the moment when Persian literary production was in its most defiant, disruptive, and emancipatory moments.

Toward the twilight of the three mighty neighboring empires—the Ottomans, the Safavids, and the Mughals—the magnitude of the Russian empire (1721–1917) and the vast riches of its literature (from Pushkin, Gogol, and Turgenev to Tolstoy, Dostoyevsky, and Chekhov) were overcoming the central Asian context of Persian literary heritage. Meanwhile in the Qajar (1785–1925) realm, which after some tumultuous intervals of the Afsharids (1736–1796) and the Zands (1750–1794) established a long and transformative sway over much of the former territories of the Safavid empire, the reigning (and mostly incompetent) monarchs had to deal with British and Russian colonial onslaughts and imperial conquest. In the Qajar realm, Persian literary outlook had a similar encounter with the rapid rise of European strategic and economic interests in the region and the wave of translations from European literatures. For all intents and purposes, Persian literary humanism produced nothing of enduring significance at the Qajar court, for by now the best and the brightest, the most imaginative and courageous had abandoned the royal courts altogether and entered the fateful encounter with European imperialism as the most powerful impetus of its creative imagination. Succeeding the Mughals in India was also the British Raj (1858–1947), where Persian literature and poetry now had to compete with and lose to English as the new imperial language, while embracing the Urdu that had emerged from within its own bosom to replicate and extend it.

From central Asia to south Asia to western Asia (Iran), Persian literary humanism saw its brightest and most promising either drawn to

European sources to agitate change in their homelands or else just traveling to Europe and to see for themselves what political, philosophical, or literary sources had animated European imperialism. If Mirza Aqa Khan Kermani (1853–1896) from the Qajar realms was the best example of the former, Muhammad Iqbal (1877–1936) from British Raj was the best example of the latter. While Kermani left his native Kerman only to go to Istanbul, where he became a vastly learned intellectual and a deeply committed political activist (for which he finally lost his life at the age of forty-three), Muhammad Iqbal traveled all the way to Europe, received advanced education in England and Germany, and returned to his homeland in soon-to-be-independent Pakistan as the shining star of both Persian and Urdu literary, poetic, and philosophical imagination. Matching these two men and mixing their politics and poetry was the extraordinary figure of Tahereh Qorrat al-Ayn (1814–1852), a revolutionary woman poet who singularly defined the rebellious disposition of her century. From Tahereh Qorrat al-Ayn who never left her homeland, to Mirza Aqa Khan Kermani who went only as far as Istanbul, to Muhammad Iqbal who traveled and studied in the heart of Europe, to Sadriddin Ayni (1878–1954), whose literary career in central Asia began and thrived under the Russians and extended into the Soviet era, the leading Persian literary humanists had categorically exited and in fact revolted against the royal courts, and entered the site of contestation with the abiding presence of European imperialism exacerbating monarchical tyrannies and corruption. Though far from each other in one way or another, these literary humanists were the harbingers of a new dispensation of the heritage they were to wed to posterity.

The seventeenth and eighteenth centuries also witnessed the fateful encounter between Persian (and other neighboring) literary humanism and the European imperial project that had code-named itself "the West" and posited itself as "modern" and everything else that it faced as "traditional" or "pre-modern." This was a time when everything in the previous history of Persian literary production suddenly became traditional, and we are told to witness the rise of modern or "modernist" Persian literature. In the panorama of the inner logic and historic unfolding of Persian literary humanism that I have presented here, this whole notion of literary "modernity" is categorically meaningless, an altogether colonial construct, and thus entirely irrelevant and distorting.

This is so because (1) Persian literature was, for about 1,000 years, changing in depth and magnitude, tropes and genres, within multiple empires and across vast global domains, and was now recasting itself within a new imperial project, something that it had done many times over; (2) this new empire had branded itself modern (because it banked on the French bourgeois revolution of 1789 and its concomitant Enlightenment project), by way of inventing "traditions" in its own past and other people's present, and that internal (provincial) proclivity had nothing to do with literary cultures it encountered; (3) for that reason the trope of modernity is categorically flawed, superfluous, and distorting, when applied to Persian literature. That modernity was received as "colonial modernity" in case of Persian (and any other colonized peoples') literary humanism"—and thus confronted by an "anticolonial modernity," if we were to understand it in those colonial terms. But what I am proposing here is a categorically different course of development—at once worldly and normative—entirely independent of the European trope of modernity as a defining category.

As Persian and other literary sites (Arabic, Chinese, etc.) were being subjected to the colonial construction of traditional or pre-modern categories, aspects of them were also being incorporated into Orientalist, romanticist, or transcendentalist movements in western European and North American contexts. These movements were in effect cannibalizing certain aspects of Persian literary humanism for their own reasons and purposes. Poets like Omar Khayyam, Sa'di, Hafez, and Rumi were paramount in these cannibal feasts on texts removed from their contexts. Against these epistemic distortions, and under the radar of Orientalist modes of knowledge production, anchored around the notion of modernity, Persian literary humanism was progressing apace through its own course of development within a new imperial setup, but this time around it was forcefully placed outside the reigning imperial courts. Persian poets and literati were alienated and estranged from those courts—they were not welcome there, or even missed. They did not exist. They were not there where it was happening, where and when Europeans were imagining their empires. This exiting the royal courts was not an entirely colonial consequence of encounters with European empires. Something had already been happening within the inner logic of Persian literary humanism. The Persian literary *logos* had become an *ethos* from within its internal developments and as it transfused itself from the Timurid into the Mughal, Safavid, and Ottoman empires. What revolutionary painters like Behzad and Reza Abbasi had done in cultivating the paralingual semiosis of Persian literary imagination, and the panorama of poets at the Mughal court had achieved in discovering the Persian *melos* or cultivating its *cosmos* in the Ottoman realms or its *polis* in the Russian empire of central Asian territories had already pushed Persian literary humanism toward an *ethos*, and ultimately *chaos*, or a *will to resist power* entirely domestic to its universal course. This was long before European imperialism had fully entered the scene. The transformation from *ethnos* to *logos* to *ethos* and eventually to *chaos* was a far superior spectrum of subjection and agency than the entire European binary between *tradition* and *modernity* could fathom or offer at the peripheralized edges of its colonial conquests. What I offer here (as I said earlier but wish to repeat) is not a theory of *alternative modernity*—it is an *alternative theory to modernity*, a theory rooted and embedded in the long history of Persian literary humanism, to which the most recent phase of encounter with European imperialism—both its *modernity* and *postmodernity*—was but one other twist in a much longer, much deeper, and much more embedded and enduring history and modality of subjection and agency.

Central Asia

Over the course of the seventeenth and eighteenth centuries, Persian literary humanism eventually packed its belongings and faded out of the defeated courts of the Mughals, the Safavids, and the Ottomans, and faded into a widening public sphere carved out between the two competing imperial projects—the Russians and the British—in three theaters of operation: central, south, and western Asia (Iran).

In central Asia, Persian literary traditions of the Timurid and the Mughal periods became the fertile ground of a renewed pact with history. In the context of two successive empires—the Russians and the Soviets—Persian *Adab* had a fateful and enduring encounter with two vastly unfamiliar imperial contexts. In these two overriding contexts, Persian literary humanism was "nationalized" as an "ethnic" component of the two imperial contexts—with a double, contradictory set of consequences. While it was rooted in a fertile public sphere of its own making in a very exciting, transformative, and revolutionary period and in a rich and diversified social and political context, it was also incorporated into the fabricated "national" regimentation of two imperial projects that by thus "nationalizing" their subject domains in effect domesticated, provincialized, and above all ethnicized and thus subjugated them to the might and majesty of the Russian empire and its literature. Russian literature, while a great literary treasure was a singular source of imperial domination in central Asia, robbing "nativized nations" of the dignity and pride of their own worldly literatures. This "ethnicization" of Persian literature by Soviet and eastern European (Marxist) Orientalism, contemporaneous with the equal ethnicization of the same literature in its west Asian (Iranian) context by western European Orientalists, was categorically antithetical to the innate self-transcendence of a worldly literary imagination by forces domestic to its dialectic. The imperial abuse of that public sphere and the literature and poetry that it had made possible and fruitful notwithstanding, the fact of that historic development had lasting impact on the character and culture of Persian literary humanism.

The origin of central Asia as a site of multiple social and cultural formations dates back to first millennium B.C.E. But since the advent of Islam in the seventh century, central Asia had been integral to the Persianate dynasties and cultures from the Samanids down to the Timurids and even as late as the Mughals. Tajik, Uzbek, Turkic, and other peoples were all integral to the multivariate polities and cultures that successive Persianate empires had formed in vast territories surrounding and including central Asia.[2] At the end of the Timurid dynasty (1370–1506), central Asia began a period of partial and eventual separation from the Persianate worlds of the Safavids, the Mughals, and the Ottomans— though the influence of Mughal poets like Bidel remained constant and even rose. As central Asia began leaving the Persianate empires (the Timurids, the Safavids, and the Mughals) behind, it became increasingly influenced by the Russian empire (1721–1917) and culture—with the Shaybanids (1500–1598) and the Khanate of Bukhara (1500–1785) as the most powerful regional powers covering the span between the decline of the Timurids and the rise of the Russian empire. Predicated on its literary traditions of the classical masters from Rudaki Samarqandi to Jami, Persian literature in central Asian territories eventually succeeded "in the creation of a standard literary language through the adoption of a new, vocalic script, and in particular by transition to the methods of socialist realism and insertion into the multinational Soviet literature."[3]

This in effect meant the relocation of Persian literary culture from Persian script into Cyrillic and from the Timurid environment into the initially Russian and subsequently Soviet (1917–1991) empires. But above all the Soviet Orientalist term of "multinational Soviet literature" is the single most important trope of "ethnicizing" the vastly cosmopolitan Persian literary heritage in its new context. This central Asian development in Persian literary humanism (and not its mechanical Marxist Orientalist reading) will have a lasting and transformative effect on the formation of a public sphere as the emerging domain of its emotive universe.

It is with the appearance of poets like Ahmad Makhdum Donish (1827–1897) that the Persian literary humanism of central Asia assumes its new urban (out of royal court) disposition, ultimately leading to the cultural movement known as *Jadidism* (Newism) with an added element of what literary historian Jiri Becka calls "Bidelism"—namely the extended influence of the Mughal poet Bidel in central Asia.[4] This body of Persian poetry produced in central Asia traced itself back to the mid-fifteenth century and the appearance of figures such as Kamalolddin Binoi (1453–1512), who was born in Herat, spent time in Shiraz and Tabriz, and then went to Samarqand in 1494 and served at the court of Muhammad the Shaybanid monarch. Kamalolddin Binoi was a poet, prose stylist, and musician, most remembered as a master of the *ghazal*. In the period between 1504 and 1510, he wrote *Futuoti Khoni*, a typical historical narrative in prose and poetry on the Timurid model.[5] Badreddin Hiloli (ca. 1471–1529), another poet of this era, thrived in Herat, but he was evidently executed because of his radical ideas. To this day he remains very popular in central Asia. As we trace the earliest signs of Persian poets leaving or denouncing the court it is crucial to remember that Hiloli, for example, had followed the example of Naser Khosrow in denouncing court poetry. It is also here that we notice the earliest signs of more liberated ideas about women. In Hiloli's rendition of "Leili and Majnun," Leili appears as "a determined woman who has the courage to reject the man she is being forced to marry."[6] This more liberated perception of women in Persian poetry is an indication of the expansion of the public sphere to include them in its historic unfolding. Yet another poet, Zainiddin Mahmud Vosif (ca. 1485–1566) traveled extensively in central Asia. He was an accomplished poet but is remembered most for his *Badaye'' al-vaqay'a* and the simplicity of his prose.

Simplification of Persian prose will become a definitive feature of the literary emancipation from the floral formalities of the court, its entrance into the public sphere, and the active cultivation of a new audience for itself.

As the Czech literary historian Jiri Becka points out, the central Asian aspect of the Persian literary traditions (*Tajik*) have not been studied by western European Orientalists—but Soviet and eastern European Orientalists like Becka have tried to cover the gap. This fact has doubly distorted the history of Persian literary humanism—once by omission and then by misappropriation. With their own penchant for incorporating Persian literature into the creation of their "national cultures" within Soviet imperialism, these Marxist Orientalists were instrumental in ethnicizing Persian literary humanism precisely at the moment of its self-sublation when it was thrice-historically removed from its originary *ethnos*. Be that as it may, predicated on the pioneering work of Tajik scholars like Sadr al-Din Ayni, Russian and eastern European Orientalists have done significant work in documenting and navigating this literature—albeit at the service of Soviet (Stalinist) ideological imperialism.

To have a complete picture of this transformative stage, we must recognize the fluidity of contact among central Asian poets irrespective of the dominant political and ideological regimes of the empires that ruled these regions. Central Asian poets were not all confined to their homeland, and the synergy among central Asia, south Asia, and western Asia (Iran) was very much open to these multiple thriving sites. Mushfiqi (1538–1587), a popular satirist, was born in Bukhara, lived in Samarqand, and traveled all the way to Delhi to the court of Akbar. Unsuccessful at the Mughal court, he returned to Bukhara and became close to a local prince, Abdullokhon (1583–1598) of the Shaybanid dynasty. He is a good example of a court poet marking the exit of the emerging generation of poets and literati.[7] What Jiri Becka has rightly characterized as "poetry of the town craftsmen" developed between the fifteenth and eighteenth centuries. The poetry of Mirobid Saiido Nasafi (fl. 1670–1679), whose significance was discovered by Sadriddin Ayni, is characterized by social themes of urban craftsmen: "Saiido was, above all, the representative and perfector of the best traditions of 'craftsmen poetry,' of poetry characterized by social themes, written for the broad masses of townspeople among whom he was extremely popular."[8] Born in Nasaf, Saiido moved to Bukhara, where he "lived and studied with the support of the craftsmen of Bukhara."⁹ The fact that he died in poverty is a clear indication of the precarious nature of this transitional period. Saiido's work is characterized by a simple prose at the service of the social themes he addressed with a penchant for folk and vernacular language.¹⁰

After the rule of Ubaidullokhon (1702–1711) was eventually weakened, Nader Shah (1711–1747) subdued central Asia and incorporated it in his Afsharid realm, and thus the first half of the nineteenth-century struggles among central Asian khanates was very much under the shadow of that monarch with his delusions of grandeur based on former Persianate empires. This is the time when Bidel and Bidelism thrived in central Asia, a clear indication that the Mughal India had persistent contact with central Asia in the wake of Russian imperial conquest of the region. The Russian empire entered the scene with the defeat of Amir Muzaffar (1860–1886). Between 1864 and 1895 the Russian capital showed "no interest in Central Asia" and then from 1895 to 1917, it began expanding "tsarist imperialism."¹¹ After the first Russian revolution, a national bourgeois movement was formed in central Asia along the lines of the New Turk movement, the so-called "Jadidism" (also known as the Young Bukhara movement). It was pan-Islamist and pan-Turkist, hated Jews and Armenians, and had contempt for Tajiks.¹² The Jadidis opposed the 1905 revolution and tried to reconcile science and Islam, thus positing themselves as *Jadidis* (the Newers) up against the *Qadimis* (the Olders).¹³ Jadidism is an expression of separation from old schools and new ideas, which in this case degenerated into reactionary hatred of others.

Incorporation into the Russian empire, of which Jadidism was a by-product, meant central Asia became integral to the Russian encounter with European modernity, elimination of slavery, introduction of European education, and the rise of a national bourgeoisie. Many progressive poets and intellectuals were the product of this encounter. Ahmad Makhdum Donish (1827–1897), born and raised in Bukhara, was an enlightened example of this period—both in his politics and poetry. His important work, *Navader al-Vaqaye'*, is devoted to the importance of "education, culture and technology."¹⁴ Another important figure of this period was Abdulqodir Khoja Savdo (1823–1873), born and raised in Bukhara—a poet, musician, painter, and satirist. Shamsiddin Makhdum Shohin (1859–1894) wrote his version of "Leili and Majnun" in this period, and he too altered the figure of Leili and gave her an emancipated and positive role. It is on the trail of this legacy that Sadriddin Ayni (1878–1954) appears, a product of the Soviet empire though deeply rooted in classical learning, which he creatively connected to social themes. Ayni is rightly considered "the founder of Socialist Realistic literature in Tajikistan.[15]

Persian literature in central Asia entered a new and entirely unprecedented phase, which Soviet and eastern European Orientalists have tried to separate and alienate from the rest of Persian literary humanism, but it is in fact the very same language and literature found under the imperial power of the Soviet Union. This "nationalization" of literature by Soviet Orientalism is entirely different from what developed in Iran, where it was from the very outset, early in the nineteenth century, decidedly anti-imperialist. In central Asia, initially under Russian and subsequently under Soviet imperialism, this "nationalization" was integral to Russian ideological hegemony, and a major component of the propaganda machinery of the empire. In central Asia, Persian was initially written in Latin (up until 1928) and then in Cyrillic (from 1940 forward). But even if it was written in the Chinese alphabet it was still Persian. Pro-Soviet Orientalists have done their best to manufacture a linguistic difference between the Persian and Tajik languages. There is no difference. Under the influence of Russian and Soviet imperialism there are obviously more Russian words in Tajik, which was written in Cyrillic, in the same way that Persian written and spoken in Iran was influenced more by French and English words but written in the Persian alphabet. But if an Iranian, a Tajik, and an Afghan were to be in the same room with a Russian or Czech Orientalist, the three of them could run circles around the Orientalist with the poetry and prose of their common heritage, while the Orientalist was still reaching for his dictionary to decipher them.

What is crucial in the emergence of Persian literary humanism in central Asia is the public space in which it emerged, and upon which the masterpieces of Russian literature had a lasting influence. Russian literature "had already made its way to central Asia before the Revolution through Azerbaijani, Tatar, Uzbek, and a few Tajik translations of Tolstoy, Gogol, Pushkin and other Russian authors, and partly too by translations from other European literatures."[16] Maxim Gorky was particularly influential among this generation of central Asian writers, and thus in the aftermath of the Russian October Revolution of 1917, the Persian literature of central Asia is heavily influenced by Maxim Gorky and Vladimir Mayakovski.[17] This creative and critical awareness of the towering figures of Russian literature and literary critics—by no means limited to Gorky and extending into far greater literary masters, including Tolstoy, Gogol, Dostoyevsky, and Chekhov—had a profound and enduring effect on Persian literary humanism of this period in central Asia and by extension in Iran.

Jiri Becka divides the Soviet-era Persian (Tajik) literary production into three periods: (1) from 1917 to 1929: "It was during this period that a new realistic literature written in the Tajik language came into being in central Asia. Ayni and Lahuti had enduring significance on this period"; (2) from 1929 to 1941: "In the 1930's there was tremendous growth in the number of readers of Tajik literature, which of course greatly spurred on literary production"; (3) from 1941 to 1945: "Although the war period covered only four years, it played an important part in the development of Tajik literature, having contributed to progress in patriotic and heroic lyrical poetry and in drama"; (4) from 1945 to the present (1968): "Tajik literature began to outgrow the local boundaries also through being translated by other nations. Its best works have been translated into more than twenty languages (mostly through Russian translations) spoken in the Soviet Union as well as into other languages"—among them Chinese, Hindi, English, French, German, Spanish, and Portuguese.[18] Social realism, expanded readership, exposure to the brutalities of war, translation from the masterpieces of European literatures, and having a global audience in mind thus come together to define the Soviet period of Tajik/ Persian literature of central Asia in this period—all of which contributed to the formation of a public sphere into which the literati immigrated from the court and thus posited the trope of "nation" as the modus operandi of their literary productions. That Soviet and eastern European Orientalists have branded this literary production ethnically "national" by way of incorporating them into Soviet imperial domination of central Asia does not compromise the autonomy and integrity (and above all the emancipatory potentials) of that public space.

The central Asian domain of Persian literary humanism produced three major figures during the Soviet era—a literature that was regionally termed "Soviet Tajik literature." Sadriddin Ayni began his intellectual and political career as a member of the Jadidism movement but later became a communist and produced prolifically during the Soviet era. His novels, branded "social realist" by Soviet scholars, deal with the Bukhara Khanate. "After 1905 Ayni became increasingly absorbed in social issues, a preoccupation that began to be reflected in his poetry."[19] The next prominent figure of this era was Abolqasem Lahuti (1887–1957), who was born and raised in the Qajar domains but eventually moved to the Soviet Union and settled in Tajikistan. He was significant both in a central Asian context and also during the Constitutional Revolution in Iran. Lahuti was instrumental in opening up new vistas of literary exploration in Persian humanism. "He used meters that were not part of the classical tradition, such as syllabic verse, and through his translation of Shakespeare's *Othello* introduced blank verse into Tajik poetry."[20] The third major figure was Mirzo Tursunzoda (1911–1977), who was an authority on oral literature, but his own poetry was mostly on contemporary social themes. During and after the collapse of the Soviet Union, central Asia (Tajikistan in particular) continued to produce a magnificent aspect of Persian literary humanism with its distinct character and flavor deeply influenced by the regional politics of the nineteenth century, the Russian revolution, and ultimately the Soviet Union in both positive and negative ways. Since the collapse of the Soviet Union in 1991, this literature has been liberated from that imperial context, and some major figures have tried to reconnect with complementary trends in Iran.[21]

A similar separation between court-affiliated literati and those exiting it and entering a public sphere is evident in the distinction between two Afghan literary masters—Mawlana Abd al-Rauf, affiliated with the court of King Habibollah (1901–1919), and Mahmud Tarzi (1865–1933), who also was deeply influenced by the Young Turk movement.[22] Mahmud Tarzi's *Seraj-al-Akhbar*, the newspaper he published (1911–1919) to propagate his ideas, was an exemplary model of journalism through which the public sphere was exponentially expanded and the increasing number of literati fully integrated into the emerging society. Though fortune at the time may seem to have thrown Persian literati an ambsace, the course of Persian literary humanism was altered for good—for it gained far more in the public sphere it crafted and defined than it lost in the royal courts it served—thus forever resolving its historic paradox. This historic overslaughing of the court for the public sphere would be the most significant event in the entire history of Persian literary humanism, emotively overtaking its royal geneaology by far more powerful moral imperatives—facilitating the move from *ethos* to *chaos* as the defining trope of Persian *Adab* in its self-sublating history.

South Asia

The ascendency of British imperial domination of south Asia and the eventual imposition of English language and literature in the subcontinent inevitably led to the decline of Persian *Adab*. At the same time, the renewed significance of the Urdu language and its literature, dating back to the fourteenth century and the exquisite legacy of the poet-musician Amir Khosrow (1253–1325), meant the eventual rise of a literary tradition in which Persian had found a renewed, vicarious, life.[23] As had happened with the rise of Turkish literature in the Ottoman territories, Persian received an extended lease on life in a different language and literature, this time in Urdu, and set off into new and uncharted territories.

In luminary figures like Mirza Asadullah Ghaleb (1796–1869) we see the rise of bilingual poets in south Asia who were "ambidextrous" in Persian and Urdu. This phenomenon in a way replicates bilingual Persian poets who were equally "ambidextrous" in Persian and Arabic early in Islamic history. Ghaleb was a very proud practitioner of Persian poetry, boasting to his contemporaries of the superiority of his Persian as opposed to Indo-Persian.[24] Ghaleb thrived in his *qasida* and *ghazals* in both Persian and Urdu—priding himself on his command of Persian, although his poetry in Urdu was far more popular. But by 1835, "the Macaulay edict abolished Persian as the official language in those parts of India that were under the British East India Company, and introduced English instead. This was a heavy blow for Muslim culture, for Persian had been, even in its late, complicated forms, the unifying element for the Indian intelligentsia, including Hindus who were often well-versed in the poetry of Hafez and Rumi."[25] The combination of the innate emergence of Urdu as a thriving literary imagination and British imperialism eventually pushed Persian to the archival memory of the subcontinent. A new empire had now overtaken India, and Persian was no longer its lingua franca. English had supplanted it. Urdu was now extending the Persian literary imagination into a different diction and dispensation.[26]

But not without one last bravura. With Muhammad Iqbal (1877–1938) the Indian subcontinent gave birth to its last, greatest Persian poet, prose stylist, philosopher, and political leader of world-historic magnitude.[27] Iqbal was the magnificent manifestation of the best literary and philosophical imagination of the Persian culture in south Asia meeting the challenge and the trauma of European imperial conquest and context. After his early education in Lahore, Iqbal was sent by his parents to Europe, where he studied in Cambridge, Heidelberg, and Munich. After his higher education, Iqbal eventually emerged as a leading Muslim revivalist of his time, with lasting influence on subsequent generations in and out of his homeland. In his *Asrar-e Khodi* (*Secrets of Selfhood*) (1915) Iqbal appealed to Muslims around the world to revive Islam as the modus operandi of a renewed pact with history. Two years later he composed *Romuz-e Bikhodi* (*Riddles of Selflessness*) (1917) and after that *Zabur-e Ajam* (*Persian Psalms*) (1927).

In all these works, Iqbal's paramount concern was to discover a new language—at once emotive and rational, Islamic and worldly—that would reaffirm Islam in confrontation with European colonial modernity. This confrontation with European modernity had drawn him deeper back toward Islam—while in the Persian language he detected a literary imagination that would speak to that purpose. But why Persian—why not Urdu or English? In Persian, Iqbal had detected a lingua franca at once integral and yet tangential to Islam, as a metaphysics that he thought needed recasting for its encounter with colonial modernity. English was too alien, Arabic too intimate to the scholastic certainties of Islam. Iqbal's prose and poetry are deeply philosophical, mystical, and above all metaphysical—and all of those in Persian, a literary lingua franca that was deliberately posited against Islamic scholasticism as the ideological foregrounding of the Arab caliphate. It is right here, in the work of Iqbal, that the metamorphic transmutation of the *ethos* of Persian literary humanism into creative *chaos* has its initial manifestations. Iqbal forced Persian poetic and philosophical imagination into a dissipative interchange at once unsettling and exciting. The world was changing fast around Iqbal, and in Persian prose and poetry he found a philosophical anchorage at once reassuring and malleable.

It is quite telling that Iqbal discovered Hafez through Goethe—a symbolic indication of how he consistently tried to navigate a path between his received Muslim heritage and his projected encounter with

European modernity through the medium of Persian literary humanism. His masterpiece, *Javid-nama*, he modeled on Dante's *Divine Comedy*— but instead of Beatrice, Rumi guides Iqbal through Paradise. "Since his early days Iqbal had been collecting material for a work comparable to Goethe's *Faust*, Dante's *Divine Comedy*, and Milton's *Paradise Lost*."[28] His *Payam-e Mashriq* was conceived as a response to Goethe's *West-östlicher Divan*. Why this approximation, this conscious and deliberate use of European masterpieces as models for his recasting of Persian humanism? Jiri Becka's judgment on Iqbal is quite harsh—that his work "reflects the philosophical insecurity and wavering of the Muslim middle classes, which had lost their bearings in the political developments between the two world wars. They may be seen as part of the wave of romantic revolutionaries that had laid hold of Indian literature at the time."[29] But nevertheless there is a ring of truth in this reading of Iqbal—for his work reflects the magnitude of a Muslim mind cracking under the pressure of exposure to European literary and philosophical monuments, which he tried to match with the book he wrote on the history of philosophy in Iran, *The Development of Metaphysics in Persia* (1908). His poetry and philosophy are fused together and informed by a thorough desire for nation-building as the simulacrum of a public sphere (an abode) where the revolutionary poet-philosopher can invite his fellow Muslims to gather, for which reason he became a champion of nationalism in Pakistan. That nationalism, as the site of contestation with "the West," was meant to provide him with a creative confidence from which to launch his poetic and philosophical manifesto. He is, as such, the product of British imperial rule, a turbulence delivered in poetic confidence, predicated on a constant attempt to confront "the West" in its own terms— terms that at once enabled and limited Iqbal.

Iqbal's final book, *Armaghan-e Hejaz* (*Gift from Hejaz*) (1938), composed in Persian and Urdu poetry and published a few months after his death, reflects his mature thoughts, getting ready in effect to meet his creator as a Muslim who had opted to speak to him and to mankind in Persian. At the center of that lifelong mission was a conception of self, who and what and whence he, as a Muslim, was.

> Peykar-e Hasti ze Asrar-e khodi-ast
>
> The embodiment of Being is a manifestation of Selfhood,
> Whatever you see is from the hidden heart of Being.

> When Selfhood awakened its Self,
> It made the thinkable world visible.
> Hundreds of worlds are hidden in its Essence,
> Its alterity is evident in Its affirmation.
> Seeds of sedition are strewn upon the world
> The Self sees itself as other than Itself . . . [30]

Iqbal's sense of the self is the microcosmic manifestation of the macro-cosmic conception of the public sphere that he was instrumental in de-fining as the modality, the template, of the nation-state. This sense of the self gives that public sphere a depth of *interiority*, in which Iqbal maps out and navigates the inner dimensions of the souls that were to populate those nations. It is not accidental that Iqbal is considered the national poet of Pakistan before Pakistan was even created. He dreamt that nation in the discursive facilities of the public space he had crafted in his Persian poetry and populated it with the souls of postcolonial people he had en-visaged, enabled, from inside out.

In the south Asian domain, Persian literary humanism was equally forced out of the royal court of the Mughals and, persona non grata at the European colonial courts, pushed toward the creation of a public sphere as the principal site of normative and emotive contestation and conversation against British imperialism—the iconic transference of an emotive universe at once frightful and exhilarating. Coming out of the royal courts and released into the uncharted territories of expansive public domains, the operative *ethos* of Persian literary humanism was now facing a historic challenge. Perhaps the greatest representative of this period in south Asia was Muhammad Iqbal, whose poetry becomes the site of a creative dialogue between Islam and Europe by way of pos-iting a public sphere on the premise of Persian poetic prowess on which he wanted to create the Pakistani nation-state, as the locus classicus of that public sphere. For that very reason, Iqbal's prose and poetry are exceedingly accessible and he has no interest in the florid language of the courts. He was fully aware of the expanded and open-ended public sphere in which his ideas were to be presented, for which reason he opted to write in Persian rather than in Urdu—a language at once uni-versal and yet native to him, the imperial language of the Mughals, which he now extended into the public sphere, the *nation*. "Iqbal com-posed the *Asrar-e Khodi* in Persian," notes the distinguished literary scholar Annemarie Schimmel, "because he rightly believed that only then would the poem have an appeal beyond the borders of India and be read by Persians and Turks as well as by European Orientalists (who for the most part were not conversant in Urdu)."[31] But that purpose is not sufficient. Persian was the lingua franca of the last Muslim empire in south Asia before the British conquest. Iqbal had "democratized" that language by bringing it out of the court and into the public sphere, allowing it to form a Muslim nationhood in south Asia.

It is in this context that Iqbal also revives Rumi and Hafez and gives them a new lease on life in his poetic universe—effectively translating their lyrical and mystical universalism into a newly globalized public domain. This awareness of the globalized public sphere is also evident in Iqbal's writing of *The Development of Metaphysics in Persia*, in which he sought to give a new reading of the history of philosophy in Islamic Iran. This book, which was in fact his doctoral thesis in philosophy at the University of Munich, traces the development of metaphysics in its Iranian context from the time of Zoroaster to the advent of Baha'ism. From prose to poetry, navigating from English to Persian to Urdu, Iqbal was fully engaged in establishing the emotive contours of a public sphere upon which a nation could be built, somewhere between the dissolving Mughal Empire, and the ascendant British imperialism—a place in Persian literary humanism where he found a lasting and enabling significance. "It seem that with Iqbal the history of Persian in the subcontinent finds its end, as a candle flickers up once more to full glow shortly before it is extinguished."[32] From the ashes of that candle have arisen the fire of literary masterpieces and professors of English and comparative literature of south Asian origin all around the world.

Iran

If Persian literature developed in central Asia in the bosom of the Russian and then Soviet empires, and it eventually faded away in south Asia under the shadow of the British Empire, in Iran of the nineteenth and twentieth centuries it went through the traumatizing rebirthing channel of exiting the royal court altogether and being born again in the context of the rivalry between the British and Russian (and subsequently Soviet and American) empires. Just as Iran was no longer the site of Persian literary humanism in the sixteenth century because the Safavids were no longer hospitable to it (except of course in multiple manners of visual humanism and architectural urbanism that resulted in a paralingual semiosis of vast epistemic and aesthetic consequences), and it found a much more rich and fulfilling domain in the Mughal empire in India (and thus the Safavids, the Mughals, and the Ottomans complemented each other in multiple registers), in the nineteenth century and during the Qajar period that dynasty was no longer the moral or imaginative frame of Persian literary humanism. The European colonial conquests and control over the Qajar dynasty and territories (Russians in the north and the British in the south) had made the European imperialism the creative context of literary imagination, and thus the significance of a crucial body of "travel literature" as well as translations from European sources into Persian. The frame of reference in Persian literary humanism has always been "power," and as the Qajars began to lose it so did poets and literati begin to wonder and wander around and be drawn to the emerging centers of power, and since they had no room in those European centers they perforce crafted and constituted a public sphere in which they would thrive on what they would begin to call their *vatan* (homeland)—and thus the origin of *vatan* (nation) and *vatanparasti* (nationalism), which at their roots remained a *literary* proposition of this historical vintage. In short: it was not political nationalism that gave birth to nationalist prose and poetry; it was (in exactly the opposition direction) nationalist prose and poetry that, positing a public sphere as its emerging locus classicus, gave rise to political nationalism.

From the rise of the Safavid dynasty in the sixteenth century to commencement of a close and fateful encounter between the Qajars and Russian, French, and British imperialism in the early nineteenth century, Persian literary imagination suffered its darkest period in Iran, a time literary historians consider a *doreh fetrat* (period of decline). The Safavid monarchs had no interest in Persian poets, especially those that praised them to the sky. Shah Tahmasp is reported to have said that poets habitually thrive on attributing exaggerated virtues to monarchs that far exceed their mortal attributes, and thus the excellence of poems is measured by how many lies can be rhymed together, while if they were to praise Muslim saints and Shi'i imams their poetry, no matter how sublime, would still fall short of those sacred entities.[33] So in a rather insightful piece of literary criticism the king had in effect posited a mimetic crisis in Persian poetic imagination: stop abusing weak metaphors and start inventing more rising allegories. That mimetic challenge turned out to be a blessing in disguise, for it forced Persian poets to pack their belongings and leave the court—and thus they were forced to think and narrate a new habitat for themselves, a public domain they will soon call *vatan*. Meanwhile, the Safavids preferred to strengthen their ideological claim to legitimacy via Shi'i saints, which resulted in perhaps the most magnificent period in Shi'i scholastic philosophy and mysticism.[34] But nothing of any enduring literary significance from Shiraz, Isfahan, Tabriz, or any other major city that had given birth to the Sa'dis or Hafezes of previous empires.

From the rise to power of Shah Isma'il (r. 1502–1524) to the ascendency of Fath Ali Shah (r. 1797–1834), a period of some 300 years, no great poet or literary prose stylist of any enduring significance emerged in Iran—a period that saw the greatest achievements of Persian *Adab* in the Indian subcontinent under the Mughals, as well as significant literary developments in central Asia under the cultural and political ascendency of the Russian empire (1721–1917), overwhelming the regional dynasties of the Shaybanids (1500–1598) and Khanate of Bukhara (1500–1785). Without simultaneous attention to these three sites, as well as to important developments under the Ottomans, with whom many Persian poets sought refuge, we will not have a clear picture of this crucial transitional period. The rise of Turkish literature in the Ottoman domain and the emergence of Urdu in the subcontinent are equally momentous substitutional literary humanisms that partake in Persian but then go their own parallel ways, giving rise to crucial traditions of their own.

For the period from the late Afsharids (1736–1796) to the early Qajars (1785–1925), eminent literary historians like Yahya Aryanpour (1907–1985) propose a *doreh-ye bazgasht* (period of return) when in the city of Isfahan, for example, we witness a resurrection of court-affiliated Persian poetry.[35] From the reign of Fath Ali Shah forward, under the patronage of such viziers as Mirza Abolqasem Qaem-Maqam Farahani (1779–1835) and with the appearance of poets like Malik al-Sho'ara Fath Ali Khan Saba (1765–1822), court poetry returned to Iran—feeble, jaundiced, entirely dispirited, and unimpressive. These poets wanted "to return" to previous masters by way of overcoming the decline of the Safavid period. This period of *bazgasht* is considered a kind of "coup" against the *Sabk-e Hendi* (Indian Style), as some later poets have put it, but it did not produce anything except some "fake Sa'dis, fake Sana'is, fake Manuchehris, etc."[36] The same is true about prose, where much weak imitation of previous historiography takes place, with the notable exception of Abolqasem Qaem-Maqam, who had a certain verve and panache in his elegant prose.[37] Qaem-Maqam was both a prominent statesman, a crucial figure in negotiating peace treaties between the defeated Qajars and the triumphant Russian empire, and a literary prose stylist. He is instrumental in the simplification of Persian prose in his mostly political (but also some private) correspondence because he was dealing with Russian and British imperialism encroaching upon his patron Qajars, and thus the forced encounter with the global powers twisted the heavily stylized Persian prose to behave and come out of its habitual courtly pomposity.[38] To be sure, court poetry continued well into the long and languorous reign of Naser al-Din Shah (1848–1896), with poets like Shahab Isfahani, Mirza Abbas Foroughi, or Soroush. Mirza Habib Qa'ani (d. 1891) is another prominent poet of the Naser al-Din Shah period who is important perhaps mostly because he refers in his poetry to crucial historical events such as the attempted assassination of Naser al-Shah by the revolutionary Babis or to the public execution of the Babis.[39] Qa'ani is now less remembered for the fact that he was also a distinguished Islamic philosopher than for the fact that he was the first Persian court poet who knew French. Why would he know French—except for the fact that the French, British, and Russian empires were calling—knocking at the gates of the Qajar courts and their attendants?

With Zarrin Taj Tahereh Qorrat al-Ayn (1814–1852), Persian poetry categorically exits the royal court and enters the emerging public domain (in this case radically revolutionary and anti-monarchic) for good. She might thus be rightly considered the mother of Persian poetry, the literary humanist par excellence, as it finally exits the royal court and enters the battlefield (literally) of history, thus positing a public sphere in which its renewed aspirations are articulated in an emancipated political environment. With Tahereh Qorrat al-Ayn the *ethos* of Persian literary humanism meets the moment of its transfusion into creative *chaos*—whereby the episteme of systematicity and coherence finally yields to the open-ended expanse of dissipative alterity, of imagining the otherwise. While Qorrat al-Ayn's significance is ordinarily assayed as a radical Babi revolutionary with daring theological ideas, it is also as a literary humanist, and above all as a poet, that she figures so prominently in the context of Persian literary humanism at this extraordinarily crucial juncture.

Tahereh Qorrat al-Ayn was born to a prominent jurist family in Qazvin and studied Islamic law and theology and Arabic and Persian languages and literatures, in her early childhood and youth. She was married off to her cousin and sent to Najaf to accompany her husband.[40] But that was not meant to be. She was soon attracted to the ideas of Shaykh Ahmadi Ahsa'i (1753–1826) and began corresponding with his disciple and successor Seyyed Kazem Rashti (1793–1843) and soon became a leading revolutionary figure in the ensuing Babi movement that was predicated on the preparatory ideas of Ahsa'i and led by Ali Mohammad Bab (1819–1850). Qorrat al-Ayn abandoned her husband and three children and became a leading figure in the Babi revolutionary uprising. She moved back to Qazvin to promote the Babi cause, but her father-in-law and uncle, a staunch enemy of the Babi movement, was murdered and she was forced to leave for Tehran (for she was a suspect) and subsequently for Dasht Badasht near Shahrud close to the Caspian Sea in northern Iran, where she unveiled herself and led a militant faction of the Babi movement. She was finally arrested and executed in Tehran in the aftermath of an assassination attempt against Naser al-Din Shah. In the figure of Tahereh Qorrat al-Ayn we see the combination of both a literary humanist and a scholastic scholar with a revolutionary bent—in her poetry and political activism the two come together to turn her into the inaugural moment of a vastly transformed emotive universe. She combined Persian and Arabic in her deeply moving and passionate *ghazals*. Nowhere else from central Asia to south Asia to Iran does any poet come close to her in her daring imagination, astonishing command of Persian and Arabic, and defiant fluency in her poetic imagination. She single-handedly delivered Persian literary humanism from its depleted and jaundiced fate at the Qajar court into the rich and rewarding public sphere she commanded for an open-ended posterity. This is one of her most famous *ghazals*:

Gar beh to oftadam nazar, chehreh beh chehreh ru beh ru . . .

If I were to see you, face to face, countenance to countenance.
I'd explain my sorrow of separation, point by point, detail upon detail.
Hoping to see you, I have become like a wind blowing through
Streets after streets, door by door, house by house, ally after ally.

Flows from my eyes, yearning for you, my bloodied heart
Just like Tigris to Tigris, sea to sea, spring upon spring,
   brook by brook.
My heart has woven your love upon the textile of my soul
Weft by weft, thread by thread, yarn by yarn, warp by warp.
Tahereh looked for you in her heart and did not find you,
Page by page, leaf by leaf, veil after veil, hiding into hiding.[41]

The Qajar encounter with aggressive French, British, and Russian imperialism began in earnest early in the nineteenth century. By mid-century, Tahereh Qorrat al-Ayn had grabbed Persian poetry by the neck and pulled it out of the Qajar court and right into the streets and alleys of urban revolutionary uprisings. Between imperial encroachments and grassroots uprisings, Persian literary humanism was where it had been historically forced out to be. By now, Persian prose and poetry had become simpler and far worldlier—and needed to reach much wider circles of readership. The introduction of the printing press was the clearest sign of the creation of the public sphere outside the court, where the illustrated manuscript was a luxurious art and a craft for the mighty, the learned, and the few. That world was now changing. Carmelite priests brought the first printing machines to Isfahan.[42] The Armenian community in Isfahan also had access to printing machines. But these were all brought by Christians for religious publications. For specifically public purposes, Mirza Saleh Shirazi, a student dispatched by Prince Abbas Mirza (1789–1833) to Europe in 1815 to learn his contemporary arts and sciences, is credited with having brought back the first printing machine from England, where he had studied.[43]

Next to the printing machine the introduction of newspapers was another major indication of the inauguration of an expansive and far-reaching public sphere. The same Mirza Saleh Shirazi is credited with establishing the first newspaper, *Kaghaz-e Akhbar* (*Newspaper*) in Iran (first published in May 1837).[44] But expatriate Iranians—those who like Mirza Saleh had left their homeland but unlike him could not return for fear of persecution, were also publishing newspapers such as *Akhtar*, published in Istanbul, where Mirza Aqa Khan Kermani, Shaykh Ahmadi Ruhi, and Mirza Mehdi Khan Tabrizi, chief among other expatriate intellectuals, published their essays. Other newspapers included *Qanun*, which was published by the leading Iranian reformist intellectual Mirza Malkam Khan (1833–1908) in London, *Hekmat* published in

Cairo, *Soraya* published in Cairo, and *Habl al-Matin* published in Kolkata. The publication of these pioneering newspapers by leading Iranian intellectuals from outside their homeland is among the first indications that the public sphere upon which the notion of *vatan* was being mapped out was in fact not limited to the emerging boundaries of Iran as a nation-state and that it was much vaster than the current boundaries of the country. It is from this wider domain that the public sphere becomes the site of the emerging nation-state. The very notion of "expatriate," as a result, becomes rather inaccurate because the combination of globalized European empires that necessitated these public spheres and domestic tyrannies that preempted them had forced these emerging domains to be transnational too, for the boundaries of the national were still territorially flexible, amorphous, and porous. For that reason the very notion of nation, predicated on this transnational formation of that public sphere is ipso facto contextual to globalizing empires—from the French and British to the Russian and even the Ottoman—to which these poets and literati were responding. The public sphere that these humanists were crafting was being carved among multiple empires and thus was transnational by definition. It is even appropriate to suggest that the very idea of "Iran" as a nation-state was in fact imagined, crafted, and narrated very much by literary intellectuals outside "Iran." The amorphous disposition of this emerging public sphere called *vatan*, as the rising locus classicus of Persian literary humanism is definitive to the transformation of its *ethos* into *chaos*.

The establishment of *Dar al-Fonun* in 1851 by the prominent Qajar Prime Minister Amir Kabir (1807–1852) as a court-initiated academy had far-reaching impact by way of bringing contemporary pedagogy and education to Iran and thus exposing the public sphere to contemporary modes of knowledge production. Though very much limited to the members of the aristocracy and the Qajar elite, *Dar al-Fonun* nevertheless was instrumental in enriching the moral and normative imagination of the public sphere at large. The establishment of these new schools did not remain limited to the aristocracy, and soon pioneering educators like Mirza Hasan Roshdiyeh (1851–1944) expanded that domain to include the public at large, initially in Tabriz but subsequently in other cities as well—much to the chagrin and anger of certain conservative forces in the clerical establishment that naturally saw in this innovation a threat to their power and prestige.[45] Roshdiyeh was a key

figure in expanding the public education in Iran and introducing regi-
mented learning, including the simplification of teaching the Persian alphabet to the younger generation. Roshdiyeh was born to a clerical family but abandoned the idea of a clerical education in favor of traveling to
the Ottoman territories and learning about new methods of education.
He learned about contemporary schooling in Beirut and became the first
teacher and founder of progressive pedagogy in Iran. These schools soon
multiplied and became a principle locus of expanding the public sphere.

Along with the establishment of public schools, the simplification
of Persian prose was equally important in facilitating the formation of
the public sphere. The eventual simplification of Persian prose and poetry, coterminous with their exiting the heavily formalized court diction, was very much indebted to the rise of a translation movement
from European sources. These translations required a command of the
original European languages, forcing Persian prose to respond to these
mostly contemporary fictional, historical, or scientific sources, access to
printing machines, and the obvious interests of an increasing reading
public. Mirza Habib Isfahani's translation of James Morier's (1780–
1849) *The Adventures of Hajji Baba of Ispahan* (1824) is perhaps the best
example of turning a vicious Orientalist spoof into a masterpiece of not
just critical thinking about corruption in the royal court but in fact the
glorious possibilities of Persian language in its newfound domains.[46]

The expatriate intellectuals played a crucial role in establishing
newspapers, translating European source materials, simplifying Persian
prose, and writing pioneering books and essays addressing the public at
large. Such leading members of the literati as Abd al-Rahim Talebof Tabrizi (1834–1911), a groundbreaking literary critic; Haji Zeyn al-Abedin
Maraghe'i (1839–1910), a pioneering novelist; Mirza Malkam Khan
(1833–1908), an Armenian-Iranian reformist committed to propagating
the rule of law in his homeland; Mirza Fath Ali Akhondzadeh (1812–
1878), a leading literary critic and playwright; and Mirza Aqa Tabrizi, a
contemporary of Akhondzadeh who is considered the father of Persian
drama, mostly thrived in central Asia and the Caucasus, as well as in the
Ottoman territories or even in Europe. In fact by virtue of their work,
these expatriate intellectuals helped to posit the public sphere upon
which they imagined their homeland and thereby projected the trope of
"coming back to Iran" to realize how backward it had remained, as it is
perhaps best evident in Haji Zeyn al-Abedin Maraghe'i's novel *Siyahat-*

nameh Ibrahim Beig (*Ibrahim Beig Travelogue*) (1903). In territorial and imaginative terms, the *patria* was thus not entirely defined yet, and as a result *expatriate* was in the process of being defined by this very genera-tion and through the very literature they were producing. As Firoozeh Kashani-Sabet has demonstrated in her exquisite study of this period, "frontier fictions" begin to get hold of Iran in the nineteenth century, when the fluctuating borders were subject to multiple imperial confron-tations, in the midst of which the land-based notion of "nation" emerges and informs a widespread interest in (among other related fields) ar-chaeology and mapmaking.[47] It is precisely at this period that Seyyed Jamal al-Din Asadabadi (1838–1897) as a leading transnational revolu-tionary becomes a clear indication that the formation of the public sphere as the bedrock of the nation was indeed as global as the globalized em-pires that it faced.[48]

It is also during this period that the figure of Mirza Aqa Khan Ker-mani (1853–1896) emerges as the leading and perhaps the first "public intellectual" in the specific sense of the term, morally and imaginatively shaped entirely outside the Qajar court and in fact in active opposition to it—for the most part as an expatriate intellectual in Istanbul and in a global context. He and his comrades Shaykh Ahmad Ruhi (1855–1896), Khabir al-Molk (d. 1896), and Mirza Habib Isfahani (1834–1894) were all "in exile" in Istanbul but—and here is the point—only as exiles they could have had the extraordinary impact they had in their homeland, both in positing a public sphere and thriving in it. It is crucial to keep in mind here that this pubic sphere is not posited against any private sphere, but against the imperial court as the locus classicus of Persian literary humanism. Persian poets and literati imagine, narrate, and de-liver this space and occupy it in juxtaposition to and in fact in defiance of their habitual habitat at the royal court. The formation of nation and thereby nation-state politicizes this literary invention and the rise of the bourgeois then populates it.

Dis-Oriented Orientalists

In south Asia, Persian literary humanism eventually lost to the colonially promoted predominance of English literature—a development that ulti-mately triumphed in the rise of such postcolonial literary achieve-ments as those of Salman Rushdie, Jhumpa Lahiri, Arundhati Roy, and Aravind Adiga—south Asians who knew English better than their parents' generation knew Persian.[49] In central Asia, it went under the influence of Russian literary masterpieces and was even written in the Cyrillic alphabet, as in the Ottoman territories; the modern Turkish literature that was inspired by it went through Kemalist reform and was even written in the Latin alphabet. In Iran, however, it eventually invented and occupied a public sphere in which it assumed anticolonial nationalist terms within the context of Russian and British (and subsequently Soviet and American) imperialism. By now the *ethos* of Persian literary humanism had reached the zenith of its tropic triumphs—from *ethnos/nezhad*, to *logos/sokhan*, to *ethos/hanjar*—and was now reaching for its iconoclastic moment of *chaos/ashub*, in which the triumphant paradigms of coherence and consistency finally yielded to the disruptive alterities of subjection and agency on multiple, variant, and inconclusive registers.

Precisely at this period of Persian literary humanism, European Orientalism produced a sustained scholarly tradition that culminated in the monumental work of E. G. Browne (1862–1926), perhaps the most eminent European Orientalist, who spent a lifetime introducing Persian literature to generations of European audiences. Although other European Orientalists have done important work on Persian literature, it was E. G. Browne that after a lifetime of scholarship, in close collaboration with such learned Iranian scholars as Mohammad Qazvini, produced a solid body of scholarship in the field. No critical stand vis-à-vis the flawed epistemic assumptions of this body of scholarship should detract from its historical significance, to which all subsequent generations of scholarship are in fact indebted.

Predicated on this history, and pacing carefully through Persian literary humanism long before and now long after the production of Orientalist scholarship over the last 200 years, I believe the reading of Persian literary humanism has been subject to two distorting wills to narrate from two diametrically opposed directions: European Orientalism and American literary criticism—one predicated on a detailed knowledge and the other on an equally massive ignorance. The focal point of their distortion is the trope of "nation" and "nationalism," which they both misread within their respective frames of references—European Orientalism reading Persian literary humanism as positing the *ethnos* of their literary historiography and thus forcing it back to its earliest period by manufacturing an ethnic nationalist narrative of Persian literature, and the other by casting it into what they alternately call "Third World literature" or even worse, "world literature." It was not only the European Orientalists, but even, or particularly, the leading American literary critics who cared to write about "Third World literature" who were in fact worse in this violent *ethnicization* of an inherently worldly literature—and here their textual ignorance of that literature mirrored the Orientalists' theoretical illiteracy of what they were perfectly capable of reading but unable to theorize (decipher its evolving literary tropes).

The greatest damage that Orientalist scholarship has done to our reading of Persian literary humanism, as best evident in the very superior example of it in E. G. Browne's *A Literary History of Persia* (1902–1920), is to recast its entire historic development into singularly ethnic nationalist terms, namely the opposite of what had inherently, historically, and narratively happened to it. Internally, Persian literary humanism had reached a complete historical self-consciousness, self-realization, and maturity, and yet Orientalist scholarship, entirely blind to this inner dynamic and reading one masterpiece after another like an archivist a dead scroll, recast it into ethnic nationalist terms. Precisely at a moment when the *ethos* of Persian literary humanism had transformed into *chaos*, the most advanced stage of its tropic developments, E. G. Browne's *A Literary History of Persia*, as the foremost and the grandest product of Orientalist scholarship on Persian literature, completely glossed over that development and produced a flat narrative tone, just like an exceedingly competent musician whistling the entire Fifth Symphony by Beethoven by repeating its four-note opening motif. The principal source of the grandest distortion of Persian literary humanism is due to two complementary regressions: (1) it is written without the slightest awareness, let alone attention, to the inner dynamics of this literary morphology (the movement from *ethnos* to *logos* to *ethos* to *chaos* as the defining morphemes of literary production) and a complete ahistorical ethnicization of a vastly worldly and cosmopolitan literary consciousness; and (2) doing so precisely at a time (1900–1930) when the *ethos* of that evolving morphology was in fact achieving a renewed pact with its ethics of responsibility in a recently globalized (colonized) world and moving toward the realization of its chaotic phase. These phases were not teleological or predetermined, but morphological, conditioned by the changing historical circumstances of literary production, and the humanism that it entailed.

De-Worlding Worldly Literatures

The groundbreaking ideas of the leading American literary critic Fredric Jameson are crucial in having shaped the perspective of generations of scholarship about what they call and consider "non-Western" or "Third World" or alternatively, "world literature"—which ranges from Persian and Arabic to Japanese and Chinese down to anything else produced in Asia, Africa, or Latin America. In effect what they call "world literature" is any literature produced outside Europe and North America. Europe and North America are not part of this "world" that produces "world literature"—they are on another planet. On this planet, called "the West," they just produce "literature," as the measure by which "world literature" on our planet is assessed and assayed. The key question of "world literature" (with its echoes going back to Goethe's *Weltliteratur* articulated in 1827), as evident in Jameson's assessment of it, is always contingent on two different and opposing trends in "Western literature": one in which it is read openly and democratically and the other that wants to guard it closely and exclusively. Both William Bennett (conservative) and Fredric Jameson (not conservative), at two opposing ends of this spectrum, approvingly quote Maynard Mack's question: "How long can a democratic nation afford to support a narcissistic mimicry so transfixed by its own image?"[50] So the idea of "world literature" is there to address this ailment (of having been transfixed on its image)—like a medicine one might be prescribed to take, an antibiotic, for example, for some bacterial infection. "World literature" is there, something that North American and western European literary scholars have discovered (invented) to attend to a deficiency (like a vitamin or mineral deficiency) in their literary imagination.

The problem with Jameson and the generation of literary scholarship that he best represents is that he only sees one (imperial) world, the one in which he lives, the one that has empowered him to write and narrate the "Third World literature," and the rest of the world is precisely that—"the rest of the world," peripheral nations that are condemned to produce "national allegories," subject to his universal will to knowledge, to be a knowing subject. From Alexander the Great to George W. Bush (retroactively strung together), leaders have enabled the pen (or the keyboard) that writes, designates, categorizes, and thus denigrates the "Third World literature." That very act of literary production might be integral to a different world Jameson does not know, does not recognize, has yet to discover; it does not occur to him, as it did not occur to generations of literary scholars all the way back to Goethe. Jameson's concern is curricular—the education of young Americans, soldiers and bankers of his empire. He believes the old notions of "world literature" are no longer sufficient and they need to be rethought (William Bennett, Jameson's interlocutor, was Secretary of Education under President Reagan)—and this necessity of rethinking is coterminous with the globalization of the American empire, which requires a corresponding conception of "world literature." The Soviet Union was about to collapse, the American empire was soon to enter its monopolar universalism, and that horizon had authored an equally global will to know the "world literature." Jameson does not beat around any proverbial bush that it is indeed "the reinvention of cultural studies in the United States [that] demands the reinvention, in a new situation, of what Goethe long ago theorized as 'world literature.'"[51] This "reinvention of cultural studies" in the United States was itself a microcosm of the globalized American empire, where inside the United States a more "multicultural" interest had become evident on university campuses by virtue of massive labor migrations in the 1970s and 1980s. The fact of a cosmopolitan culture inside and the presumption of an empire outside had given this generation of literary scholars, just like their counterparts from the Ghaznavids to the Mughals, the compelling illusion that they own the world and need to imagine it in their literary dreams.

From Goethe to Jameson, the invention of "world literature" had always had something to do with the body and soul of other people's worldly literature, robbing it of that innate worldliness by casting it into the no-man's-land of the "Third World." What Jameson calls "Third World literature," which as he says, "is not necessarily a narrower subject," is of the same sort: reinventing the First (his own) World by cannibalizing other people's *worldly* literature, irrespective of or else indifferent to the living organicity of those literatures. Jameson does not even shy away from asserting empathically "Third World cultures offer a more unvarnished challenging image of ourselves."[52] This "ourselves" is the people of North America and western Europe, people of the empire, who read and produce literature. They have "a more unvarnished" and "challenging" image, Jameson believes, that is fortunately still extant for archeological and anthropological investigation in Asia, Africa, and Latin

America—which they can excavate and investigate for a better understanding of their own "varnished image." Such vintage racism, from the vantage point of a colonial (yet to be varnished) perspective, coming from a leading American Marxist, is quite refreshing, but it should not detract from the more fundamental issue in Jameson's project, for he believes that not just the "Third World literature," but in fact "world literature" is instrumental for "a new view of ourselves." "Ourselves" is the nondenominational "West" that has wiped out—both physically and metaphysically—its own internal as well as external alterities. The world outside this "West" exists only so far as it can serve as an inanimate mirror in which "the West" can see itself. That world, thus turned into a "thing," a mirror, has no worldly reality sui generis, for unless the metaphysical eye of "the West" can see itself in it, it does not exist. In contemporary figures such as Fredric Jameson we can well imagine the nature and disposition of Arab imperialism and the production of Arab *Adab*, and in turn the multiple Persianate empires, and the production of Persian *Adab*, in which the imperial foregrounding is the *condito sine qua non* of a worldly, global imagination. Jameson at the heart of the American empire is identical to al-Jahiz (781–869) or Khwajah Nasir al-Din al-Tusi (1201–1274) in the Arab and Persianate courts, respectively.

Equally unabashedly, Jameson predicates his reading of "Third World literature" on the Eurocentric genealogy that delegates "the rest of the world" to "primitive or tribal" (Asian), or else Asiatic/Oriental despotism (China and India).[53] Upon this classification, his categorical pronouncement is that "All Third World literatures are necessarily . . . allegorical—and this in a very specific way: They are to be read as what I will call national allegories, even . . . when their forms develop out of essentially Western machines of representation, such as the novel."[54]

The number of ways in which this phrase, issued from the self-assured imperial hubris of its author's moment in history, is flawed is staggering. "Third World" is the invention of the colonizing mind of the triumphalist world that calls itself "the First" or "the West"—otherwise it has no reality sui generis, and thus it cannot have a literature. The conventional phrasing is a cliché with no referent. It is a self-serving, self-firsting, denigrating phrase that ipso facto casts what is categorically unknown to the literary critic to a third-rate status, site unseen. There is no such thing as "Third World literature." It is a product of North American departments of English and comparative literature (as the literary accoutrement of American empire) that nobody buys anywhere around the globe—except of course graduate students implicated in these programs. No professor of English and comparative literature can decide for literature produced even in his own backyard what it must or must not "necessarily" do or be—except by assuming the imperial distance that his accidental birth has given him. Above all, the literatures produced around the globe—from Chinese and Bengali to Persian, Arabic, Swahili, Igbo, Hausa, Amharic, Yoruba, and so on—are categorically *not* "national allegories," whether they are produced as novels, novellas, short stories, poetry, drama, or anything else in between. All "national literatures" are sites of contestation between defeated (but defiant) imperial domains, dominant imperial hegemonies, and above all the public sphere they have managed to create and craft—and thus by definition *not* national allegories.

Empires and Nations

Both the territorial space of nation/state and the political ideology of nationalism emerged from the literary constitution of a public sphere for Persian literary humanism, fresh out of the royal courts to find a new habitat within which to articulate a renewed dispensation for itself. What I propose here is that the idea of the nation/state and thus nationalism are essentially literary productions manufactured deliberately at a crucial juncture in the history of Persian literary humanism when it had exited the Persianate courts (its locus classicus) and had to carve out a new location for itself. Here I take the words of the leading Iranian nationalist poet of the Constitutional Revolution (1906–1911) Aref Qazvini (1882–1934), quite literally, when he said that before his poetry scarce anyone knew what *vatan* even meant.[55] Of course they did not. He invented it—poetically, as a space into which Persian literary humanism would transmigrate body and soul for a renewed historical dispensation. Aref Qazvini and other nationalist poets invented and occupied *vatan*/homeland/nation as the site of their literary imagination outside the royal court.

This idea of *vatan* or homeland, however, was not of identical disposition in all its relevant domains (central Asia, south Asia, and Iran) as Persian literary humanism began its historic journey of moving away from the royal court and into the public sphere of its own making. In central Asia, the idea of "the nation" and the national space were entirely *subservient* to initially Russian and subsequently Soviet imperialism—but it kept the language and literature alive and thriving in exceedingly important domains, despite the fact that it was cast into the imperial alphabet of Cyrillic. In south Asia it was *conversant and cajoling* with British imperialism but eventually lost to the might of English language and literature and at the time of the partition of India in 1948 it also lost to an ostensibly Islamist/Hindu binary reading of "nation." Meanwhile in Iran it remained adamantly resistant and antagonistic and above all defiant to both Russian and British imperialism (later to be replaced by American-Soviet imperialism), and thus kept the idea of the nation/state and perforce nationalism, as constitutionally literary. The cultivation of the public sphere as the *nexus classicus* of Persian literary humanism had three different but complementary registers in central Asia, south Asia, and Iran—three variants on a common theme as literary imagination found new bearings out of the Persianate royal court and into a site of contestation with new imperial projects.

Nation and nationalism as public sphere were the link between the faded imperialisms in which Persian literary humanism was paramount and the emerging imperialism (eventually code-named "Western") in which it was not—and by virtue of which exclusion it was finally delivered from its historic paradox and was no longer an instrument of a will to power but integral to a will to resist power. As the Ottoman-Safavid-Mughal empires collectively faded into the dominance of European empires, national territories and nationalism emerged as the site of the public sphere for articulating literary humanism outside the royal court—in opposing (Iran), accommodating (central Asia), or conversing (south Asia) with the imperialism it faced, but all the while occupying a public domain outside its habitat of the royal Persianate courts. Alienated from the European courts and their languages and literatures of conquest, Persian literary humanism was actively cultivating a public sphere for its renewed articulation. This is the period when Persian prose and poetry is radically simplified for a mass readership, printing machines are brought in and mass circulation newspapers and other periodicals begin to appear, translation from non-Persian languages begin to be produced and circulated (mostly in Ottoman and central Asian territories), and thereby the public sphere is defined, articulated, constituted, and incessantly expanded until the Constitutional Revolution, which can be considered the first rebellion of a literarily constituted public domain against the royal court and Russian and British imperialism.

In his *Imagined Communities* (1983), Benedict Anderson's thoughts on the process of nation-building as the construction of an imaginative community are insightful but limited. A *nation* for Anderson is a community of people who are in an imaginative recollection of themselves as a people. In an "anthropological spirit," as he stipulates, a nation is "an imagined political community—imagined as both inherently limited and sovereign. It is imagined because the members of even the smallest nation will never know most of their fellow-members, meet them, or even hear of them, yet in the minds of each lives the image of their communion."[56] Anderson is very insightful about the manner in which members of a nation imaginatively partake in the collective image they have constructed of themselves, even though they may never see each other face to face. Nations are thus posited as both limited in their boundaries (where other nations begin) and also as sovereign. Anderson traces the origin of the idea of nation to the end of divine and dynastic sovereignty. "Print-capitalism" he suggests has been instrumental in the making of these imagined communities. These are all apt and verifiable observations so far as the modus operandi of nations and nationalism as a mode of imagining communities and purposefully committing to them are concerned. But Anderson has nothing to say, except the formation of nations marking the end of divine and dynastic power, about the empowering engine of nations—while I suggest the exiting of the Persian literati from the Muslim royal courts and their nonadmittance into the European imperial courts forces them into a public sphere crafted in between the two, and it is that public sphere that the literati term "the nation," poetically imagining and coining it, and the rest of society then follows suit by virtue of both physically being on that public sphere and co-imagining it with their poets and literati. Nationalism does not *mark* the end of dynastic or divine legitimacy—it is the code-name of the public space that poets and literati manufacture to occupy outside the dynastic courts. The end of the divine or the dynastic legitimacies is coterminous with the formation of nations—not its cause. You may have dynasties (Qajars and Pahlavis), empires (Russian/Soviet), and assumptions of divine dispensations (United States, the Islamic Republic) claiming nations and their nationalisms. But the positing of the public sphere as the site of the nation has to do with poets and literati imagining a habitat for their legitimacy and operation. In the public sphere of nations, Persian poets and literati not only find a new modus operandi but in fact resolve their historic paradox of at once serving and subverting the royal power that embraced them. The principle agents in "imagining" the nation, quite obviously, are poets and the literati, people in the business of imagining things. But that imagination has a material force, which is the world-historic exiting of the poets and literati from the dynastic courts and the royal elite, where they made their livelihood.

In his *Nation and Its Fragments* (1993), Partha Chatterjee's thoughts on nationalism are a vast improvement on Benedict Anderson's but are still very much bogged down in the circuitous issue of "alternative modernities," and as such is entirely inattentive to the force that begins the process of imagining the nation in the first place.[57] The advantage of Chatterjee's reading of nationalism is that it consciously posits itself on the colonial site and thus effectively exposes Benedict Anderson's typically Eurocentric take on nationalism and equally typical proclivity to universalize that location. On the colonial site, however, Chaterjee rightly considers the rise of nationalism as predicated not on *identity*, as Anderson had suggested, but in fact on *difference*. Chatterjee distinguishes between *political nationalism* and *communal nationalism*, which he traces back to the colonial moment when anticolonial nationalists first crafted the idea of "nations" and then put it to political use. He in effect posits the community nationalism of a specific site like Bengal against the political nationalism of India. He thus distinguishes between material and spiritual domains for the idea of nationalism, where nation was first imagined in its spiritual dimensions before it was later put to political use. If the dominant ideas of anticolonial nationalism was very much informed by the globalized market economy, its alterity, communal nationalism was entirely homegrown and in fact disrupted the hegemony that colonialism had extended from the European Enlightenment to conquered lands.

The problem with Chatterjee's otherwise excellent counter-reading of nationalism from the colonial site is that it is too dialogical against the colonial reading of anticolonial nationalism—effectively accepting the binary between tradition and modernity and thus at best offering an alternative route between nations and their modernities. But what I suggest here, again, takes its point of departure from the moment when Persian literati exited the Mughal, the Safavid, and the Ottoman courts perforce (and as a material force) and, not being admitted to the imperial project that had landed on them, were forced into a tertiary space that they thus constituted, theorized, sang, populated, and above all imagined as the nation. Chatterjee in effect agrees with Anderson that nation-building is an imaginative enterprise but differs with his statement that the European manner of imagining the nation provides a model for the rest of the world. But Chatterjee's issue, like many other south Asian subalternists, dwells in the preoccupation with always finding alternative modes of producing (noncolonial suppositions of) modernities. They take the European imperial trope of modernity for granted and never build an alternative theory *to* modernity rather than an alternative theory *of* modernity.

The other problem with Chatterjee's formulation is that it is very much Bengal-specific and is unresponsive to cases we encounter in central Asia, where nationalism was formed not in opposition and contestation but in fact by way of accommodating initially Russian and subsequently Soviet imperialism. In the Iranian case, which faced both British and Russian imperialism, the constitution of nations was far more intimately connected to the formation of a combative confrontation. The intimate link between colonial domination and anticolonial responses that Chatterjee best theorizes is in fact very much a south Asian trait specific to encountering British imperialism—an intimacy perhaps best captured by the exquisite essay of Ashis Nandy, "Intimate Enemy."[58] This very much limits how much Chatterjee is willing to depart from Anderson—for in producing modernities they remain thoroughly connected—while the advantage of Chatterjee is that he goes down to the site of contestation for producing imaginative nationhood. But again he takes such tropes as nations, secularism, modernity, civil society, and so on, all for granted and tries (successfully) to offer alternative readings of them from ground up. Chatterjee thrives on finding manners in which the notion of "the East" is disturbed by local traditions of multiple worlds. But that is the extent of his vision and ambition. He just wants to prove "the East" is not "the East" that "the West" had imagined. That is a good and worthy but very limited project. Chatterjee's project is not nativist, which is good, but it is oppositional and reactive, which is limited. It is from within the three sites of encounter between Persian literary humanism and the empires they faced—in central Asia, south Asia, and Iran—that I suggest the literary citation of the public sphere as the modus operandi of nations and nationalism—a reading that is no longer trapped within the trope of European modernity or even anticolonial modernity.

That nations are imagined communities is a truism; that on the colonial site that imagination has a reality sui generis and is not following the Western model is equally valid and insightful. But if one of these two insights takes the Western experience as universal and exemplary, the other takes the colonial site as a reality sui generis and scarcely thinks historically through the forms of subject formation prior to the ascendency of European imperialism, namely the history of the subcontinent under the Mughal Empire, and what was the role of literary imagination at that court, and what happened to the matter and manner of literary production once it exited that court perforce and faced the might and majesty of a European imperialism into which it had no literary access or import. The public sphere that Persian literary humanism thus posited and cultivated for itself, I consider and submit as the territorial disposition of nation and thus nationalism.

Orientalism East and West

In the course of the eighteenth and nineteenth centuries, Persian literary humanism eventually found itself in a new and unprecedented imperial setting. In this imperial project, the trope of (capitalist) modernity was an Enlightenment legacy, celebrating its triumphant victory at the expense of effectively dismissing, denigrating, historicizing, and overcoming both its own European past and the cultures and climes of resistances it met at the peripheralized borders of its colonial conquests and imagination. The modernity of the European Enlightenment was coterminous with an innately global capitalism and in its missionary zeal it dismissed any mode of resistance to its instrumental rationality as "traditional"—as much in its own European past as in the present history and geography of lands it conquered. Receiving European modernity through the gun barrel of colonialism was the fate of much of the globe. Being told that "man" was now free to think precisely at the moment that colonized men and women were enslaved to the superior military might of their conquerors was a contradiction in terms, while at the same time, and ipso facto, those conquerors nullified, disregarded, ignored, and altogether distorted whatever mode of agential formations or subjections they had cultivated in their own worldly and imperial cultures.

For the internal logic of Persian literary humanism, as I have outlined it in detail in this book, this European modernity, in its originary disposition or colonial rendition, was an extraneous imposition. It was an imperial category thematically and theoretically forced by colonial might and facilitated by colonized minds upon the surface of a literary humanism (*Adab*) that had its own internal logic, external texture, worldly dispensation, imperial pedigree, historical depth and longevity, geographical expanse, and moral imagination. The systematic, gradual, and logical transformation of the originary *ethnos* of Persian literary humanism into *logos*, and then *ethos*, and finally toward a radically transformative *chaos* was and remains a far richer texture and *topoi* for enduring subjection, historical agency, and normative and moral authority. Blind to its inner logic and rhetoric, literary morphology and manners of subjection, European Orientalists and American literary comparatists alike mutilated the history of Persian literary humanism and carved it violently into "classical," "medieval," or "modern" (or any other variation on that theme) slices. This act of literary cannibalism was a by-product of colonial modernity and as such not only distorts Persian literary humanism but in fact discomposes the innate logic of its historic and narrative unfolding.

Orientalism of western European vintage (best exemplified by E. G. Browne's exemplary scholarship) took the "Persian" designation in the entire history of Persian literary humanism as the marker of a national designation and not as the lingua franca of multiple empires, and thus categorically cast Persian literary history in ethno-nationalist terms *(ethnos)* and thereby glossed over and pacified the inner tensions of Persian literary humanism, its driving force from one empire to another. The ethnic nationalism of the Reza Shah era, beholden to German National Socialism, led the leading Iranian literati to deeply internalize that ethnic nationalism and replicate Browne and other European Orientalists' historiography in multiple and varied registers. This categorical ethnicizing of a vastly more complicated literary imagination deboned a literary cosmogony and concealed its innate power of agential subjection in multiple tropic (axiomatic) registers. At the same time, Russian and by extension eastern European Orientalism, obviously influenced by a mechanical Marxist historiography (best exemplified by the exquisite scholarship of Jan Rypka), sought to incorporate it into a universal socialist narrative of revolt. The fate of Persian (or any other non-European) literary history was not any better in the hands of American literary comparatists (as best exemplified by the distinguished literary and cultural critic Fredric Jameson), for they in effect theorized the "non-Western" literature into a vacuous and unnerved "Third World," or even worse, "world literature," which was the selfsame ethnicization of Orientalists minus their detailed learning and erudition. So in effect, while Orientalism did this distorting ethnicization of Persian literary humanism (at the height of its metamorphic self-sublation into *chaos/ashub*), in substance, theorists of "(Third) World literature" did it in theory—both in effect pacifying the inner dynamics of a literary legacy that had remained for both camps a terra incognita.

I am not offering this literary cosmogony and the trajectory of multiple agential subjections it had historically enabled, from *ethnos* to *logos* to *ethos* to *chaos*, as an alternative theory *of* modernity. I have discovered this genealogy in Persian literary humanism and suggest it as an alternative theory *to* modernity.

8

~~⟹◆⟸~~

The Final Frontiers

New Persian Literary Humanism (1906 to the Present)

THE COSMOPOLITAN worldliness of Persian literary humanism commenced in a confrontation with the alienating imperium of Arab domination soon after the Muslim conquest of the Sassanid empire. Phase after phase this worldliness has planted itself in the context of multiple and successive global empires. The retrieving of these successive global worldings of Persian literary humanism from the sixteenth century forward narratively confronts its systematic de-worlding by both European Orientalism and its twin peak of colonially manufactured ethnic nationalism. Our understanding of Persian literary humanism has as a result been subjected to systematic appropriation and dispossession with every learned word that European Orientalists have uttered about its "history"—a history they have narrated (not out of any malice but by the force of history blowing to their side) by way of ending with European "modernity" as the crowning achievement of humanity.

Under the pressure of the Arab invasion, Persian literary humanism moved toward a new cosmopolitan worldliness, which from the ninth to the sixteenth centuries systematically worked within successive self-conscious registers of worldliness. With the distancing memories of the Sassanid empire and under the imperial domination of the Umayyads and the Abbasids, we have the rise of Turkic and Mongol empires, in which Persian literary humanism altogether abandoned its inaugural formation around the *ethnos* of its narrative coagulation for a definitive transformation into the *logos* of the language it was now celebrating. "Persian" was now a marker of eloquence in a language and not an ethnic designation that would contradict the transnational formation of that *logos*. From the Iranian empire to the Turkic empire to the Mongol empire, these morphological self-transmutations finally emerged as full self-recognition during the Turko-Mongol Timurid Empire when Persian language and literature fully recognized and discovered itself as a globally anchored literary humanism. The period from the sixteenth to the twenty-first centuries is the next phase in the self-transformation of Persian literary humanism, when its *logos*, having overcome *ethnos* in the earlier phases, is now itself overcome by and eventually yields to a universalizing *ethos* that renders the literary language autonomous and self-referential. Beginning in the sixteenth century, Persian literary humanism spread deep into the Indian subcontinent, encountered European imperialism, eventually lost to British colonialism, marked by the Macaulay Act (English Education Act) of 1835, and from that fateful encounter it finally exited the royal court altogether, and through this historic move the central paradox of Persian literary humanism was categorically resolved and a public space was formed upon which it now had a new rendezvous with history.

This final phase of *Adab* concludes with the most recent episode (1906 to the present), when Persian literary humanism reached a fully self-conscious worldly cosmopolitanism outside any royal court and firmly grounded in the public space of its own making, which it calls *vatan* (homeland, nation). In a fateful encounter with European colonialism, Persian literary humanism meets in a public space the people it had figuratively imagined and liberated from imperial domination, whereby it reached for a postcolonial cosmopolitanism. From the sixteenth century forward, Persian *Adab* faced European imperialism, losing the imperial cosmopolitan confidence it had cultivated over the centuries in its natural habitat in the royal court, until eventually it regained it in the twentieth century, and through the crucibles of fiction, poetry, and film fully realized its worldliness, and thus worked toward a renewed self-conscious cosmopolitanism. As the Orientalists were busy casting Persian literary humanism in ethnic nationalist terms, Iranian poets and literati were busy recasting themselves in a renewed cosmopolitanism, on the dominant map of the world, as evident in Nima Yushij's poetry or Sadeq Hedayat's fiction—as indeed in all other related fields of drama, cinema, photography, etc. In this context, Iranian poets, literati, and artists picked up from where their predecessors had left behind, in the de-sedimentation of the subject, moving the *ethos/hanjar* of their literary heritage toward the creative *chaos/ ashub* of the world they were claiming, in which the subject was now dissolving in uncertain terms.

In reading the historic manner of subjection in and through Persian literary humanism, Michel Foucault's take on power and its discursive sedimentation appears thoroughly ethnocentric in its European disposition. Power in fact articulates itself in Europe in part by way of effacing the multiple manners of subjection in non-Europe, in the other-than-Europe, which fact facilitates and enables its self-Europeanization, as is evident in the Orientalist project, integral to the European project of self-subjection into modernity, but catastrophic to others by its erasure of their worldliness and submersion into "the Orient"—which for Immanuel Kant (the towering figure of the European Enlightenment) meant the entire world minus western Europe. Foucault's "classic age" is precisely the age of colonialism, of which he takes no theoretical notice and the fact of which is entirely tangential to his theories (and thus the origin of Edward Said's work). The process of subjection in "the Orient" (thus Orientalized and self-alienated) was eclipsed by the European worldliness concealing non-European worlds and their worldlinesses. Against the grain of that systematic erasure, from the seventh to the twenty-first centuries there was a pyramidal expansion of the initial *ethnos* of Persian literary humanism into *logos* (seventh to fifteenth centuries—from the Samanids to the Timurids), and then from *logos* to *ethos* (fifteenth to twentieth centuries—Timurids to the Qajars), and from *ethos* to *chaos* (twentieth to twenty-first centuries—Pahlavis to the present). In the *ethnos* stage, the emerging literary subject ethically asserted itself against the Arab invasion in order to identify itself. In the *logos* stage, the selfsame subject actively de-ethnicized itself by the force of successive imperial contexts. In the *ethos* stage, the subject ethicized itself by a combination of internal combustions and external encounters. In the final stage the subject disperses itself in multiple creative registers and dispensations. After every stage the moral and material base of Persian *Adab* expands and transforms itself until it ultimately realizes itself in the public space it crafts in the nineteenth and twentieth centuries and calls *vatan* (homeland, nation).

I offer Persian literary humanism as a poetics of alterity that has historically posited itself as a decentered and decentering form of resistance against a recalcitrant accoutrement of (imperial) power. It has been a creative catalyst that exposes the structural functionality of power, as a participating observer that both facilitated and subverted the constitution of the power of subjection—of making and breaking the proposition of being *human*. I offer Persian *Adab* as the antithesis of *regimes of governmentality*—medieval and modern—evident and embedded in Islamic scholasticism in general and in the *nomocentricity* of the Islamic law and the *logocentricism* of Islamic theocentric philosophy in particular. The sheer *linguisticality* of Persian *Adab* as a hermeneutic project overrides even the *homocentricity* of Islamic mysticism and releases it in open-ended, literary directions. The free-floating, counterdiscursive disposition of Persian *Adab* will only make sense when read against the violent discursive subjection of Muslims (qua Muslims) in either nomocentric (juridical) or logocentric (theophilosophical) terms. The individual was made a subject, the *human* of humanism, by virtue of the counterdiscursive disposition of Persian literary humanism—the subject of this destabilizing project was itself unstable and thrived on that instability.

The human at the center of Persian *Adab* was a literary subject, formed narratively, morphologically self-transformative, open-ended, transversal, inconclusive, unsettled, unsettling, but always agential. Through that agency Persian literary humanism has historically posited a space for questioning the *regime du savoir* embedded in Islamic scholasticism, not by way of offering an alternative to it but by way of suspending any assumption of a knowing subject—and doing so by example. If we were to use the language of the Italian philosopher Gianni Vattimo, Persian literary humanism has been predicated on an *il pensiero debole* (weak thought): it was never conducive to the formation, let alone the sovereignty, of an all-knowing subject; it has been predicated on the will to resist power, ipso facto, by way of substituting the sovereign, subjecting the absolutist, king by and to the uncertain human. This subversive power has expanded from the political realm into its discursive renditions. The nomocentricity of the Islamic law and the logocentricity of Islamic scholasticism, both squarely at the service of the successive imperial dominations from the Ghaznavids to the Ottomans, posited and legislated the "Muslim subject." Persian literary humanism de-sedimented this dominant matrix of subjection. The "Muslim subject" was subject to Islamic law and Islamic scholasticism, and that subjection made Muslims as Muslim subjects tied to and embedded in their own "knowledge" of themselves. Persian literary humanism was the way out of that trap.

Persian literary humanism was posited against what Michel Foucault has (in the Christian context) called "pastoral power," though obviously within an Islamic frame of reference and against clerical domination and its scholastic discourses. The pastoral, or clerical, power of Islam as a network of discourses was first and foremost embedded in the nomocentricity if its law, extended into and exacerbated by the logocentricity of its scholasticism, and subsequently evanesced into the theoeroticism of its mysticism. Persian literary humanism never became *discursive*, always remaining subject-forming in an inconclusive manner, predicated on a *differed defiance*—just like a mighty river running under your feet, shaping the universe of your habitat and imagination as you walk on that bridge, crossing transversally over it. Persian literary humanism has thus been a *remissive* space (Philip Rieff's words) posited in between the *interdictory* injunctions of the God-terms of Islamic scholasticism and the *transgressive* urges that have historically challenged those injunctions.

The trajectory of the internal transmutation of Persian literary humanism in the empowering context of multiple empires from the Samanids down to the Qajars is precisely what is concealed and covered under the rubric of Orientalist knowledge production that came in the aftermath of European colonialism from the late eighteenth century forward. My contention is that the bugbear of "modernity" was a colonially transported ideological trope that glossed over these historic developments in the cosmopolitan worldliness of Persian literary humanism—where the splitting of the focal fissure of the un/knowing subject has traversed in multiple directions, a fact and phenomenon categorically ignored by the overriding Orientalist reading of Persian *Adab*. This innate self-transformative force within Persian literary humanism has remained completely hidden to the naked eye of the Orientalist and North American comparative literary studies alike. From classical Orientalism down to area studies and beyond, these successive *regimes du savoir* (predicated on the European imperial *la volonté de savoir*) have not only been incapable of detecting this morphological transmutation of the subject at the heart of Persian literary humanism, they have been in fact invested in glossing over it. My detection and theorizing of that morphology of the subject in Persian literary humanism is a trajectory that I have posited here against (not adjacent to) the European predicament of modernity—a predicament that Europe has universalized by the imperial power of its autonormative knowledge production.

A Constitutional Revolution

Resuming our story of Persian literary humanism in its fateful encounter with European imperialism, we reach the cataclysmic events of the Constitutional Revolution of 1906–1911, which reads like the festive birth of Iran as a nation-state, populated by self-conscious citizens mobilized to define their inalienable rights in a free and democratic polity. The poetry of this nascent period in particular became the traumatic birth channel of the inaugural ideas of *vatan* (homeland, nation) and *vatanparasti* (nationalism). The Constitutional Revolution was the first political expression of the public sphere that poets and literati, now completely out of the royal courts, had crafted with diligence and steadfast determination. The Constitutional Revolution was a vast social uprising that was not initiated by a rising dynasty against another—and thus it did not result in the collapse of the Qajars and the ascendency of another monarchy. More than a decade after the success of the Constitutional Revolution, another dynasty, the Pahlavis, came to power through a military coup sponsored by the colonial interest of the British in the region, in direct opposition to the equally colonial interests of the Russian empire, which had a powerful presence in the Qajar court. But the revolution itself was the political manifestation of a pubic sphere now fully cognizant of itself. It was a revolution that was initiated by the emerging citizens of a potentially democratic polity based on their newly minted public sphere. It was a revolution from the public sphere, by the public sphere, and for the public sphere. Constitutional revolution was the crowning achievement of that public sphere and the singularly influential poet Aref Qazvini was its singer and songwriter.

> Az khun-e javanan-e vatan laleh damideh . . .
>
> From the blood of the youth of this homeland
> Tulips have grown,
> Mourning their tall fallen figures
> Cypress is bent,

From this sorrow, under the shade of the rose
The Nightingale has hidden.
From sadness of this loss,
The Rose, just like me, has torn its shirt.
Oh how cruel art thou fate![1]

The revolutionary uprising that resulted in the drafting of a constitution limiting the absolutist monarchy began during the reign of the feeble and corrupt Qajar king Mozaffar al-Din Shah (1896–1907). His reign coincided with the height of colonial interest in Iran, with the Russian and British empires competing for control of his court, as he borrowed money from the Russians to finance his vacations in Europe, while the state was going to ruins under the control of his corrupt courtiers. Massive street demonstrations began late in 1905 with a historic alliance between the clergy and the merchant class, a collaboration that went back to the 1892 Tobacco Revolt, which protested the Qajar court having granted a British merchant exclusive rights to cultivation and trade in tobacco. A revolutionary component of the clerical class in alliance with the rising Iranian bourgeoisie was thus striking an alliance for the control of the public space specifically targeting the court. By January 1906 the king had agreed to dismiss his prime minister and establish an *Edalat-khaneh* (*House of Justice*). The truce, however, was temporary and the confrontation between the royal court and the revolutionaries soon resumed. In the summer of 1906 the revolutionaries in their thousands gathered in the garden of the British embassy, where they gave political speeches and cemented their claim on the public space, which now incorporated a global attention via the British embassy, demanding an end to absolutist monarchy and the establishment of a parliament. By August the king agreed and by the fall of that year the first elections were held. By October 1906, the Constitutional Assembly was formed and forced the reigning Qajar monarch to sign the constitution. Soon after signing the document Mozaffar al-Din Shah died. His son Mohammad Ali Shah reneged on his father's agreement and signature and bombarded the parliament, and the Constitutional Revolution thus extended well into the next decade, with Russian and British imperialism interfering, impeding, but ultimately grounding the public domain that the revolutionaries had founded. The ideal of a collective, revolutionary will was thus manifested in the course of a cataclysmic social uprising.

The political fruits of the Constitutional Revolution were not to last for long. By 1926, a British-sponsored coup brought Reza Shah (r. 1925–1941) to power and changed the dynasty from the Qajars to the Pahlavis, a catastrophic development for the cause of liberty in Iran that extended well into the twenty-first century and resulted in a militant Islamist takeover of Iranian political culture in the course of 1977–1979 revolutions. Between the Constitutional Revolution and the Islamic Revolution of 1977–1979, a succession of military coups brought the first and kept the second Pahlavi monarch to and in power—two foreign interventions by the British and the Americans that paved the way to a clerical theocracy that continues to rule Iran to this day. Both the Pahlavis and the Islamists kept themselves in power by brute and naked violence, one worse than the other—while the consolidation and expansion of the public sphere continued apace despite the illegitimate rules that categorically fail to represent the multivariate fact of the polity they have usurped from its legitimate occupants. Between the Constitutional Revolution and the Green Movement of 2009–2011, that public space has seen uninterrupted and repeated manifestations of violent or peaceful revolts, each expanding exponentially in range and depth. At the heart of these revolts remains the transmutation of Persian literary humanism from the *ethos/hanjar* of its normative creativity to the *chaos/ashub* of multivariate sites and citations of defiant agency. The more brutally the states have tried to homogenize and neutralize the public space, the more varied, multifaceted, amorphous, and evasive have been the varied forms of creative resistance to the state.

A key factor in defining the terms of that creative resistance is how the windows of Persian literary humanism are opened wide to new syncretism in this period. The rediscovery of the Greek sources in the nineteenth and twentieth centuries, for example, puts forward a renewed conception of humanism into the emerging public space and gives an anthropomorphic disposition to the ensuing political discourse. Platonic ideas had of course a lasting influence in the changing conception of humanism in Persian as in all other Islamic discourses.[2] But the idea of humanism as it emerged from within the matrix of Persian *Adab* with its own cosmopolitan disposition—which includes Platonic influences but is not reducible to them—very much continued apace. A key factor in the Constitutional Revolution period, however, is that there were many references to humanism that went beyond the inherited

literary traditions. For example, the prominent statesman Mirza Malkam Khan (1833–1908) had organized an association he called *Majma-e
Adamiyat* (The Assembly of Humanism).[3] Such uses are clear indications that old and new conceptions of humanism from within and without the Persianate world were entering the public domain for a new
register of *Adab*.

The Poetry of a Public Revolt

Having exited the royal court for good, Persian literary humanism has
been singularly responsible for crafting the public space on which it
thrives and populating it with the citizens of a nation-state built upon
that space. From the preparatory stages of the Constitutional Revolution
of 1906–1911 forward, we navigate through layered formations of literary, poetic, visual, and performing arts successively defining the creative
and critical imagination of one generation after another of Iranians (thus
defined by the literary humanism that had narratively imagined them).
The center of Persian literary humanism could no longer be held by one
genre or another and the *ethos* at its epicenter is now exploding into multiple *chaotic* registers, dodging domination, appropriation, stagnation.

Between 1900 and 1930, Persian poetry is the first and foremost
form of creative outburst in tune with the vastly changing political circumstances of the time, giving emotive and visionary expressions to
the political aspirations of the nation it has, ipso facto, constituted. The
Constitutional Revolution, in which the absolutist monarchy of the Qajars was forced to accept the authority of a national assembly (*Majlis*),
gave full, colorful, and enduring expression to hopes, fears, and aspirations of a *vatan* (homeland, nation) in the making—and the poets were
there to name and register this momentous occasion in their passionately nationalist lyricism. In the hands of these revolutionary poets,
Persian poetic metaphors were retrieved and recast into the formative
mold of a whole new aesthetic plane matching the new moral imagination of the age. In the process Persian language and diction were in effect liberated from old and tired repetitions of outdated sensibilities. The
revolutionary effervescence created by the poetry of the Constitutional period continued well into the 1920s and 1930s as the most accurate barometer of the political temperature of the revolutionary society at large.

The poetry of the Constitutional Revolution is star-studded with an astounding cast of characters—as if the hidden and repressed soul of Persian humanism had finally erupted with volcanic verve and power. This time around the humanism at the heart of literary imagination was targeted toward a public space, a collective persona, in which liberated humanity was in pursuit of its historically denied liberties—a will not just to free itself from the yoke of tyrannical absolutism that had historically denied its humanity (thus being redefined), but also to exercise a drive toward liberties in markedly public, namely democratic, terms. Aref Qazvini (1882–1934) is a typical example, the example par excellence, of a poet who defined the moral imagination of his time. His is both the spirit of his age and the spirit that defined his age. An exceedingly popular lyricist, singer, songwriter, and musician, Aref Qazvini's name became synonymous with the revolution he sang and celebrated in his music and lyricism. It is in fact safe to suggest that the active formation of Iranian political culture at the time and beyond was very much indebted to memorization and popular recitations of Aref Qazvini's songs of liberty. Aref Qazvini invented *vatan* (homeland, nation) as a nationalist metaphor.

> Payam dusham az pir-e mey forush amad
> Benush badeh keh yek mellati beh hush amad. . . .

> The old wine seller told me the other day:
> Drink and be merry that a nation has finally awoken!
> One thousand veils has tyranny torn in Iran,
> Thousands of thanks that Constitutionalism has covered its wounds
> From the dust of the grave of pure martyrs of freedom
> Look how the blood of Seyavash is boiling![4]

What made poets like Aref so definitive to their age was the danger always implicit in their work, for they had dared the elements exiting the secure walls of royal courts, coming out to find and define a new habitat for humanity at large. Not only were the poets no longer at the service of the court—they were in fact opposing and thus at the mercy of monarchs. Mirza Mohammad Farrokhi Yazdi (1887–1939) was a poet and political activist who was killed in Reza Shah's dungeons, for Farrokhi Yazdi had decidedly anti-monarchic and socialist ideals. Definitive to Farrokhi Yazdi's poetry was a radical socialism that gave his readers a fresh and invigorating new take on Persian poetry—politically committed and socially revolutionary. Farrokhi Yazdi is an excellent example of a poet who was now following the dreams and aspirations of a public interest that he was in fact as much serving as in fact dreaming and defining.[5]

What is equally important in this era is the group of poets among the aristocracy who join the public and become instrumental in defining a national domain and a collective interest beyond and in fact opposed to their own class interests. In his eloquent poetry and biting satire, Prince Iraj Mirza (1874–1926) was a key force—now best remembered for the ease and facility with which he simplified Persian poetry and even brought foreign (French) words into his satire, overcoming anxieties of "the purity" of the language. Iraj Mirza was born and raised as a member of the aristocratic elite, and yet he put his exquisite learning and erudition squarely at the service of the emerging public interests. Among other aspects of his socially pathbreaking poetry, it can be seen that Iraj Mirza was a progressive feminist deeply concerned about the emancipation and civil liberties of women. Equally important is the freedom with which poets began adapting non-Persian forms and genres of poetic compositions, one such poet being Mirzadeh Eshghi (1893–1924), who had learned French in the Ecole d'Alliance, moved to Istanbul for a while, and later became particularly famous for writing the opera *Rastakhiz Iran/Resurrection of Iran*, which was a reflection of his patriotic spirit. Composition of opera was a formal innovation that enriched and enabled the public domain in unprecedented manners. Eshqi was equally adamant about women's rights and the necessity of incorporating them into the national uprising and the corresponding expansion of the public domain.[6]

Poets of the Constitutional period were multitasking, spreading themselves to the organic diversity of the civil society they were defining, mobilizing, constituting. Mohammad-Taqi Malek al-Sho'ara Bahar (1884–1951) was a typical example of a poet who was an equally accomplished scholar, politician, journalist, historian, and professor of Persian literature. His patriotic poetry is marked by decidedly innovative and iconoclastic force. Equally multitalented was Allameh Ali Akbar Dehkhoda (1879–1956), a linguist, encyclopedist, and journalist, but perhaps above all a satirist of unsurpassed talent and tenacity. Dehkhoda wrote newspaper columns that to this day are considered classic examples of political satire. The writing of an encyclopedia, a herculean task undertaken by Dehkhoda, was a nationalist project in which the Persian language was now transformed into a public property, rather than the private possession of the royal court. Neither the genre of writing nor the political boundaries that separated the emerging states could contain the rebellious soul of these poets. Iran as an emerging nation-state by no stretch of imagination was the exclusive domain of these poets, for a markedly transnational setting was definitive to their historic tasks. Abolqasem Lahuti (1887–1957), for example, was a poet and political activist who was active in Iran during the Constitutional Revolution but (as noted in Chapter 7) was equally crucial in central Asia. New nation-states were emerging in the imperial territories of former or emerging empires—but first and foremost these poets were committed to the public sphere that was the principal source of their legitimacy, irrespective of the fact that this space at times could trespass the emerging and fluctuating borders of the nation-state.

Women poets were integral to this claim on the public space. Generations of women poets from Zarrin Taj Tahereh Qorrat al-Ayn (1814–1852) forward were key forces in disallowing men to have an exclusive claim on the emerging agenda of the nations. Shams Kasma'i (1883–1963) was the first Iranian poet ever to break the metric rules of Persian classical prosody. Her poetry was combined with a fiery political disposition. She was a pioneering poet with articulate political and social themes making her thoughts widely responsive to the tumultuous events of her time. Another great poet, Parvin E'tesami (1907–1941), was such a powerful and popular force that her male contemporaries denied her the authorship of her work and believed her poems were by her father. She was a very strict follower of classical prosody and remained in this respect a very conservative poet. But she and other female or feminist poets of this period were instrumental in multiplying the public domain of the emerging nation-state by the factor of gender.

That these poets were doing something new and that the whole society was in fact contingent on what they were doing is perfectly evident in a figure like Taqi Raf'at (ca. 1885–1920), a leading political activist, poet, and literary critic who joined the revolutionary uprising of Shaykh Muhammad Khiabani (1880–1920) and pursued his poetic and political activism with the same tenacity and conviction. Raf'at had studied in Istanbul and taught French in Tabriz and became a leading intellectual force of his time. He was the standard-bearer of an *osyan-e adabi* (literary rebellion) to which many young poets and political activists were attracted. Opposing these reformers were the classicists who were adamant in defending the canonical tropes of Persian poetry. The battle between the reformers and the classicists not only did not weaken the public domain—it in fact rooted and strengthened it.[7] Whether they defended classicism or else advocated radical reform in poetic diction and composition, Persian poets were now claiming for themselves the whole public domain upon which the nation was erected.

The Poetics of the Public Space

The consolidation of the public space as the site of a national identity formation from the Constitutional Revolution forward fades in comparison with what happens in the aftermath of the establishment of Radio Iran in 1940, which was a momentous occasion in exponentially expanding the public domain far beyond the few urban centers and well into the remotest corners of the nation-state. The construction of the network of a national railroad, the establishment of telephone and telegraph, printing of a standardized currency, the consolidation of a national education system, and many other similar matrixes of national identity that eventually emerged from the late Qajars to the early Pahlavis were all instrumental in sculpting this public sphere and giving it meaning and significance. Along the same lines, the establishment of Radio Iran standardized Persian language and prose and began cultivating a canonical body of prose, poetry, and music that at once defined the public space and incorporated the nation that was built on it into a common normative denomination.

By no stretch of imagination was Radio Iran the solitary source defining the contours of that public space, nor was it immune to abuses of the Pahlavi monarchy for state propaganda purposes. But nevertheless it was instrumental in expanding and consolidating the collective consciousness of the nation beyond anything achieved before. It was not accidental that occupying Radio Iran and broadcasting a message to the nation was the single most important symbolic sign of either a military coup or a revolutionary takeover in the course of Iranian history since its establishment. Occupying that symbolic and functional site was commanding the public space upon which the nation was built and through which it recognized itself. Later, during the reign of the second Pahlavi monarch, Mohammad Reza Shah Pahlavi (r. 1941–1979), national television was added to the radio, as were numerous national newspapers and magazines, all of which were to explode in the age of the Internet and social networking. But the inaugural moment of Radio Iran was instrumental in staging the national identity and expanding the public space it claimed on a collective plane that made "Iran" what we conceive it to be today.

Perhaps the most significant aspect of Radio Iran programming that spread the domain of Persian literary humanism beyond anything achieved before was a succession of classical music and poetry programs known as *Barnameh-ye Golha* (*Program of Flowers*), a vastly popular radio show that was the joyous companion of millions of Iranians for generations and eventually became integral to the collective consciousness of the entire nation. Davud Pirnia, a prominent lawyer from a Qajar aristocratic background who had an exquisitely cultivated love for music, launched *Barnameh-ye Golha* in 1955, and it continued under multiple names and innovative programming, featuring classical and contemporary poetry, until 1971, by which time a canonical collection of classical Persian music and lyricism was deeply archived in people's emotive imagination. It was through the musical programming of Radio Iran and *Barnameh-ye Golha* in particular that classical Persian music, an otherwise elitist art that had hitherto been limited to its master practitioners and their immediate disciples, now found a national audience. Composers such as Ali-Naqi Vaziri, Javad Ma'rufi, Ruhollah Khaleqi, Morteza Mahjubi, and Ali Tajvidi, along with virtuoso vocalists such as Elaheh, Golpayegani, Banan, Marziyeh, Shajarian, and Haideh, among scores of other deeply cultivated and vastly popular musicians and lyricists became household names to young and old, men and women, city-dwellers and villagers, ordinary folks, scholars, intellectuals, civil servants, and even the younger generation of seminarians. *Barnameh-ye Golha* was Persian literary humanism wrapped into a bouquet of fresh flowers and thrown across centuries and epochs like a gift to the public at large.[8]

Women vocalists were particularly important in this period. Such widely popular singers as Qamar al-Moluk Vaziri (1905–1959) became legendary performers, allowing, among other things, for the voice of an Iranian woman to be heard singing from one end of the land to another. It is impossible to exaggerate the significance of this voice for the cause of women's rights and the expansion of the public space to include women in its domain. Qamar al-Moluk Vaziri began singing as a young girl in religious congregations with her grandmother, who was a prominent preacher. Equally popular was Moluk Zarrabi (1910–1999) who became initially famous through her popular gramophone recordings but was later popularized through Radio Iran. Other women singers such as Ruh Bakhsh (d. 1989) broadcast the voice of Iranian women with lyrical melodies and endearing love songs to which young Iranians grew up, fell in love, married, aged, and watched their own children and grandchildren do the same with a new generation of popular singers. The older generation of master musicians and vocalists soon gave rise to new ones and the names of such singers as Mohammad Reza Shajarian, Shahram Nazeri, Alireza Ghorbanifar, and Sepideh Raissadat spread widely on the Internet, connecting Persian speakers across the globe.

Words cannot express the unsurpassed joy, sense of bliss, and boundless feeling of happiness that these songs have given their audiences for generation after generation and through the thick and thin of Iranian history—war, peace, revolutions, natural catastrophes, deep social anomie, inspired political movements. It is equally impossible to imagine the Constitutional Revolution without the lyrics of Aref Qazvini, or the Islamic Revolution without the voice of Mohammad Reza Shajarian, who has stayed the course with his people to the rise of the Green Movement and beyond. Shajarian's rendition of "Rabbana" (a pious prayer popular during the month of Ramadan) has trespassed the boundaries between the sacred and the profane and carved a niche in which binaries melt into a third dimension. With the memorable melodies that Shajarian and other classical musicians create, Iranians laugh, cry, hope for better days, pour into their streets for liberty, hide in the innermost sanctities of their being, and there and then discover the concealed interiorities of their souls otherwise unknown and undiscovered to them. The names of Marziyeh, Delkash, Pouran, Elaheh, Parvin, Sima Bina, Parisa, and then even more widely into the more popular music domains, Ramesh, Googoosh, Ahdiyeh, Haideh, Mahasti, and many more, are markers of generational leaps, the songs, lyrics, and melodies of their music the accompaniment of the most noble, memorable, or else playful moments of a people's lives. With these songs generations have been born to their mothers' lullabies, grown up with avalanches of loving memories, touched the budding sensuality of each other's bodies and souls, fallen in love, married, and then sung these songs again as lullabies to their own children. These melodies are the soundtracks of lives lived with memories worthy of a people's noblest sense of selfhood. You will hear mothers whispering these songs to their sleeping infants from Tajikistan to Afghanistan to Iran, and from there, and through the cycles of labor migrations and by the force of political turmoil, into the cold nights of Scandinavian countries and western European capitals, and from there to the East and West coasts of North America. Old masters of *ghazals*, the younger generation of poets, classical musicians, talented and popular vocalists were the gifts from which a national operatic repertoire was created that kept generations happy, singing, hopeful, and determined in and toward their innate humanity. Persian literary humanism was never sung on a grander public space or staged as a vaster spectacle than this—ever!

> Yaram gereh bar mu zadeh
> Gol bar sar-e gisu zadeh. . . .
>
> My beloved has tied her hair into a knot,
> Placed a flower on her hair,
> Her eyes have drunken a magical wine,
> Her eyes are my wine, my goblet,
> Her eyes my pitcher of wine, her eyes my wine cellar,
> Rosewater drops from her face . . . [9]

Poetry Matures, Fiction Rises

As the first three decades of the twentieth century witnessed the rise of Persian poetry in a new and invigorated register, both formally and thematically, claiming and calling the public space it crafted the *vatan* (homeland, nation), the next thirty years were the time for the rise of fiction, while simultaneously the poetry of the Constitutional Revolution period yielded to the Nimaic revolution in Persian prosody.

If the poetry of the Constitutional Revolution gave birth to the Iranian "nation" as the normative polity in which an emerging sense of citizenship was crafted, the Nimaic revolution in Persian poetics liberated that nation from the metric measures historically bonding the elegiac expressions of its humanity. Ali (Nima) Esfandiari, who gave himself the nom de plume Nima Yushij (1897–1960), the founding father of New Persian poetry (*She'r-e No*), gave full theoretical and poetic expression to a whole new universe of imagination. There is no historical comparison to what Nima did in Persian poetics in the millennium-old history of Persian poetry. Through a sustained theoretical and practical rethinking of the very nature of the poetic act, Nima revolutionized Persian poetry to the marrow of its bones and opened a vast spectrum of creative reconception of poetically being-in-the world. Against tremendous odds, antagonized by generations of hostile contemporaries, Nima single-handedly made a convincing case for a radical rethinking in the very constitutional configuration of sensibilities that make a particular worlding of the world "poetic." Nima radically questioned the validity of all received prosodies and persuasively argued for what he considered the innate, "natural," musicality of the poetic narrative itself as it emerges from the creative imagination of the poet. Nima argued that the dictatorial imposition of no extrapoetic prosody should hamper that innate force and presence of the poetic wording itself. The aesthetic origins of the Nimaic revolution cannot be reduced to vague and conventional references to "Western influences." In his major theoretical manifesto, *"Arzesh-e Ehsasat dar Zendegi-ye Honarmand"* ("The Significances of Sensibilities in the Life of an Artist"), Nima makes as many references to Russian, French, and German poets and theorists as he does to classical Persian and Arab prosodists. But all these theorizing acts are in fact ex post facto, by way of explaining in prose what he had already done, thought through, and performed in his poetry. His argument, theoretical as is indeed the very reading of his poetic rebellion, is sui generis. Undoubtedly Nima's knowledge of his contemporary Russian and French poetics was as much a part of his radical rethinking of Persian poetics as was his knowledge of his own classical heritage. But no amount of historical or geographical genealogy or archeology can account for the unprecedented daring of his poetic revolution. Nima changed the landscape and the topology of Persian poetic imagination, the very terms and thrusts of its worldly engagements, self-consciousness, and confidence.[10]

The first volume of Nima's poetry, *Qesseh-ye Rang-e Parideh* (*The Story of the Faded Color*) (1921) was still very much engaged in classical Persian prosody—but a new set of poetic imageries had already started percolating in his poems, in which he treats nature (sea, mountain, jungle, rain, cloud, fog, etc.) as a living agent rather than an object of romantic adulation. Classicist poets like Malek al-Sho'ra Bahar reacted quite negatively to Nima's entry into the Persian poetic scene. Bigger shifts in the formal diction of Nima's poetics become increasingly evident in his subsequent works, in which we are listening to a decidedly different music hitherto untapped by the formalized and rhythmic tyranny of Persian prosody. It is also precisely at this time that Nima begins to explain his thoughts on poetry in a series of letters to his wife Aliyeh Khanom. Nima believed that classical prosody forces an artificial music on the language, and that poets must uncover the innate musicality of the poetic utterance. The emotive description of nature in Nima's poetry eventually yields and morphs into a description of his own emotional discoveries.

> Mitaravad Mahtab,
> Miderakkshad shabtab,
>
> The moonlight is shining,
> The fireflies sparkle—
> Not for a moment do the sleepers awake,
> Though the sorrow of those asleep
> Keeps me awake. . . .

With Nima the subject embedded with and in Persian literary humanism is finally *liberated* from the arbitrary litigations of a mandated prosody legislating its emotive universe—its normative *ethos* formally exploded into a creative *chaos*. The Nimaic revolution in Persian poetry results in a formal destruction of the subject with vastly emancipatory consequences in Persian literary humanism.[11] Precisely for that reason, singing Nimaic poetry in classical Persian musical *dastgahs* is such an unqualified failure, because no similar formal destructions have occurred in Persian classical music until recently with the appearance of Mohsen Namjoo (b. 1976) in the first decade of the twenty-first century. Mohsen Namjoo did for and to Persian classical music what Nima did for poetry—the formal destruction of its knowing, feeling, performing subject.

As Persian poetics went through a cataclysmic transformation in the aftermath of the Nimaic revolution between the 1930s and 1960s, Persian fiction received its greatest narrative impetus, initially from Muhammad Ali Jamalzadeh (ca. 1892–1997) but ultimately from Sadeq Hedayat (1903–1951). With such works as *Yeki Bud, Yeki Nabud* (*Once upon a Time*) (1921) and *Sar-o Taha Yek Karbas* (*Cut from the Same Cloth*), Jamalzadeh successfully brought earlier attempts at a simplified prose to an effective and promising conclusion in producing the first works of fiction commensurate with the renewed conditions of his society. Jamalzadeh built on decades of revolutionary, simplified, prose and earlier attempts at fiction writing from the Constitutional Revolution period and thus helped to rescue that prose from the depleted energy of the Qajar period. Jamalzadeh wrote and published *Once Upon a Time* in Berlin, where the transnational formation of the public sphere ipso facto had a global disposition. Jamalzadeh's fiction invested a narrative enthusiasm in and about all the ups and downs of the new transformative circumstances, with the paramount preoccupations being tropes of progress and reason. In his short stories and novellas, colloquial and conversational Persian effortlessly enters the writing drama of works of fiction. Meanwhile, in the public domain an expansive readership was being constituted, as the language was stripped of its formal baggage.

While Jamalzadeh's simple, effective, and colorful colloquialism provided ample opportunity for Persian prose to cultivate expressions of diverse social types and groupings, Sadeq Hedayat took that prose and drove it into the darkest and most unexplored corners of the Iranian psyche. If Jamalzadeh drew a panorama of Persian prose ready for literary exploration, Hedayat unpacked the subconscious of that prose. Hedayat's *The Blind Owl* (1937) is the first and the most successful attempt to reach for and achieve a literary narrative in frightful tune with the irreducible (at times even ahistorical) anxieties of being-in-the-world, the renewed world of yet to be fathomed dimensions.

Sadeq Hedayat was a European-educated aristocrat, deeply rooted in the texture and tonality of Iranian culture. He published his *The Blind Owl* in India. Paramount in this unsurpassed masterpiece of Persian fiction is the naked, brutally honest, intense and disturbing audacity of the prose announcing the birth of literature as literature. This is not religious revelation, or historical narrative, or scholarship, or poetry (that hides itself in its own poesy). It is pure literature, and as a work of literature it is about nothing. For the first time we hear someone talking to us and we do not know who it is. It is about itself. The first line is the birth of Persian fiction—not only the birth of a narrator, but the birth of its own readership as well. Here the reader is entirely at the mercy of the narrator. The opening lines are truth statements, absolute, atemporal, playful, sublime, certain, frivolous—you can read them in any tone of voice, and they will speak to you. The way *The Blind Owl* starts breaks the emotive decorum of Persian literature—for good. The fact that this was written by an actual person, a human being, an author, disappears in the face of the narrative facticity of it. You are left alone with the narration. It can do to you whatever it pleases. The eternal here becomes accidental, atemporal temporal, the world fragile, the narrator flippant.

In *The Blind Owl*, Sadeq Hedayat places the narrative outside the realms of history, religion, sanctity, everything—the literary narrative becomes a reality sui generis, an end in and of itself: pure literary performance on full display. Here fiction has the bizarre power to make the reader not only complicit—it infects the reader with the writer's "disease." We have sympathy with the narrator because we have become the writer, writing the story with him. The narrator cuts so deeply into the notion of the collective "I," of the inner anxieties of a people, that when translated to the societal level it becomes the flip side of "reason and progress." Revealing those narrative anxieties becomes arresting. The lack of trustworthiness in the narrator reflects the fragmentation of the subject precisely when we have no choice but to trust him. The narrator's ability to stare into the abyss remains unparalleled, coterminous with Reza Shah's push to the thing called "modernization." With Hedayat the subject embedded with and in Persian literary humanism is finally fractured from within its formative coherence—its tonal ethos is atonally liberated into uncharted, chaotic, territories. It is the normative (as Nima's was formal) destruction of the subject.[12]

Film Now Uplifts Fiction and Poetry

In the next phase of this transmutation of Persian literary humanism, mapped out between 1960 and 1979, poetry thrives apace, fiction matures, and now cinema emerges as the combination and sublation of both into the visual register. Nima's formal destruction of the postcolonial subject was matched and mixed with Hedayat's normative destruction and augmented by the lyrical effervescence of the destabilizing subject singing newer dreams from Radio Iran. The rise of Iranian cinema now turned the feast into a visual carnival.

In the three decades leading to the Iranian revolution of 1977–1979, Nimaic poetry thrived in multiple and diverse directions. Nima had to suffer the consequences of his poetic genius. With few but crucial exceptions, his contemporaries had no taste or patience for his radical reconfiguration of Persian poetics. Powerful and influential neoclassicists vehemently opposed him. But a group of young and inspired poets picked up where he had left off. Chief among these young followers was Ahmad Shamlou (1925–2000), who pushed the Nimaic poetics to even fresher, physically more tangible, edges. The radical physicality of Shamlou's poetry, and ultimately his daring experimentation with the full potentialities of Persian language, and the progressive politics that run through the lyrical veins of his poetry gave a supremely elegant twist to every possibility of poetic materialism available in Persian language. In his hand, and through the effervescent force of his creative imagination, Persian poetic drive was pushed to exhilarating edges of radical narrativity. In his poetry, all extrapoetic realities dissolve and rise obediently to meet the poetic.[13] Another major voice in the Nimaic movement was arguably the most eloquent feminine voice in the entire history of Persian poetry: Forough Farrokhzad (1935–1967). No woman had hitherto dared to subvert so much so publicly in so short a span of time. Forough Farrokhzad's decidedly feminine voice settled a millennium-old account of suffocating silence imposed on the Iranian woman in her relentlessly patriarchal society. Farrokhzad's naked, exquisite, beautiful, and daring subversion of Persian cultural taboos was so radical that it would take generations of her readers to map out the range of physical sensibilities with which she dared to experiment.[14]

Mehdi Akhavan Sales (1928–1990) was yet another forceful poetic voice that successfully and convincingly combined the best and the most eloquent potentialities of the classical poetic sensibilities with an unflinching political commitment to radical recasting of the Persian poetics. The result was a nuanced and barely noticeable balance between a poetic narrative that had nothing but its own story to tell and a relentless engagement with the political predicament of the time. Akhavan's poetry is a nostalgic reading of a glorious past that may or may not have been there and yet is narratively put there to make the present read a particularly powerful song. His poetry then became the conscience of a whole generation of poetic politics: a poetry that took zest and momentum from life, a politics that was embedded in the humanizing force of poetry. In the same category of the master lyricists of the New Persian poetic imagination is Sohrab Sepehri (1928–1980), who gave momentous, elegant, and stunningly beautiful expression to a radical physicality in his poetry. A painter-poet, Sepehri used almost identical strokes of simple, articulate, and deceptively naive staccatos to create sheer astonishment at the awesome physicality of the mere act of living, of the forceful, absolutist, conception of existence.[15]

In many respects a follower of Akhavan in poetic diction and sentiment is Esma'il Khoi (b. 1938) who, from an early romantic beginning, grew to fruition in the post-Islamic Revolution period as a poet of massive rhetorical skills put squarely in the service of a severe, almost debilitating, anticlerical sentiment. Khoi's poetry in the 1980s emerged as the most articulate voice of an Iranian diaspora in total disillusion with the consequences of the Islamic Revolution in Iran. Two unusually gifted poets—Ahmad Reza Ahmadi (b. 1940) and Manuchehr Yekta'i (b. 1921)—took the Nimaic revolution in poetic narrative in yet another— even freer and more experimental—direction. Fuller experimentation with the aesthetic possibilities of the poetic narrative became paramount in Ahmadi's poetry. Having lived most of his adult life in New York, Manuchehr Yekta'i, yet another painter-poet in the Nimaic tradition, has been in a state of near-obsession with narrative experimentation. Coming to him from a distance, as it were, has made the poetic daring of Nima something of a linguistic fable for Yekta'i, folding and unfolding itself in self-descriptive directions.

Closer to popular taste but with no particularly significant connection to these revolutionary changes in Persian poetics were a number of poets, such as Fereydun Moshiri (1926–2000), Fereydun Tavalloli (1919– 1985), Houshang Ebtehaj (H. I. Sayeh, b. 1927), Simin Behbahani (b. 1927), and Nader Naderpour (1929–2000). At times virtuoso performers of pictorial and emotive imageries, these poets had no particularly powerful connection to their time and space and spoke mostly of outdated and even irrelevant sentimentalities. The effective shock of the Islamic

Revolution, however, had a considerable impact on some of these poets—for example, Houshang Ebtehaj and Simin Behbahani—but not to such a degree as to cause a drastic, qualitative change in their poetic diction or the narrative force of their creative imagination.

The Islamic Revolution in Iran subjected Persian poetry to a major political shock. The leading poets of the early 1970s, whose mode of thinking was established by the political and poetic power of Ahmad Shamlou, fully participated in the course of the revolution so far as they thought it a democratic uprising. In the wake of the revolution, Shamlou moved to London and published *Iranshahr,* a journal that took full political and intellectual account of the cataclysmic event. After the success of the revolution and the commencement of its Islamization, Shamlou moved back to Iran and started a new journal, *Jame'eh,* to which the leading intellectuals contributed. With the successful Islamization of the revolution, Persian poetic imagination went into a major period of hiatus characterized by effective neoclassical Islamization (perhaps best represented by Tahereh Saffarzadeh [1936–2008]), silenced commitment (represented by Ahmad Shamlou), and radical exilic defiance (best voiced in the most recent poems of Esma'il Khoi). In the meantime, a new generation of Iranian poets was coming of age and fruition—some inside Iran, others in exile. This generation was too young to remember with any degree of intensity the particular package of sensibility carried for so long by the no longer so "new" poetry. The rising spirit that informed and animated this generation was now bilingual to its very soul.

Looking at the crucial years of 1960–1979, we can see the main contours of the Nimaic poetic revolution in comparative terms—where Forough Farrokhzad's poetry appears irreducibly physical: the material, corporeal, love verbalized. Hers was ecstatic love—fleshly, orgasmic, defying taboos, exploring the forbidden. She was the long, repressed, desired, denied, and suddenly coagulated, defiant physical love, unabashed, pulsating. Compared to Forough Farrokhzad (and she is the standard), Nima is Olympian, inaugural, prophetic. He had gone up to the mountain and came down with his oracular tablets: *She'r e No* ("New Poetry"). He was the sun of the recently discovered solar system: magnetic;, and in godly terms: oracular. Ahmad Shamlou was Nima's vernacular, forward-looking, unpacking, happy, frivolous, flirtatious, lyricist of revolutionary defiance of the status quo. Mehdi Akhavan Sales was

Zarathustra, having come back, descended, and celebrated the past for the future, a model of the future in its ideality. Sohrab Sepehri was saintly, presential, gnostic, dwelling in the here and now, sunk and soaked in being, without any metaphysics. His is the poetics of being dissolved in the ephemeral, of which, in his poetry, he made an ontology.

As the Nimaic revolution thus radically destabilized and set flying onto uncharted territories a new generation of poets as defiant subjects between 1960 and 1979, Persian fiction matured beyond its inaugural registers by Sadeq Hedayat. Although many prominent writers, such as Bozorg Alavi (1904–1997), Sadeq Chubak (1916–1998), Mahmud E'temad-zadeh (also known as Behazin, 1915–2006), and Jalal Al-e Ahmad (1923–1969), followed Hedayat's socially conscious fiction, no other author matched, let alone surpassed, him in his existential excavations in *The Blind Owl*. The only exception to this statement is the exquisite achievement of Ebrahim Golestan (b. 1922), who took up and developed a particularly compelling aspect of Hedayat's legacy, namely, an unswerving penchant for the primacy of aesthetic narrativity. In such staccatos as *Az Ruzegar-e Rafteh Hekayat* (*Once Upon a Time*), and *Ju va divar-e Teshneh* (*The Brook and the Thirsty Wall*), Golestan created and sustained flawless sketches of a descriptive self-signification that always surpassed and overcame the traces of its own acts of meaning. What exactly these highly stylized, judiciously crafted, narratives "mean" or "signify" almost fades under the dazzling dominance of the aesthetic act of narrativity itself. Standing exactly at the opposite side of Ebrahim Golestan is Jalal Al-e Ahmad, who took Hedayat's social realism and carried it to thinly fictionalized political manifestos. Infinitely more effective as an essayist and an engagé intellectual, Al-e Ahmad's perhaps most successful fiction was *Nun va al-Qalam* (*By the Pen*), in which he borrowed from older forms of storytelling to depict a revolutionary society in the wake of a popular uprising.[16]

In the same generation, and somewhere between Golestan's aesthetic narrativity and Al-e Ahmad's excessive realism, is Sadeq Chubak, one of the most prolific writers of his generation. In such works as *Tangsir* and *Atari keh Lutiasb Mordeh bud* (*The Baboon Whose Master Had Died*), Chubak paid critical attention to the narrative realism of his craft. Having been born and bred in southern Iran, Chubak was chiefly responsible for introducing a whole new repertoire of southern sensibilities to the literary lexicon of Persian fiction, a trend that was then successfully pursued by Ahmad Mahmud in such works as *Hamsayeh-ha* (*Neighbors*) and *Za'eri dar Zir-e Baran* (*A Pilgrim under the Rain*). The more aesthetically serious work that commenced with Hedayat and continued with Golestan was subsequently picked up by perhaps the most brilliant writer of his generation, Houshang Golshiri (1938–2000). Golshiri's *Prince Ehtejab* reads in the same vein as Hedayat's *The Blind Owl* and Golestan's *Az Ruzegar-e Rafteh Hekayat*. Manipulating the tormented consciousness of a Qajar prince, Golshiri masterfully recreates in *Prince Ehtejab* the social and psychological malaise of a whole cycle of corruption and decay. Love and loyalty, power and seduction, corruption and decay, are the undercurrents of a narrative labyrinth that weaves its own story around itself.[17]

Women writers have a singularly significant role in the making of modern Persian fiction. Simin Daneshvar (b. 1921), Mahshid Amirshahi (b. 1937), Shahrnoush Parsipour (b. 1946), Ghazaleh Alizadeh (1947–1996), Moniru Ravanipour (b. 1952), and scores of other women have been the leading female novelists of their generation, with vastly popular output and readership. Simin Daneshvar's *Savushun* (*Requiem*) (1969) became the most widely read work of fiction in the entire history of the genre. Shahrnoush Parsipour's *Tuba va Ma'na-ye Shab* (*Tuba and the Meaning of Night*) (1989) and *Zanan bedun-e Mardan* (*Women without Men*) (1989) explored deeply the labyrinth of feminine consciousness in history and politics. Ravanipour's *Ahl-e Ghargh* (*The People of Ghargh*) (1989) opened a whole new vista of southern mythical sensibilities in Persian fiction.

The publication of Mahmud Dolatabadi's (b. 1940) ten-volume epic *Klidar* in the late 1970s must be considered a major event in the history of Persian fiction. Centered on a fictionalized version of a local hero in Khurasan, *Klidar* is a majestic narrative of legendary proportions. Dolatabadi constructs a full-bodied epic in which love and adventure, atrocity and nobility are woven together and led toward a uniquely ennobling tragedy. The setting of Dolatabadi's *Klidar* is the rural and pastoral highlands of Khurasan, which he successfully incorporated into the literary geography of his homeland.[18]

Immediately related to the rise and development of Persian fiction in this period was a simultaneous flourishing of drama. From such traditions of performing arts as romance literature—*Shahnameh-Khani, Ta'ziyeh, Ru-Hozi, Siyah-Bazi, Kheymeh-Shah-Bazi*—in conjunction with widespread exposure to other theatrical influences from the Arab world, India, central Asia, China, Turkey, and eastern and western Europe, a thriving drama emerged in the middle of the nineteenth century. In the wake of the Constitutional Revolution drama took center stage in the creative imagination of dramatists and artists. Mirza Fath Ali Akhondzadeh (1812–1878) and Mirza Malkam Khan (1833–1908) were the forerunners of social realism and political satire in Persian drama. Translations from Russian, French, and English plays increased dramatically after World War II, while such talented dramatists as Abd al-Hossein Nushin (1906–1971) gave institutional recognition to the genre. During the 1960s and 1970s Persian drama reached its creative zenith when leading playwrights such as Gholam Hossein Sa'edi (Gowhar-e Morad was his nom de plume, [1935–1985]), Akbar Radi (1939–2007), Bahram Beizai (b. 1938), and Abbas Na'lbandiyan (1949–1989), among many others, took full advantage of drama to address prevailing social and political issues. Sa'edi, in particular, explored the deepest corners of anxiety (he was a trained psychologist) in foreign and familiar characters and cultures beyond the reach of Tehran-based café intellectuals. Bahram Beizai soon linked his interest in theater to a brilliant career in cinema and created a whole spectrum of dramatic and visual sensibilities entirely his own.[19] Another major playwright/director of considerable talent is Parviz Sayyad (b. 1937), who has successfully bridged a wider gap between popular and avant-garde arts.[20]

In the context of Persian literary humanism and the public sphere it crafted and commanded over the last 200 years, the novel as the site of a democratic space, following Bakhtinian theory of the genre, gave narrative spectrum to characters and plots to pull their readers into open-ended events, in which the narrator might be omniscient but never omnipotent. The relationship between novel and democratic institutions reflects the correspondence between the site of literature and bourgeois democratic aspirations—abstract in their diction and disposition, specific in the political agenda they engender. In the Iranian context the multiplicity of narratives that mark Persian fiction—from Hedayat to Parsipour—amounts to the fragmentation of the knowing subject in critical but stable circumstances. Almost every major figure in the history of Persian fiction comes with a different fragment of the knowing subject and that amounts to the absence of an authorial homogeneity through which the narrator could possess the narration. If you string together the history of Persian fiction chronologically, you see from one extremity of broken narrative (Hedayat) to another (Parsipour), disallowing the formation of any claim to any metaphysics and yet enabling and agential in specific historical terms.

Squarely rooted in Persian fiction and poetry, cinema emerged in the course of the twentieth century as an increasingly public form of art and entertainment with the widest conceivable appeal, exponentially expanding the sphere of Persian literary humanism into visual and performing arts.[21] From its very inception, the formation of any "national cinema" has also been a global phenomenon, wedding universalized technological virtuosity and regional themes and subjects. The history of art in general, but cinema especially, is at the same time full of influences from Iranian minorities: Armenians, Jews, and Zoroastrians have been definitive to the rise of Iranian cinema as a nondenominational public sphere in which artists have crafted a common aesthetic field entirely independent of their creed and religious heritage. Though the origin of Iranian cinema goes back to the late nineteenth/early twentieth century, it is in the 1950s that cinema becomes an art form, with filmmakers such as Farrokh Ghaffari (1921–2006) having studied in Europe and returned to their homeland to create a national cinema. In the 1960s, the pioneering work of Forough Farrokhzad, *The House Is Black* (1962), introduced the combination of documentary and poetry that has ever since remained definitive to Iranian cinema.[22] By the late 1960s, Iranian cinema had reached a level of maturity that could now attract a global attention. Daryoush Mehrjui's *Cow* (1969), a psychodrama about a man who so dearly loves his cow that upon its death he becomes the animal he loves, put Iranian cinema on the global map. If in the figure of Forough Farrokhzad we had a prominent poet becoming the pioneering visionary of Iranian cinema, in Mehrjui's we witness an effective link between the psychological depth of Persian drama and the rising cinematic humanism. In two complementary directions, Iranian cinema expanded its domestic boundaries of the public space and integrated that space into a far more global sphere than any other form of visual, performing, or literary arts.

The successive traumas of the 1977–1979 revolution and the 1980–1988 Iran-Iraq war gave Iranian cinema a transformative and imaginative boost. Amir Naderi's (b. 1946) *The Runner* (1985) is a vintage product of this period, first and foremost the sublime example of his cinema of solitude, balanced by moments of cathartic ecstasy. The story of a poor and lonely child who lives in an abandoned ship and whose sole source of solace is to run, *The Runner* turned the attention of a global audience to postrevolutionary Iran. Now in full view of global audiences, Iranian cinematic humanism is entirely indebted to Naderi for having cultivated a psychological *interiority* for it. Equally iconic for this period is Bahram Beizai's *Bashu: The Little Stranger* (1986), the story of a young boy from southern Iran who runs away from the war-torn Khuzestan to find himself in the luscious greenery of Northern Iran, where he meets Na'i, a young mother of two young children who manages her life in the village separated from her husband, who is away at the front in the Iran-Iraq war. In the course of their encounter Na'i gives symbolic birth to Bashu through a visually modulated suggestion of an "Immaculate Conception." The mythic disposition of Beizai's cinema has been definitive to suspending the structural-functional reading of humanity and its potential for liberation.[23]

Iranian cinema was catapulted to the global limelight soon after the end of the Iran-Iraq war in 1988, and Abbas Kiarostami was the locomotive, as a French film critic once put it graphically, that pulled other Iranian filmmakers along to world attention, thus globally multiplying the public space that Persian humanism covered and in which it thrived. Whether political, like Mohsen Makhmalbaf, or apolitical, like Abbas Kiarostami, this cinema had found its bearing as a global spectacle, owning a world that was hitherto alien to it. Mohsen Makhmalbaf (b. 1957), *Once Upon a Time, Cinema* (1991), and Abbas Kiarostami's *Through the Olive Trees* (1993) are the hallmarks of this period, which ultimately witnessed Jafar Panahi's (b. 1960) *Crimson Gold* (2003) as its finest achievement.[24] The factual realism of Abbas Kiarostami's cinema, in which a matter-of-fact realism is exposed in its full visual proportions, combined with Makhmalbaf's *virtual realism,* in which reality is vacated and reduced to its virtual forces, came together in this decade to explore the hitherto hidden dimensions of Persian humanism in a cinematic register and for a mesmerized global audience to behold. Upon what Kiarostami and Makhmalbaf had built, Jafar Panahi, in such films as *Crimson Gold* and *Offside* (2006), explored a visual realism in which that humanism had finally achieved its absolute semiotic heteronormativity.

In the course of the twentieth century, visual and performing arts drastically widened the *social space* to non-Persian-speaking audiences in and out of Iran, and people hitherto branded as "minorities" entered that space with equal claims and contributions. The notion of *vatan* (homeland, nation) as the simulacrum of the public sphere on which the artists and literati thrived expanded exponentially in both material and imaginative ways. Aesthetically, this was the most extreme complication of Persian literary humanism since the Timurid and the Safavid periods when paralingual semiosis had transformed its *logos* into *ethos*. After the celebration and assimilation of Persian miniature paintings and poetry by the Orientalists for their own purposes, this was the most global recognition of an aspect of literary and aesthetic humanism beyond its immediate surroundings. In this newest phase, the European film festivals did manage to exoticize and at times even Orientalize what they were watching, but at the same time the entry of Iranian cinema into global limelight provided a critical venue for a larger transnational public to see and celebrate it and become integral to its sense of self-awareness. The transnational aesthetics celebrated in Iranian cinema and transfused into the audience it attracted managed to overcome both the censorship it faced at home and the exoticization it endured abroad and turn them both around to its own advantage. The radical humanism evident and celebrated in this cinema pushed forward the paralingual semiosis it had inherited from earlier phases of Persian humanism, while the *mimetic dissonance* at the heart of this cinema, a *Verfremdungseffekt* of its own making, became the sublime example of the creative *chaos* to which earlier morphological phases of Persian literary humanism had given birth.

A Revolutionary Trauma

The public space in which Persian literary humanism found a new habitat away from its habitual abode in the royal court emerged from the interface between the dying Qajar dynasty and the emerging European empires that had immediate colonial interest in the region. This encounter vastly expanded the public space and eventually produced a postcolonial subject repressing the successive historical self-transmutations of its identities and alterities in the context of the overwhelming European empires and in defiance of its globalized power. Nima Yushij's formal destruction of that subject, coupled with Sadegh Hedayat's normative undoing, combined with the lyrical and visual transfiguration of that subject to eventually give birth to a full-bodied postcolonial subject that has historically and habitably arisen in revolutionary defiance of tyranny. That postcolonial subject has historically been far more conscious of its colonial encounter with "modernity" than cognizant of its preceding imperial formations. My entire project in retrieving Persian literary humanism might be considered an attempt to bring back that self-transmutation of the subject to full consciousness, overriding the false anxiety of an encounter with European modernity that has been falsely globalized by the power invested in it by a Eurocentric conception of the world.

The revolution of 1977–1979 and its immediate Islamization by the victorious faction introduced the combined forces of a triple imperative in the Persian literary imagination: the first formed by those who opted for an exilic life over enduring the militant censorship of a theocracy; the second shaped by those who ideologically, or as a matter of principle, chose not to oppose the political formation of a theocracy and in fact initially thrived in it (they call themselves *roshanfekr-e dini* [*religious intellectuals*]); and the third, grouped by those opposition intellectuals who preferred to stay inside Iran and continue with their work under dire circumstances. The dramatist Gholam Hossein Sa'edi and the poet Esma'il Khoi (b. 1938) are prime examples of Iranian literati who left their country and became the acid-tongued expatriate intellectuals. The poet Tahereh Saffarzadeh and novelist and scholar Shams Al-e Ahmad (1929–2010), the brother of the towering intellectual Jalal Al-e Ahmad, are among those members of the literati who wholeheartedly celebrated the Islamic Revolution, remained in Iran, and continued to be productive in the new political environment. But not all who remained inside Iran advocated for or even accepted the radical and forced Islamization of their culture. Ahmad Shamlou, Ahmad Reza Ahmadi, Houshang Golshiri, Mahmoud Dolatabadi, Simin Daneshvar, Abbas Kiarostami, and Bahram Beizai, among scores of other poets, novelists, playwrights, and filmmakers, continued to produce in active or tacit celebration of an autonomous creative imagination in opposition to the militant occupation of their public space by censorial ideologues of a militant Islamist theocracy. Whether they left their homeland or stayed put, the Iranian artists and literati enriched and empowered the public space that had given autonomy and legitimacy to them, thus ipso facto discrediting the militant occupation of their homeland by a totalitarian militancy institutionalized as a dictatorial Islamist theocracy.

In the meantime, the younger generation of poets, novelists, dramatists, filmmakers, and public intellectuals were charting their own separate courses into the future and thus reclaiming their public domain. The radical implications of an Islamic revolution had stirred up the deepest emotions and anxieties among the children born to that revolution. A flood of literary and visual outputs marked the younger generation's creative response to a world-historic revolution, the unfathomable sacrifices endured during the eight-year war with Iraq, and the continued agitations of a collective imagination not at peace with itself. Millions of Iranians now lived around the world, and whatever the language of their culture, they tried to teach Persian to their children. These children were growing up to express the configuration of their history and identity in the language of their adopted culture, with the accent of a Persian intonation to their moral and intellectual imagination. Persian language, meanwhile was thriving with steadfast confidence in the works of novelists like Moniru Ravanipour and Shahriar Mandanipour (b. 1957); filmmakers like Mohsen Makhmalbaf and Jafar Panahi (b. 1960); musicians, singers, and songwriters like Mohsen Namjoo and Shahin Najafi (b. 1980)—all leading a new generation that had come to fruition in the unknown and uncharted territories of the aftermath of the Islamic Republic.

The hostile Islamist takeover of the cosmopolitan Iranian political culture (which includes Islam but is not limited to it) was predicated on suppressing the multifaceted ideological formation in the postcolonial period that had anticipated the 1979 revolution. The active composition of Iranian political culture was never exclusively Islamist (Shi'i). Three modes of ideological mobilization—militant Islamism, Third World socialism, and anticolonial nationalism—were at once challenging the reigning monarchy and competing against one another. These ideologies had emerged against and in the context of European colonialism. In the 1940s, it was the Tudeh Party socialism that was the most defining point of Iranian political culture; while in the 1950s, the anticolonial nationalism of Mohammad Musaddiq had mobilized the nation against British colonialism; and in the 1960s, the militant Islamism of

Ayatollah Khomeini had seriously challenged the Pahlavi monarchy. These forces were simultaneously present in the 1970s as the revolutionary mobilization took advantage of all of them to topple the monarchy. The Islamist ideology was integral to this mobilization but not definitive to it. The Islamic Republic that was violently imposed on the country at large has been an aberration, a corruption of Iranian political culture, a kidnapping of it. The theocracy has always thrived on regional wars, such as the Israeli invasion of Lebanon, the continued crisis in Palestine, the U.S.-led invasions of Afghanistan and Iraq. Over the course of its militant ascendency, the Islamic Republic sought radically to over-Islamize the revolution it had hijacked and thereby over-Islamized the public space it had violently occupied. The so-called "religious intellectuals," even those who opposed the atrocities of the Islamic Republic, were instrumental in this militant distortion of a cosmopolitan culture. Even when they were opposing the atrocities of the Islamic Republic they were in fact even more deeply entrenching an exclusively Islamist reading of the Iranian political culture in that public domain. As a distortion of Iranian political culture, the Islamic Republic has never been able to drop its guard and see a day of peace in its turbulent history—and it has faced one form of social uprising or another, all of them culminating in the Green Movement of 2009 in the aftermath of a widely contested presidential election. These social uprisings—now imbedded in women's rights, labor unions, and student assemblies, have continued a face-off with the Islamic Republic for the ownership of the public domain.

The Widening Gyre

Between the Constitutional Revolution of 1906–1911 and the Islamic Revolution of 1977–1979, successive narrative breakthroughs and the formal destruction of the creative subject gave Persian literary humanism an increasingly decentered disposition. Never content or satisfied with one form or another, the spirit of the creative subject wandered around the firmament of Persian literary humanism in search of one mode of expression or another. Promiscuous, meandering, restless, and wavering, it went through multiple genres and engendered varied registers of its moral and normative whereabouts—in poetry, prose, drama, cinema, and then more. The widening phases of aesthetic imagination that run through this period may first be located in the years 1900–1930, with poetry as the paramount mode of cultural expression. This period entered a new phase during the years 1930–1960, when the Qajars yielded to the Pahlavis, as poetry went through the Nimaic revolution precisely when Sadeq Hedayat inaugurated a vigorous crescendo of Persian fiction. During the years 1960–1979, and as the trauma of the 1953 U.S. Central Intelligence Agency–sponsored coup settled in the soul of the nation, Persian poetry continued to thrive in the blood of a new generation, while fiction matured, and cinema emerged as the formal sublimation of all its previous art forms.

These cycles of socially significant and normatively self-transformative creativity in the arts came to an end in the course of the cataclysmic events of the 1977–1979 revolution, when we witness a paradigm shift in which both poetry and fiction effectively reached a cul de sac. In the aftermath of the revolution, cinema continued apace, now using the mostly vacated platform of poetry and fiction as its new launchpad. Between 1980 and 1998, Iranian cinema became the singular carrier of these successive phases of creativity, using the trauma of the 1977–1979 revolution and the Iran-Iraq war of 1980–1988 as the social grounding of its aesthetic sublation. It was now possible to see successive generations of filmmakers leading the poetry and the prose of Persian literary humanism into uncharted visual domains. The first generation of Iranian filmmakers (including figures like Ebrahim Golestan and Forough Farrokhzad) were in fact poets and novelists who had now emerged as filmmakers; in the second generation (including Daryoush Mehrjui and Bahman Farmanara) filmmakers were creatively connected to poets and novelists but charted a new visual vocabulary; in the third generation (from Amir Naderi to Abbas Kiarostami) filmmakers ultimately emerged as visionaries of the sign, standing apart from poets and novelists, thus giving birth to cinema as an autonomous art form.

Predicated on the internal exhaustion of its aesthetics, the height of Iranian cinema ended in 1998 with a major student uprising, when Iranian filmmakers no longer had much to offer Iranian society (though Iranian cinema continued to travel the international festival circuits), and thereafter the combative and beleaguered press became paramount, and thus the 1998–2009 period is the era of groundbreaking journalism as the vanguard of safeguarding the public domain. The urgency and immediacy of events were now the characteristics of the new journalistic narratives in the agent of the Internet. The severe crackdown on newspapers coincided with the rise of underground music and a plethora of bloggers between 2000 and 2009. When the Green Movement started in 2009, soon to be followed by the Arab Spring, the postcolonial public space had finally cracked open to new possibilities, a seismic change that had begun changing the moral map of "the Middle East." Among other things, the Green Movement staged the power of Persian blogging.[25] The prose of the blog was fast, furious, impatient, iconoclastic, spontaneous, fragmentary. This was accompanied by the rise of underground music (rap especially) as a crucial component of cultural production. As perhaps best represented by Shirin Neshat, the art of photography and video installation now vastly globalized both the particulars of Persian humanism and the public domain in which it thrived. By the first decade of the twenty-first century, the scattered attention span of Facebook "friends" and members of other forms of social networking had moved into allegorical de-sedimentation of the subject into cyberspace.

Public Sphere Writ Global

The morphological transformation of the central trope of Persian literary humanism from *ethos/hanjar* to *chaos/ashub* meant the multiplication of the manners, modes, and genres of creativity in multivariate registers, meaning creativity became promiscuous, unstable, mobile, multifarious. The more the public space of these creativities went global, the more exponentially this creativity metamorphosed.

In the aftermath of the Islamic Revolution of 1977–1979 and the establishment of the Islamist theocracy, some of the leading members of the Iranian literati could not take the intolerable circumstances and left their country, others stayed and continued to work—but in either case the public space both groups occupied in and out of their homeland had become even more interpolated and globalized. Meanwhile, the massively globalized circulations of labor, capital, and commodity, combined with the dire consequences of the political upheavals, revolutions, and wars that they caused catapulted Iran and Iranians (like everyone else) into the global scene. Over the last 200 years, Iranian intellectuals, scholars, artists, literati, and political activists have been moving in and out of their homeland for short or long periods of time or at times even permanently. In recent history, Mirza Saleh Shirazi was dispatched by Prince Abbas Mirza to Europe to study the contemporary fields of social sciences and the humanities, and Shirazi came back with a printing machine to establish the first newspaper and publish his travelogue in much-simplified Persian prose. Some half a century later, Mirza Aqa Khan Kermani (1853–1896) was the first major public intellectual to move to Istanbul for fear of persecution and to develop his pioneering literary ideas. He was arrested, extradited to Iran, and executed instantly, along with his two other comrades—Shaykh Ahmad Ruhi and Khabir al-Molk. In subsequent generations, Seyyed Hasan Taqizadeh (1878–1970) was a major force during the Constitutional Revolution of 1906–1911, and subsequently a towering intellectual figure who reached moral and intellectual maturity mostly in western Europe and North America. Considered by many the founding father of Persian fiction— short stories and novellas in particular—Mohammad Ali Jamalzadeh (ca. 1892–1997) came to complete literary fruition in Europe and spent most of his life in Geneva.

A serious contender from the left, Bozorg Alavi (1904–1997) reached literary maturity in Europe and lived and died in Germany. The enduring significance of Sadeq Hedayat was formed in Europe, in France in particular, where he finally committed suicide. In the aftermath of the Islamic Revolution of 1977–1979 Ebrahim Golestan moved to the United Kingdom, where he continued with his literary production, though on a much smaller scale. Gholam Hossein Sa'edi also moved out of Iran after the Islamic revolution and died in Paris. Esma'il Khoi was another writer who left his homeland soon after the 1977–1979 revolution, but he remained both politically and poetically active in England. Shahrnoush Parsipour left Iran after spending time in jail and moved permanently to the United States. The common denominator of all these members of the literati is that in or out of their homeland they have written mostly if not exclusively in Persian and addressed their readers in and out of Iran, a clear indication that the public space in which Persian as a literary language has developed is not limited to Iran and the notion of *vatan* as the simulacrum of the pubic space is not limited to the geographical boundaries of Iran.

Other artists like Amir Naderi, Sohrab Shahid-Sales (1944–1988), Shirin Neshat (b. 1957), and Marjane Satrapi (b. 1969)—whether they moved out of their homeland after they had established a name and a reputation for themselves or else have in fact come to full fruition in Europe or the United States—expand the public sphere in which they have performed their art in more specifically global terms. Filmmakers like Amir Naderi have completely abandoned thematic and narrative concerns with Iran, with not a single Iranian reference remaining in their cinema, traveling even to Japan, where Naderi made his *Cut* (2011), making movies without a trace of anything Iranian. This does not mean that the cinema of filmmakers like Abbas Kiarostami who have made most of their films inside Iran is exclusively Iranian—in theme or in form—and immune to non-Iranian influences: yet another indication that the public space they occupy and upon which they stage is innately global. The same is true about Shirin Neshat and Marjane Satrapi—a video installation artist and a graphic novelist—whose works are conceived in fact entirely outside the political boundaries of Iran. The collective effect of these Iranian artists, intellectuals, artists, and literati is not a mere assumption of being in exile or diaspora or being expatriates. They were in fact just expanding the public sphere in which they were working, and from which they had originated.

The case of Marjane Satrapi's *Persepolis* (2000) and her other graphic novels poses quite an intriguing case. The author comes from a prominent elite family with a privileged education in the French lycée in northern Tehran, by no stretch of imagination representative of the overwhelming majority of her people. The elitist origin of the author defines the air of the comic strip, though not its politics, which are fairly open-minded and at times even progressive. Though the author's range of representation is of course fairly limited and privileged, this does not compromise the inaugural excitement and novelty of the work. It locates and situates her power of representation within a social space that extends from her limited experiences in Iran to her formal virtuosity in adapting the genre of *bande dessinée.*

Throughout these developments, that public space that Iranian literati in or out of their homeland were occupying was being exponentially expanded, interpolated, exacerbated, imploded in texture and dexterity—

whereby the trope of *ethos* was being transformed toward successively creative *chaos*.

An Alternative Theory to Modernity

What I have put forward in this book is a theory of subjection from within the historical matrix of Persian literary humanism to which the entire European spectrum of tradition, modernity, and postmodernity is entirely tangential. This is a reading of Persian literary humanism that in fact overcomes the notion of "modernity" altogether by way of a sustained progression of autonormativity that effectively gives birth to its own alterities and it thus thrives on a differed form of heteronormativity, whereby its subject formation is never final but always suspenseful. Whereas for the Eurocentricity of the project of "modernity," the breakdown of instrumental reason was the downfall of logocentricity of subjection, this very project was always spelled out as "colonial modernity" for the rest of the world. The transformation of the techniques of *biopower* (Michel Foucault's thinking), both disciplinary and discursive, yield to the formation of the subject to forces within and without itself. The discursive formation of biopower is constitutionally logocentric—whereas Persian literary humanism, as I have offered it here, has always been a mobile body of metaphors, moving (self-transformative) from *ethnos* to *logos* to *ethos* to *chaos*.

By *chaos* in this last stage of Persian literary humanism I mean the splitting of its formative *ethos* into divergent directions, its transmutation into multiple registers, which results in alternating and unstable creative formations. Literary and artistic creativity in the chaotic mode becomes dissipative, with tropic turbulence at the heart of a disequilibrium that emanates from politics to poetics and aesthetics, whereby the works of literary art becomes politically stochastic.[26] In terms of literary production, this chaotic mode amounts to a historic unfolding in which Persian literary humanism keeps changing from prose to poetry, from complicated to simplified prose, from metric classical to the Nimaic model, from poetry to painting, from fiction to film, from painting to photography, from scholarship to journalism. The more unstable these systems are, the more destablizing they become to the tyrannical ruling regimes. The ruling regimes are farthest removed from—and thus always deligitimated by—the destablizing fact of these alternating systems. Persian literary humanism keeps dodging power and meta-morphosing itself, from one genre to another, and no ruling regime is ever able to lay claim to it. Thus, at its *chaotic* register Persian literary humanism overcomes the all-knowing subject not just by incessantly splitting it but by preempting it from devouring the world through its would-be objects of knowledge.

Conclusion

Literary Humanism as an
Alternative Theory to Modernity

ABU AL-HASAN Ali ibn Osman al-Jollabi al-Hujwiri al-Ghaznavi (ca. 990–1077) was a prominent Sufi master who was responsible for spreading both Persian literary prose and, through it, Sufism in south Asia. He was born in Ghazni in contemporary Afghanistan during the Ghaznavid empire and died and is buried in Lahore, in contemporary Pakistan, where to this day his mausoleum is a major site of pious pilgrims from the farthest corners of the Muslim world. Al-Hujwiri's principal work, *Kashf al-Mahjub* (*Unveiling the Veiled*) is considered among the first and finest Sufi treatises written in Persian. Early in this text when al-Hujwiri is explaining what "Sufism" actually means, he quotes a certain Sufi master, Abu al-Hasan Fushanjeh, for having once said that "Today Sufism is a name with no reference to any truth, while before it was a truth that had no name."[1] Early in the eleventh century, and already "Sufism" has become a signifier with a vanishing signified—a term with no referent, a word with no meaning. Al-Hujwiri's paradox (via attribution to an earlier Sufi master) emphasizes that when there was Sufism there was no name for it and when there was a name for it there was no Sufism! But how can that be? How can there be something with no name or a name that does not refer to something? In explaining this paradox al-Hujwiri suggests that during the time of the companions of the Prophet the truth of Sufism was there without its actually having a name. Further explaining the assertion, he adds: "The *signified practices* [*mo'amelat*] were *definite* [*ma'ruf*], but the *signifier* [*da'va*] indefinite [*majhul*]; while now *the signifier is definite*, but *the signified practices indefinite*." What al-Hujwiri stipulates here is an im/possible act of mimesis that at one and the same time both posits a knowing subject and dismantles and discredits it. In that very short hermeneutic gesture, we see in a nutshell the central paradox of subjection—making human fallible— that is at the heart of Persian literary humanism. Consider the fact that al-Hujwiri's *Kashf al-Mahjub* is the inaugural text of a massive body of literature on Persian Sufism—a pious knowledge generated about something that does not exist, by a knowing subject that, vacating himself, gets to know more about nothing—and yet in the process that very literary act enables the human as the author of humanity.

A Cosmopolitan Worldliness

How do people become "human"—and what does that exactly mean? I have thought this question through a literary humanism that expands over 1,400 years, extends over vast global empires that culminate in the Mongol conquest of the vastest imperial territory in human history, and finally divides into three magnificent Muslim empires of the Mughals, the Safavids, and the Ottomans, before it faces the catalytic effects of the mighty European imperialism. My central thesis in this book is predicated on a systematic articulation of a theory of subjection (how do people become human?) embedded in the heart of Persian literary humanism—a theory that proposes a *metamorphic sublation* of a succession of defining tropes that lead it from one phase to another, from its initial *ethnos/nezhad* when it was formed in opposition to Arab imperialism of the seventh century, to its definitive *logos/sokhan* when an expansive number of transnational empires took over the region, to its transformative *ethos/hanjar* when the fragile knowing subject at the heart of Persian poetic imagination became self-evident, and ultimately to its defiant *chaos/ashub* when it exited its habitual habitat at royal courts under the duress of its fateful encounter with European imperialism and perforce crafted for itself a *public space* it called *vatan* (homeland, nation). The self-transformative disposition of this fragile subject has been at the heart of Persian literary humanism and its cosmopolitan worldliness. My principal objection to the present state of literary studies is that the current location of this panoramic development under the self-designated "Western" hegemony has hitherto preempted the theoretical assessment of its metamorphic history. I have sought to expose and overcome this blind spot.

I propose this *metamorphic transformation* of the central tropes of Persian literary humanism to be a far more thematically accurate register of normative subjection and moral agency than a generic, Eurocentric, or even anticolonial mode of subject formation, which is the most recent globalized context in which Persian literary humanism has found itself, performing in the shadow of European imperialism. This imperialism should not be privileged over all the preceding forms of imperialism—from the Achamanids and the Sassanids in the pre-Islamic period to the Arabs in the seventh century to the Mongols in the thirteenth century or the Mughals or the Ottomans in the sixteenth century. I have sought to give historical depth and geographical range to our understanding of literary humanism as the modus operandi of subjection. When the transnational empires of the Ghaznavids and Seljuqids took over from the early Iranian dynasties of the Saffarids and the Samanids, they forced the early transformation of *ethnos* into *logos* because *sokhan* was now the paramount factor of Persian literary humanism and not the presumed ethnicity of the poet or the literati. When the global empire of the Mongols took over, the *logos* of Persian literary humanism was at the center of its self-universalizing literary cosmopolitanism and pushed the *logos* toward the formation of an *ethos* as the matrix of the multiple measures of being human. From the Timurid period forward, the eventual formation of a *paralingual semiosis* at the juncture of Persian poetry and painting extended the potential transmutation of *ethos* into *chaos* in the context of the four adjacent empires of the Mughals, the Safavids, the Ottomans, and the Russians, where the tropic transfusion was exacerbated in the context of encounter with a fifth, aterritorial, constellation of empires, approaching from Europe. This latest encounter finally forced Persian literary humanism out of its habitat inside the royal court, while disallowing it entrance into the new imperial formation, which was decidedly against any privileging of the Persian language and literature—as best evident in the Macaulay Act (English Education Act) of 1835. This fortuitous development finally resolved the historical paradox of Persian literary humanism and forced it to craft and cultivate a tertiary space—between its own courts that it had abandoned and the European courts that did not welcome it—which became the public space it now termed *nation* and *nationalism,* in which Persian literary humanism effectively set up its own edifice, finally in its new home, where it belonged.

This whole process has resulted in a manner of literary subjection as a self-conscious worlding of the world that European Orientalism and American literary criticism alike have silenced by their respective narrative urges to flatten out the world against the presumed centrality of the allegory of "the West" that they habitually take for real by way of allegorizing the rest of the world. The literary nationalism of the postcolonial world has unknowingly corroborated this episteme by competing in producing ethnic nationalist historiographies of their own. Contrary to the very grain of this train of thinking about literary history and theory, the locus classicus of the first three phases of Persian literary humanism—from *ethnos* to *logos* to *ethos*—has been the royal courts of vast empires, while the location of the very last phase, *chaos,* is the public space that Persian literary imagination has termed *vatan* (homeland, nation) and *vatanparasti* (nationalism) and carved in between the courts it exited and the courts into which it had no entry. Both European Orientalism and American literary criticism have misread this notion of *vatan* (homeland, nation)—one by *ethnicizing* Persian literary humanism in its entirety and the other by colonizing it as "Third World literature," or even worse "world literature," and thus declaring "all Third World texts . . . are national allegories."[2] This collusion of false readings is an expression of nothing more innocent/sinister than simply being embedded in one imperial imaginary—the one that calls itself "the West"—that has imperially overcome and glossed over the historical fact and continued resonance of other worldly empires—and is now casting its extended shadow over the long history that has preceded it.

The final phase of Persian literary humanism in its encounter with European imperialism was in fact a liberating and emancipatory moment in its long and adventurous history. Persian literary humanism was formed and coagulated in an initial encounter with Arab imperialism in *ethnic* terms (Persian vs. Arab). It went through multiple transformative phases and was finally delivered to a renewed cosmopolitan worldliness in its encounter with European imperialism—though this time around it was not confined within the royal courts but acted from the assured centrality of a public space it had in fact envisioned, imagined, articulated, and inhabited. The success of the Constitutional Revolution of 1906–1911 was interrupted by a corrupt monarchy (the Pahlavis) and an even more tyrannical theocracy (the Islamic Republic)—a historical development that was nevertheless necessary to get rid of two overriding illusions that the monarchy and the theocracy had any claim over that public space, which was not theirs. The royal courts and the juridical scholasticism had been identically overcome and run over by that public space. Successive revolutionary uprisings in Iran from the mid-nineteenth century forward effectively claimed that public space for the democratic aspirations that had initiated it in the first place and filled it with poets, musicians, dramatists, filmmakers, journalists, scholars, each in his or her own way articulating the specifics of that public sphere.

The cosmopolitan worldliness embedded in Persian literary humanism enters a renewed pact with its history in this final phase. By *chaos/ashub* in this phase I mean a morphological transmutation of the *ethos/hanjar* of Persian literary humanism into multiple registers, thematically and formally alternating and unstable in its multiple formations, positing a dissipative mood of creativity that dismantles any regime of *knowledge/power* production and its presumed subject.[3] *Chaos* is a condition of dissolute creativity whereby the positivist epistemes of *systematicity*, *longevity*, *endurance*, or even *coherence* finally yield to the open-ended expanse of a dissipative alterity. Poetry, fiction, drama, journalism, photography, music, and film keep producing, exhausting, and overcoming one another's capacities. Creative turbulence and formal disequilibria become the markers of a *mood* in the literary act that breaks any appearance of symmetry or systematicity and becomes negatively stochastic, formally disruptive—as perhaps best evident in Nima's poetic revolution, Hedayat's subversive fiction, or Kiarostami's fusion of fact and fantasy in his cinema. The creative mood remains constant in its synergy but keeps changing from prose to poetry, from complicated to simplified verse, from metric prosody to Nimaic revolt, from poetry to painting, from fiction to film, from painting to photography, from scholarship to journalism, etc. The more unstable these systems become, the more tyrannical and solid do appear the ruling regimes—which are farthest removed from the destablizing fact of these alternating subsystems. In its varied and evasive forms, literary humanism keeps dodging power and metamorphosizing itself, from one genre to another, so that no *ruling regime* ever would be able to lay any claim to it. The transmutation of *ethos* into *chaos* is the last and most creatively dissipative disposition of Persian literary humanism—a creative effervescence corresponding to the globality of the public space that it has crafted and that it commands.

The Contingent Subject of Literary Humanism

The historical unfolding of Persian literary humanism has been predicated on a *contingent* subject, a mode of metamorphic subjection that has achieved self-consciousness precisely through that formative fragility. The history of this mode of subjection is entirely autonomous (until the commencement of colonial modernity) from the one we witness in the history of European capitalist modernity—which has now fetishized itself as the only viable mode of subjection, in conformation or rejection. But within the European philosophical tradition itself serious challenges have been made to the overarching and totalizing claims of all-knowing European subject formations. In his *Against Epistemology* (1956) Theodore Adorno (1903–1969) turns his metacritical edge against Husserl's phenomenology and through that encounter we obtain the enduring insight of how both the European bourgeoisie and its transcendental philosophies have tried to contain the central paradoxes of the project of capitalist modernity. Speaking of Husserl, Adorno writes: "All bourgeoisie—all first—philosophy has struggled in vain with contingency. For every such philosophy seeks to reconcile a really self-antagonistic whole."[4] The factor and force of "contingency" is what halts the all-knowing violence of the subject. "Philosophical consciousness," Adorno suggests, "qualifies the antagonism as one of subject and object. Since it cannot sublate the antagonism in itself; it strives to remove it for itself, i.e. through reduction of being to consciousness."[5] This amounts to a philosophical resolution of a political paradox. In Adorno's words:

> Contingency remains, however, the "Menetekel" of lordship. This is always covert, though lordship eventually openly confesses it: Totalitarianism. It subsumes as chance whatever is not like it, the slightest non-homonymy. One has no power over what occurs by chance. No matter where contingency arises, it gives the lie to the universal mastery of spirit, its identity with matter. It is the mutilated, abstract shape of the in-itself from which the subject has usurped everything commensurable. The more recklessly the subject insists upon identity and the more purely it strives to establish mastery, the more threateningly looms

the shadow of non-identity. The threat of contingency is simply advanced by the pure a priori which is the enemy and should allay it.[6]

What the European treatment of the all-knowing subject has subsumed as chance, in Adorno's terms, Persian literary humanism centers as an identity that keeps altering itself. Adorno insists: "The false point of departure of the philosophy of identity comes to light in the insolubility of contingency. The world cannot be thought as a product of consciousness. Contingency is frightening only in the structure of delusion."[7] That contingency—the *ethnos* that awaits to become *logos, ethos,* and ultimately *chaos*—is intuitive in the sense of subjection I have detected and suggested in Persian literary humanism.

As Adorno notes, there is a link between the bourgeois will to dominate and the will of the subject of its modernity to know/own everything. What Adorno left out (typical of all European philosophers—even the most critical) was the colonial extension of that bourgeois will and stayed the course only on its European domain. But his critique of Husserl's epistemology is also the theoretical foregrounding of a critique of the European subject that comes from the peripheralized edges of European imperialism. Yet that critique of the subject must be from the ground up, retrieving the multiple worlds in which varieties of subjection have been historically formed. In this book and in the context of Persian literary humanism, I have offered a reading of the fragmentary subject, contingent on its own manner of self-transcendence, by way of overcoming the colonial extension of the European crisis of the subject, whereby "the Third World" (as they call it) has found itself engaged in a debate that is none of its business. But that engagement has even more critically covered other world-historic modes of subjection extending from Asia to Africa to Latin America. These modes of subjection, just like the one Adorno criticizes, have been covered and camouflaged by the fact and phenomenon of European imperial sovereignty, the modes of knowledge it has generated, and even (or particularly) the sites of resistance it has seen resisting its operation.

Walter Benjamin's (1892–1940) theory of allegory is yet another way of confronting the European will to knowledge that ipso facto posits its all-devouring subject. In contradistinction to the dominant will to know and narrate, Benjamin's theory of allegory charts an apprehension, a sudden staccato recognition of the world as impermanence, of reality as irreality, of life marking mortality, of seeing in mortality the sign of an inconclusive encounter.[8] As both fragmentary and enigmatic, allegory marks a constellation of signs, the privation of the material world into its own semiology. In 1927, Benjamin began working on his *Das Passagenwerk* (*The Arcades Project*) as a study of nineteenth-century Parisian life.[9] Three years later, in 1930, he published a revision of his *habilitation* dissertation *Ursprung des Deutschen Trauerspiel* (*The Origin of German Tragic Drama*). Walter Benjamin's *Passagenwerk* thrives on and celebrates a reading of reality by way of *collage* and *montage*—the art of quoting things out of context and thus allowing them to generate their own context. Avoiding totalism, Benjamin's reading of allegory, as a fragment of a totality, assigns to it the composition of a collage by way of dismantling the autonomy and authority of the subsumed totalities. Benjamin's critique of capitalist modernity led him to a complete abandonment of linear logic:

> Benjamin was at least convinced of one thing: what was needed was a visual, not a linear logic: The concepts were to be imagistically constructed, according to the cognitive principles of montage. Nineteenth-century objects were to be made visible as the origin of the present, at the same time that every assumption of progress was to be scrupulously rejected.[10]

Benjamin's turn to a visual rather than a linear logic is one way of overcoming the assumption of the all-knowing subject in fragmentary (montage) terms. This in part is a reaction to the totalizing consequences of the European Enlightenment as the ideological foregrounding of capitalist modernity. On the site of the colonial consequences of that modernity, the knowing subject is nonexistent, for the colonial qua colonial is the knowable object of that omniscient narrator that calls itself "the West." But taking the question upstream, in the context of Persian literary humanism, I have suggested a different route—historically anchored and textually articulated—for the formation of that fragile subject. Retrieving successive modes of historical self-worlding against the presentist de-worlding effects of European imperialism, I have outlined a grounded mode of subjection from the fertile field of literary humanism. Here I have demonstrated how the central paradox of Persian literary humanism dwelled in its worldliness having been formed at imperial courts, while its final exit from the court was under the duress of

European imperialism. Persian literary humanism is the historic self-realization of a people, coming to meet them where they had invented it in their imaginative anteriority. In it people see themselves reflected, just like Simurgh casting a glance upon a mirror on Mount Qaf—and they see themselves reflected in the historic consciousness of their ancestral alterity.

The crisis of the subject that Adorno and Benjamin had tried—each in his own way—to address finally came to a crescendo in Michel Foucault's more radical critique of Enlightenment modernity. Foucault's *The Order of Things* (*Les Mots et les choses*) (1966) is by now the most compelling account of how "man" as a knowing subject is discursively constituted via the three human sciences of *linguistics, biology,* and *economics.* Foucault's critique of the subject—in both *The Birth of the Clinic* (*Naissance de la clinique*) (1963) and *The Order of Things*—posits "man" as having recently emerged as an object (and thus paradoxically subject) of knowledge. "When natural history becomes biology," Foucault famously concluded, "when the analysis of wealth becomes economics, when, above all, reflection upon language becomes philology, . . . then, in the profoundest upheaval of such an archeological mutation, man appears in his ambiguous position as object of knowledge and as subject that knows: enslaved sovereign, observed spectator, he appears in the place belonging to the king, which was assigned to him in advance by *Las Meninas*, but from which his real presence has for so long been excluded."[11] Foucault's was an archeological undoing of the all-knowing subject of capitalist modernity that had conquered Europe and colonized the world alike.

Foucault's project, here worked out through modern European social and biological sciences, loses momentum in the context of a literary humanism in which the absence of gender-specific pronouns in the language makes it impossible even to surmise if the central figure of the *ma'shuq* (beloved) is male or female, earthly or spiritual, physical or metaphoric. In the context of Persian literary humanism, the knowing subject is self-destructive, and all the knowledge s/he produces suspect, and thus there is no objectivizing the subject. Persian literary humanism has been decidedly de-objectivizing—the mad is the most sane, the most sick is the most healthy, the criminal is the saintly—the subject, thus constantly re/formed, cannot turn himself/herself into anything other than the other than itself.

An Alternative Theory to Modernity

As both a philosophical predicament and a social phenomenon, "modernity" was and remains a principally European problem—while grappling with it in either hermeneutic or postmodern directions provides comparative clues as to how the question of the subject is to be understood or overcome on the colonial domains of that globally presumptuous "modernity." To the degree that it became a global issue, whether by the colonized imagination of those who wanted "to modernize," or else the modernity of the means of colonial conquest and domination,[12] it has cast a European imperial map on the mind, body, soul, and history of the people thus dominated, "modernized," and ruled. Even in the moments of their defiance, colonized people under the normative and imaginative spell of "the modern West" have reversely corroborated the European condition of "modernity" as their problem too.

What I have offered in this book on Persian literary humanism (*Adab*) is not in opposition to the European project of modernity—which remains a perfectly valid and thriving issue in its immediate European context (however falsely globalized). What I have outlined in some historical and textual detail is an alternative vision of subjection, whereby humans become human, in the very last stages of which, when the literary manner of subjection moved from the centrality of *ethnos*, to *logos*, to *ethos*, to *chaos* it was in fact eventually located and articulated within the European imperial context—carrying (obviously) the stamp of its previous imperial framings into newer encounters. In doing so, I have altogether discarded the "tradition *versus* modernity" binary—itself a manufactured opposition superimposed on Persian literary humanism to further universalize the European project of modernity. The far more accurate, grounded, and nuanced morphological succession of *ethnos, logos, ethos,* and *chaos* within successive imperial contexts includes, but does not privilege, the encounter of this humanism with European empires. It does not deny the historic significance of European imperialism—but it does not privilege it with deciding the entire history of the human race. What I have offered here, as a result, is not a theory of alternative modernity—but an alternative theory *to* modernity, the vision of an inner dynamic to the logic and rhetoric, poetic and aesthetic of Persian literary humanism, of its manner of subjection, of how was it that it made humans all too human.

Though I have narrated my story within the vast imperial context of Persian literary humanism, it would still be an exercise in futility and entirely self-delusional to purpose any idea of "humanism" a decade into the twenty-first century and not to confront the traumatizing matter of European philosophical antihumanism or pretend that it did not exist, or otherwise introduce and treat the masterpieces of a rich literary tradition like relics of bygone ages gathered in a museum. My intention has been to produce an account of Persian literary humanism that will speak directly to the challenging traumas of our time and not turn a magnificent literary heritage into an object of Orientalist curiosity, fetishized items of a nationalized literary history, or else the exclusive and privileged scholarly preoccupation of academically secluded "Persianists." I have offered a theory of Persian literary humanism as the modus operandi of a sustained historical mode of subjection as an alternative theory to European modernity, and I have defended the case of a literary humanism based on the particular, contingent, and unstable mode of subjection integral to this humanism. At the receiving end of European imperialism and perforce its philosophical predicaments, the normative hegemony of European humanism and antihumanism requires a sustained argument from within the context of historical experiences silenced precisely by that hegemony.

In making my case, I have also suggested that the literary act creates its own autonomous and even sovereign truth claims, so that through a Bakhtinian act of *heteroglossia* it becomes self-propelling, a kind of detranscendentalized alterity, its signs meaning nothing outside their signature in the text they signal, whereby everything that is said is said through an always already decentered and mislaid knowing subject that denies itself evident agency precisely at the moment that it authors itself. The mortal fragility of *Adami (*human) that keeps historicism at bay but incorporates history into the literary is such that the literary become self-revelatory, positing an evident historicality to the literary act. The autonomous fragility of *Adami* at the heart of Persian literary humanism joins the parabolic prose and poetry that Sa'di had made proverbial to stage the indeterminacy of the knowing subject and the effective dissolution of the narrator to present it as not just autonomous of the scholastic but in fact defiant of its own sovereignty over the fate of successive empires it served and subverted at one and the same time.

The problem of antihumanism is internal to the European philo-sophical crisis, globalized by virtue of the power of philosophical narra-tives that have subsumed the non-European philosophical domains to their self-assured dominance. Positing literary humanism by way of overcoming the problem of the subject points to the evident fact that the self-revelatory disposition of Persian *Adab* has no false self-systematizing subject to authorize or de-authorize it. Edward Said could not resolve the problem of humanism because he remained very much limited within Aristotelian (Western) mimesis and never worked seriously through any other literary tradition than English—Arabic or otherwise. So theoretically he opted for a *quantitative* resolution of the problem of the subject by asking that more "world literature" be added to the re-pository of English and comparative literature project. This does not resolve the issue—it in fact exacerbates it if it ends up assimilating other worldly literatures into what the English and comparative literature pro-grams call "world literature." English and comparative literature in fact digests and absorbs anything that comes its way—whether through Franco Moretti's "distant reading,"[13] Gayatri Spivak's "close reading,"[14] David Damrosch's "world literature,"[15] or Edward Said's "critical humanism"[16]—all housed and launched in and from the English and comparative literature departments. The sovereign subject (falsely self-conscious) continues to gobble up all you feed it into something the (Eu-ropean) knowing subject can grasp and thus devour. The whole idea of "world literature" is an English and comparative literature department menu of exotic appetizers to wet the dulled appetites of their professors (there is only so much Dickens and Austen that one can have)—and scarce has anything to do with worldly literatures they thus carve up and serve to one another. Said's idea of including more "world literature" in the arsenal of "Western humanism" not only does not cure that glut-tonous appetite for exotic food—it positively fattens the self-totalizing subject to disfigured proportions.

Working the problem through Persian literature (or the writing idiomaticity and reading protocols of any other non-European litera-ture) reveals a variety of ways in which the sovereign subject is never formed to falsely organize any knowledge to begin with, for it to be in need of an antihumanism to dismantle it, for the "human" at the heart of (Persian) literary humanism is no knowing subject you can corner and name. The self-signifying literary act is always cognizant of its idiomaticity and as such has no false systematizing subject at its center to decenter, for its shifting, lyrical "heart" cannot hold, for its mimetic acts are always already momentary and indivisible into subject and object, and ipso facto self-destruct, for that "self" is always already somewhere else.

Literature and Transnational Empires

To come to terms with the cosmopolitan worldliness of Persian literary humanism and the enduring significance of the manner in which it has posited the very fragile notion of *human*, it is imperative not to reduce it to a "national literature" and at this stage in fact to reverse the combined distortions of the Orientalist and nationalist readings of it back to its imperial history, and thus come to terms with its transnational, and even more accurately non-national, origins and disposition. The idea will be unsettling to ethnic nationalists of all sorts—Iranians, Afghans, Tajiks, Indians, Turks, Arabs, and so on—but the transnational and imperial context of this literary humanism is written into the very textual and contextual facts of its history, the very global disposition of its idiomaticities.

Because it emerged and thrived in multiple and multinational empires, Persian literary humanism does not exclusively belong to any single, contemporary, postcolonial nation-state. Afghanistan, India, Iran, Pakistan, Tajikistan, and any number of other central Asian states have identical claim on its long and meandering history—and rightly so. Ferdowsi, Nezami, Rumi, Sa'di, Hafez, and so on—these are the master practitioners of Persian poetry performed within multiple imperial contexts, having emerged on a continuum that has thrived on the primacy of *logos* and not *ethnos*—so that by "Persian" we mean, and we can only mean, a *language* and not any false pretense to a *race* or *ethnicity*, which in this case is entirely meaningless. There are no people, no nation, no race, and no ethnicity called "Persian." Any such assumption is entirely fictitious. There is only a language called *Farsi*, or *Dari*, or *Tajik* in Iran, Afghanistan, or Tajikistan, respectively—for all of which there is only one word in English: Persian.

It is thus fundamentally flawed to call Ferdowsi's *Shahnameh*, for example, an "Iranian national epic." It is not. It is as much Afghanistan or Tajikistan's "national epic" as it is Iran's—if we are to commit the fallacy of attributing a product of an *imperial* age to a postcolonial nation-state. Ferdowsi's *Shahnameh* is not a *national* epic of Iran or any other postcolonial nation-state. It is an *imperial* epic, like all other epics, as indeed all epics are products of imperial imaginations—empires that by nature are transnational—in this case Iranians, Turks, Mongols, Indians, and so on. The contemporary Iran, Afghanistan, Tajikistan, Pakistan, India, an so on, have been integral to multiple empires over the last 1,400 years and beyond. It is that historic fact that must inform our reading of their literary products, and not the postcolonial nation-states that are, without a single exception, the product of the encounter of the last of those empires with European imperialism. Ferdowsi's *Shahnameh* belongs to Persian literary humanism so far as "Persian" is the linguistic designation of a *literary* tradition and not the *racial* register of any postcolonial nation and its anxiety of longevity and authenticity. Today when we say "English literature" it will have to include anything from Shakespeare to Hemingway, to Salman Rushdie, to Nadine Gordimer, to V. S. Naipaul—meaning various literary expressions in English and within the real or imaginative contours of the British Empire, and thus "English" here means a language and not a race, an ethnicity, or a breed. The same is true for French or Spanish literature. Spanish literature includes anything from Cervantes to Juan Goytisolo, to Gabriel García Márquez, to Mario Vargas Llosa. It is a literary allusion predicated on a language that was made imperially global, and certainly not on a race. The same is true for "Persian literature"—it can only mean the language, for there are no people called "Persians." Today, there are Iranians, Indians, Pakistanis, Afghans, Tajiks, and so on, as the nationals of various postcolonial nation-states—and they all have identical claims on various stages of Persian literature. Understood in its own terms, Ferdowsi's *Shahnameh* was and remains an imperial epic, produced in the context of two successive and transnational empires, about another forgone imperial age—half-legendary and half-historical. This is not to rob Iranians, Afghans, and so on, of their "national epic"—it is to give it back to them with a far more global imaginary in which they should read their epic.

Ferdowsi's *Shahnameh* was and has remained an imperial epic, transnational, multinational, cross-national, and thus nonnational, for the simple reason that the current postcolonial national boundaries have been drawn over and against multiple imperial mappings from the Samanids to the Safavids down to the Qajars. *Shahnameh* is the product and the manifestation of an imperial imagination. The problem becomes particularly jarring when contemporary Iranian scholars, staunch and fanatical nationalists against the very grain of historical facts, call *Shahnameh* "their" national epic, and then if the Turks or the Afghans call Rumi "their" poet or the Azerbaijanis call Nezami "their" poet, the nationalists get very angry. Ferdowsi's birth and death place of Tus is much closer to Herat and Samarqand than it is to Tehran or Shiraz or Ahvaz. By what authority or reason can an Isfahani or a Tabrizi or an Ahvazi have a claim to the *Shahnameh* that a resident of Herat or Samarqand or Dushanbe does not? If the fact that Ferdowsi's birthplace is within the current borders of Iran were to be the measure, then Iranians will instantly lose Rumi who was born in Balkh in Afghanistan and died in Konya in Turkey. And if they were to cite the fact that Rumi wrote much of his poetry in Persian, they would then instantly lose Avicenna and al-Ghazali and al-Tabari who wrote most of their significant work in Arabic—and thus Iraqis, Egyptians, Kuwaitis, Bahrainis, and Qataris have more right to them than would the people of Hamadhan, Tabarestan, or Tus.

All of these false problems arise when we juxtapose the colonially calibrated postcolonial map of the world—a gift of European colonialism that keeps giving—on the historical mapping of the world in which these poets and by extension Persian literary humanism wrote and was produced. The historical experience of Persian literary humanism is predicated on the fact that it began as the ethnic assumption of Iranians in juxtaposition to a racialized Arab sense of superiority in the late Umayyad and early Abbasid dynasties. But as soon as the Saffarids and Samanid dynasties yielded power to the Turkic empires of the Ghaznavids and the Seljuqids, that *ethnos* as the trope of Persian literary humanism had moved to become a *logos* and "Persian" meant language, not race or ethnicity, for it was, in discourse and disposition, the imperial language and culture of vastly transnational—if we were to use the term *national* ahistorically here—empires. But even that *logos* did not stand still, and because of developments internal to Persian literary humanism and external to its varied imperial contexts, it transmuted to *ethos* during the Timurid period—a development that was exacerbated during the Mughal, Safavid, Ottoman, and Russian empires. But even that *ethos*, put into full practice in the crucible of its encounter with European imperialism, initially in India but later in the rest of the Persianate world, eventually transmuted into *chaos/ashub* as the productive trope of Persian literary humanism in the age of its active interface with colonial domination in the age of European imperialism. Precisely at the moment of its highest self-transcendence, European Orientalism recast it in *ethnic* terms and, in the work of E. G. Browne in particular, drew it toward *ethnos*. In this flawed and misbegotten (even catastrophic) development, European Orientalists like Browne were still infinitely superior to American postmodernist (even Marxist) literary theorists like Fredric Jameson—for if the ethnicizing of Persian literary humanism by the Orientalists was predicated on deep knowledge but poor theory, the postmodernists misapplied European theories that were, and have remained, constitutionally blind to alternative imperial maps of the world before their empire took over and shaped their critical imagination.

The problem with nationalist literary history is not just historical. It is also categorical. It creates much confusion and anarchy for the literary historian who insists on forcefully nationalizing a transnational history. Here is the late Zabihollah Safa, the preeminent Iranian literary historian, trying to explain what he is doing in tracing that history in India:

> A point that needs to be explained is that in this chapter more than in others the domain of my discussions will cross the boundaries of Iran and extend to all those lands/sarzamins that Persian poetry and Adab has reached. I will go after Persian speaking/Farsi-guy poets, writers, and their patrons and those who have served Persian Adab anywhere in Asia Minor/Rum, India, and Transoxiana, that is necessary. I will discuss the life and work of any master Persian-speaker that I find in these lands, whether Iranian, Indian, or from Asia Minor/Rum. Every patron of Persian poets and prose stylists in these discussions is like a brother to me, who has arisen from my Kuy-o-Barzan/ neighborhood and has lived with me—be he a Turk, a Tajik, someone from Asia Minor, or an Indian. I very much hope that this task, which is diluted by no political intentions, will not become an excuse for [scurrilous] interpretations of the sort we have known and recognize—and that no dust of gloom is caused by the steps taken by my thoughts.[17]

This anxiety is caused when the literary historian crosses the current borders of Iran and moves to India to complete his historical narrative. But that anxiety becomes entirely misplaced when we remember that Persian literature produced in the Mughal court or in south Asia had a perfectly natural habitat within an empire adjacent to the Safavid and

Ottoman empires, long before the European empires eventually took them over and redrew the map of the world, within which Zabihollah Safa found himself when writing his history. Literary historians must be able freely to navigate from the Timurids to the Mughals back to the Qajars and so on without the slightest sense of anxiety if they cross over the political boundaries of the map that European empires have imposed on them and their world. Without that crossing over something constitutional, something definitive to Persian literary cosmopolitanism will be lost to the historian.

Another effect of this forced nationalization of literature is the racialization of literary taste, as is evident in the expression *Sabk-e Hendi*, propagated at the height of Reza Shah's ultra-nativist nationalism by the Iranian literary critic Mohammad Taqi Bahar, who in a poem said:

> Their thoughts were weak and their imagination weird;
> Poetry was filled with themes but non-attractive—
> Devoid of elegance.
> Every poet was carrying the burden of meaning;
> Much painfully—
> For which reason Sabk-e Hendi was so garish.[18]

Upon this racialized characterization and dismissal of a literary taste in the Mughal court, yet another literary historian, Yahya Aryanpour, further adds his own gloss and in fact endorses it by saying that at this point "poetry [had] left the royal court and degenerated in the hands of the masses *(beh dast-e ammeh oftad)*."[19]

The same racialization of literary taste is also evident in the thinking of Orientalist scholar Jan Marek about Persian literature in India: "It might indeed be difficult to point out a comparable example in the history of the world literature of a language being adopted, and to find another country having mastered a foreign language to such a degree as was the case with Persian in India. The Indians have contributed very really to the rise of Persian literature, and to them we owe many of its most brilliant pages."[20] Persian was not "adopted" in the Mughal court, nor was it a "foreign language" to its domain. Indians have as much contributed to Persian, Hindi, or English literature as to Bengali, Guajarati, or Marathi—and they are all "their own languages." Here is the perfect example of how Orientalist ethnic nationalization of Persian literature completely distorts the imperial (transnational) context of

Persian language and alienates people from their own language and literature.

Against the grain of these false categories, and placing Persian literary humanism in its proper context of successive empires, I have suggested in the unfolding of Persian literary humanism as a historic event the successive formation of four nodal tropes—*ethnos, logos, ethos,* and *chaos*. If I were to give a comparative example of this idea it would be Hayden White's *Metahistory*, in which he suggests the historical unfolding of four major tropes (from *metaphor* to *metonymy*, to *synecdoche*, and finally *irony*).[21] White offers these tropes by way of alerting historians to the use of linguistic devices in the writing of history. I offer these four morphological tropes by way of an historical unfolding of the modus operandi of literary production, moving from one imperial setting to another, and thus repositing the un/knowing subject at the heart of the literary act. This succession of the tropics of subjection in Persian literary imagination is to me a far more accurate and rooted grounding of historical agency than the European project of modernity. If we follow this train of thought and course of development internal to the logic and rhetoric of Persian literary humanism in multiple imperial contexts over a period of 1,400 years, the question is no longer the possibility of an alternative modernity, but the fact that this course of development is an entirely indifferent, autonomous matrix of subjection to the European philosophical problem of modernity and its contingent crisis of the subject. The imperial and discursive force of European modernity and particularly its gestation as "colonial modernity" have forced themselves on our reading of the non-European worlding in those imported and super/imposed terms. The question here is not to disregard, bypass, or ignore the historical fact of European imperialism, but not to privilege it over all the other previous imperial settings in which Persian literary humanism has been acted out. The Seljuqid, Mongol, Timurid, Mughal, and Safavid empires each had their own distinct impact on Persian literary humanism. Against the grain and texture of this history, the "nationalization" of Persian literature has been instrumental in deworlding it—unplugging it from its historical habitat and casting it into a postcolonial context that assigns it a "Third World" status and glosses over its historic worldliness. My insistence in this book on restoring its historicity and denationalizing its imperial context is to retrieve its cosmopolitan worldliness and its multiple manner of subjection that includes *ethnos* but is not limited to it.

Farewell to Our Orientalists

The enduring impact of Orientalism, ethnic nationalism, and area studies on the study of Persian (and all other non-European) literary humanism has been quite dire. Up until now, the study of Persian literature, both classical and modern, has suffered from a depth of theoretical poverty that it has inherited from Orientalism and extended into nativist nationalism—an aversion to theory that mirrors a tired and belabored face-off between the two overlapping narratives of Orientalism and ethnic nationalism. This poverty of insight is a closed-circuit system that has now degenerated into an Islamic Republic giving lip service to "the glorious Iranian culture" by way of covering up its atrocious abuses of a world religion. Exceedingly competent textual criticism has of course created reliable and heavily glossed texts—from Ferdowsi's *Shahnameh* to Mehdi Akhavan Sales's poetry—but the reading of those texts very much suffers from an analytical positivism that has very little beyond a nativist-nationalist, analytical regurgitation of old-fashioned Orientalism. Outside Iran the scene is not any better with a bizarre combination of watered-down Orientalism and literary comparatist cross-breeding in the impoverished field of "Iranian Studies." The answer to all of this is not an "application" of high theory to "Third World literature"—an even more paralyzing cliché. What is needed is theorization of the history of this literature from within itself, predicated on a detailed textual hermeneutics that is informed by larger theoretical concerns in an organic (not mechanical) way—and always in conversation with other literary settings but not beholden to them.

As Orientalism alienated and othered Persian literature to its own authorship and readership, Iranian literary nativism allegorized it for a nationalist politics, both concealing the worldliness of Persian literary humanism—which in the twentieth century ran away from strictly literary terms and manifested itself in cinema, art, music, drama, and so on. The driving forces of Persian literary humanism became runaway metaphors—decentering it into multiple subject formation. While Orientalist and ethnic nationalist narratives assimilated Persian literary humanism into the colonial and postcolonial world, in parallel terms, English and comparative literature de-worlded it altogether by considering it part of "the Third World Literature." What I have sought to do in this book is to retrieve its historic worldliness, a worldly cosmopolitanism that extends from India through Iran to the Mediterranean basin. That world is now lost to the overextended narratives of Orientalism and ethnic nationalism competing, complementing, and even cross-metaphorizing each other.

The European Orientalist writing on Persian literary history, best exemplified by E. G. Browne and continued to this day with full force and through multivolume projects, has categorically glossed over the inner dynamics of its emotive universes and assimilated downward toward the colonial context of its reception. Browne and other European Orientalists cast Persian literary humanism in ethnic nationalist terms precisely at a moment when for more than 1,000 years after the successful transmutation of its *ethnos* into *logos* and then to *ethos,* it had finally reached a momentous point of self-transmutation into *chaos*—bringing the paralingual semiosis it had achieved during the Timurid and Safavid eras to full literary production within the European imperial context and the creative formation of a public space. Entirely blinded to this tropic development, E. G. Browne and other Orientalists, deeply learned as they were, wasted their vast knowledge of Persian literature on a theoretically flat-footed narration of Persian literary humanism in an *ethnos* tone from beginning to end.

Recasting the masterpieces and thereby the history of Persian literature into a decidedly different narrative than the one canonized by Orientalists and exacerbated by the nativist nationalists, I have offered literary humanism as a key concept in comparative literary studies. I use and locate the concept of "literary humanism" somewhere between its articulation by the detailed textual hermeneutics of George Makdisi and its later comparative theorization by Edward Said and then extend it into a specifically Persian literary context. Persian literature has historically been cast into the shadow of Arabic literary humanism, which in turn prevented George Makdisi from seeing and realizing that humanism was a reality sui generis and should not be framed in the shadow of "Western" literary humanism or Islamic scholasticism. The domain of Persian (or Arabic, Turkish, Urdu) literary humanism was the vast arena of worldly literatures (in the plurality of worlds they have occupied and most certainly not as "world literature," a historical fact that Edward Said never seriously studied during his lifelong preoccupation with humanism, with a mode of knowledge production that did not implicate an all-knowing, imperial, subject position. My objective has been to posit literary humanism as a reality sui generis, autonomous of any alterity to "Western humanism," and adjacent to Islamic scholasticism (my conversation with George Makdisi), and to predicate it on an autonormative constellation of subject positions that posits humanism without implicating an all-knowing subject in the making of a cosmopolitan worldliness (my conversation with Edward Said). Thus, in conversation with two monumental figures in the study of literary humanism, I have sought to make my case.

Worlding the World

The ethnic nationalization of worldly literatures—a project begun by the Orientalists in the context of European imperialism and sustained by literary nationalists in the context of postcolonial nation-building—categorically de-worlds them against the very grain of their historical unfolding. Re-worlding Persian literary humanism means rescuing it from both Orientalism and nativist nationalism, and thus restoring the cosmopolitan worldliness of its historic experiences.

Preempting worldly literatures like Persian, Arabic, Turkish, Urdu or any other similar literature has been the singular, exclusive worlding of what they have consistently called "Western literature." In his *Modern Epic*, Franco Moretti begins with "the world system" and uses it as the foregrounding for an imperial literature that has a universal claim on humanity.[22] The overriding assumption of this idea is that no other literary cosmopolitanism the world has experienced is predicated on a "world system"—if not capitalism at its advanced stages, then imperialism of varied sorts that preceded European imperialism—perfectly capable of having "systematized" their world in terms of the political and economic parameters of their time, and the ideological registers they entailed. Delegating other world literatures to the rank of "world literature," the imperial authority of what calls itself "Western literature" assumes a renewed globality, to the point of even claiming, as Moretti does, Gabriel García Márquez's *One Hundred Years of Solitude* as "Western epic." The same disregard for worlds outside the purview of "Western literature" is even evident in Edward Said's *Culture and Imperialism*, in which he posits the global domination of "Western" imperialism, the literature that it entailed, and the literature that opposed it, all within the global imaginary of "Western literature."[23] In other words, "non-Western" literatures appear as contrapuntal, oppositional, reduced only to the rank of defiance against "Western" domination, and thus ipso facto are denied the fact of worlding their own world. Multiple worlds "other" (thus othered) than this "Western world" and their literary and cultural foregrounding are categorically eclipsed under this "Western" imagination. David Damrosch, for example, categorically declares that world literature has scarcely anything to do with national literatures and is an "elliptical" take on them for consumption in the category of "world literate."[24] The problem with all these readings is their common presentism. They take the current condition of "Western" imperialism and its self-globalization and catapult it across time and space. That other imperial imaginaries have also produced not just their literary cultures but also claimed a world with it, and that the one in which they live is not as dominant ideologically as they think it is does not seem to occur to them.

The only way we can overcome one sovereign, self-conscious worldliness is for the non-English ("non-Western") worlds (now, as the non-Arab empires then) to become conscious of their own worldliness. Arabic literature at the commencement of the Islamic empires and English literature at the height of American imperialism achieved that worldliness at the expense of others by becoming imperially self-conscious, and self-consciously embodying themselves in their canons, into which body they have cannibalized and digested other people's worlds and literatures that today literary theorists call "world literature."

For a world to achieve self-consciousness it must realize the conditions in which the dominant ("Western") world has achieved its exclusive self-assertion as the measure of humanity at large. Antonio Gramsci's take on Immanuel Kant's notion of "the categorical imperative" in his *Groundwork of the Metaphysics of Morals* (1785)—"I ought never to act in such a way that I could not also will that the maxim on which I act should be a universal law"[25]—points to the worldly condition in which the mere supposition of this universality is posited. It is revealing to note, at the very outset, that in the *Prison Notebooks* (1930s) Gramsci in fact slightly (but crucially) misquotes Kant. The way Gramsci remembers the famous quote in prison is this: "Act in such a way that your conduct can become a norm for all men in similar conditions."[26] In other words he replaces "universal law" with "similar conditions." This is an exceedingly insightful piece of misremembering, because it is precisely that unique European (Enlightenment) presumption of universality that preempts the possibility of "similar conditions" to be noted or cultivated in non-European contexts. Conscious of the subalterns of the earth, and in the dungeons of Mussolini's Fascism, and by that act of crucial mis-remembering, Gramsci in effect de-Europeanizes the transnational possibilities of that mode of transcendental universalization. In the clarity and equanimity of his own imagination, Gramsci sees that universality as the possibility of "similar conditions." So he rightly observes that this dictum "is less simple and obvious than it appears at first sight." But how does he dismantle and reconfigure that universality—and make it accessible to the "non-West"?

Gramsci picks up precisely on the point of his misquoting Kant and asks, "What is meant by 'similar conditions?' "—namely he chooses for his hermeneutic unpacking precisely the phrase that he has misremembered from Kant and that Kant in his uncompromising Eurocentric philosophical imagination never used. So Gramsci in fact interprets something that Kant never said, but Gramsci wished and willed him to have said. The answer to this wrong question is the key to Gramsci's path beyond Kant's Eurocentric limitations. There are two kinds of conditions, Gramsci stipulates, under which this universality can be assayed: "the immediate conditions in which one is operating," and then "the complex and organic general conditions, knowledge of which requires long and critically elaborate research." The difference between the two conditions is precisely the difference between the *particular (nativized)* and the *universal (globalized)*—and the universal is nothing but the particular having achieved the self-confidence of projecting itself globally and thus materializing its worldliness. My suggestion is that without the European imperial confidence, Kant would have lacked the universal poise to write such a grand moral narrative, or even if he did it would have never been read as globally consequential. The range and depth of Kant's metaphysical confidence, and the universal implication with which it has been read, I suggest, is proportionate to European imperial conquests.

From this premise Gramsci then moves to say that on the surface Kant's proposition is "a truism . . . since it is hard to find anyone who does not act in the belief that in the conditions he is in everyone else would act in the same way. A man who steals for hunger maintains that hungry people steal; a man who kills his unfaithful wife maintains that all betrayed husbands should kill, etc. It is only 'madmen,' in the clinical sense, who act without believing to be in the right." From here, then Gramsci moves to conclude that: "(1) everyone is indulgent towards himself . . . and (2) everyone acts according to his culture."[27] So what is it that raises a mere truism into the status of an axiom, of categorical imperative in Kant's ethics? From these two premises, Gramsci makes the crucial observation that "Kant's axiom presupposes a single culture, a single religion, a 'world-wide' conformism."[28] All of these are then the premise upon which Gramsci comes across the enduring wisdom that:

> Kant's maxim is connected with his time, with the cosmopolitan enlightenment and the critical conception of the author. In brief, it is linked to the philosophy of the intellectual as a cosmopolitan stratum. Therefore the agent is the bearer of the "similar conditions" and indeed their creator. That is, he "must" act according to a "model" which he would like to see diffused among all mankind, according to a type of civilization for whose coming he is working or for whose preservation he is "resisting" the forces that threaten its disintegration.[29]

The crucial point of Gramsci here, that "Kant's maxim presupposes a single culture, a single religion, a 'world-wide' conformism," is the principal predicate of the more critical argument that the conceptual universalization of the European particular is a European consciousness, a "civilizing mission," which the cosmopolitan Enlightenment, predicated on European imperialism, had made possible. The imperial *Aufgehoben* (sublation) of the European particular to a globalized universal is the condition of the worlding of the world in a manner that a single European can think that his action must be the dictum of a universal mandate. To be sure, there is nothing unusual about Kant's confident universalization of his particular, for this is precisely the way Arab or Persianate literati and philosophers thought of themselves when they were universalizing *their* particular at the heights of, say, the Abbasid or Mongol empires. But the presentist disposition of contemporary Euro-American literary criticism takes that Kantian penchant for self-universalization and globalizes it across time and space.

Gramsci's decoding of Kant's self-universalizing confidence makes it possible for the rest of the world, and the rest of the worlds, to realize that their equally legitimate worlding of the world must reach an identi-

cal self-conscious universalism, minus the imperial hubris, and cultivated in the public space evident in between empires. With a similar
sentiment, but disregarding Gramsci's crucial insight, Edward Said went
after a mechanical (quantitative) expansion of the literary to balance
the limitations of Eurocentric humanism. But you cannot correct a
limited but self-universalizing literary humanism by just accepting the
European take on it as the point of departure and then simply adding to
it. To do so you must recognize their independent, autonomous, historically rooted, and even sovereign worldliness—in the case of Persian literary humanism predicated on four successive tropics of subjection
categorically different from the European condition of "modernity."
Worldliness is not just starting from English (or any other imperial) comparative literature and exponentially globalizing its central tropes. That
worldliness was imperial—picking up from the Sassanids and running
it through the Abbasids—the Samanids, the Tahirids, the Ghaznavids,
the Seljuqids, the Mongols and the Timurids, and then the three empires
of the Mughals, the Safavids, and the Ottomans. That imperial context
of Persian literary humanism then resumed its worldly cosmopolitanism
via its encounter with and response to European cosmopolitan imperialism. From David Damrosch to Franco Moretti and Gayatri Spivak and
Edward Said, whether they want to read other literatures closely, from
a distance, through an ellipsis, or not at all, they do so by disregarding
their worlds, decontextualizing their texts, and categorically assimilating them into their disciplinary domain of English and comparative literature via what Spivak has termed a "sanctioned ignorance." Against
the grain of such de-worldings, by identifying Persian literary humanism as an autonomous and even sovereign domain, I have sought to read
it as the poetic subtext of successive empires throughout the last 1,400
years until it comes to a decisive encounter with European imperialism
in the context of which what calls itself "Western literature" has systematically de-worlded other worldly literatures—while, paradoxically,
and by the force of the opposition that it has engendered, it has in fact
enabled the historical consciousness that it has sought to disable.

The World Regained

After a long and lasting history, Persian literary humanism finally
achieved a renewed cosmopolitan consciousness, a self-awareness, in a

globalized context, overcoming its imperial designation and denial of agency at one and the same time by the creative effervescence of a defiant subject at home in a worldly abode with its own sign and signature on it. To be at home now with this humanism is to descend gently into a vast, generous, warm, comforting, forgiving sea. The current condition of its self-worlding keeps moving from one creative register to another—from film to fiction, poetry, drama, photography, and any number of other visual, performing, and literary arts, all perceived, conceived, and delivered on a vastly expansive public domain. The democratic uprising known as the Green Movement is the most potent social register of this retrieval of its cosmopolitan worldliness, remembering itself, summoning all the other social revolutions from the past, in search of liberty, in want of happiness, in quest of assurances on the uncertain edges of being, of becoming human. You may watch this shimmering wonder shy of a revelation in a Jafar Panahi's film, or else listen to it in a song of Mohammad Reza Shajarian, or behold it in the photography of Bahman Jalali, or get lost finding it in the sinuous prose of a Houshang Golshiri novel. The confidence of Abbas Kiarostami behind his camera, the furious frivolity of Mohsen Namjoo in his music, the seductive solace of Shirin Neshat in her photography and video installations, the mysterious meanderings of Shahrnoush Parsipour in her fiction, or even the childish musings of Marjane Satrapi in her graphic novels are all the scattered indices of a globality of vision that has given birth to new shoots from very distant and robust roots. The shoots grow, the roots deepen, the music resonates, the images multiply, mirrors reflecting mirrors: behold an infinity—life is repeated in the pulsating palpitation of every birthing of an emotion with a pronouncedly Persian lyric and melody to it. Whence the time, wherefore the space: homeland is but a dream a poet once sadly sang. The world, a new world, a world embraced by these visionaries of our hidden and most sacrosanct, or else by the emancipatory uprisings of a people, their better angels singing in their dreams, seeking their otherwise, is now the home of this worldly homecoming, running through it like a mighty river, like the Karun of my memories, self-confident, indifferent to its own majesty, attending to the world it must irrigate—lovingly. In this, its ultimate mode and melody, its resting place, Persian literary humanism has achieved the voice of that world that has given birth to it in its sublimest moments of self-revelations—subjecting and de-subjecting itself, at one and the same time—not by being, but by becoming human, all-too-human:

> Miveh bar shakheh shodam,
> Sangpareh dar kaf-e kudak
>
> I became a fruit upon a branch
> And a stone in a child's hand—
> Just a miracle might save me
> From my own harm—thus determined
> That I am
> Assaulting myself . . .
> Who said I am the last
> Remaining sage of this earth—I am
> That magnificent monster
> Standing upon the equator of this night—drown
> In the crystal clearance of all the waters of the universe—
> From whose devilish vision
> A star is about to rise.
> I have a hut at the end of the earth
> Where the solidity of the soil—just like
> The dancing of a mirage—
> Relies
> On the deceit of thirst.
> Yes—in between man and God—
> In between dust and void—
> I have a ramshackle hut.[30]

Notes

Introduction

1. My translation of a story from Sa'di's *Golestan*, from the critical edition of Gholam Hussein Yusefi, *Golestan* (Tehran: Khwarizmi Publishers, 1368/1989), 58–59.

2. I borrow the title of this section from the seminal work of Philip Rieff, *Freud: The Mind of the Moralist* (Chicago: University of Chicago Press, 1959).

3. I take Sa'di's biographical data, based on the earliest extant sources, from the exquisite work of Zabihollah Safa's *Tarikh-e Adabiat dar Iran* [History of literature in Iran] (Tehran: Tehran University [and other] Press, 1959–1989), vol. III: sec. i: 584–614.

4. See the brief but learned introduction of Mohammad Ali Foroughi, one of the most prominent literary figures of the twentieth century in Iran, to his critical edition of Sa'di's oeuvre, *Kolliyat-e Sa'di* (Tehran: Amir Kabir Publishers, 1984), xiv.

5. Ibid., xii.

6. For a comprehensive history of Mongol conquest, see J. J. Saunders, *The History of the Mongol Conquests* (Philadelphia: University of Pennsylvania Press, 2001).

7. See M. M. Bakhtin, *The Dialogic Imagination: Four Essays*, ed. Michael Holquist, trans. Caryl Emerson and Michael Holquist (Austin: University of Texas Press, 1981).

8. The poem is cited in a story from *Golestan*, in which Sa'di reports he was visiting the mausoleum of John the Baptist in Damascus when an Arab prince approached him and asked him to pray for him, for he was about to face a mortal enemy. "Be merciful to your weak subjects, so you won't be harmed by your mighty enemy," Sa'di responded and then cited this poem for him. See Yusefi, *Golestan*, 66.

9. Ibid.

10. Foroughi, *Kolliyat-e Sa'di*, xiii.

11. In his *Dawn of Historical Reason: The Historicality of Human Existence in the Thought of Dilthey, Heidegger and Ortega Y Gasset* (New York: Peter Lang, 1994), Howard N. Tuttle offers a comparative reading of three different takes on the evident historicality of human life. Dwelling on the thoughts of Wilhelm Dilthey (1833–1911), Martin Heidegger (1889–1976), and Jose Ortega y Gasset (1883–1955), Tuttle narrows in on multiple and varied readings of historicality. Heidegger's *Dasein* here becomes a recasting of Dilthey's historicality of the human condition, lifting Dilthey's epistemology to Heidegger's ontology, and from there to Ortega's insistence that there is no nature to humanity except our history, which ultimately results in the proposition of historical reason. In my reading of the act of the literary, that sense of historicality is self-evident and will not be falsely attributed to a falsely organizing subject.

12. For the original text of the story, see Yusefi, *Golestan*, 162–168.

13. For an excellent example in Christian context, see James H. Overfield, *Humanism and Scholasticism in Late Medieval Germany* (Princeton: Princeton University Press, 1984). See also Erika Rummel, ed., *Biblical Humanism and Scholasticism in the Age of Erasmus* (Leiden: Brill, 2008).

14. See George Makdisi, *The Rise of Colleges: Institutions of Learning in Islam and the West* (Edinburgh: Edinburgh University Press, 1981); and *The Rise of Humanism in Classical Islam and the Christian West: With Special Reference to Scholasticism* (Edinburgh: Edinburgh University Press, 1990).

15. Makdisi, *Rise of Humanism*, xix.

16. Ibid.

17. Yusefi, *Golestan*, 171.

18. Ibid., 170.

19. Makdisi, *Rise of Humanism*, xix.

20. Ibid., xx.

21. I have in part developed the central role of Persian vizierate in this capacity in the following essay: "The Philosopher/Vizier: Khwajah Nasir al-Din al-Tusi and His Isma'ili Connection." In *Studies in Isma'ili History and Doctrines*, ed. Farhad Daftari (Cambridge: Cambridge University Press, 1996).

22. Makdisi, *Rise of Humanism*, xx.

23. Ibid.

24. Ibid.

25. My translation of *"Hameh omr bar-nadaram sar az ain khomar-e masti. . . ."* For the original Persian, see Foroughi, *Kolliyat-e Sa'di*, 606.

26. See Martin Heidegger, "Letter on Humanism," in *Basic Writings* (New York: Harper & Row, 1977), 189–242.

27. For more on the idea of *il pensiero debole* (weak thought), see Gianni Vattimo and Pier Aldo Rovatti, eds., *Il Pensiero Debole* (Genova: Feltrinelli, 2010). "Weak thought," as Daniel Barbiero succinctly summarizes the idea,

"entails a reevaluation of philosophical reason . . . as a discourse that suppresses, or is not equipped to address, the ruptures and discontinuities that present themselves in our experiences of the world. Against philosophical reason, with its emphasis on the 'strong' values of logic and continuity, weak thought proposes the construction of a philosophical discourse sensitive to the ruptures of experience, as well as the largely metaphorical language deemed necessary to encompass experience" ("Weakness for Heidegger: The German Root of Il Pensiero Debole," *New German Critique*, no. 55 [Winter 1992]: 159–172).

28. See Edward Said, *Orientalism* (New York: Penguin Books, 1995), 340.

29. Ibid., xvii.

30. See Edward Said, *Humanism and Democratic Criticism* (New York: Columbia University Press, 2004), 9–10.

31. Ibid., 10.

32. Ibid., 10–11.

33. See R. Radhakrishnan, "Edward Said's Literary Humanism," (*Cultural Critique*, 67 (Fall 2007): 16.

34. Ibid.

35. Ibid., 17.

36. Ibid., 21–22.

37. Frantz Fanon, *Wretched of the Earth* (New York: Grove Press, 1963), 311.

38. Said, *Humanism and Democratic Criticism* (op. cit): 54.

39. Ibid., 55.

40. A volume of Ehsan Yarshater's projected multi-volume *History of Persian Literature*, now in preparation, is dedicated to the "Oral Literature of Iranian Languages: Kurdish, Pashto, Balochi, Ossetic." This is a welcome addition to a fuller understanding of Persian literary humanism.

41. See Yusefi, *Golestan*, 36.

42. Ibid., 32.

43. For further details on this genre, see the introduction to the critical edition of Farid al-Din Attar's *Asrar al-Tawhid fi Maqamat al-Sheikh Abu Sa'id* [Secrets of unification: on the spiritual attainments of al-Sheykh Abu Sa'id]. Edited with notes and introduction by Mohammad Reza Shafi'i-Kadkani (Tehran: Agah, 1987), 96–100.

44. Judith Butler, *Bodies That Matter: On the Discursive Limits of Sex* (London: Routledge, 1993), x.

45. Ibid., 116.

46. See Erving Goffman, *The Presentation of Self in Everyday Life* (New York: Anchor Books, 1959), 252. Goffman traces the origin of his ideas at least back to Charles H. Cooley and his *Human Nature and the Social Order* (New Brunswick, NJ: Transactions Publishers, 1922/1983). See Goffman, 35.

47. Ibid.; Cooley, *Human Nature*, 35.

48. Ibid., 252.

49. Of course in Søren Kierkegaard, Jacques Derrida, and John Caputo there is a common trace of resolving this question of the subject via the idea of God as "the possibility for me to keep a secret which is inwardly visible but outwardly invisible," on the basis of which Kierkegaardian/Derridian idea Caputo then suggests, "What I call God, God in me, calls me to be myself, the interior I, which Kierkegaard calls 'subjectivity.'" This subject, Caputo then adds, "posits one of the most fascinating tensions in which is its simultaneous destruction of Cartesian subjectivity." (See John D. Caputo, *The Prayers and Tears of Jacques Derrida: Religion without Religion* [Bloomington: Indiana University Press, 1997], 215–216.) In the mystical dimension of Persian literature we might consider a similar resolution.

50. As now fully demonstrated by Massad in his *Desiring Arabs*, 107–109, 121–123, et passim.

51. See Foroughi, *Kolliyat-e Sa'di*, 205.

52. For the original version of this story, see Foroughi, *Kolliyat-e Sa'di*, 919–921.

1. The Dawn of an Iranian World in an Islamic Universe

1. For the most recent scholarship on the Sassanid empire, see Touraj Daryaee's *Sasanian Iran (224–651 CE): Portrait of a Late Antique Empire* (Costa Mesa, CA: Mazda Publishers, 2008), and his *Sasanian Persia: The Rise and Fall of an Empire* (London: I. B. Tauris, 2009).

2. For a history of the Byzantine Empire during the rise of Islam, see Robert Browning, *The Byzantine Empire* (Washington, DC: Catholic University of America Press, 1992), 1–40.

3. For a groundbreaking new work on the decline and fall of the Sassanids, see Parvaneh Pourshariati's *Decline and Fall of the Sasanian Empire: The Sasanian-Parthian Confederacy and the Arab Conquest of Iran* (London: I. B. Tauris, 2008).

4. For a recent narrative of the early Muslim conquest, see Hugh Kennedy *The Great Arab Conquests: How the Spread of Islam Changed the World We Live In* (New York: Da Capo, 2007).

5. For a detailed examination of the Arab conquest of Iran, see Abdolhossein Zarrinkub's "The Arab Conquest of Iran and Its Aftermath," in *The Cambridge History of Iran*, vol. 4, *The Period from the Arab Conquest to the Saljuqs*, ed. R. N. Frye (Cambridge: Cambridge University Press, 1975), 1–56. See also E. G. Browne, *A Literary History of Persia* (Cambridge: Cambridge University Press, 1902), I:127–247.

6. See Abdolhossein Zarrinkub, *Do Qarn Sokut* [Two centuries of silence] (Tehran: Javidan, 1951). For the most recent scholarship on the Umayyad dynasty, see G. R. Hawting, *The First Dynasty of Islam: The Umayyad Caliphate AD 661–750* (London: Routledge, 2000).

7. R. A. Nicholson, *A Literary History of the Arabs* (Cambridge: Cambridge University Press, 1907), 278.

8. See Morteza Ravandi, *Tarikh-e Ijtema'i Iran* [Social history of Iran] (Tehran: Amir Kabir, 1974), II:114–115.

9. For a detailed account of the Abbasid caliphate in Iran, see Roy Mottahedeh, "The Abbasid Caliphate in Iran," in Frye, ed., *Cambridge History of Iran*, 4:57–89.

10. For a pioneering study of the contribution of Iranian literati to Arabic literature, see Victor Danner, "Arabic Literature in Iran," in Frye, ed., *Cambridge History of Iran*, 4:566–594.

11. Ibn Khaldun, cited in Nicholson, *Literary History of the Arabs*, 278.

12. Ibid., 281.

13. Ibid., 277.

14. For a general account of Iran in the early Abbasid period, see Browne, *Literary History of Persia*, I:251–336.

15. Nicholson, *Literary History of the Arabs*, 279.

16. Ibid., 280.

17. For a study of these sectarian revolutionary uprisings, see B. S. Amoretti, "Sects and Heresies," in Frye, ed., *Cambridge History of Iran*, 4:481–519.

18. For more on the history of the Tahirids and the Saffarids, see C. E. Bosworth, "The Tahirids and Saffarids" in Frye, ed., *Cambridge History of Iran*, 4:90–135.

19. For further on Ya'qub bin Laith as-Saffar's attention to Persian language and poetry, see Zabihollah Safa, *Tarikh-e Adabiyat dar Iran* [History of Persian literature in Iran] (Tehran, Ibn Sina, 1959), I:39, 166.

20. For a study of the Buyid dynasty in this period, see Heribert Busse, "Iran under the Buyids," in Frye, ed., *Cambridge History of Iran*, 4:250–304.

21. For a study of the rise of Persian language in the immediate aftermath of the Arab conquest, see G. Lazard, "The Rise of the New Persian Language," in Frye, ed., *Cambridge History of Iran*, 4:595–632.

22. For the most recent and comprehensive study of this transitional period, see Mohammad Mohammadi Malayeri, *Tarikh va Farhang-e Iran dar Doran-e Enteqal as Asr-e Saasani beh Asr-e Islami* [The history and culture during the transition period from the Sassanids to the Islamic period], 6 vols. (Tehran: Tus Publication, 2000).

23. For an introduction to pre-Islamic literature in Iran, see Otakar Klima, "Avesta, Ancient Persian Inscriptions, Middle Persian Literature," in *History of Persian Literature*, ed. Jan Rypka (Dordrecht, The Netherlands: D. Reidel, 1968), 1–67.

24. For an account of the earliest archeological inscriptions of pre-Islamic origin, see Browne, *Literary History of Persia*, I:3–38.

25. As quoted in *Persian Literature* ed. Ehsan Yarshater (New York: State University of New York Press 1988), 5–6.

26. Ibid., 6.

27. For further details, see Mary Boyce, *A History of Zoroastrianism* (Leiden: Brill, 1975).

28. For a detailed discussion of the Avestan literature in this period, see Dale Bishop's *"Literary Aspects of the Avesta,"* in Yarshater, ed., *Persian Literature,* chap. 2.

29. For more details on the literary heritage of this early period see Browne, *Literary History of Persia,* 88–123.

30. Yarshater, ed., *Persian Literature,* 10–11.

31. Ibid., 10.

32. Ibid.

33. For a recent English translation of which, see Fakhraddin Gorgani, *Vis and Ramin,* trans. Dick Davis (Washington, DC: Mage, 2009).

34. For more on Zoroastrian-related literature in the aftermath of the Muslim conquest see J. de Menasce, "Zoroastrian Literature after the Muslim Conquest," in Frye, ed., *Cambridge History of Iran,* 4:543–565.

35. For a pioneering study of the rise of Persian prose after the Arab invasion, see Rypka, ed., *History of Persian Literature,* 108–125.

36. For a learned discussion of these initial texts, see Mohammad Qazvini, "Qadimitarin Ketab dar Zaban-e Farsi Haliyeh [The oldest book in contemporary Persian]," in *Bist Maqaleh Qazvini* [Twenty essays by Qazvini] (Tehran: Donya-ye Ketab, 1984), I:64–65.

37. For further details, see ibid., I:65.

38. For more details on the Samanid dynasty, see R. N. Frye, "The Samanids," in Frye, ed., *Cambridge History of Iran,* 4:136–161.

39. Ibid., *Bist Maqaleh Qazvini.*

40. Ibid., II:16–18.

41. The origins of this genre of *Khwaday-namag* are in fact deeply rooted in the pre-Islamic dynasties, and the connection of this genre to the eventual writing of Ferdowsi's *Shahnameh* is the subject of extensive scholarship. For the most recent and comprehensive study of this subject, see Jalal Khaleqi-Motlaq, "Az *Shahnameh* ta *Khwaday-namag* [From *Shahnameh* to *Khwaday-namag*]," Noufe website: http://noufe.com/persish/Khaleghi/pdf/azshahnametakhoday name.pdf (accessed January 15, 2009).

42. Qazvini's critical edition of this text, from which I translate, is in "The Oldest Book in Contemporary Persian," II:30–31.

43. This assertion of Abu Mansur al-Mu'ammari that Ibn Muqaffa' brought *Panchatantra* to al-Ma'mun's attention is actually false and anachronistic. Ibn Muqaffa was killed in 757 by the Abbasid caliph al-Mansur (r. 754–775). He could not have done any such thing during the reign of caliph al-Ma'mun (813–833) more than half a century after he was dead. This is a famous error in the preface of Abu Mansur's *Shahnameh,* which Ferdowsi repeats almost verbatim in his subsequent poetic rendition. Qazvini and other *Shahnameh*

scholars in fact cite the repetition of this error as proof that Ferdowsi was following his prose exemplar very closely.

44. Qazvini, "The Oldest Book in Contemporary Persian," II:44.

45. For further details on the sources of, see Khaleqi-Motlaq, "From *Shahnameh* to *Khwaday-namag*."

46. Qazvini, "The Oldest Book in Contemporary Persian," II:69–70.

47. For more on the significance of the Samanid period, see Rypka, ed., *History of Persian Literature*, 126–171.

48. For more on the origin of Persian poetry in the aftermath of Arab invasion, see Safa, *Tarikh-e Adabiyat dar Iran*, I:163–182.

49. See Qazvini, "Qadimitarin She'r-e Farsi [The oldest Persian poem]," in *Bist Maqaleh Qazvini*, 35.

50. As cited in Ibid., 41.

51. Ibid., 43–44.

2. The Persian Presence in the Early Islamic Empires

1. This old story, which has subsequently been depicted in many manuscript illustrations, dates back to the earliest manuscripts of Ferdowsi's *Shahnameh*, such as the famous Florence manuscript of 1217, in which there are two prose introductions, in one of which this story appears. Mahmoud Omidsalar, the distinguished contemporary *Shahnameh* scholar, believes that "it is a literary use of the traditional motif of poetic ability tested, motif H509.4 of Thompson's Motif-Index. [S. Thompson. Motif-index of folk-literature: a classification of narrative elements in folktales, ballads, myths, fables, medieval romances, exempla, fabliaux, jest-books, and local legends. Revised and Enlarged Edition. (Bloomington, IN: Indiana University Press, 1955–1958)]." He dates the story as early as ca. 1150. I am grateful to Mahmoud Omidsalar for this explanation.

2. Nicholson, *Literary History of the Arabs*, 266.

3. For an English translation, see Abu al-Hasan al-Mawardi, *al-Ahkam al-Sultaniyyah* [The laws of Islamic governance], trans. Asadullah Yate (London: Ta-Ha Publishers, 1996).

4. These Persian political treatises are the subject of extensive scholarship by Seyyed Djavad Tabataba'i. See, e.g., his *Daramadi bar Tarikh-e Andisheh Siasi dar Iran* [An introduction to the history of political thought in Iran] (Tehran: Islamic Republic Foreign Ministry Publications, 1988). In English see the equally important scholarship of A. K. S. Lambton, *Theory and Practice in Medieval Persian Government* (London: Variorum Reprints, 1980).

5. Seyyed Djavad Tabataba'i is particularly attentive to what he considers the "Iranshahri/Persepolis" dimensions of these Persian political discourses.

6. See Amir Unsur al-Ma'ali Keikavus ibn Iskandar ibn Qabus ibn Vushmgir ibn al-Ziyar, *Qabusnameh*, ed. Gholam Hossein Yusefi (Tehran: Elmi va

Farhangi, 1966), 86–87. One might think that Amir Unsur al-Ma'ali is unabashedly "bisexual" in his inclinations, except he does not seem to think that there is a shift in a man's sexuality if he goes with one sort in summer and another in winter. For him it is just a matter of bodily and political balance, e.g., similar to having too much of the same fruit. Women (*zanan*) and slave boys (*gholaman*) are interchangeable object of a man's sexual pleasure (*tamatto'*). He partakes in one on certain occasions and in another on others.

7. Ibid., 144.

8. Nicholson, *Literary History of the Arabs*, 267.

9. Ibid., 266.

10. Edward W. Said, *Culture and Imperialism* (New York: Knopf, 1993), xii.

11. Ibid., xv–xvi.

12. To this day, Iranian historiographies are traumatized by accounts of these atrocious records. For a very sedate account, see Hasan Pirnia and Abbas Iqbal Ashtiani, *Tarikh-e Iran* (Tehran: Khayyam, 1967), 90.

13. Said, *Culture and Imperialism*, xiii–xiv.

14. Ibid., xii.

15. See Joseph Massad, *Desiring Arabs* (Chicago: University of Chicago Press, 2007), 108. The central thesis of Massad, that "modern and contemporary Arab historiography developed to a considerable extent around the repudiation not only of men's love for boys but also of all sexual desires it identified as part of the Arab past which the European present condemns and sometimes champions" (1), is entirely contingent on the manufacturing of "an Arab past" in which Persians were the contaminant of its virtuous characters.

16. Ibid., 109.

17. Ibid., 108.

18. One must not of course overgeneralize this point, for there was much cross-national anticolonial solidarity that linked Arab, Iranian, and south Asian nationalism. To this day, streets in Cairo are named after Mohammad Musaddiq.

19. Massad, *Desiring Arabs*, 122.

20. Ibid., 218.

21. Ibid., 63, 218.

22. Leila Ahmed, *Women and Gender in Islam: Historical Roots of a Modern Debate* (New Haven: Yale University Press, 1992), 19.

23. Ibid., 28.

24. Ibid., 77.

25. For more on Persian court poetry, see Julie Scott Meisami, *Medieval Persian Court Poetry* (Princeton, NJ: Princeton University Press, 1987).

26. For a full discussion of the prominent features of court poetry in this period, see Jerome E. Clinton's "Court Poetry at the Beginning of the Classical Period," in Yarshater, ed., *Persian Literature*, 75–95.

27. See Safa *Tarikh-e Adabiyat dar Iran*, I:449–451.

28. For a pioneering history of Persian epic poetry in the Islamic period, see Zabihollah Safa, *Hamaseh Sara'i dar Iran* [Epic poetry in Iran] (Tehran: Amir Kabir, 1990).

29. As I noted in the case of *Qabusnameh*, the appellations of "homosexuality" or "heterosexuality" as we understand them today are not categorically applicable to Iranian or any other non-Eurocentric contexts. The author of *Qabusnameh* clearly instructs his son to have sex with *gholam* (slave boys) and *zanan* (women) intermittently, as a matter of balance and the golden mean, and by way of not exaggerating in one way or another. Central in *Qabusnameh*, which was meant as an instructional manual for a civilized life, is the primacy of masculinist sexual desires that can be satisfied in two equally normative ways. So the assumption of heteronormativity, or a fortiori homonormativity, is not applicable here at all. Ferdowsi's cryptic reference to Daghighi's "*khu-ye bad* [bad habit]" might be his own personal stand, but it does not mean "homosexuality" (thus qualified) was not acceptable in the medieval world. For a critical assessment of this point, see the excellent arguments of Joseph Massad in his *Desiring Arabs*.

30. For an excellent poetic rendition into English, see Dick Davis's translation, *Shahnameh: The Persian Book of Kings* (New York: Viking, 2006).

31. For two excellent essays on *Shahnameh*, see the articles by William L. Hanaway, "Epic Poetry" and Amin Banani, "Ferdowsi and the Art of Tragic Epic," in Yarshater, *Persian Literature*, 96–108 and 109–119, respectively.

32. See Antonio Gramsci, "What Is Man?" in his *Modern Prince and Other Writings* (New York: International Publishers, 1957), 76–81.

33. Ibid., 77.

34. Ibid., 78.

35. Ibid., 78–79.

36. Ibid., 80.

37. Mohammad Dabir Siyaqi, ed., *Divan-e Manuchehri Damghani* (Tehran: Zavvar, 1984), 27–28.

38. Ibid., 72.

39. For an English translation of the story of "Rostam and Sohrab," see Abolqasem Ferdowsi, *In the Dragon's Claws: The Story of Rostam and Esfandiar from the Persian Book of Kings*, trans. Jerome W. Clinton (Washington, DC: Mage, 1999).

3. The Prose and Poetry of the World

1. See for example Allan Megill's cogent readings in his *Prophets of Extremity: Nietzsche, Heidegger, Foucault, Derrida* (Berkeley: University of California Press, 1985), 2–3.

2. For a classical study of the general condition of Central Asia that includes the Seljuqids in a much larger frame of reference, see René Grousset, *The Empire*

of the Steppes: A History of Central Asia (New Brunswick: Rutgers University Press, 1970). For the most recent scholarship on the Seljuqids, see Osman Aziz Basan, *The Great Seljuqs: A History* (London: Routledge, 2010).

3. For the historical context of the rise of the Seljuqids, see C. E. Bosworth, "The Political and Dynastic History of the Iranian World (A.D. 1000–1217)," in *The Cambridge History of Iran*, vol. 5, *The Saljuq and Mongol Periods*, ed. J. A. Boyle (Cambridge: Cambridge University Press, 1968), 1–202.

4. For more on the administrative apparatus of the Seljuqids, see A. K. S. Lambton, "The Internal Structure of the Saljuq Empire," in Boyle, *Cambridge History of Iran*, 5:203–282.

5. For more on the Isma'ili branch of Shi'ism and its revolutionary uprisings, see Hamid Dabashi, *Shi'ism: A Religion of Protest* (Cambridge, MA: Harvard University Press, 2010), 132–158.

6. Hans-Georg Gadamer, *Truth and Method* (New York: Crossroad, 1975), 401.

7. Ibid.

8. For further details on Nezam al-Molk's Persian writings on politics, see Zabihollah Safa, *Tarikh-e Adabiyat dar Iran* (Tehran, Ibn Sina, 1959), II:904–909.

9. Nezam al-Mulk, *The Book of Government or Rules for Kings*, trans. Hubert Darke (London: Routledge & Kegan Paul, 1960), 9. Hubert Darke had done this translation based on his own critical edition of *Siasatnameh* (Tehran: Bongah Tarjomeh va Nashr-e Ketab, 1976).

10. For the critical edition of *Nasihat al-Moluk*, see Imam Mohammad ibn Mohammad ibn Mohammad al-Ghazali al-Tusi, *Nasihat al-Moluk*, ed. Jalal Homa'i (Tehran: Babak, 1982).

11. For more on the centrality of *justice* in Persian political thought, see A. K. S. Lambton, "Justice in the Medieval Persian Theory of Kingship," *Studia Islamica* XVII(1956); reprinted in *Theory and Practice in Medieval Persian Government* (London: Variorum Reprints, 1980), 91–119.

12. For more details on al-Ghazali's political thought, see A. K. S. Lambton, "The Theory of Kingship in the *Nasihat ul-Muluk* of Ghazali," *Islamic Quarterly* I(1954); reprinted in *Theory and Practice in Medieval Persian Government*, 47–55.

13. See the editor's introduction to al-Ghazali, *Nasihat al-Moluk*, 81.

14. For more on Persian political thought, see A. K. S. Lambton, "Quis custodiet custodes: Some Reflections on the Persian Theory of Government," *Studia Islamica* V/VI (1956); reprinted in *Theory and Practice in Medieval Persian Government*, 125–146.

15. I have developed this idea of "philosopher-vizier" in an essay on another major political thinker (of the Mongol period), Khwajah Nasir al-Din al-Tusi. See Hamid Dabashi, "The Philosopher/Vizier: Khwajah Nasir al-Din al-Tusi and His Isma'ili Connection," in *Studies in Isma'ili History and Doctrines*, ed. Farhad Daftari (Cambridge: Cambridge University Press, 1996).

16. I have dealt in some detail with the political power of Tarkan Khatun in the matter of succession to her husband Malik Shah in my *Truth and Narrative: The Untimely Thoughts of Ayn al-Qudat al-Hamadhani* (London: Curzon, 1999), chap. 10.

17. For more on Seyyed Javad Tabataba'i's notion of *Iranshahri/Persopolitan* see his *Daramadi Falsafi bar Tarikh Andisheh Siasi dar Iran* [A philosophical introduction to the history of political thought in Iran] (Tehran: Political and International Studies Publications, 1988).

18. For more on the social and economic conditions of the Seljuqid period, see M. A. Dandamaev et al., *Tarikh-e Iran* [History of Iran] trans. Kikhosrow Keshavarzi (Tehran: 1980), 197–212.

19. For more on the Isma'ili revolutionary movements in this period, see Dabashi, *Shi'ism*, 103–131. For a more detailed treatment, see Farhad Daftary, *The Isma'ilis: Their History and Doctrines* (Cambridge: Cambridge University Press, 1992).

20. For an introduction to the famous Danesh-nameh Ala'i and his major philosophical text in Persian, see Hamid Dabashi, "Danish-namah-yi 'Ala'i" in *Encyclopedia Iranica,* http://www.iranicaonline.org/articles/danes-nama-ye-alai -persian-philosophical-treatise-written-by-avicenna-q, (accessed September 15, 2011).

21. For more on Nasir Khosrow, see Dabashi, *Shi'ism*, 103–131; for a more detailed account of his life and thoughts, see Alice C. Hunsberger, *Nasir Khusraw: The Ruby of Badakhshan: A Portrait of the Persian Poet, Traveler and Philosopher* (London: I. B. Tauris, 2003).

22. Nasir Khosrow, *Divan*, ed. Mojtaba Minovi, annot. Ali Akbar Dehkhoda, with an introduction by Hasan Taghizadeh (Tehran: Donya-ye Ketab, 1988), 14. This obvious reference to Matt. 7:6—"Do not give dogs what is sacred; do not throw your pearls to pigs. If you do, they may trample them under their feet, and then turn and tear you to pieces"—is a clear indication of Nasir Khosrow's knowledge of the Bible (King James translation).

23. Onsori was a prominent poet of the Ghaznavid era, and Ammar ibn Yasir and Abu Dharr al-Ghifari were two of the closest comrades and companions of Prophet Muhammad.

24. For an excellent introductory essay on the life and thought of Suhrawardi, see Hossein Ziai, "Shihab al-Din Suhrawardi: Founder of the Illuminationist School," in *History of Islamic Philosophy,* ed. Oliver Leaman and Seyyed Hossein Nasr, (London: Routledge, 2001), 434–464.

25. See Shahab al-Din Yahya Suhrawardi, *Majmu'eh Mosannafat Shaykh Ishraq* [Collected works of Shaykh Ishraq], vol. 3, ed. with commentaries and an introduction by Seyyed Hossein Nasr, with a French introduction by Henry Corbin (Tehran: Académie Imperiale Iranienne de Philosophie, 1977), 197–205. For an English translation of these allegories, see Shihabuddin Yahya Suhrawardi, *The Mystical & Visionary Treatises of Suhrawardi,* trans. W. M. Thackston

Jr. (London: Octagon, 1982). I use the original Persian and provide my own translations.

26. For more on Baba Taher Oryan, see Safa, *Tarikh-e Adabiyat dar Iran*, II:383–386. See also the excellent essay of L. P. Elwell-Sutton in *Encyclopedia Iranica*, "BĀBĀ ṬĀHER ʿORYĀN" http://www.iranicaonline.org/articles/baba -taher-oryan (acccessed September 30, 2011).

27. For an excellent introduction to Omar Khayyam's life and works, see Mehdi Aminrazavi, *The Wine of Wisdom: The Life, Poetry, and Philosophy of Omar Khayyam* (Oxford: Oneworld, 2005).

28. For a classical study of the hidden side of Victorian morality, see Steven Marcus, *The Other Victorians: A Study of Sexuality and Pornography in Mid-Nineteenth-Century England* (New York: Basic Books, 1974).

29. For a short introduction to Ayn al-Qudat's life and thought, see Hamid Dabashi, "Ayn al-Qudat al-Hamadhani and the Intellectual Climate of His Time," in *History of Islamic Philosophy*, ed. Oliver Leaman and Seyyed Hossein Nasr (London: Routledge, 2001), 374–433. For a much more extensive study, see Dabashi, *Truth and Narrative*.

30. Ayn al-Qudat al-Hamadhani, *Nameh-ha/Makaib* [Letters], 2 vols., ed. Alinaqi Monzavi and Afif Osayran (Tehran: Golshan, 1969–1972), II:81–82.

31. Ibid., II:189–199.

32. For an English translation, see Farid al-Din Attar, *The Conference of the Birds*, trans. Afkham Darbandi and Dick Davis (London: Penguin Classics, 1984).

33. Peter Brook and Shirin Neshat have done theatrical renditions of *The Conference of the Birds*. For more details, see Hamid Dabashi, "It Was in China, Late One Moonless Night, *Social Research* (70, no. 3 (Fall 2003).

34. For a pioneering study of the relationship between mysticism and Persian literature in larger context see Annemarie Schimmel, *As Through A Veil: Mystical Poetry in Islam* (Oxford: Oneworld, 2001).

35. For a comprehensive essay on *Vis and Ramin*, see M. J. Mahjoub's introduction to his critical edition of the text, Fakhraddin Gorgani, *Vis va Ramin*, ed. and annot. with an introduction by M. J. Mahjoub (Tehran: Nashr-e Andisheh, 1959). There are two translations of this text into English: F. A. Gorgani, *Vis and Ramin*, trans. George Morrison (New York: Columbia University Press, 1972); and Fakhraddin Gorgani, *Vis and Ramin*, trans. (Washington, DC: Mage, 2008).

36. For an excellent study of Nezami's life and work, see Abdolhossein Zarrinkub, *Pir-e Ganjeh: Dar Josteju-ye Nakoja-abad: Athar va Andishe-ye Nezami* [The Master from Ganjeh: in search of Utopia: the works and thoughts of Nezami] (Tehran: Nashr-e Sokhan, 1993).

37. For an excellent introduction to Nezami's poetry, see Peter Chelkowski's "Nezami: Master Dramatist" in Yarshater, ed., *Persian Literature*, 179–189; J. C. Burgel's *"The Romance,"* in the same volume, 9: 161–178, is a comprehensive introduction to the genre.

38. This section has unfortunately been left untranslated in the excellent translation of Afkham Darbandi by Dick Davis in *The Conference of the Birds*. For the original, see Shaykh Farid al-Din Attar, *Manteq al-Tayr*, ed. Seyyed Sadeq Goharin (Tehran: Entesharat Elmi va Farhangi, 1963), 246–253.

39. For a critical edition of *Samak Ayyar*, see Faramarz ibn Khodadad ibn Abdollah al-Kateb al-Arjani, *Samak Ayyar*, 6 vols., ed. with an introduction and notes by Parviz Natel Khanlari (Tehran: Bonyad Farhang Iran, 1958–1974).

40. For more details on the context and content of Samak Ayyar, see Safa, *Tarikh-e Adabiyat dar Iran*, II:990.

41. See the introduction of Khanlari, *Samak Ayyar*, 1:5–12; and the entire sixth volume, which is dedicated to an excellent scholarly examination of the text.

42. For a superb translation of the Amir Hamza story from a south Asian version, see Ghalib Lakhnavi and Abdullah Bilgrami, *The Adventures of Amir Hamza*, trans. Musharraf Ali Farooqi (New York: Modern Library, 2007).

43. For a biographical essay on Abu al-Fazl Bayhaqi, see Gholam Hussein Yusefi's entry under "Bayhaqi, Abu'l-Fazl" in *Encyclopedia Iranica* online, http://www.iranicaonline.org/articles/bayhaqi-abul-fazl-mohammad-b. (accessed October 15, 2011).

44. For a critical edition see Abu al-Fazl Bayhaqi, *Ta'rikh-e Bayhaqi*, ed. Ali Akbar Fayyaz (Mashhad: Mashhad University Press, 1996).

45. There is an excellent study of Bayhaqi's *History* by the late Marilyn Robinson Waldman in her pioneering work *Toward a Theory of Historical Narrative: A Case Study in Perso-Islamicate Historiography* (Columbus, OH: Ohio State University Press, 1980).

4. The Triumph of the Word

1. This statement was uttered by a resident of Bokhara who had escaped the Mongol massacre and run away to Khurasan, where, upon being asked what had happened, he uttered these swift and effective words. The report is first recorded by the great historian of the early Mongol period, Ata-Malik al-Jovayni in his *Ta'rikh-e Jahan-gusha* [History of the world conqueror], 3 vols., ed. Mohammad Qazvini (Leiden: E. J. Brill, 1912), 1:83. Upon recording these words, al-Jovayni adds, "all those learned people who were present and heard these words concurred that one cannot be more precise and brief in the Persian language" (83).

2. For more on the history and conquests of the Mongol Empire, see Peter L. Brent, *The Mongol Empire: Genghis Khan: His Triumph and His Legacy* (London: Weidenfeld & Nicholson, 1976); René Grousset, *The Empire of the Steppes* (New Brunswick, NJ: Rutgers University Press, 1970); Thomas T. Allsen, *Mongol Imperialism: The Policies of the Grand Qan Möngke in China, Russia, and the Islamic Lands, 1251–1259* (Berkeley: University of California Press, 1987).

3. For a detailed account of Ata-Malik al-Jovayni's life and career, see Mohammad Qazvini's learned introduction to his critical edition of *Ta'rikh-e Jahangusha*, 1:128.

4. For an account of the Mongol history in Iran, see Judith Kolbas, *The Mongols in Iran: Chingiz Khan to Uljaytu 1220–1309* (London: Routledge, 2006).

5. The best study of the abusive relation of Mongol warlords toward the peasantry and the rise of the Sarbedar movement is by the Russian scholar Ilya Pavlovich Petrashevsky, *Keshavarzi va Monasebat-e Arzi dar Iran-e Ahd-e Moghol* [Agriculture and feudal relationship in Mongol Iran], 2 vols., trans. Karim Keshavarz (Tehran: Nil Publications, 1968).

6. I have elaborated this primacy of *narrative* over *truth* in my *Truth and Narrative*.

7. For an excellent essay on Baba Afdal's life and work, see William Chittick's entry in *Encyclopedia Iranica* online, http://www.iranicaonline.org/articles/baba-afzal-al-din (accessed October 15, 2011). For Baba Afdal's complete philosophical treatises, see Afdal al-Din Kashani, *Mosannafat* [Works], ed. Mojtaba Minovi and Yahya Mahdavi (Tehran: Khwarizmi Publications, 1987).

8. Chittick, *Encyclopedia Iranica*.

9. Ibid.

10. Mostafa Faydi et al., eds., *Divan Hakim Afdal al-Din Kashani* [Complete poems of Baba Afdal] (Tehran: Zavvar, 1984), 1.

11. For a collection of Semnani's poetry and a biographical account, see Abd al-Rafi' Haghighat (Rafi'), ed., *Divan-e Kamel-e Ash'ar-e Farsi va Arabi Sheikh Ala' al—Dowlah Semnani* [The Complete divan of the Persian and Arabic poetry of Ala' al-Dowlah Semnani] (Tehran: Sherkat Moallefan va Motarjeman Irani, 1985).

12. For a collection of Semnani's treatises, see Najib Mayel Heravi, ed., Ala' al—Dowlah Semnani, *Mosannafat Farsi* [Works in Persian] (Tehran: Sherkat Entesharat Elmi va Farhangi, 1990).

13. For a critical edition of this text, see Najib Mayel Heravi, ed. Ala' al—Dowlah Semnani, *Al-Urwah li-Ahl al-Khilwah wa al-Jilwah* [The pillar for the people of solitude and epiphany] (Tehran: Khusheh Publications, 1983).

14. For more details see Sa'id Niyaz Kermani, ed., *Khamseh Khwaju-ye Kermani* [The quintet of Khwaju Kermani] (Tehran: Kerman University Press, 1991).

15. For a comprehensive essay on Khwajah Nasir al-Din al-Tusi, see Hamid Dabashi, "Khwajah Nasir al-Din al-Tusi: The Philosopher/Vizier and the Intellectual Climate of His Times," in Leaman and Nasr, eds., *History of Islamic Philosophy*, 527–584.

16. I have developed the idea of "philosopher-vizier" in my essay "The Philosopher/Vizier: Khwajah Nasir al-Din al-Tusi and His Isma'ili Connection," in Daftari, ed., *Studies in Isma'ili History and Doctrines*.

17. For an assessment of al-Tusi's scientific significance, see George Saliba, *Islamic Science and the Making of the European Renaissance* (Cambridge: The MIT Press, 2011). See also George Saliba's *A History of Arabic Astronomy: Planetary Theories During the Golden Age of Islam* (New York: New York University Press, 1995). Khwajah Nasir al-Din Tusi's student Qotb al-Din Shirazi (1236–1311) continued with much of his teacher's scientific research.

18. See Safa, *Tarikh-e Adabiyat dar Iran*, II:560, for a discussion.

19. For further details, see J. T. P. De Bruijn, *Of Piety and Poetry: The Interaction of Religion and Literature in the Life and Works of Hakim Sana'i of Ghazna* (Leiden: E. J. Brill, 1983).

20. For an excellent study of Sana'i's poetics, see De Bruijn, *Of Piety and Poetry*.

21. For a critical edition of Attar's *Ilahi-Nameh*, see Seyyed Sadeq Goharin, ed., *Ilahi-Nameh* (Tehran: Zavvar, 1959).

22. For the English translation of Rumi's *Mathnavi*, see Jalal al-Din Rumi, *The Mathnavi of Jalalu'ddin Rumi*, ed., trans., and annot. by Reynold A. Nicholson (London: Luzac, 1925–1940).

23. For an exquisite study of Rumi's work. see Frank Lewis, *Rumi: Past and Present, East and West: The Life, Teachings and Poetry of Jalal al-Din Rumi* (London: Oneworld, 2004).

24. For an excellent introduction to Rumi's mysticism. see William C. Chittick, *The Sufi Doctrine of Rumi* (London: World Wisdom, 2005).

25. There is a new and excellent translation of Rumi's *Mathnavi* being done by the great Rumi scholar Jawid Mojaddedi. For the initial volume done by Jawid Mojaddedi, see *The Masnavi, Book One* (Oxford: Oxford World's Classics, 2008).

26. See Paul Ricoeur, *Time and Narrative*, 3 vols., trans. Kathleen McLaughlin and David Pellauer (Chicago: University of Chicago Press, 1990), 1:52.

27. For a discussion of Persian lyric poetry, see Heshmat Moayyad's "Lyric Poetry," in Yarshater, ed., *Persian Literature*, chap. 7:120–146.

28. Foroughi, *Kolliyat-e Sa'di*, 556, *ghazal* number 391 (my translation).

29. Badi' al-Zaman Foruzanfar, ed., *Kolliyat-e Shams, Ya Divan-e Kabir* [The complete works of Shams or the grand divan] 10 vols., (Tehran: Amir Kabir Publishers, 1960), 5:64, *ghazal* number 2219 (my translation).

30. Mohammad Qazvini and Qasem Ghani, eds., *Divan Khwajah Shams al-Din Mohammad Hafez Shirazi* (Tehran: Zavvar, 1941), 114, *ghazal* number 169 (my translation).

31. There have been many attempts at rendering Hafez into English. A representative case is Gertrude Bell's *The Garden of Heaven: Poems of Hafiz* (New York: Dover Thrift Editions, 2003). Another good sample from this Orientalist tradition is A. J. Arberry's *Fifty Poems of Hafiz* (London: Routledge, 1995). For a more recent attempt, see Robert Bly and Leonard Lewisohn, *The Angels Knocking on the Tavern Door: Thirty Poems of Hafez* (New York: Harper Perennial, 2009).

32. Sa'di's *Bustan* has been a favorite for Orientalist rendition and has been translated into most European languages. For a typical translation, see A. Hart Edwards, trans., *The Bustan of Sadi by Muslih-ud-din Sadi* (IndoEuropean Publishing Amazon Digital Services, Kindle Edition, 2011).

33. The critical edition of *Bustan* is the result of the exquisite scholarship of the late Gholam Hussein Yusefi. See his *Bustan Sa'di* (Tehran: Khwarizmi, 1980).

34. Yusefi, *Bustan Sa'di*, 17.

35. For a bilingual edition of Golestan in Persian and English, see Shaykh Mushrifuddin Sa'di of Shiraz, *The Gulistan (Rose Garden) of Sa'di: Bilingual English and Persian Edition with Vocabulary*, trans. Wheeler M. Thackston (Washington, DC: IBEX, 2008).

36. The critical edition of *Golestan* is also the result of the untiring scholarship of the late Yusefi. See his *Golestan Sa'di* (Tehran: Khwarizmi, 1989).

37. Yusefi, *Golestan Sa'di*, 30.

38. To this day al-Mas'udi's *al-Tanbih wa al-Ashraf* is of utmost interest to Iranian scholars. See Abu al-Hasan al-Mas'udi, *al-Tanbih wa al-Ashraf*, ed. and trans. Abolqasem Payandeh (Tehran: Nashr-e Elmi va Farhangi, 1970).

39. See Abu Ishaq Ibrahim al-Istakhri, *Masalek va Mamalek*. ed., with an introduction and commentary by Iraj Afshar (Tehran: Sherkat Entesharat-e Elmi va Farhangi, 1968), 89.

40. Abu Ishaq Ibrahim al-Istakhri, *Masalek va Mamalek*, 5–7.

41. See Muhammad Ibrahim Ayati's introduction to Ahmad ibn al-Ya'qubi, *al-Buldan* (Tehran: Bongah Tarjomeh va Nashr-e Ketab, 1963), 9–17.

42. Ibn Hawqal, *Surat al-Ard*, ed. and trans. into Persian with an introduction and commentary by Jafar Sha'ar (Tehran: Entesharat-e Bonyad-e Farhang, 1966).

43. Anonymous, *Hudud al-Alam min al-Mashriq ila al-Maghrib*. ed. Manuchehr Sotudeh (Tehran: Tahuri, 1983).

44. Ibid., 8.

45. Abu al-Fida', *Taqwim al-Buldan*, ed. and trans. into Persian with an introduction and commentary by Abd al-Mohammad Ayati (Tehran: Entesharat-e Bonyad-e Farhang, 1970).

46. See Hamdollah al-Mawstawfi, *Nuzhat al-Qolub*, ed. Guy le Strange (Tehran: Donya-ye Ketab, 1915).

47. For a partial translation, see H. A. R. Gibb, trans., *Ibn Battuta Travels in Asia and Africa* (London: Routledge, 1929).

48. Ibn Rustah, *al-A'laq al-Nafisah*, ed. and trans. into Persian with an introduction and commentary by Hossein Qarachanlu (Tehran: Amir Kabir, 1986), 139–152.

49. For more details, see George Saliba, *A History of Arabic Astronomy: Planetary Theories During the Golden Age of Islam* (New York: New York University Press, 2008). Saliba's pioneering work is now augmented by an impressive

doctoral dissertation by Kaveh Niazi, "A Comparative Study of Qotb al-Din Shirazi's Models on the Configuration of the Heavens" (Columbia University, 2011).

50. Gayatri Spivak, *Other Asias* (Oxford: Blackwell, 2008), 97.

5. The Lure and Lyrics of a Literature

1. For an account of Timur's life, see Justin Marozzi, *Tamerlane: Sword of Islam, Conqueror of the World* (New York: Da Capo, 2006). Equally insightful on the shapes of the world affected by Timur's conquests is John Darwin's *After Tamerlane: The Global History of Empire Since 1405* (New York: Bloomsbury, 2008). For an account of the Timur's era in central Asia, Iran, south Asia, and Asia Minor, see H. R. Roemer, "Timur in Iran," in *The Cambridge History of Iran*, vol. 6, *The Timurid and Safavid Periods*, ed. Peter Jackson and Laurence Lockhart (Cambridge: Cambridge University Press, 1986), 42–97.

2. For more details, see Safa, *Tarikh-e Adabiyat dar Iran*, IV:471–475.

3. See Mawlana Sharaf al-Din Ali Yazdi's *Zafarnameh*, 2 vols., ed. Mohammad Abbasi (Tehran: Amir Kabir, 1957). There is also a more recent edition of this book, edited by Abdolhossein Nava'i and Seyyed Sa'id Mir Mohammad Sadeq (Tehran: Ketabkhaneh-ye Majles-e Shora-ye Islami, 1998).

4. Mawlana Sharaf al-Din Ali Yazdi's *Zafarnameh*, 2 vols., ed. Mohammad Abbasi (op. cit.): I:1–7.

5. Ibid., I:7–17.

6. Ibid., I:21.

7. Ibid., I:458–467.

8. Zabihollah Safa gives a full description of the literary and poetic elegance of Sharaf al-Din Ali Yazdi's *Zafarnameh*. See Safa, *Tarikh-e Adabiyat dar Iran*, IV:483–486.

9. Véronique M. Fóti in her *Heidegger and the Poets: Poiêsis/Sophia/Techné* (London: Humanities Press, 1992) proposes that "what Heidegger's interlocution with the poets calls for is an articulation of the chiasm linking the ontological and ethical aspects of alterity, namely, responsiveness to the enigma of manifestation and responsibility for the Other" (114). This "enigma of alterity" is precisely what I believe has taken place in the *poiêsis* of history, where the literary act sustains an authorial voice in humanism without assuming the sovereignty of the subject in it.

10. For a general assessment of Persian literature during the Timurid period, see Safa, "Persian Literature in the Timurid and Turkmen Periods," in Jackson and Lockhart, eds., *The Cambridge History of Iran*, 6:913–928.

11. For a general introduction to Turkish literature, see Talat S. Halman, *A Millennium of Turkish Literature: A Concise History*, ed. Jayne L. Warner (Syracuse, NY: Syracuse University Press, 2010). Older but with still solid scholarship is Alessio Bombaci's *Histoire de la littérature turque* (Paris: C. Klincksieck, 1968).

12. For the critical edition of Jami's romances, see Abd al-Rahman Jami, *Haft Awrang* [Seven thrones], ed. Morteza Modarres Gilani (Tehran: Sa'di Publishers, 1959). For a detailed study of Jami's poetry and prose, see Hashem Razi, *Divan-e Kamel Jami* [The complete divan of Jami] (Tehran: Piruz Publishers, n.d.). For a comprehensive study of Jami's life and ideas, see Ali Asghar Hekmat, *Jami* (Tehran: Heydari, 1984).

13. Safa, *Tarikh-e Adabiyat dar Iran*, IV:354.

14. Ibid., IV:354–355.

15. Ibid., IV:357.

16. For the critical edition, see Mawlana Abd al-Rahman Jami, *Baharestan Jami*, ed. and with an introduction by Isma'il Hakemi (Tehran: Ettela'at Publishers, 1988).

17. For a selection of his works, see Nezam al-Din Obeyd-e Zakani, *Obeyd-e Zakani: Ethics of The Aristocrats and Other Satirical Works*, ed., trans., and with an introduction by Hasan Javadi (Washington, DC: Mage, 2008).

18. For the collection of Obeid Zakani's oeuvre, see the critical edition by Parviz Atabaki, ed., *Kolliyat-e Obeid Zakani* (Tehran: Zavvar Publications, 1957). There is a more recent critical edition by the late Iranian literary scholar Mohammad Ja'far Mahjoub, ed., *Kolliyat-e Obeid Zakani* (New York: Bibliotheca Iranica, 1999).

19. Atabaki, *Kolliyat-e Obeid Zakani*, 268.

20. Ibid., 265.

21. For an excellent study of Obeid Zakani's work, see Yusefi, "Shukh-tab'i Agah [A humorous wise man]," in his *Didari ba Ahl-e Qalam* [A rendezvous with people of the pen], (Tehran: Ferdowsi University Press, 1976): 1:285–312.

22. For a fine essay on Persian satire and Obeid Zakani, see Paul Sprachman, "Persian Satire, Parody and Burlesque," in Yarshater, ed., *Persian Literature*, 226–248. Equally insightful is Yusefi, "Latifeh-pardazan/Satirists," in his *Didari ba Ahl-e Qalam*, 1:313–341.

23. See Yousofi, "Shukh-tab'i Agah," in his *Didari ba Ahl-e Qalam*, 1:288.

24. See B. S. Amoretti, "Religion in the Timurid and Safavid Periods," in Jackson and Lockhart, eds., *The Cambridge History of Iran*, 6:610–655.

25. For more on the Hurufiyyah movement and other revolutionary uprisings in the Timurid period, see I. P. Petrashevsky et al., *Tarikh-e Iran* [History of Iran], (op. cit.): 236–237.

26. For more details on these events, see Safa, *Tarikh-e Adabiyat dar Iran*, IV: 61–66.

27. For more on the historical link of the Hurufiyyah movement between the Isma'ilis and the Babis, see Hamid Dabashi, *Shi'ism: A Religion of Protest* (Cambridge: Harvard University Press, 2011), 340–341, et passim.

28. For more on the revolutionary character of the Hurufiyyah movement, see Said Amir Arjomand, *The Shadow of God and the Hidden Imam: Religion, Political*

Order, and Societal Change in Shi'ite Iran from the Beginning to 1890 (Chicago: University of Chicago Press, 1984), 72.

29. See Amoretti, "Religion in the Timurid and Safavid Periods," 624.

30. Ibid., 644.

31. Sheila Blair and Jonathan Bloom, *The Art and Architecture of Islam 1250–1800* (New Haven: Yale University Press, 1994), 63.

32. Ibid.

33. Ibid.

34. Ibid., 64.

35. Ibid.

6. The Contours of a Literary Cosmopolitanism

1. For further details about the rise of Shi'ism as the state religion during the Safavids, see Dabashi, *Shi'ism*, chap. 5.

2. For more details and the most recent scholarship on the Safavid empire, see the excellent book of Andrew J. Newman, *Safavid Iran: Rebirth of a Persian Empire* (London: I. B. Tauris, 2006).

3. For an English translation of Babur's autobiography, the best introduction to the Mughal Empire, see Wheeler Thackston, ed. and trans., *The Baburnama: Memoirs of Babur, Prince and Emperor* (New York: Modern Library Classics, 2002).

4. For more on the illustrious reign of Shah Abbas I, see H. R. Roemer, "The Safavid Period," in Jackson and Lockhart, eds., *The Cambridge History of Iran*, 6:262–278.

5. For more on the Safavid-Mughal relationship, see Ibid., 244–245, 299–301.

6. Safa, *Tarikh-e Adabiyat dar Iran*, (op. cit.) 5 (1):28.

7. For a history of the Mughals with a particular reference to arts and literature, see Annemarie Schimmel, *The Empire of the Great Mughals: History, Art and Culture* (London: Reaktion Books, 2006).

8. For an introduction to the history of the Ottoman Empire, see Donald Quataert, *The Ottoman Empire, 1700–1922* (Cambridge: Cambridge University Press, 2005).

9. For more on the geopolitics of the region and the rivalries along the Russian, Ottoman, and Safavid porous borders, see Dominic Lieven, *Empire: The Russian Empire and Its Rivals* (New Haven: Yale University Press, 2002), chaps. 4 and 6.

10. See Safa, *Tarikh-e Adabiyat dar Iran*, (op. cit.) 5 (1):53.

11. Ibid., (op. cit.) 5 (1):57–58.

12. For a detailed discussion of the political context of contact between European powers and the Muslim domains during the Timurid and Safavid periods in which these literary and cultural contacts take place, see Laurence

Lockhart, "European Contacts with Persia: 1350–1736," in Jackson and Lockart, eds., *The Cambridge History of Iran*, 6:373–411.

13. For a pioneering study of the history of the European and American reception of Persian literature, see John D. Yohannan, *Persian Poetry in Europe and America: A 200-Year History* (Delmar, NY: Caravan Books, 1977).

14. See Safa, *Tarikh-e Adabiyat dar Iran*, (op. cit.) 5 (1):71–72.

15. For a detailed discussion of international trade in this period, see Ronald Ferrier, "Trade from the Mid-14th Century to the End of the Safavid Period," in Jackson and Lockart, eds., *The Cambridge History of Iran*, 6:412–490.

16. For an assessment of the economic condition of the Safavids in particular, see Bert Fragner, "Social and Internal Economic Affairs," in Jackson and Lockart, eds., *The Cambridge History of Iran*, 6:491–567; and F. Spuhler, "Carpets and Textiles," in Jackson and Lockart, eds., *The Cambridge History of Iran*, 6:698–727.

17. For an assessment of the status of exact sciences at this point, see E. S. Kennedy, "The Exact Sciences in Timurid Iran," in Jackson and Lockart, eds., *The Cambridge History of Iran*, 6:568–580; and H. J. J. Winter, "Persian Science in Safavid Times," in Jackson and Lockart, eds., *The Cambridge History of Iran*, 6:581–609. For an even more extended assessment of science in the Muslim world and its impact on Europe, see George Saliba, *Islamic Science and the Making of the European Renaissance* (Cambridge: The MIT Press, 2007).

18. For an extensive coverage of literary production in this period, see 7. Safa, "Persian Literature in the Timurid and Turkmen Periods," in Jackson and Lockart, eds., *The Cambridge History of Iran*, 6:913–98 and 948–964; and Ehsan Yarshater, "Persian Poetry in the Safavid Period," in Jackson and Lockart, eds., *The Cambridge History of Iran*, 6:965–994. For the territorial domain of Persian literature in this era, see esp. the last essay (Ibid., 977–979).

19. For a discussion of the role of language and literature in the Mughal era, see Muzaffar Alam, "The Pursuit of Persian: Language in Mughal Politics," *Modern Asian Studies*, 32, no. 2 (May 1998): 317–349. See also Juan R. I. Cole, "Iranian Culture and South Asia, 1500–1900," in *Iran and the Surrounding World: Interactions in Culture and Cultural Politics*, ed. Nikki Keddie and Rudolph P. Matthee (Seattle: University of Washington Press 2002), 15–35.

20. For a detailed history of the later Mughal period, see William Dalrymple, *The Last Mughal: The Fall of a Dynasty: Delhi, 1857* (New York: Knopf, 2007).

21. Safa, *Tarikh-e Adabiyat dar Iran*, (op. cit.) 5 (1): 373.

22. Ibid., (op. cit.) 5 (1):373–374.

23. See Gauri Vishwanathan, *Masks of Conquest: Literary Study and British Rule in India* (New York: Columbia University Press, 1989).

24. For more on Shah Taher Dakani and other prominent poets of this period, see Nabi Hadi, *Dictionary of Indo-Persian Literature* (New Delhi: Indira Gandhi National Center for the Arts, 1995).

25. Safa, *Tarikh-e Adabiyat dar Iran*, 2:1766–1770.

26. For an English translation, see Prince Muhammad Dara Shikuh *Majma'ul Bahrain* or *The Mingling Of Two Oceans*, Bibliotheca Indica Series, ed. and trans. M. Mahfuz-ul-Haq (Kolkata: Asiatic Society, 1929/2007).

27. For an excellent assessment of one of famous poems in praise of Shi'i imams, see Gholam Hussein Yusefi, *Cheshmeh-ye Roshan* [Bright Spring] (Tehran: Entesharat-e Elmi, 1990), 278–288.

28. Safa, *Tarikh-e Adabiyat dar Iran*, (op. cit.) 5 (2):1170–1181.

29. For more on the poetic output of this period, see Waris Kirmani, *Dreams Forgotten: An Anthology of Indo-Persian Poetry* (Aligarh: Academic Books, 1986).

30. Safa, *Tarikh-e Adabiyat dar Iran/History of Persian Literature in Iran*, 5 (2):897–916.

31. Ibid., 5 (2):1044.

32. See Mohammad-Reza Shafi'i-Kadkani, *Sha'er-e Ayeneh-ha: Barrasi Sabk-e Hendi va She'r-e Bidel* [The poet of mirrors: an inquiry on the Indian Style and the poetry of Bidel] (Tehran: Agah Publications, 1987). Before this, Bidel was the subject of critical examination by Jiri Becka, "Tajik Literature from the 16th Century to the Present," especially the section on Bidel and Bidelism in Jan Rypka, *History of Iranian Literature* (Dordrecht, The Netherlands: D. Reidel, 1968), 515–520.

33. Rypka, ed., *History of Iranian Literature*, 517.

34. Shafi'i-Kadkani, *Sha'er-e Ayeneh-ha*, 78.

35. For an excellent review of scholarship on "Sabk-e Hendi," see Shamsur Rahman Faruqi, "Stranger in the City: The Poetics of Sabk-e Hendi," http://www.columbia.edu/itc/mealac/pritchett/00fwp/srf/sabkihindi/srf_sabk_i_hindi.pdf (accessed October 15, 2011). Equally insightful are Shams Langerudi, *Sabk-e Hendi va Kalim-e Kashani* [Indian Style and Kalim Kashani] (Tehran: Nashr Markaz, 1993); Ehsan Yarshater, "The Indian Style: Progress or Decline" in Ehsan Yarshater, ed., *Persian Literaure* (op. cit): 249–290, and Paul E. Losensky, *Welcoming Fighani, Imitation and Poetic Individuality in the Safavid-Mughal Ghazal* (Costa Mesa: Mazda, 1998).

36. Faruqi, "Stranger in the City," 3.

37. Ibid.

38. Shafi'i-Kadkani has developed this and his other literary ideas over the expanse of a lifetime of groundbreaking scholarship. He is also an eminent and vastly popular poet. Particularly important in regard to his ideas about the periodization of Persian poetry are Mohammad-Reza Shafi'i-Kadkani, *Sovar-e Khiyal dar She'r-e Farsi* [Images of imagination in Persian poetry] (Tehran: Agah, 2000); and Mohammad-Reza Shafi'i-Kadkani, *Musiqi She'r* [The music of poetry] (Tehran: Agah, 2000). His application of these theories to Sabk-e Hendi and Bidel are in Shafi'i-Kadkani, *Sha'er-e Ayeneh-ha*, 37–72.

39. Shafi'i-Kadkani, *Sha'er-e Ayeneh-ha*, 40–72.

40. All these themes are abundant in Bidel's poetry. See Ibid., 115–302.

41. Jan Rypka comes close to recognizing this melodious aspect of Persian poetry at the Mughal court when he metaphorically refers to it as "baroque." But he does not pursue the matter and is distracted by the verses "being like labyrinth, riddles that often make the impression of being soluble only with the aid of geometry and astrolabe" (*History of Iranian Literature*, 295).

42. For a thorough review of Persian *Adab* in the Mughal era, see Jan Marek, "Persian Literature in India," in Rypka, *History of Iranian Literature*, 711–734.

43. For a study of how the development of a postcolonial national culture in India used classical music to manufacture a tradition predicated on colonial and exclusionary practices—exclusion of Persian (Muslim) musicians by the Brahmanic elite to manufacture a "Hindu" national tradition—see Janaki Bakhle, *Two Men and Music: Nationalism in the Making of an Indian Classical Tradition* (Oxford: Oxford University Press, 2005).

44. See Safa, *Tarikh-e Adabiyat dar Iran*, I:353–354.

45. See David Michael Hertz, *The Tuning of the Word: The Musico-Literary Poetics of the Symbolist Movement* (Carbondale: Southern Illinois University Press, 1987).

46. Ibid., xii.

47. See "Minute by the Hon'ble T. B. Macaulay, dated the 2nd February 1835," http://www.columbia.edu/itc/mealac/pritchett/00generallinks/macau lay/txt_minute_education_1835.html (accessed August 15, 2011). Also, G. M. Young, ed., *Macaulay, Prose and Poetry* (Cambridge: Harvard University Press, 1957), 721–724.

48. Ibid.

49. See Qazi Mir Ahmad Qomi, *Golestan Honar*, ed. and with notes and introduction by Ahmad Soheili Khwansari (Tehran: Manuchehri Publishers, 1972).

50. Ibid., 139–140.

51. The Maktab-e Isfahan/School of Isfahan in painting is not to be confused with "The School of Isfahan" in Islamic philosophy of the same period. For more on the philosophical school, see Dabashi, *Shi'ism*, chap. 5.

52. For a detailed account of this vandalism, see Souren Melikian, "Destroying a Treasure: The Sad Story of a Manuscript," *International Herald Tribune*, April 27, 1996, http://www.cais-soas.com/CAIS/Art/manuscript.htm. Torn pages of this *Shahnameh* have been sold in European and American auction houses for millions of pounds or dollars. For the details of one such sale see http://www.iran-times.com/english/index.php?option=com_content& view=article&id=1657:single-miniature-from-shahnameh-sells-for-12m& catid=99:whats-mid&Itemid=425 (accessed August 15, 2011).

53. See Blair and Bloom, *Art and Architecture of Islam*, 168. For a more detailed study of the history of illustrated *Shahnameh*, see Marianna Shreve Simpson's essay on "Shahnameh Illustration" in *Encyclopedia Iranica* online, https://

www.iranica.com/articles/sah-nama-iv-illustrations (accessed September 15, 2011).

54. Ibid.

55. Blair and Bloom, *Art and Architecture of Islam*, 168. A few of the pages were sold at auctions, a few were given to the New York Metropolitan Museum, and the rest were later swapped with a work of Willem de Kooning, "Woman III," and returned to Iran in 1996. For the cloak-and-dagger details of the swap in the international zone of the Vienna airport, see Melikian, "Destroying a Treasure." What this manuscript amounted to was in effect a sizable mobile museum—and vandalizing it as Houghton did was like planting a bomb at the Uffizi and then auctioning the masterpieces of Renaissance art that are strewn on the site to the highest bidder.

56. Blair and Bloom, *Art and Architecture of Islam*, 178.

57. Ibid.

58. Ibid., 179.

59. Ibid.

60. Ibid.

61. Ibid., 179–180.

62. As cited, pictured, and translated in the text in Blair and Bloom, *Art and Architecture of Islam*, 180. A *man* is a unit of weight, anda *bisti* is a monetary unit of the time.

63. Ibid.

64. Ibid.

65. Ibid.

66. Ibid., 181.

67. Ibid.

68. For more on Mohammad Zaman, see A. A. Ivanov, "The Life of Muhammad Zaman: A Reconsideration," *Iran* 17 (1979): 65–70. See also Amy Landau, "From Poet to Painter: Allegory and Metaphor in a Seventeenth-Century Persian Painting by Muhammad Zaman, Master of Farangi-Sazi (the Europe-anized Style)" *Muqarnas* 28, (forthcoming). Amy Landau has also written her doctoral dissertation on Mohammad Zaman, "Farangi-sazi at Isfahan: The Court Painter Muhammad Zaman, the Armenians of New Julfa and Shah Sulayman (1666–1694)." For more on the painting styles of the period, see "Persian Painting in the Eighteenth Century: Tradition and Transmission," *Muqarnas* 6 (1989): 147–160.

69. I have discussed the architectural formation of the public space in the Safavid period in *Shi'ism*, chap. 5.

70. For an overview of Judeo-Persian literature, see Jan Rypka, "An Outline of Judeo-Persian Literature," in *History of Iranian Literature*, 735–740.

71. For a thorough review of central Asian Persian literature of this period, see Jiri Becka, "Tajik Literature from the 16th Century to the Present" in Rypka, *History of Iranian Literature*, 483–545.

7. The Dawn of New Empires

1. For a now classic study of European imperialism and its corresponding culture of domination, see Said, *Culture and Imperialism.*

2. For a comprehensive account of literary production in central Asia, see Becka, "Tajik Literature from the 16th Century to the Present," 483–606.

3. Ibid., 487.

4. Ibid., 489.

5. Ibid., 497–500.

6. Ibid., 500–501.

7. Ibid., 502–504.

8. Ibid., 509.

9. Ibid.

10. Ibid., 509–510.

11. Ibid., 521.

12. Ibid., 523.

13. Ibid.

14. Ibid., 531.

15. Ibid., 535.

16. Ibid., 549.

17. Ibid., 550.

18. Ibid., 553–559.

19. See Keith Hitchens, "Modern Tajik Literature" in Yarshater, ed., *Persian Literature,* 459.

20. Ibid., 463.

21. For the more recent developments in the central Asian context, see ibid., 462–475.

22. For more on Mawlana Abd al-Rauf, Mahmud Tarzi, and other aspects of Afghan literature (1911–1978), see Ashraf Ghani, "The Persian Literature of Afghanistan," in Yarshater, ed., *Persian Literature,* 428–453.

23. For an Introduction to Urdu literature, see Shamsur Rahman Faruqi, *Early Urdu Literary Culture and History* (Delhi: Oxford University Press, 2001).

24. See Annemarie Schimmel, "Persian Poetry in the Indo-Pakistani Subcontinent," in Yarshater, ed., *Persian Literature,* 405–421.

25. Ibid., 420.

26. A magnificent achievement of this period of Urdu literature is *The Adventures of Amir Hamza* by Ghalib Lakhnavi and Abdullah Bilgrami, now available in an exquisite translation by Musharraf Ali Farooqi (New York: Modern Library, 2007).

27. For a detailed examination of the significance of Iqbal in modern south Asian history see Ayesha Jalal, *Self and Sovereignty: Individual and Community in South Asian Islam since 1850* (London: Routledge, 2001).

28. Schimmel, "Persian Poetry in the Indo-Pakistani Subcontinent," 425.

29. Becka, "Tajik Literature from the 16th Century to the Present," 732.

30. A vast archive of the masterpieces of Persian literature and poetry has now been made available on the Internet on the Ganjur website. The works of Muhammad Iqbal are archived here. *Asrar-e Khodi/Secrets of Selfhood* can be found at http://ganjoor.net/iqbal/asrar-khodi/sh3/ (accessed August 15, 2011).

31. Schimmel, "Persian Poetry in the Indo-Pakistani Subcontinent," 422.

32. Ibid., 421.

33. Yahya Aryanpour, *Az Saba ta Nima* [From Saba to Nima] and *Az Nima ta Ruzegar-e Ma* [From Nima to our time: Tarikh-e 150 Sal Adab-e Farsi: 150 years of Persian literature], 3 vols. (Tehran: Zavvar, 1971–1995), I:8.

34. For more on these achievements under the Safavids, see Dabashi, *Shi'ism*, chap. 5.

35. Aryanpour, *Az Saba ta Nima*, I:13.

36. Ibid., I:19.

37. Ibid., I:46.

38. Ibid., I:65–66.

39. Ibid., I:101. For more on the nineteenth-century Shi'i Babi revolutionary movement, see Dabashi, *Shi'ism*, chap. 6.

40. For more on Qorrat al-Ayn and her revolutionary career, see Dabashi, *Shi'ism*, chap. 6.

41. Aryanpour, *Az Saba ta Nima*, I:132 (my translation).

42. Ibid., I:228.

43. For more on Mirza Saleh Shirazi, see Hamid Dabashi, *Iran: A People Interrupted* (New York: The New Press, 2007), chap. 2.

44. Aryanpour, *Az Saba ta Nima*, I:236.

45. For more on Mirza Hasan Roshdiyeh and his pioneering work in education, see Ahmad Kasravi, *Tarikh-e Mashrutah-ye Iran* [History of Iranian Constitution] (Tehran: Amir Kabir, 1984), 18–21.

46. For more on James Morier's *The Adventures of Hajji Baba of Ispahan* and its Persian translation by Mirza Habib Isfahani, see Dabashi, *Iran*, chap. 2.

47. See Firoozeh Kashani-Sabet, *Frontier Fictions* (Princeton: Princeton University Press, 2000).

48. For more on the itinerant disposition of Seyyed Jamal al-Din Asadabadi, see Dabashi, *Shi'ism*, 284–294.

49. See Vishwanathan, *Masks of Conquest*.

50. See Fredric Jameson, "World Literature in an Age of Multinational Capitalism," in *The Current in Criticism: Essays on the Present and Future of Literary Theory*, ed. Clayton Koelb and Virgil Lokke (West Lafayette: Purdue University Press, 1986), 139.

51. Ibid.

52. Ibid., 140.

53. Ibid., 140–141.

54. Ibid., 141.

55. For more on Aref Qazvini and his poetry during the course of the Iranian Constitutional Revolution, see Dabashi, *Iran*, chap. 3.

56. Benedict Anderson, *Imagined Communities: Reflections on the Origin and Spread of Nationalism* (London: Verso, 1991), 6.

57. Partha Chatterjee, *The Nation and Its Fragments: Colonial and Postcolonial Histories* (Princeton: Princeton University Press, 1993).

58. See Ashis Nandy, *The Intimate Enemy: Loss and Recovery of Self Under Colonialism* (Oxford: Oxford University Press, 1989).

8. The Final Frontiers

1. For more on Qazvini's life and poetry, see Aryanpour, *Az Saba ta Nima*, II:146–168.

2. For an account of the influence of Platonic ideas on Muslim thinkers, see Muhsin Mahdi, *Al-Farabi's Philosophy of Plato and Aristotle* (Ithaca: Cornell University Press, 1962). See also Erwin I. J. Rosenthal, *Political Thought in Medieval Islam* (Cambridge: Cambridge University Press, 1958).

3. According to E. G. Browne, there was even a newspaper called *Aflatun* (*Plato*) during the Constitutional period. See *Press and Poetry of Modern Persia* (Cambridge: Cambridge University Press, 1914), 44.

4. Aryanpour, *Az Saba ta Nima*, II:149.

5. For more on these poets and their significance in the course of the Constitutional Revolution, see Dabashi, *Iran*, 98–104.

6. For more on Eshqi and his poetry, see Aryanpour, *Az Saba ta Nima*, II:361–381.

7. For more on the battle between the reformists and the classicists, see Ibid., II:436–466.

8. For more on the history of classical Persian music, see Ruhollah Khaleqi, *Sargozasht-e Musiqi Iran* [The story of Iranian music], 2 vols. (Tehran: Safi Ali Shah, 1974). See also Hasan Mashhun, *Tarikh Musiqi Iran* [History of Persian music], 2 vols. (Tehran: Nashr-e Simurgh, 1994).

9. Lyrics by Bizhan Tarraghi from *Barnameh-ye Golha Number 461*, vocalist Elaheh, music composed by Homayun Khorram.

10. For a close examination of the Nimaic revolution, see Aryanpour, *Az Nima ta Ruzegar-e Ma*, III:567–639.

11. For further reflections on the significance of Nima's poetry, see Hamid Dabashi, "Nima Yushij and Constitution of a National subject," *Oriente Moderno* 22, no. 33 (2003): 93–129.

12. For an excellent English translation see Sadegh Hedayat, *The Blind Owl*, trans. D. P. Costello (New York: Grove Press, 1994).

13. For further reflections on Ahmad Shamlou's poetry, see Hamid Dabashi, "Ahmad Shamlou and the Contingency of our Future" in *Intellectual*

Trends in Twentieth-Century Iran: A Critical Survey ed. Negin Nabavi (Tallahassee: University Press of Florida, 2003), 53–90.

14. For a pioneering examination of the life and poetry of Forough Farrokhzad, see Michael Craig Hillmann, *A Lonely Woman: Forough Farrokhzad and Her Poetry* (Washington, DC: Three Continents Press, 1987). For more on her poetry and other women poets and writers, see Farzaneh Milani, *Veils and Words: The Emerging Voices of Iranian Women Writers* (Syracuse: Syracuse University Press, 1992). For further reflections on the significance of her poetry, see Hamid Dabashi, "Forough Farrokhzad and the Formative Forces of Iranian Culture," In *Forough Farrokhzad: A Quarter Century Later,* ed. Michael C. Hillmann, Literature East and West (Austin: University of Texas Press, 1988).

15. For a sample translation of these poets' work, see Ahmad Karimi-Hakkak, trans., *An Anthology of Modern Persian Poetry* (Washington, DC: Westview, 1978).

16. For an excellent translation, see Jalal Ale Ahmad, *By the Pen*, trans. M. R. Ghanoonparvar (Austin: University of Texas Press, 1989).

17. For an excellent collection of short stories from these and other Iranian writers of fiction, see Heshmat Moayyad, ed., *Stories from Iran: A Chicago Anthology 1921–1991* (Washington, DC: Mage, 1992).

18. For more on Mahmoud Dolatabadi's *Klidar,* see Hamid Dabashi, "Who's Who in *Klidar?* Society and Solitude in the Making of a Character," in *Iranica Varia: Papers in Honor of Professor Ehsan Yarshater,* Acta Iranica 30, Volume XVI (Leeuwen, The Netherlands: Peeters, 1990), 48–59.

19. For detailed examination of the works of Sa'edi and Beizai, see Hamid Dabashi, *Masters and Masterpieces of Iranian Cinema* (Washington, DC: Mage, 2007).

20. For more on Parviz Sayyad, see Hamid Dabashi, *Parviz Sayyad's Theater of Diaspora: Two Plays* (Costa Mesa: Mazda, 1992).

21. For a detailed account of the history of cinema in Iran, see Hamid Naficy, *A Social History of Iranian Cinema,* 4 vols. (Durham: Duke University Press, 2011).

22. For a series of reflections on the leading Iranian filmmakers, see Dabashi, *Masters and Masterpieces of Iranian Cinema.*

23. For more on Beizai's cinema, see Hamid Dabashi, *Close Up: Iranian Cinema, Past, Present, Future* (London: Verso, 2001), chap. 3.

24. For more on Kiarostami's cinema, see Dabashi, *Close Up),* chap. 2. For more on Makhmalbaf, see Hamid Dabashi, *The Making of a Rebel Filmmaker: Makhmalbaf at Large* (London: I. B. Tauris, 2007).

25. For a pioneering study of blogging in Iran, see Nasrin Alavi, *We Are Iran: The Persian Blogs* (Berkeley: Soft Skull Press, 2005).

26. See Barbara Riebling, "Remodeling Truth, Power, and Society: Implications of Chaos Theory, Nonequilibrium Dynamics, and System Science for the Study of Politics and Literature," in *After Poststructuralism: Interdisciplinary*

and Literary Theory, ed. Nancy Esaterlin and Barbara Riebling (Evanston: North-western University Press, 1993), 177–201.

Conclusion

1. See Abu al-Hasan Ali ibn Osman al-Jollabi al-Hujwiri al-Ghaznavi, *Kashf al-Mahjub* [Unveiling the veiled], ed. V. Zhokovsky (Tehran: Tahuri Publications, 1979), 49.

2. Jameson, "World Literature in an Age of Multinational Capitalism," 141.

3. This notion of *chaos,* which I detect as the last mode of subjection in Persian literary humanism, is very much akin to what Riebling theorizes in her "Remodeling Truth, Power, and Society," 177–201.

4. Theodor W. Adorno, *Against Epistemology: A Metacritique—Studies in Husserl and the Phenomenological Antinomies* (Cambridge: The MIT Press, 1984), 82.

5. Ibid., 83.

6. Ibid.

7. Ibid., 83–84.

8. For an excellent essay on Walter Benjamin's theory of allegory, see Bainard Cowen, "Walter Benjamin's *Theory of Allegory,*" *New German Critique* 22 (Winter 1981): 109–122.

9. Walter Benjamin, *The Arcades Project,* trans. Howard Eiland and Kevin McLaughlin (Cambridge: Belknap Press of Harvard University Press, 2002).

10. See Susan Buck-Morss, *The Dialectics of Seeing: Walter Benjamin and the Arcades Project* (Cambridge: The MIT Press, 1991), 218.

11. Michel Foucault, *The Order of Things: An Archaeology of the Human Sciences* (New York: Vintage, 1994), 312.

12. The best example of how "modernizing" was "colonizing" for the non-European world is in Timothy Mitchell's classical study, *Colonizing Egypt* (Berkeley: University of California Press, 1991).

13. For Franco Moretti's notion of "distant reading," see his "Conjectures on World Literature," *New Left Review* 1 (January–February 2000), http://www.newleftreview.org/A2094.

14. For a rebuttal to Moretti's position on "distant reading" and articulation of her notion of "close reading," see Gayatri Chakravorty Spivak, *Death of a Discipline* (New York: Columbia University Press, 2005).

15. See Damrosch, *What Is World Literature?* (Princeton, NJ: Princeton University Press, 2003).

16. See Said, *Humanism and Democratic Criticism,*

17. See Safa, *Tarikh-e Adabiyat dar Iran,* (op. cit.) 5: I:420.

18. See Aryanpour, *Az Saba ta Nima,* I:9.

19. Ibid., I:8.

20. See Rypka, *History of Iranian Literature,* 732–733.

21. See Hayden White, *Metahistory: The Historical Imagination in Nineteenth-Century Europe* (Baltimore: Johns Hopkins University Press, 1975).

22. See Franco Moretti, *Modern Epic: The World-System from Goethe to Garcia Marquez* (London: Verso, 1995).

23. See Said, *Culture and Imperialism.*

24. See Damrosch, *What Is World Literature?*

25. Immanuel Kant, *The Groundwork for the Metaphysics of Morals* (Cambridge: Cambridge University Press, 1998), 15.

26. Antonio Gramsci, *Selections from the Prison Notebooks*, ed. and trans. Quintin Hoare and Geoffrey Nowell Smith (New York: International Publishers, 1971), 373. The editors and translators note the misquoting in n. 70 on this page. In the new, vastly improved, English translation of Gramsci's *Prison Notebooks* by Joseph A. Buttigieg, "similar conditions" has been translated as "same circumstances" (New York: Columbia University Press, 2007), III:323. Buttigieg notes the original Kantian phrase in his editor's note (III:608) but does not note the discrepancy between Kant's phrasing and Gramsci's misquote. Hoare and Nowell Smith do. Much has been said, and rightly so, of the superiority of Buttigieg's translation and edition, but this crucial difference escapes his attention.

27. Gramsci, *Selections from the Prison Notebooks*, 374.

28. Ibid.

29. Ibid.

30. Ahmad Shamlou, "Oqubat/Punishment," in Ahmad Shamlou, *Majmu'eh Ash'ar* [Collected Poems], 2 vols. (Giessen, Germany: Bamdad, 1989), I:955–959 (my translation).

Acknowledgments

It took me exactly one year to write this book—some sixty years to sort it out in my mind and soul. My mother's lullabies must have been the first whispers nodding me toward this book. Songs of my motherland, my youthful poetries, music to my adolescent ears, poring over dusty *divans* for a lifetime—Persian literature is a treasure trove, a sea full of seafarers and their stories. We needed an angle of vision, a window to open and look at it anew.

I am eternally indebted and grateful to Sharmila Sen, my editor at Harvard University Press, for giving me the gift of this journey of joy and rediscovery—for goading me to write this book. Heather Hughes, Editorial Assistant in the Humanities at Harvard University Press, has been a constant source of support and encouragement—punctiliously keeping me on schedule. My dear old friend Mahmoud Omidsalar is the most learned source of Persian literary texts among my colleagues—always ready and gracious with his encyclopedic knowledge. Generations of scholars have been at work for me to be able to write this book. It is not a sign of ingratitude that I have at times parted ways with them in reading Persian literature. Without their exquisite scholarship, this book would have been impossible.

Two anonymous colleagues read an earlier draft of this book and generously gave me both the gracious endorsement of my work and their exquisite suggestions as to how to buttress its arguments more effectively. I am grateful to them.

I thank my wife, Golbarg Bashi, for her precious trust and encouragement to write this book. I dedicate this book to her as a bouquet of flowers thrown to her place of origin, Shiraz—in gratitude for having given the world Sa'di and Hafez—and then her to me.

I have had the unsurpassed pleasure of listening to passages of this book read back to me out loud by my eldest daughter, Pardis Dabashi, as she went meticulously through the last page proofs to catch typos and other infelicities.

Words cannot describe my joy at listening to my words come through the mind and soul and voice of my daughter.

Persian literary humanism is a gift—to humanity at large. For sixty years, and then for a year, I have been blessed to be possessed by it. You do not write Persian literary humanism. It writes you—it authors your humanity.

Index